D1595300

THE IMAGINARY VOYAGE
IN PROSE FICTION

» » »

THE IMAGINARY VOYAGE IN PROSE FICTION

» » A History of Its Criticism and a Guide for Its Study, with an Annotated Check List of 215 Imaginary Voyages from 1700 to 1800 » »

BY PHILIP BABCOCK GOVE » »

THE HOLLAND PRESS

1961

First published 1941
This edition   1961

Printed by
Lowe & Brydone (Printers) Ltd., London, N.W.10
and published by
The Holland Press Ltd.
112 Whitfield Street, London, W.1

To

Grace Potter Gove

for, among other virtues, inestimable contribu-
tory sacrifices, for uncounted hours of secretarial
assistance, and for constructive use of a critical
blue pencil

Preface

When I first became interested in the content and the technique of a few imaginary voyages and began to lay the groundwork for a study of them, I became involved in unanticipated problems in bibliography and definition. Critical commentary was random, disparate, even (as one of my predecessors has stated) chaotic. Professor Bernbaum wrote in 1926 that "there is as yet no history . . . of the criticism of prose fiction" (*Publications of the Modern Language Association,* XLI, 424 n. 1). Although a few books and articles have since then begun to make good this deficiency, the statement is, nevertheless, still applicable to the imaginary voyage. I saw the need and (I thought) the value of a book which would organize and epitomize in one place all the relevant critical material, and I found that my investigation was forming the basis for such a book, which had to be written before the study which I once intended could even be planned. To concentrate upon what others have written about imaginary voyages is to get *temporarily* one step away from the imaginary voyages themselves. But no single imaginary voyage can be thoroughly studied or appreciated without a knowledge of the background of similar works and critical discussion of them.

These studies of the imaginary voyage I have traced chronologically, and I have found that many of the critics have attempted to classify the genre by rigid definitions. Sometimes, for purposes of analyzing a particular small group of works, these definitions are useful and tenable for the nonce, but almost all of them break down when pressed to serve another group of works. The imaginary voyages of the early eighteenth century furnish the basis for one definition; those of a later period, the basis for another. The two definitions are not always compatible. So too, a definition based on the imaginary voyages in one language differs from a definition based upon those in another language. Still further divergences result from considering some imaginary voyages not as fiction but as social documents. Hence, there has been much quibbling over definitions and much discrepancy whenever imaginary voyages have been classified under mutually exclusive headings. No matter how unimportant these discrepancies may be, a student concerned with the history of imaginary voyages continually meets them and, because they exist, must, sooner or later, bring them together even if only to discover that they resolve into little of constructive value. This groundwork I hope to have done once for all.

I have tried to follow understandingly the methods and the reasoning of each critic and classifier before suggesting wherein his definition or delimited conception of the imaginary voyage as a genre may or may not be acceptable. Thus I have been led into what may often seem hypercritical analysis leading to no significant conclusion. However, my purpose throughout has been to demonstrate by cumulative evidence that the imaginary voyage constitutes an organic, shifting division of fiction, recognizable, but indefinable as a static, fixed, and exclusive genre. Genres in fiction are far from rigid anyway; their usefulness as conventions often depends upon their flexibility (cf. Harold E. Mantz, "The Reality of Types," *Journal of Philosophy,* XX, 1923, 404). But *definitions* are rigid, and those who wish to form a definition of a genre should not forget that such a definition is only a temporary and arbitrary means to an end (cf. Charles E. Whitmore, "The Validity of Literary Definitions," *Publications of the Modern Language Association,* XXXIX, 1924, 729). Though I have sometimes found fault with the definitions of others, it has not been with the intention of clearing the way for my own. I have none. Nor have I solved all the confusing problems; *Gulliver,* for example, still belongs to "a literary genus full of grotesque and anomalous forms," as Leslie Stephen wrote (*Swift,* English Men of Letters, p. 172), and *Robinson Crusoe* still is one of the fictions "qui échappent à toute classification" (see my note 233).

This is a book which I hope can show others where to begin, on which others can rely temporarily, and to which others can relate separate studies. The fact that I have kept constantly in mind the possible uses of this book as a guide explains the fullness of references and of quotations, many of which come from books not everywhere available. I do not disavow the intention of detailing a critical history that makes sense and completeness in itself. When, however, enough monographs shall have clarified enough problems, perhaps some historian of fiction will write a more comprehensive volume on the imaginary voyage. The late Hermann Ullrich, whose knowledge of the influence of *Robinson Crusoe* has probably never been equaled, put on the title page of his bibliography of robinsonades in 1898 "Teil I," to be continued by a history and criticism; when he died in 1932, the second volume had never been completed, partly, to be sure, because of competing obligations and interests but partly, too, and admittedly, because of the largeness of the subject. Except for the imaginary voyages of a few first-rate writers such as Defoe, Swift, Schnabel, and Holberg, there is hardly a main entry in my check list that does not require

a separate, detailed study—separate but not unrelated to the
large group of which it is a part.

Why, it may be asked, does the check list in this book
confine itself to the eighteenth century? Partly, I admit,
because life is short, but principally because that century is,
as Professor Pons has called it, "l'âge d'or du voyage imaginaire." A list before 1700 must be drawn up sometime; but
its few-score imaginary voyages, though presenting their
own problems and characteristics, would be collectively only
a prelude to the following century. How many hundreds
have been written since 1800 I should not care to be precise
about now, but experience with this book warns me that the
obvious totals of a dozen easily recollected authors would
constitute only a scant beginning in this type of fiction
which, whatever its fluctuations, has not been without its
current examples right down to the present day. The sum
total from the earliest prototypes down to the fiction of 1940
might prove surprising. The eighteenth century, nevertheless, provides the best approach to the imaginary voyage of
all centuries and all languages.

I wish to acknowledge with thankful appreciation all the
help I have received from colleagues and librarians. To
name them all with statements of my particular indebtedness
for large and small favors would require several pages. At
least one member of the staff of every library in which I have
worked or from which I have sought information by correspondence has freely given me time and help none the less
generous and none the less appreciated because scholars have
come to take for granted such aid of which any rare exception serves only as an emphatic reminder. Miss Ella M.
Hymans, as curator of rare books in the library of the University of Michigan, has contributed much to the extent and
accuracy of my information by verifying with scrupulous

care the title pages of many volumes in the Hubbard Collection of Imaginary Voyages, but I alone am responsible for any errors concerning these books that may have crept into my final pages.

For a helpful reading and criticizing of the manuscript I wish to thank Professor Norman L. Torrey of Columbia University and Dr. L. F. Powell of Oxford. To Professor George Sherburn of Harvard University I am deeply grateful for valued suggestions and criticism continued throughout a period of many months. I am most indebted to Professor Ernest Hunter Wright of Columbia University, who saw the work begun several years ago in his seminar in eighteenth-century literature and who has encouraged and helped me with valuable criticism and advice all along the way to completion. I am also happy to express an abiding gratitude to the Trustees and various officers of Columbia University for appointing me William Bayard Cutting Traveling Fellow for 1939-40 and thus enabling me to carry out part of my research in England.

PHILIP BABCOCK GOVE

Brown House
New York University
December, 1940

Contents

PART ONE

*A History of the Criticism
of the Imaginary Voyage*

A History of the Criticism
of the Imaginary Voyage » » » » »

i. Widespread but Indefinite Use of the Term
"Imaginary Voyage"

Once upon a time there was an aspiring scholar who set out
to write a history of the imaginary voyage in English literature. He followed the tracks of others as far as they went
and then plunged into uncharted realms, gathering voyages
real and fictitious, possible and impossible, extraterrestrial
and subterranean, occidental and oriental, preadamitical and
millennial. He became uneasy. He saw that many of these
voyages were unified not so much by the fact that they were
voyages as by the fact that they were evidence of the activity
of the human mind, and he found that the voyage-form was
basically an often-employed vehicle which took all knowledge to be its province. Its study became a part of the history
of locomotion and of human aspiration, and its scope led into
the realms of geographic knowledge and discovery, of philosophy, of political science, of sociology, of religion, and, in
addition, of such a *comparatively* minor matter as the development of fiction from folklore and geographic myth
through romance of adventure to novel. The exploration of
a channel in the stream of fiction—a channel demanding but
defying full exploration[1]—was tempting the discoverer to

[1] Compare C. W. Kent, prefatory note to Carl Holliday, *English Fiction
from the Fifth to the Twentieth Century* (New York, 1912), p. xiii.

lose himself in little more than footnote material to a grand encyclopedia of universal knowledge as conceived in the minds of imaginary voyagers in all languages.

It is not surprising, therefore, that no completely satisfactory definition of the imaginary voyage as a type of literature has ever been devised. Indeed, doubt that the type even exists as such is engendered by the fact that no definition is to be found in more than 150 dictionaries and encyclopedias.[2] That *voyage* may refer to a kind of composition, to a narration itself, has long been recognized.[3] That it may further apply to a mental act totally unconnected with physical locomotion is not unrecognized.[4] But that it may, with or without

[2] It is difficult to explain why in Paul Rouaix, *Dictionnaire-manuel-illustré des idées suggérés par les mots* . . . , 15e éd. (Paris, 1926), among 124 words or phrases suggested by *voyage* the phrase *voyage imaginaire* is not included, and in Elvire D. Bar, *Dictionnaire des épithètes et qualificatifs* (Paris, 1930), among 82 adjectival expressions qualifying *voyage* the word *imaginaire* is not given although *extraordinaire* is.

[3] For example, "A written account of a voyage . . . 1587"—*Oxford English Dictionary;* "an account of, or a work dealing with, a voyage . . ." —*Webster's New International Dictionary,* 2d ed. Cf. H[enri] Barbieux, *Antibarbarus der französischen Sprache* . . . (Frankfurt am Main, 1862) *s.v. voyageur:* "Bemerkenswerth ist folgende Stelle, wo dieses Wort für das *Werk* eines Reisenden gebraucht wird: 'Ne soyez pas étonné, si ma relation diffère en quelques points de celles que vous avez pu lire *dans d'autres voyageurs.'* "

[4] For example, Pierre Richelet, *Nouveau Dictionnaire francois* . . . (Rouen, 1719) *s.v. voiager:* ". . . Se dit figurément de ceux qui étudient la géographie. (Cet homme a bien *voiagé* dans les cartes & dans les livres.)"; Antoine Furetière (apparently amplifying Richelet), *Dictionnaire universel* (La Haye, 1727) *s.v. voyager:* ". . . se dit figurément en parlant de ceux qui étudient la Geographie & l'Histoire, qui apprennent la situation des lieux, les mœurs des peuples, aussi bien que ceux qui *voyagent* effectivement. Cet homme a bien *voyagé* dans les cartes, dans les livres"; M. N. Bouillet, *Dictionnaire universel* . . . (Paris, 1908) *s.v. voyages:* "Il existe aussi des relations de *Voyages imaginaires,* les uns écrits dans un but tout scientifique . . . ; les autres comme œuvres de fantaisie et de pure imagination . . ."; and *Enciclopedia universal ilustrada* . . . (Bilbao [etc., 1929]) *s.v. viaje* (p. 420): "Finalmente, cabe mencionar aquellas obras que, en parte, son producto de la fantasía, pero

the qualifying word *imaginary,* signify the product of crea-
tive imagination is attested not by lexicographers and en-
cyclopedists but by authors of fiction and their critics. The
duty of the dictionary-maker, it should be conceded, does
not include defining fictional but nonfigurative uses of
words: the *horse* of Squire Western and the *horse* of the
Duke of Marlborough are lexicographically and semasiologi-
cally the same; so, the *voyages* of Lemuel Gulliver and the
voyages of Captain James Cook.

However, the imaginary voyage does exist as a literary
genre, as evidenced particularly by its use as a term of classification by literary historians and writers on fiction. But
one kind of evidence often available in the study of a literary
genre, designation by the author himself, is completely lacking. An author may announce in title or subtitle that he is
writing a fable, an oriental tale, a humorous story, or a historical novel, but he is not likely to say that his voyage is
imaginary. I know of no work before the nineteenth century
in any language in which an author so informs his readers
by specific use on the title page of the phrase *imaginary voyage,* although there is no mistaking the fictional implications
of clearly impossible voyages and of transparent pseudonyms.
Examination of the titles included by librarians under the
subject heading "Voyages, imaginary"[5] will reveal the wide
range of this classification but will not help to define it, for
the librarian is not concerned with establishing mutually exclusive subject headings; the more ways a book can be classified the more useful is the catalogue as an aid in the search
for books. But so uncertain are the limits of the imaginary

llevando el ropaje de la descripción, las llamadas *robinsonadas,* y las
descripciones científiconoveladas de Julio Verne." Such statements in
dictionaries are surprisingly rare; I have found no similar statement in
an English dictionary.

[5] As used by the Congressional, Columbia, Harvard, Yale, and other
libraries.

voyage that in 1935 the New York Public Library abandoned this subject classification as too indefinite;[6] in the cataloguers' guidebook opposite this printed term now stands the notation "Do not use," and the list of subject headings on any card prepared by this library has, in the place where a Library of Congress card for the same book carries "Voyages, imaginary," instead "No subject." Such books are now classified under "Fiction" and its linguistic and chronological subdivisions. Mr. C. W. Perley, chief of the Classification Division of the Library of Congress, responding to a request for information, writes:

The distinction between the three subject headings "Voyages, Imaginary," "Utopias," and "Robinsonades," seems to us clearly defined, at least as regards the last two. "Utopias" imply social ideals, the ideal commonwealths of Plato and Sir Thomas More being the best examples. "Robinsonades" are of course stories of the Robinson Crusoe type, adventures of castaways on desert islands. "Voyages, Imaginary" would include fictional accounts of imaginary travelers to real or imaginary lands and seas not covered by the other subject headings.[7]

These distinctions, satisfactory in the use for which they are intended, do not bring one any nearer to qualities which might distinguish the imaginary voyage as a literary genre.

Numerous allusions by literary critics indicate acceptance of the term as a literary classification. Professor Bernbaum in the introduction to his edition of *Gulliver's Travels* writes that "Swift chose, as suitable forms, the imaginary voyage and the moral allegory," Professor Seccombe mentions "va-

[6] Conversation (July, 1936) with Mr. Wyllis Wright, Chief Cataloguer of the New York Public Library. The subject-heading is retained in the files for a few works *about* imaginary voyages.

[7] Letter of March 21, 1932, printed by permission of Mr. Perley, who has since retired. The letter is addressed to the director of the University Heights Library of New York University, Professor Theodore F. Jones, to whom I am indebted for help on several occasions.

rieties of the type of *voyage imaginaire*," and Professor
Baker speaks of a "combination of the imaginary voyage
with the story of erotic adventure." [8] Even more specific are
these sentences: "[Of] five minor forces in fiction . . . one
was the *voyage imaginaire*, consisting in an unrelated series
of adventures, determined by a 'purpose' either satirical . . .
diverting . . . or reformatory . . . ," and ". . . it was only
natural that the authors of the *chronique scandaleuse*, the
voyage imaginaire, and the short romantic novel, the types
flourishing from 1700 to 1719, should attempt to parade their
fictions as fact. . . ." [9] Joseph Jacobs, though not actually
using the term, is referring to the type when he says that "the
Odyssey itself may be regarded as the grandest specimen of
this *genre* of literature." [10] In 1842 the *Encyclopedia Britannica* notes that "in France the pastoral romances . . .
and the heroic romances . . . were succeeded by an inunda-
tion of *contes des fees* and *voyages imaginaires*" but follows
the sentence with a discussion of only the fairy tales, "this
species of nursery literature." [11]

Similarly, among French writers. According to Zevort,
the prose fictions preceding the Greek novel "se rattachent à
trois classes distinctes: les *Milésiennes*, les *Métamorphoses*
. . . et les *Voyages imaginaires*. Tous ces genres sont an-
térieurs au roman proprement dit, qui souvent ne fait que
les copier et les combiner." [12] Alexis Chassang in his *Histoire*

[8] Respectively, *Gulliver's Travels* (New York, 1920), p. xv; *Age of
Johnson* (London, 1926), p. 190; and *The History of the English Novel*
(London), I (1924), 37; see also III (1929), 47 and 91.
[9] Arthur J. Tieje, "The Critical Heritage of Fiction in 1579," *Englische
Studien*, XLVII (1913-14), 417, and Joseph B. Heidler, *The History, from
1700 to 1800, of English Criticism of Prose Fiction*, University of Illinois
Studies in Language and Literature, XIII, No. 2 (Urbana, 1928), 168;
see also similar statements on pp. 28, 29, 32, 34, 35, and 42.
[10] *Book of Wonder Voyages* (New York, 1896), p. [213].
[11] [George Moir], article "Romance," 7th ed. (Edinburgh, 1842), p. 352.
[12] Ch. Zevort, *Romans Grecs* . . . (Paris, 1856), I, x f.; also, on p. xvi:

du roman . . . *dans l'antiquité* writes: "Dans l'époque Romaine, la fantaisie des rhéteurs et des philosophes prend avec la géographie des libertés encore plus grandes [than in 'l'époque Attique et l'époque Alexandrine']. C'est alors que se développe et que grandit un genre illustré depuis par les auteurs de *Gulliver* et de *Robinson;* nous voulons parler des *voyages imaginaires.*" [13] Among more recent examples M. Lachèvre speaks of "le cadre de voyages imaginaires." [14] In all these ten quotations the conception of the imaginary voyage as a literary genre is indisputable. [15]

The term is in some degree interlingual; occasionally to German writers it seems so apposite that it is not translated, although usually applied to either French or English works. Hettner, for example, writes: "Bei den Franzosen lassen sich die Einwirkungen [of *Robinson Crusoe*] weniger deutlich wahrnehmen, weil diese schon an und für sich eine weitschichtige Literatur von *Voyages imaginaires* hatten." [16]

"il fallut que ce genre [voyage imaginaire] fût tombé dans un profond discrédit par son extravagance. . . ."

[13] Second ed. (Paris, 1862), p. 375.

[14] Frédéric Lachèvre, *Les Successeurs de Cyrano de Bergerac* (Paris, 1922), p. x.

[15] Often the construction or content of a sentence is such that the intention of the author is not indisputable. For instance, R. S. Crane: "some of the less familiar imaginary voyages of the middle of the eighteenth century"—*Philological Quarterly*, XI (1932), 182, and "the relations between *Gulliver* and earlier imaginary voyages"—*ibid.*, VII (1928), 186; Walter Raleigh: "Imaginary voyages and travels cannot, for the most part, be regarded as pure romances . . ."—*The English Novel* (London, 1894), p. 136; Olivier de Gourcuff: "Deux Voyages imaginaires écrits par des Bretons"—articles in *Revue de Bretagne de Vendée & d'Anjou*, VI (1891), [215]-223, [306]-315; and Daniel Mornet: "Voyages imaginaires [et] . . . utopies qui se multiplient à la fin du xviie et au commencement du xviiie siècles"—*La Pensée française au XVIIIe siècle* (Paris, 1926), p. 33. In these quotations I believe the writers imply *imaginary voyage* as a genre, but one could contend instead that they are merely qualifying *voyage* by an appropriate adjective.

[16] Hermann Hettner, *Literaturgeschichte des achtzehnten Jahrhunderts*, 5 Auf. (Braunschweig, 1894), I, 285.

More significant are certain passages in Liebrecht's translation of Dunlop's *History of Prose Fiction*. The English phrase, "Fairy Tales, to which may be associated the French imitations of the Oriental Tales, and the Voyages Imaginaires," becomes "Feeenmärchen, zu denen man auch noch die französischen Nachahmungen der morgenländischen Märchen und die *Voyages Imaginaires* rechnen kann." [17] In four other passages the German translator employs the English writer's French term, although twice Liebrecht does translate literally by *imaginäre Reise* and once freely by the single word *Reise*.[18] The translation *imaginäre Reise,* however, loses the full connotation of *voyage imaginaire,* for the adjective qualifies the noun but seems in actual usage not to combine with it to name a literary genre as in the French or the English. This is true also of *fingierte Reise* and *erdichtete Reise;* in a sentence such as the following the suggestion of genre comes not from the phrase itself but from the whole passage: "Es wurde Mode, im Anschlusz an diese Vorbilder fortan die Einkleidung des Romans in eine fingierte Reise zu bevorzugen; zwar war diese Form nicht neu und ist von Lucian bis Jules Verne in allen erdenklichen Variationen ausgebeutet; fabelhafte Länder, bis zum Mittelpunkt der Erde und bis in die Tiefe des Meeres, Sonne, Mond und Sterne wurden als Reiseziel gewählt, und der ausschweifendsten Phantasie wurde der ungemessenste Spielraum eröffnet." [19]

[17] John C. Dunlop, ed. Henry Wilson (London, 1896), II, [447]; Felix Liebrecht, John Dunlop's *Geschichte der Prosadichtungen* . . . (Berlin, 1851), p. [387]. The first edition of Dunlop (Edinburgh, 1814) I have not seen, but the second edition (Edinburgh, 1816), which Liebrecht used (Vorrede, p. vi n.**), contains the above phrase.

[18] Pages 417, 419, 426, 427; p. 421 (eine imaginäre Reise) = Dunlop, II, 527; p. 450 (die imaginären Reisen) = Dunlop, II, 587; and p. 427 (als jene Reisen) = Dunlop, II, 539. Note that *eine imaginäre Reise* (p. 421) is also the translation for *an imaginary expedition* (II, 526).

[19] Karl Rehorn, *Der deutsche Roman* . . . (Köln & Leipzig, 1890), pp. 39 f.

Referring to the early eighteenth century, Rudolf Fürst
uses the phrase, "Die neu erwachte Neigung zu den '*Voyages Imaginaires*,'" and he says later: "Eine reiche Anregung
für jene Gruppe von Wundergeschichten, die mit den '*Voyages imaginaires*' des Cyrano . . . in Verbindung stehen, gab
Swifts unsterblicher 'Gulliver'. . . ." [20] According to Dr.
A. J. Tieje, Rohde in *Der griechische Roman* "traces the development of the *voyage imaginaire*, allowing both for such
Oriental sea-voyages as the *Ursindbad* and for the Greek
Utopias . . . ," to its culmination in the sea-voyage of Iambulus.[21] But Rohde, although he read Liebrecht's translation of Dunlop, does not adopt the term itself; instead he
employs several synonyms, which, though not the exact
equivalents of *voyage imaginaire*, are often interchangeable:
*Reisedichtung, Reisebeschreibung, Reiseroman, Seefahrt(en),
Reiseabenteuer, Reisemärchen, Reisebericht,* and *Reisefabulistik.*[22]

Although all these words seem to classify as well as to describe, only three unmistakably denote fiction: *Reiseroman,
Reisemärchen,* and *Reisefabulistik,* and of these the first is
the most frequent equivalent of *voyage imaginaire.* After
using the phrase "der grotesk-komische Reiseroman Gullivers Reisen" one German writer summarizes his remarks
introductory to *Robinson Crusoe:* "Zuerst war der Ritterro-

[20] *Die Vorläufer der modernen Novelle im achtzehnten Jahrhundert*
. . . (Halle a.S., 1897), pp. 53 and 97; see also pp. 69 and 71.
[21] A. J. Tieje, *loc. cit.,* p. 438.
[22] Erwin Rohde, *Der griechische Roman und seine Vorläufer* (Leipzig,
1914), pp. 177, 178, 178, 178 n.2, 180, 183, 234, and 242 respectively; my page
numbers are those of the first edition (1876) which are given marginally
in the editions of 1900 and 1914. On p. 5 n.1, he says, referring to Dunlop,
"ich benutze, wie billig, die Liebrechtsche Übersetzung"; see also pp.
180 ff., n.1. A necessary supplement to Rohde's valuable book is R.M.
R[attenbury], "Romance: Traces of Lost Greek Novels," in *New Chapters
in the History of Greek Literature Third Series* . . . , ed. J. U. Powell
(Oxford, 1933), pp. [211]-257.

man, dann der Schäferroman an die Reihe gekommen. . . .
Jetzt kam der Reiseroman auf. . . ." [23] *Reiseroman,* however, often includes both the imaginary voyage and the sea
novel,[24] and here again the names are confusing. *Reiseroman, Seeroman,* and *Seefahrt* are likely to be employed
synonymously in the same short criticism,[25] and "der 'Kapitän Singleton' nimmt den späteren Seeroman à la Marryat
voraus." [26] Another recent writer explains parenthetically
that he prefers *Reisebeschreibung* as the equivalent of the
French term: "Beide Werke [Cyranos] sind eigentlich keine
richtigen Romane, sondern gehören der Gattung der *phantastischen Reisebeschreibungen (Voyages imaginaires)* an,
und der Verfasser erscheint darin mehr als Philosoph,
Physiker und Satiriker denn als Erzähler." [27] Similar examples could be added indefinitely, but it should be clear
that, substantive value aside, discussion in German with its
characteristic facility in compounding nouns can supply only
indirect information about the ways in which the term
imaginary voyage itself is used. This information does indicate uncertainty about its meaning, for whereas some
literary terms (like *chivalric romance* and *pastoral romance*)
have invariably only one German equivalent, *imaginary
voyage* has nearly a dozen.[28]

[23] Johannes Scherr, *Allgemeine Geschichte der Literatur* (Stuttgart, 1875), II, 59 and 61.
[24] For remarks on the difference, see pp. 164-67.
[25] Karl Bleibtreu, *Geschichte der englischen Litteratur im neunzehnten Jahrhundert* (Geschichte der Weltlitteratur in Einzelsdarstellungen, Bd. IV, Leipzig, [1887]), pp. 532 f.
[26] Carl Busse, *Geschichte der Weltliteratur* (Bielefeld und Leipzig, 1910-13), II, 128.
[27] Wolfgang von Wurzbach, *Geschichte des französischen Romans . . .* (Heidelberg, 1912), I, 337. On p. 346 the author quotes from Dunlop and twice uses *Voyages imaginaires* untranslated.
[28] Five other German quotations which have relevant interest are: (1) "Endlich ist noch auf jene Werke hinzuweisen, die durchaus Produkte

ii. *The Antiquity of the Imaginary Voyage*

Whatever uncertainty may exist about the name for the type of literature under discussion, its antiquity, as some of

der Phantasie, aber in das Gewand einer Reisebeschreibung gekleidet sind: die sogen. Robinsonaden und die fingierten naturwissenschaftlichen Reisebeschreibungen, wie sie neuerdings J. Verne mit Erfolg gepflegt hat." —*Meyers groszes Konversations-Lexikon,* 6 Auf. (Leipzig und Wien, 1909) *s.v. Reisebeschreibung.* (2) "Seefahrer-Geschichte und Mährchen sind bisweilen Synonymen."—*Allgemeine deutsche Bibliothek,* LXXXVIII (1789), ii, 177. (3) "Er [Cyrano de Bergerac] gab die Anregung für die späteren allegorisch-satirischen Reisebeschreibungen, unter welchen Voltaire's 'Micromégas' hervorragt, und Swift's 'Gulliver' als unübertroffenes Werk allen voransteht."—Ferdinand Lotheissen, *Geschichte der französischen Literatur im XVII. Jahrhundert* (Wien, 1879), II, 461 f. (4) "Die sonstigen Abenteuer Münchhausens, in denen man zumeist directe Entlehnungen Bürgers aus Lucian erkennt, gehören zu denjenigen, die den Inhalt der eigentlichen Reiseberichte, der *Voyages imaginaires* bilden, einer Gattung von Erzählungen, die zwar auch πολλὰ τεράδτια χαὶ ἀλλόχοτα ["Lucian, ed. Bekker, I, 211, 7"] ersinnen und erdichten, deren Darstellung jedoch eine von der vorliegenden gesonderte sein müsste."—Carl Müller-Fraureuth, *Die deutschen Lügendichtungen bis auf Münchhausen* (Halle, 1881), p. 84. (5) Reiseroman: "eine Gruppe von Romanen, die mit der Beschreibung einer Reise oder Zuständen in fremden, meist exotischen Ländern dichterische Absichten verbinden. Dadurch gerät der R. in die Verwandtschaft des Abenteuer-, Lügen-, Schelmenromans, er wird zu satirischer und humoristischer Dichtung oder gestaltet utopische Zustände im Staatsroman. . . . Danach erst, im 18. Jh., entsteht die beliebteste Art der R., die Robinsonaden."—Hans Röhl, *Wörterbuch zur deutschen Literatur,* 2 Auf. (Leipzig u. Berlin, 1931). I have found the untranslated term twice used significantly in Dutch texts: (1) "In de eerste heft der 18e eeuw begon de sympathie van 't volk voor 'Aenmerckelycke voyagien, Schipbreuken en Lotgevallen van zeeroovers' gedeeld te worden met die voor de zoogenaamde voyages imaginaires, die, uit het engelsch overgezet, met graagte gelezen en herlezen werden en nog heden eene plaats in de volksbibliothek bekleeden. Boven alle anderen gaf men de voorkeur aan *Robinson Crusoë* en *Gullivers Reizen*."—G. D. J. Schotel, *Vaderlandsche Volksboeken en Volkssprookjes van de vroegste Tijden tot het Einde der 18e Eeuw* (Haarlem, 1873-74), II, 158. (2) "Voorts had zich, ook alreede vóór Defoe, de fantazie van ons onderwerp meester gemaakt en 'voyages imaginaires' geschapen, waarin den held een soortgelijk lot treft als Robinson."—W. H. Staverman, *Robinson Crusoe in Nederland* . . . (Groningen, 1907), p. [45].

the references have already indicated, is unquestionable. The beginning lies in the first deviation from the truth in some prehistoric travelogue. Speculations about the working of the primitive imagination and its manifestations in folklore lie beyond the scope of this book. Two observations, however, are too well attested to be speculative: Always there have been travelers who have lied, and always man has been interested in the far places where others have been. The combination sufficiently explains the simple elements constituting the basis of all imaginary voyages. "Wherever Mandeville goes, or Marco Polo, whether to Persia or the pole, on elephant or automobile or on his two feet, there will be travelers' tales, because there is a traveler. It is an Ancient Mariner that we cannot choose but hear. . . . It is that charming person who called himself Mandeville. There is a traveler's tale wherever there is a man with the wit to travel." [29] That natural man of the eighteenth century, Hermsprong, took no offense when his account of American savages was regarded suspiciously. "Travellers have always imposed upon credulity," he said; "and sensible men receive their reports now more circumspectly." [30] A few years earlier Diderot's *Encyclopédie* was citing Strabo as classical authority for his observations on voyagers. "Ils ajoutent presque toujours aux choses qu'ils ont vues . . . ils rapportent ce qu'ils ont lu dans les auteurs. . . . Il y a bien peu de relations auxquelles on ne puisse appliquer ce que Strabon disoit de celles de Ménélas: je vois bien que tout homme qui décrit ses voyages est un menteur." [31] Exactly what inter-

[29] [Charles S. Baldwin] "Travel," *Atlantic Monthly*, XCIX (1907), 871 f.; also *Essays Out of Hours* (New York, 1907), p. 14.
[30] Robert Bage, *Hermsprong* (1796), chap. x; in *British Novelists* (London, 1810), XLVIII, 50.
[31] *Encyclopedie ou dictionnaire raisonné*, nouv. éd. (Genève, 1778), *s.v. voyageur;* the article is signed "D.J.," the chevalier de Jaucourt. Strabo's sentence in the *Geography* (I.2.23) is: ἀλαζὼν δὴ πᾶς ὁ πλάνην

pretation of travelers' wanderings from the truth Strabo wished to convey is not clear even from his own words, which translators render in sentences of widely differing connotation. "Every one is prone to romance a little in narrating his travels" is not the same as "Everybody who tells the story of his own travels is a braggart," and neither precisely corresponds to the translation of the *Encyclopédie*. An anthology of statements about travelers' lies could fill many volumes, perhaps more than the lies themselves.

Many and curious are the attempts to account for the prevalence of these lies. "Some of the legends of *'lying travellers'* are not unpleasing to the imagination" is William Lisle Bowles's tolerant note on Cornelius Scriblerus's interdiction of maps and travelers' legends for his son Martin.[32] Not content apparently with the succinct statement that the mixture of a lie doth ever add pleasure, an anonymous reviewer of Anson's and Byron's *Voyages* writes:

The accounts of the first voyagers are mingled with fabulous tales of giants and monsters, that could only have existed in the imagination of the writer; or, what is more probable, they were introduced by artful and designing men, for the purpose of deterring other adventurers from exploring the same spot, and enriching themselves with the supposed treasure it contained. . . .[33]

Probably even closer to an understanding of human nature is Fielding's explanation in the preface to his *Journal of a Voyage to Lisbon:*

αὐτῶν διηγούμενος. The elliptical construction makes it difficult to determine whether ἀλαζών is noun or adjective, which in the Liddell-Scott *Lexicon* have slightly different connotations. The translations which follow are respectively by H. C. Hamilton in Bohn's Classical Library (London, 1903), I, 47, and H. L. Jones in Loeb Classical Library (London and New York, 1917), I, 111.

[32] *Works of Alexander Pope*, ed. W. L. Bowles (London, 1806), VI, 66 n. n.

[33] *Retrospective Review*, X (1824), ii, 286.

What motive a man can have to sit down, and to draw forth a
list of stupid, senseless, incredible lies upon paper, would be difficult to determine, did not vanity present herself so immediately as
the adequate cause. The vanity of knowing more than other
men, is, perhaps, besides hunger, the only inducement to writing,
at least to publishing, at all. Why then should not the voyage-
writer be inflamed with the glory of having seen what no man
ever did or will see but himself? This is the true source of the
wonderful in the discourse and writings, and sometimes, I believe, in the actions of men.[34]

An essentially similar point of view, approached less cyni-
cally, is Professor Atkinson's statement:

Le voyageur de tous les temps, en essayant de prouver à ses com-
patriotes qu'il a bien fait de voyager, s'efforce de trouver des
raisons à sa conduite, et raconte volontiers les merveilles qu'il a
vues aux pays lointains. C'est une tendance qui est née lors du
premier voyage fait par les hommes, un penchant profondément
humain. . . . Ceux qui font de longs voyages doivent à leur
amour-propre d'insister sur les beautés des terres lointaines.[35]

The practical poet Shenstone thought more simply that "the

[34] *Works*, ed. James P. Browne (London, 1903), X, 194. Cf. Shaftesbury's
"Advice to an Author": "Yet so enchanted we are with the travelling
memoirs of any casual adventurer, that be his character or genius what it
will . . . no sooner has he taken shipping at the mouth of the Thames
. . . than straight our attention is earnestly taken up . . . with all . . .
his personal dangers and mischances on land and sea. And thus, full of
desire and hope, we accompany him till he enters on his great scene of
action, and begins by the description of some enormous fish or beast.
From monstrous brutes he proceeds to yet more monstrous men. For in
this race of authors he is ever completest and of the first rank who is able
to speak of things the most unnatural and monstrous."—*Characteristics
of Men, Manners, Opinions, Times, etc.* (London, 1900), I, 223. To this
the editor, J. M. Robertson, adds a note saying "that it is not unlikely to
have influenced Defoe towards the artistic restraint which marks his story
[*Robinson Crusoe*] in comparison with the class of narratives here described."

[35] Geoffroy Atkinson, *Les Relations de voyages du XVIIe siècle et
l'évolution des idées* (Paris, [1924], pp. [63] and 65.

many lies, discernible in books of travels, may be owing to accounts collected from improper people." [36] Whether the motive be traced to artistic inventiveness, pure mendacity, avarice, vanity, or ignorance, or to any of several other possibilities, matters not here. What does matter is that in fabrication lies a timeless and universal source of fiction and, whenever that fabrication concerns travel, of the imaginary voyage.[37]

All extended attempts to seek the possible origins of fiction must mention in some manner this combination of travelers' tales, real or imagined, and interest in distant lands, known or unknown. Consideration of the relation between real and imagined voyages will be given later. Atkinson, writing of the French Renaissance, indicates sufficiently for the present how popular interest in voyages concerns voyage literature from Homer to the present day:

. . . le genre des "Voyages" a toujours plu au grand public. A toutes les époques, ceux qui ont goûté les voyages d'Ulysse et de Jason ont été pour le moins aussi nombreux que ceux qui ont compris et qui ont aimé les spéculations des philosophes grecs. Il n'est pas sans importance que, dans les chefs-d'œuvre littéraires, il se trouve des histoires dont les héros sont des voyageurs, et qu'Homère, Dante, Rabelais, Cervantès et De Foë se soient assuré l'attention du grand public en décrivant de tels héros. Personne ne croit que, de nos jours, ce soit l'intérêt scientifique qui pousse les rédacteurs à mettre les "voyages véridiques" dans la stratosphère en première page de nos journaux. L'homme ordinaire, qui ne comprend guère pourquoi certaines expériences délicates réussissent très loin de la surface terrestre, se plonge

---

[36] William Shenstone, "On Writing and Books," *Works,* 4th ed. (London, 1773), II, 171.

[37] Some provocative but admittedly fanciful remarks about the relation between the lie and fiction in general may be found in Charles F. Horne, *The Technique of the Novel* . . . (New York and London, 1908), pp. 8-10.

néanmoins avec avidité dans l'histoire d'un être humain qui se déplace, qui monte très haut.[38]

Professed history and romance, the true and the false, in both ancient and medieval writing, often entwine so inseparably that today it is impossible to decide between what an early writer believed and what he knew to be fictitious, if indeed he himself had any clear conception of what the difference might be. Sir Gaston Maspero, commenting on the "récits de voyages merveilleux . . . dans la bouche des matelots," says relevantly that

les *Mille et une Nuits* ne sont pas ici plus mensongères que les histoires sérieuses du moyen âge musulman. Aussi bien le bourgeois du Caire qui écrivit les sept voyages de Sindbad n'avait-il pas besoin d'en emprunter les données à un conte antérieur: il n'avait qu'à lire les auteurs les plus graves ou qu'à écouter les matelots et les marchands revenus de loin, pour y recueillir à foison la matière de ses romans.[39]

Fabulous voyages [writes Baker] have always played a momentous part in the establishment of prose fiction as a new literary genre. They first appear as attested records of travel in the vast regions known to all mankind; and then merely as the picturesque framework for a Utopia, as in Plato's account of Atlantis in the *Timaeus;* for love adventures, as in *The Incredible Things beyond Thule;* or for satire, as in Lucian's *True History.* . . . The ancients likewise had their Mandevilles and their Defoes, as well as their Swifts and their earnest delineators of various kinds of Utopias. . . .[40]

Voyez leurs romans les plus importants, il n'y en a pas un où les

[38] Geoffroy Atkinson, *Les Nouveaux Horizons de la Renaissance* (Paris, 1935), preface, p. x.
[39] *Les Contes populaires de l'Égypte ancienne,* 4e éd. (Paris [1911]), introduction, p. lxxi.
[40] E. A. Baker, *op. cit.,* I, 36.

3

récits de voyages ne jouent un rôle considérable, qui même ne soit présenté en grande partie sous forme de récit de voyage.[41]

Rohde too makes the *Reisefabulistik* a basic element in the development of "eine besondere Gattung prosaischer Dichtung."[42] He sees in Antonius Diogenes the whole direction of later romance,[43] although other scholars have not accepted this opinion;[44] but the choosing of one particular work is not essential to the argument.

Even if a prototype for the imaginary voyage could be found, it would have origins now certainly indeterminable, and had its author expressed himself in a critical foreword, he could have said with Cervantes, in his preface to *Don Quixote,* "I do not so much as know what authors I follow. . . ."[45] Chassang, having written that "l'ouvrage de Ctésias est le plus ancien recueil tératologique de l'antiquité," makes clear the same point: "Est-ce à dire que Ctésias invente tout cela [peuple fabuleux, animaux moitié lions moitié oiseaux, etc.]? Nullement. Il ne fait que répéter les traditions répandues sur l'Inde chez les Perses. . . ."[46] The very existence of Lucian's burlesque of the imaginary voyage sufficiently indicates the ancient popularity of the type, for, as Chassang says, "Lucien n'était pas homme à aiguiser ses épigrammes contre un genre tombé en désuétude."[47] Cen-

---

[41] Chassang, *op. cit.,* p. 130.

[42] Rohde, *op. cit.,* p. 242.

[43] *Ibid.,* pp. 275 f.: ". . . die ganze Richtung der späteren Romane in diesem älteren Vorbild [Antonius Diogenes] schon vorgezeichnet ist. . . . Es scheint aber als ob Diogenes nicht nur in der Darstellung eines Liebespaares auf Reisen und der Gefahren und Abenteuer . . . den späteren Romanschreibern zum Muster gedient habe, sondern auch in der leichtfertigen Motivierung dieses ziellosen Wanderns und Schweifens, und somit in dem ganzen lockern Aufbau der eigentlichen Geschichte."

[44] See S. Gaselee, "Appendix on the Greek Novel," *Daphnis and Chloe,* Loeb Classical Library (London and New York, 1916), pp. 403-16.

[45] Modern Library ed., p. xx.

[46] *Op. cit.,* p. 34.

[47] *Ibid.,* p. 379. Cf. also Baker, *op. cit.,* I, 37, and Rohde, *op. cit.,* p. 273.

turies before Lucian, before Antonius Diogenes, even before Ctesias, were the voyages of Odysseus, drawn from the past by a poet who called upon the Muse—one of the daughters of Mnemosyne—for the power to remember.[48] Oriental sources harbor in some obscure age an Ursindbad. More than a thousand years before Homer, in the twelfth Egyptian dynasty, existed one of the earliest datable stories known, *Le Naufragé*, an imaginary voyage about a lone castaway on a marvelous island.[49] Much of the earliest recoverable information about the origins of fiction is, it should not need to be further urged, also the history of the imaginary voyage and therefore establishes clearly its antiquity.

iii. Earliest Discoverable Uses of the Term "Imaginary Voyage"

Old as the imaginary voyage is, the designation itself did not come into existence until many years after literary criticism had added fiction to its province. Three of the best-known and earliest critics of fiction do not employ the term:

[48] See J. A. K. Thomson, *The Art of the Logos* (London, George Allen & Unwin [1935]), p. 117. Homer does not name the Muse. M. Victor Bérard believes that, though Homer did not know the geography of Odysseus' travels, the route can be followed on modern maps: "Il me semble désormais indiscutable que le poète odysséen fut un disciple des Phéniciens, dont il connut et traduisit les livres et contes de navigation. . . ."—"Les Navigations d'Ulysse," *Revue des deux mondes,* 7e pér. LIV (1 nov. 1929), p. 202. Upon this long-argued controversy I am not competent to pass judgment. G. H. Palmer in "A Retrospect" (1920) on his famous prose translation says that his publishers added a mythical map "to curb thought and give school-teachers the comfort of certainty on matters about which the rest of the world is content to remain in romantic ignorance."—*Odyssey* (Boston [etc., c.1921]), p. [xxvii].

[49] From an Egyptian papyrus discovered at St. Petersburg in 1880 by Woldemar Golénicheff, who translated it into French (Leipzig, 1881); reproduced with slight modifications in Maspero, *op. cit.,* pp. [104]-114; and in Mrs. C. H. W. Johns's English translation of Maspero (New York and London, 1915); also in W. M. Flinders Petrie, *Egyptian Tales . . . First Series,* 3d ed. (London [1918]), pp. 81-96.

Charles Sorel in his *Bibliotheque françoise* (1664),[50] Pierre Huet in *De l'origine des romans* (1670),[51] and the abbé Nicolas Lenglet du Fresnoy in *L'Usage des romans* (1734).[52] The abbé was able to think of fourteen different kinds of romances, the last of which was "Romans divers qui ne se raportent à aucune des classes précédentes." Into this class went *Robinson Crusoe, Gulliver's Travels,* and many other imaginary voyages.

In 1741 the imaginary voyage was called to the attention of the French Academy, when on St. Louis day of that year François Augustin Paradis de Moncrif, in a dissertation entitled *Réflexions sur quelques ouvrages faussement appelés ouvrages d'imagination,* condemned it before that learned body. Since I have found no earlier critical recognition of the term as a literary classification,[53] the address is entitled

[50] Licensed 1659. Sorel quickly dismisses the "Voyages fabuleux" of Jason, Odysseus, and Aeneas and discusses the useful instruction to be derived from reading "Voyages veritables": "on trouue toufiours quelque matiere d'instruction, & en tout cecy le profit est grand de visiter tant de pays sans danger, & de faire le tour du Monde sans sortir d' vne chambre." —2e éd. (Paris, 1667), p. 146.

[51] Reprinted in J. R. de Segrais, *Zayde* (Paris, 1764), I, i-c. "On le met toujours à la tête de toutes les Editions de la *Zayde.*"—Lenglet du Fresnoy, II, 1.

[52] "Par M. le C. Gordon De Percel [pseud.]."

[53] No doubt there are earlier examples, probably in French journals. R. C. Williams, *Bibliography of the Seventeenth-Century Novel in France* (New York, 1931), p. 65, lists under Eustache Le Noble de Tennelière, who died in 1711, a work entitled *Voyages imaginaires,* s.l.n.d., with a Bibliothèque Nationale shelf number Y². 9291 (2). I have a photostat and a letter from the Office de Documentation of the Société des amis de la Bibliothèque nationale showing that Y². 9291 is a separately catalogued Volume 29 of Garnier's collection (see my notes 65 *et seq.*), Amsterdam and Paris, 1788, which contains as (2) Lenoble's *Voyage de falaise.* He did not use the term *voyage imaginaire* as a title. The *Catalogue général des livres imprimés de la Biblio. nat.* (Paris, 1929) *s.v. Lenoble* gives an index of over 300 titles and subtitles of 171 books by him, including every book mentioned by Williams except Y². 9291 (2). In the abbé Desfontaines's preface to his translation (1727) of *Gulliver's Travels* occur the

to the distinction which priority usually confers, although a distinction out of proportion to intrinsic value. Accordingly, I quote from it the relevant parts:

Par quelle prévention de certains Ecrits sont-ils communément regardés comme des fruits d'une belle imagination? Qu'on les examine ces Ecrits si favorablement jugés; on s'apperçoit, & il est bien aisé de s'en convaincre, qu'ils sont en eux-mêmes plus dénués d'imagination, que beaucoup d'autres Ouvrages qui semblent n'avoir aucun rapport avec cette partie de l'esprit, & qui cependant ne peuvent se passer de son secours.

. . . Je vais parler avec bien peu d'éloges des *Romans* qui ne sont fondés que sur le *merveilleux & le surnaturel,* des *Voyages imaginaires,* & enfin des *Contes de Fées & d'Enchanteurs.* Non assurément que je prétende conclure qu'on doit mépriser des compositions dignes d'amuser même les gens de goût; elles ont un prix dès qu'elles remplissent leur objet: le mien est uniquement d'indiquer le rang qui leur appartient parmi les Ouvrages d'esprit. Il me suffira, dans cette vue, d'approfondir ce qu'il en

---

following sentences: "J'ai dit que cet Ouvrage étoit neuf & original en son genre. Je n'ignore pas cependant que nous en avons déjà de cette espèce. Sans parler de la *République* de Platon, de l'*Histoire véritable* de Lucien, & du *Supplément* . . . , on connoît l'*Utopie* . . . , la *Nouvelle Atlantis* . . . , l'*Histoire des Sevarambes,* les *Voyages de Sadeur, & de Jacques Macé* & enfin le *Voyage* . . . de Cyrano de Bergerac. Mais tous ces Ouvrages sont d'un goût fort différent, & ceux qui voudront les comparer à celui-ci, trouveront qu'ils n'ont rien de commun avec lui, que l'idée d'un voyage imaginaire, & d'un pays supposé."—*L'Esprit de l'Abbé Desfontaines* . . . (Londres, 1757), IV, 323. Here *voyage imaginaire* seems to me to be no more than a chance combination of words, in no sufficient sense implying literary genre, and the same reasoning, if acceptable, applies to repetitions of the phrase in reviews of Desfontaines's translation, as in the *Mercure de France* for May, 1727, pp. 956 and 967. Many other such combinations in several languages can undoubtedly be found long before the eighteenth century. The *Bibliothèque historique à l'usage des dames,* B [II] (1779), 171, has *Lamekis, voyage imaginaire* as if this were the title of the chevalier de Mouhy's romance published at Paris, 1735-38. But the first edition was entitled *Lamekis, ou les voyages extraordinaires d'un Égyptien dans la terre intérieure* . . . , and I can find no evidence that *voyage imaginaire* was ever a part of the title.

coûte à l'esprit pour saisir ces sortes de matières & les mettre en œuvre: je le suivrai dans ses démarches qu'on apperçoit sans peine; & l'on verra qu'il agit toujours avec succès, sans que l'imagination le secoure, & sans qu'il ait jamais besoin d'elle. On conçoit sans doute que j'entends ici par imagination ce qu'on appelle *Invention, Génie, Idées neuves,* ou du moins rendues d'une manière *originale.*

Si nous recherchons les sources où l'on peut puiser toutes sortes de Contes & d'Histoires fabuleuses, nous allons trouver qu'elles se réduisent à quatre; que ces sources se présentent à presque tout le monde, & que l'une d'elles peut fournir à l'Auteur le moins abondant en tout autre genre de quoi écrire toute sa vie, & accumuler volumes sur volumes.

La première est un simple renversement des principes ou des usages communs à toutes, ou du moins à presque toutes les Nations; un déplacement fait sans aucun fondement, de quelques propriétés reconnues dans de certains êtres, & qu'on attribue à d'autres êtres à qui la nature a refusé de tels avantages: deux moyens qui ne supposent aucune invention dans l'esprit, & qui ont suffi pour composer presque tous les Voyages imaginaires qu'on lit avec quelque plaisir. [Par exemple] . . . femmes ayant l'empire sur les hommes . . . cette République, où sous le nom d'*Houynhnhnis,* les chevaux ont la raison des hommes. . . .

Les sujets que présente la seconde source exercent un peu plus l'esprit: c'est de mettre un ou plusieurs personnages dans quelques situations extraordinaires & embarrassantes. . . . Tel est Robinson dans son Isle déserte. . . .

Robinson, seul habitant d'un désert, est sans doute un objet intéressant. Mais faut-il de l'imagination pour concevoir un naufrage, & un Voyageur jetté dans une Isle inhabitée? On voit naître au premier coup d'œil mille événemens que cette situation amène. . . . Si parmi les personnes qui pensent différemment de moi . . . , il s'en trouve quelqu'une qui soit bien convaincue de n'avoir point du tout d'imagination, qu'elle donne une heure seulement à penser & à écrire ce qu'on peut faire d'un Robinson; je lui suis garant que sans rien dérober au Roman Anglois, elle en composera un qui plaira aux amateurs des Oùvrages de ce genre.

La troisième source n'est que l'art d'étendre ou de réduire la forme de certains êtres: on voit que je parle des *grands hommes* & des *petits hommes de Gulliver*. J'avouerai qu'un Ouvrage dont toute l'invention consiste à me montrer des hommes plus que *Géants,* ou moindres que *Pigmées,* me paroît commencer & finir à la première page; tout le reste n'est que redite. . . . l'Auteur de Gulliver [bien qu'un homme d'esprit] . . . ne me fait voir dans ces mêmes objets que ce que j'y découvre sans autre secours que celui de mes yeux. . . .[54] [This opinion anticipates Dr. Johnson's famous remark of thirty-four years later: "When once you have thought of big men and little men, it is very easy to do all the rest."]

Without paying any attention to the lucubrations of Moncrif the marquis de Paulmy, in his monthly periodical *Bibliothèque universelle des romans,* begun in July, 1775,[55] reduced Lenglet du Fresnoy's fourteen classes to a more reasonable eight, of which

La huitième & dernière classe, comprendra tous les *Romans merveilleux.* Les Contes de Fées, les Voyages imaginaires, les

---

[54] *Œuvres,* nouv. éd. (Paris, 1768), II, 93-98. The "quatrième source" concerns Génies and Fées. If the passage quoted does not speak for itself, Moncrif's insufficient qualifications for literary criticism and for admission to the Academy are interestingly set forth by Augustin Thierry, "Les Amuseurs d'autrefois," *Revue des deux mondes,* 6e pér. XXII (15 juil. 1914), [342]-377; reprinted in *Trois Amuseurs d'autrefois* (Paris, [1924]), pp. 3-69. See also Edmond Pilon, *Portraits français (XVIIIe et XIXe siècles)* (Paris, 1904), I, [50]-78.

[55] Paris. The marquis's full designation, variously listed alphabetically, is Marc Antoine René de Voyer, marquis de Paulmy d'Argenson (1722-1787). The *Biblio. univ. des romans* was left to be carried on by others when in 1778 he turned his attention to another large work, his *Mélanges d'une générale bibliothèque.* See Hippol. de Laporte, article "Voyer-D'Argenson," Michaud, *Biographie universelle,* 2e éd. (Paris, 1842-65). Several others were associated with him in the former work; see A. A. Barbier, *Dictionnaire des ouvrages anonymes,* 3e éd. (1872), I, 421.

Romans Orientaux dans lesquels il est question de génies &
d'esprits élémentaires. L'empire de l'imagination, pays si vaste,
& qui n'a, pour ainsi dire, aucune limite, s'étend sur tous les
Romans en général: mais ce genre est bien plus particulièrement
de son ressort; c'est sa plus brillante carrière; & il seroit difficile
d'ennuyer ses Lecteurs, en la parcourant. On pourroit cependant
les fatiguer en les arrêtant trop longtemps sur des chimères d'un
genre trop uniforme: mais nous aurons soin de varier cette classe,
de même que les précédentes; & nos ressources sont si abondantes,
que nous serons plus dans le cas de les ménager avec soin & avec
goût, que de chercher à les multiplier.⁵⁶

Fairy tales dominate this last class so completely that the
imaginary voyage seems to have been forgotten, at least for
sixteen months after the first issue. Then, preceding a
résumé of Cyrano, appears this note: "Pour laisser un peu
reposer la Féerie qui, après tout, ne doit faire que partie de
cette Classe-ci, nous allons donner un Voyage Imaginaire,
& nous ne pouvons nous dispenser de commencer par celui
de Cyrano Bergerac, qui a servi de modèle à tant d'autres
Ouvrages de ce genre, écrits en François ou en Anglois." ⁵⁷

⁵⁶ I, 23 f. The other seven classes are traductions des anciens Romans
Grecs & Latins (later changed to Romans étrangers); Romans de Cheva-
lerie; Roman historique; Romans d'amour; Romans de spiritualité, de
morale & de politique; Romans satyriques, comiques & bourgeois; and
Nouvelles historiques & les Contes. As the work progressed, some changes
were made, one class was eliminated, and towards the end the classifications became very loose and were sometimes omitted altogether. The
classes are used as the basis for the section "Des Romans" in the Nouvelle
Bibliotheque d'un homme de gout, ou, tableau de la littérature ancienne &
moderne (Paris, 1777), IV, [1]-109. When "une société d'hommes de
lettres" in Paris undertook in 1799 to continue Paulmy's bibliography
under the title Nouvelle Bibliothèque universelle des romans . . . , it took
over the same classes except for dropping the "Romans étrangers"; see I,
iv and x.

⁵⁷ Octobre, 1776, ii, 165. On this important seventeenth-century imaginary voyage see particularly, for editions, Leo Jordan, Savinien de

A year later the editors turned their attention to Holberg's *Niels Klim,* classifying it directly both as *roman de spiritualité, de morale, & de politique* and as *roman satyrique, comique & bourgeois,* and indirectly as imaginary voyage: "Il y a même une autre Classe où il pourroit être rangé, c'est celle des Romans merveilleux & des voyages imaginaires." [58] A few other imaginary voyages considered appear in other classes, three of them under the convenient but undiscriminating heading *romans étrangers:* Longueville's *Philip Quarll,* which one of the editors calls "une imitation de *Robinson Crusoé,* dont nous n'avons point rendu compte, parce que ce Livre est dans les mains de tout le monde"; Berington's *Gaudentio di Lucca;* and Gain de Montagnac's

---

Cyrano Bergerac's L'Autre Monde ou les états et empires de la lune nach der pariser und der münchener Handschrift sowie nach dem Drucke von 1659 . . . (Dresden, 1910; Gesellschaft für romanische Literatur, Bd. 23), and *Les Œuvres libertines de Cyrano de Bergerac* . . . , 2 vols. (Paris, 1921; Le Libertinage du XVIIe siècle, VIII); for further commentary see Victor Fournel, *La Littérature indépendante et les écrivains oubliés* . . . (Paris, 1862), pp. 95-118; E[rwin] Hönncher, *Fahrten nach Mond und Sonne* . . . (Oppeln und Leipzig, 1887); H. Dübi, "Cyrano de Bergerac (1619-1655), sein Leben und seine Werke," *Archiv für das Studium der neuern Sprachen und Literaturen,* CXIII (1904), [352]-373; CXIV (1905), [115]-145, [371]-396; CXV (1906), [133]-161; and J. F. Normano, "A Neglected Utopian: Cyrano de Bergerac, 1619-55," *American Journal of Sociology,* XXXVII (1931-32), 454-57. Eddy, *op. cit.* (see my note 74), p. 32 n. 14, states: "There is no record of any eighteenth century English writer who connected *Gulliver* with the works of Cyrano. As a matter of fact, the latter seems to have been virtually unknown to English readers before 1800." But the two are connected in Orrery's *Remarks on the Life and Writings of Dr. Jonathan Swift,* Letter xi (London, 1752), p. 99, and the paragraph there was reprinted in the *Monthly Review,* IX (1753), 314 f., as a commentary on Samuel Derrick's translation of Cyrano, entitled *A Voyage to the Moon: with Some Account of the Solar World* (London, 1754). Cf. Eddy, p. 61 n. 57.

[58] Septembre, 1777, p. 6. For imaginary voyages in the eighteenth century see the annotations in my check list, cross references to which I have generally omitted.

Chevalier Kilpar.[59] A prefatory note to Foigny's *Jacques Sadeur* explains that

Le goût des voyages a toujours piqué la curiosité des Lecteurs. Nous sommes tous avides de choses merveilleuses, & nous avons bien plus plaisir avec l'Abbé Prévost & le Capitaine Cook, qu'avec le plus beau Livre de morale. Un Moine saisit ce penchant naturel des hommes, pour faire ce Roman extraordinaire.[60]

After ten years of digesting several hundred fictions the editors included *Gulliver's Travels* (as a *roman merveilleux*) and *Robinson Crusoe,* despite the earlier excuse for omitting it. Of this last work, which is unclassified, the editors say: "Il n'est pas douteux qu'il ne doive tenir le premier rang dans la classe des voyages imaginaires." [61]

This attention, even though infrequent, accorded to the imaginary voyage in the *Bibliothèque universelle des romans* helped to establish the genre in subsequent bibliographies. The author of the *Bibliothèque historique à l'usage des dames,* begun a few years later, used Paulmy's work as a basis[62] for his "Catalogue de six cents volumes qui doivent composer la Bibliotheque romanesque." Of his eight classes one is "Contes de Fées, Romans merveilleux, & Voyages imaginaires," listed without distinction and further confused by a separate class of "Romans traduits" into which fall *Robinson Crusoe* and *Gulliver's Travels* along with *Don Quixote, Tom Jones,* and *Clarissa.* The first two are, however, dis-

[59] Mars, 1779, pp. 39-59; octobre, 1784, pp. [3]-81; and avril, 1785, i, [3]-70, respectively. The reference to *Quarll* and *Robinson* on p. 59 is signed by [Charles Joseph de] Mayer.

[60] Février, 1786, i, 182. The account runs only to p. 190.

[61] Mars, 1787, pp. 62-192 (*Gulliver*), and juillet, 1787, ii, [3]-146 (*Robinson;* the quotation is on p. 4). The volume for mai, 1787, [3]-120, is taken up with *Sévarambes* without any class heading.

[62] B [II] (1779), 1-3 and *passim.* This second volume is entitled *Manuel des chateaux, ou lettres contenant des conseils pour former une bibliotheque romanesque. . . .*

cussed briefly in another place as imaginary voyages.[63] The term is also to be found in the Vallière catalogue of about the same time. It is there not a division of romances but a subheading under "Voyages" and bears the connotation of apocryphal voyages without regard to literary form.[64]

iv. History of Critical Discussion and of Bibliography

A. GARNIER'S "VOYAGES IMAGINAIRES"

Bibliographic recognition of the imaginary voyage in France at the beginning of the fourth quarter of the eighteenth century undoubtedly influenced the appearance of the thirty-six volumes which constitute the most important single publication in the history of the genre in any language:

VOYAGES IMAGINAIRES, SONGES, VISIONS, ET ROMANS CABALISTIQUES. Ornés de Figures . . . A AMSTERDAM, Et se trouve à PARIS, RUE ET HÔTEL SERPENTE, M.DCC.LXXXVII [-M.DCC.LXXXIX].[65]

---

[63] *Ibid.*, pp. 171-72; 143-45.

[64] Guillaume de Bure, *Catalogue des livres de la bibliothèque de feu M. le Duc de la Valliere* . . . (Paris, 1783-84), 1e pte., III, 39; 2e pte., V, 321.

[65] Commonly catalogued as in 39 volumes, 1787-89, or sometimes 1787-95 (Library of Congress), and as at Amsterdam (Peabody Institute Library), at Amsterdam and Paris (Columbia Library), or at Paris (British Museum Catalogue). All my references are to the Columbia Library set in which Vols. 1-18 are dated 1787; Vols. 19-20, 1788; Vol. 21, 1787; Vols. 22-34, 1788; Vols. 35-36, 1789. Vol. 20 was published at Astemrdam [*sic*]; other sets have Amsterdam.

In 1781 had appeared at Rheims in three parts *Relations d'infortunes sur mer* . . . , ed. by J. L. H. Simon Deperthes (1730-92), a barrister and collector of books, especially voyages (C. [de] T[aiz]y in Michaud, *op. cit.*). This work was reprinted under the title *Histoire des naufrages, ou recueil des relations les plus intéressantes des naufrages, hivernemens, délaissemens, incendies, famines, & autres evènemens funestes sur mer* . . . (Paris, 1789), 3 vols., and became Vols. 37-39 of *Voyages imaginaires*, with half titles reading: *Supplément aux voyages imaginaires, contenant un recueil de naufrages véritables, pour faire suite aux naufrages apocriphes qui sont*

The half title of Volume One:

VOYAGES IMAGINAIRES, ROMANESQUES, MERVEIL-LEUX, ALLÉGORIQUES, AMUSANS, COMIQUES ET CRITIQUES. SUIVIS DES SONGES ET VISIONS, ET DES ROMANS CABALISTIQUES.

The editor, Charles Georges Thomas Garnier (1746-95), knew at least two of the editors of the *Bibliothèque universelle des romans,* le comte de Tressan and Charles Joseph de Mayer, and perhaps Paulmy himself, and one may even speculate that Garnier had some hand in editing the earlier work. Only a few years before, he and Mayer had begun to edit the *Cabinet des fées, ou collection de contes des fées et autres contes merveilleux* (Amsterdam et Paris, 1785-89) in forty-one volumes.[66] To literary men associated in these

dans la première division, & qui forment les tomes X, XI & XII de la collection. These three volumes containing 39 shipwrecks, etc., were separately reprinted (and augmented) several times during the next 50 years (see *Cat. gén. des livres impr. de la Biblio. nat., s.v. Deperthes*), but I do not know of a second edition of the 36 volumes of *Voyages imaginaires.* The *Supplément* has on the title pages: A Paris, Chez Cuchet, Libraire, rue & hôtel Serpente. Except for uniform bindings (with *Voyages imaginaires* on the spines), for the half-title sheets in Vols. 37-39, for the address rue et hôtel Serpente, and for four pages bound in at the end of Vol. 39 (see my note 70, part 3), nothing in the make-up (title pages, *avertissements, préfaces,* cross references, *approbation* or *privilège*) indicates any internal relationship between Vols. 1-36 and Vols. 37-39. Cf. also my notes 70 (4), 77, and 85.

According to Henri Cohen, *Guide de l'amateur de livres à gravures du XVIIIe siècle,* ed. Seymour de Ricci (Paris, 1912), col. 1050, the 70 plates in the 36 volumes are "par [Clement Pierre] Marillier, gravées par Berthet, Borgnet, Croutelle, Delignon, Delvaux, de Ghendt, Le Villain, Langlois, Delaunay, Giraud, Patas, Maillet, Dambrun, . . . Viguet et Mme. de Monchy, plus 6 figures des mêmes pour l'*Histoire des Naufrages.*" George S. Layard, "Robinson Crusoe and Its Illustrators," *Bibliographica,* II (1896), 181-203, gives a description of the plates for *Robinson* and says they are the "most important of those up to" 1787 (pp. 190-92).

[66] Published also at Genève, 1785-89. The volumes themselves do not carry the names of the editors. The card catalogues of the Congressional,

two large undertakings attractive plans for a collection of imaginary voyages would be obvious,[67] especially when they could see that the type was not adequately represented in the *Bibliothèque universelle*. Garnier was no hack writer soliciting popular response to an ephemeral *omnium gatherum;* he was a barrister with a record of distinguished public service, a literary student and antiquarian, a writer on jurisprudence and contributor to the *Mercure de France,* a translator, and editor of the works of le comte de Caylus, le comte de Tressan, and Regnard. "Toutes ces différentes publications sont faites avec le soin et la conscience d'un homme qui, étranger à toute spéculation mercantile, se plaît dans son travail, et se fait un amusement de ses recherches."[68] His brief introduction to the *Voyages imaginaires* points out significance and unity in a collection which at first might appear to be solely for the reader's amusement and not at all for his edification. Written in 1787 it is, too, an interesting footnote to the study of prerevolutionary France, overlooked by students of the *philosophes:*

L'histoire nous peint les hommes tels qu'ils ont été ou tels qu'ils sont; les romans nous les peignent tels qu'ils devroient être; le voyageur décrit les terres qu'il a parcourues, fait le récit de ses

---

New York Public, and Columbia libraries give Charles Joseph de Mayer as editor with no mention of Garnier; likewise, Gustave Lanson, *Manuel bibliographique* . . . nouv. éd. (Paris, 1921), No. 394. Against these is the reliable evidence of the *Catalogue général* of the Bibliothèque nationale, which enters under Garnier as editor and under Mayer as editor, with the same shelf-numbers, both the Amsterdam and Paris edition and the Genève edition. Also Michaud, *op. cit.,* article "Garnier," includes the *Cab. des fées* among his works. Mayer's connection with the *Bibliothèque univ. des romans* is mentioned in the *Cab. des fées,* XXXVII, 186.

[67] George Saintsbury in his *History of the French Novel* (London, 1917-19), I, 271, speaking of the popularity of the fairy tales in the eighteenth century, refers to the "national characteristic, the as yet incurable set of the French mind towards types."

[68] Michaud, *op. cit.,* article "Garnier."

découvertes, & raconte ce qui lui est arrivé chez des peuples jusqu'alors inconnus & dont il nous transmet les mœurs & les usages: mais le philosophe a une autre manière de voyager; sans autre guide que son imagination, il se transporte dans des mondes nouveaux, où il recueille des observations qui ne sont ni moins intéressantes ni moins précieuses. Suivons-le dans ses courses, & soyons assurés de rapporter autant de fruit de nos voyages, que si nous avions fait le tour du monde.

Nous le voyons d'abord solitaire dans l'*Isle de Robinson,* jeté loin de ses semblables; c'est en vain que la fortune lui fournit tout ce qui est nécessaire à la vie; si ses premiers soins tendent à la conserver, le dégoût & l'ennui la lui rendent bientôt un fardeau insupportable. Les facultés de son ame, devenues inutiles dans sa profonde solitude, se flétrissent; notre voyageur va descendre dans le tombeau qui se creuse insensiblement sous ses pas; un homme paroît & vient lui rendre la joie, la santé, ou plutôt une nouvelle vie. Cet homme, dont il a le bonheur de conserver les jours, lui est attaché par les liens sacrés de l'amitié & de la reconnoissance; liens inestimables qui ont uni les premiers l'homme à l'homme, qui ont établi cette subordination noble, douce & tendre, & le principal fondement de la société humaine.

Il est d'autres liens, plus doux encore, qui charment la solitude de notre voyageur dans l'*Isle inconnue,* si toutefois on peut appeler solitaire un père de famille entouré de sa femme & de ses enfans: n'est il pas plutôt le premier des hommes sortant des mains du Créateur & s'occupant sous ses yeux du soin de peupler la terre & de la cultiver?

Après avoir vu les sociétés naître & se former, notre voyageur se trouve au milieu de peuples de sages; nous l'accompagnons chez les *Sevarambes* & chez les *Mezzoraniens.* Que l'air que l'on respire dans ces heureuses contrées est pur & salutaire? Les douces haleines des innocentes créatures qui les habitent, ne peuvent le corrompre. Nous aurons de la peine à quitter ces nations vertueuses; nous allons néanmoins les abandonner, pour être témoins de spectacles faits pour déchirer les ames sensibles, mais qui ne sont pas inutiles à un philosophe.

La mer & son inconstance, la perfidie des hommes, la cruauté des pirates, l'inclémence des saisons, l'ingratitude du sol, vont nous fournir une galerie de tableaux tristes à la vérité, mais intéressans. Une foule de maux assiégeoit déjà l'humanité; la présomptueuse témérité de quelques mortels en a beaucoup augmenté le nombre. Ne placerons-nous pas, avec Horace, une triple plaque d'airain sur la poitrine de celui qui le premier hasarda sa vie au milieu des mers? *Illi robur & aes triplex.* Les naufrages & les sinistres aventures qui vont s'offrir à nos yeux, nous ferons partager les plaintes & les regrets du poëte latin.

Tels seront les principaux événemens que nous ferons parcourir à nos lecteurs dans cette première partie des voyages imaginaires. . . . Critique, morale, philosophie, peintures intéressantes: nous comptons parler alternativement à l'esprit, pour l'amuser & l'instruire; & au cœur, pour le toucher.[69]

To amuse, to instruct, and to purge (what more could editor promise or reader ask?) Garnier chose seventy-one works written originally in seven languages, not including feigned translations from Persian and Egyptian manuscripts.[70] From the Greek came D'Ablancourt's translation

[69] "Avertissement de l'éditeur," I, [1]-4. I know of no evidence that the *nous* here and *passim* is anything but the editorial singular. Cf. the opening sentence with Gustave Vaperau, *Dictionnaire universel des littératures* (Paris, 1876) *s.v. roman:* "Pourquoi, en effet, tandis que l'histoire peint forcément les hommes tels qu'ils sont, le roman ne les peindrait-il pas tels qu'ils doivent être? A une condition toutefois: c'est que les fictions édifiantes ou consolantes du roman ne se mêleront pas aux témoignages de l'histoire pour les altérer et fausser les leçons, tristes ou sévères, qu'ils contiennent." Although the dual purpose suggested by *amuser* and *instruire* was well established in literary criticism long before the eighteenth century, Garnier may have seen and remembered a review of *Gulliver* in the *Journal des Sçavans,* LXXXIV (janv. 1728), p. 87: "Nous ne finirions pas, si nous voulions nous attacher à tous les endroits, qui peuvent plaire & instruire. . . ."

[70] Lists of the contents may be found in the *Catalogue of the Library of the Peabody Institute* (Baltimore, 1885) *s.v. Garnier;* in the *Catalogue of the London Library,* ed. C. T. H. Wright and C. J. Purnell (London,

of Lucian's *True History* (2d century); from the Latin, De
Mauvillon's translation of Holberg's *Nicolai Klimii iter sub-
terraneum* (1741); from the Portuguese, Pinto's *Peregrinação*
(1614) and an episode from Camoens's *Os lusiadas* (1572);
from the Spanish, Béraud's translation from Quevedo y
Villegas's *Sueños y discoursos* (1627); and from the Italian,
De Mailly's translation of Armeno's *Peregrinaggio di tre
Giovani Figliuoli del Re di Serendippo* (1557). Over two-
thirds are French, of which the best known are Cyrano de
Bergerac's *Histoire comique de la lune et du soleil* (c. 1650),

---

1914), *s.v. Voyages imaginaires;* and in J[ulien] V[inson], "Bibliographie
du Folk-Lore," *Revue de linguistique et de philologie comparée,* XXXIX
(1906), 201-7. I know of no collation of various sets, which may differ in
some respects, but the sources of some of the misinformation frequently
given about the contents may be traced: (1) the Peabody catalogue omits
Montesquieu's *L'Histoire des troglodites* in Vol. 10 and enters the 39 shipwrecks, etc., of Vols. 37-39 under one title, Lucian and D'Ablancourt's continuation in Vol. 13 under two titles, and the voyages of Boyle and Castleman in Vols. 10-11 under two titles. This division of what Garnier included as a unit is logical but inconsistent; (2) the London Library catalogue omits the *Démon de Socrate* in Vol. 33 and enters the 39 shipwrecks
under one title, the two separate works of Néel and Lottin in Vol. 30
under one title, and the *Description du sabbat* in Vol. 36, which is a part
of the *Histoire de M. Oufle,* under a separate title; (3) in the "Liste des
Ouvrages qui composent la Collection des Voyages imaginaires . . ." at
the end of the *Supplément,* III, one work is omitted: *La Relation de l'isle
imaginaire, & l'histoire de la Princesse de Paphlagonie,* attributed to Jean
R. de Segrais, in Vol. 26; (4) one work is printed twice, in Vols. 12 and
39, and owners of some sets may have followed the instructions in the
Supplément, III, [ii] (half-title sheet verso): "On trouvera dans ce Volume
le Naufrage de Madame Godin, qui est déjà imprimé dans le Tome XII de
la Collection. C'est un double emploi qu'il n'est plus tems d'éviter; mais
heureusement il n'est pas considérable, & on peut réparer cette difformité,
en supprimant & détachant du Tome XII les 36 dernières pages qui contiennent ce Naufrage"; (5) Vinson, *loc. cit.,* omits the *Fragment d'un
voyage d'Espagne* in Vol. 28; his article, presented as a complete bibliographical description of his own set, gives condensed titles and contains
several misprints.

Foigny's *La Terre australe connue* (1676), Veiras's (or Vairasse's) *Histoire des Sévarambes* (1677), and Voltaire's *Micromégas* (1752). Eight English works are included:

Vols. 1-3—Defoe's *Robinson Crusoe* (1719), translated by Themiseul de Saint-Hyacinthe and J. Van Effen (1721)
4 —Longueville's *Hermit: or, the Unparallel'd Sufferings . . . of Philip Quarll* (1727)
6 —Berington's *Gaudentio di Lucca* (1737), augmented by Dupuy Demportes (1753)[71]
10-11—Chetwood's *Voyages of Captain Robert Boyle to Which Is Added the Voyages of Richard Castleman* (1726), translated 1730
14 —Swift's *Gulliver's Travels* (1726), translated by the abbé Desfontaines (1727)
22 —Paltock's *Life and Adventures of Peter Wilkins* (1750), translated by Philippe Florent de Puisieux (1763)
24 —Fielding's *Journey from This World to the Next* (1743), translated by Kaufmann (1768)
28 —Sterne's *Sentimental Journey* (1768), translated by Frénais (1769)[72]

Even this partial list of eighteen titles indicates the diverse material that Garnier wished to unify under one general title for the thirty-six volumes. "Je ne connais pas," warns Professor Chinard, "de lecture plus effarante et je ne crois pas que jamais on ait compilé une plus extraordinaire encyclo-

[71] Garnier's phrase (VI, x) is "faite sous les yeux & par les soins de" Demportes; André Lichtenberger, *Le Socialisme au XVIIIe siècle . . .* (Paris, 1895), p. 45 f. n. 5, says that Dupuy-Demportes "y avait ajouté un grand nombre de fragments de son cru, en feignant d'avoir retrouvé les cahiers qui, d'après l'auteur primitif, avaient dû être perdus à la douane de Marseille. C'est cette édition qui est reproduite dans la *Bibliothèque des voyages imaginaires*."
[72] The authors, titles, dates, and translators in this list are not taken from Garnier, whose information about such matters is often incomplete or incorrect.

4

pédie des inventions qui peuvent passer par la tête des hommes." [73]

First Garnier set up three classes: *voyages imaginaires,* comprising fifty-seven works, in which are included all those I have so far named; *songes et visions,* four works; and *romans cabalistiques,* ten works. The first class he then subdivided into four: *romanesques,* including the first four English titles in the list given; *merveilleux,* including the next three English titles; *allégoriques,* exemplified by Bougeant's *Voyage merveilleux du Prince Fan-Férédin dans la romancie,* 1735; and *amusans, comiques & critiques,* including the eighth English title. Obviously this illogical division required arbitrary decisions; some works could be put into more than one group. But examination of the results rather than of the terms per se reveals that Garnier was not without a workable plan satisfactory for his purposes and equal in merit to many later attempts to subdivide into types fiction, or essays, or poetry, by scholars with shelves of monographs and bibliographies to consult.[74] It should be remembered that in Garnier's time no one had yet written a history of fiction in several volumes or classified romances helpfully, but illogically, into mythical, legendary, fabulous, and historical, or oriental tales into imaginative, moralistic, philosophic, and satiric. Professor J. A. K. Thomson, having

[73] Gilbert Chinard, *L'Amérique et le rêve exotique dans la littérature française au XVIIe et au XVIIIe siècle* (Paris, 1913), p. 408.

[74] William A. Eddy, *Gulliver's Travels: a Critical Study* (Princeton, 1923), p. 12, believes that the types are "hopelessly confused." With this I do not agree. Confusion *is* caused by the fact that two volumes are incorrectly labeled on the title pages: in Vol. 29 "IIIe division" should read "IVe division"; and in Vol. 30 "Deuxième division de la première classe, contenant les voyages imaginaires *merveilleux*" should read "Quatrième division de la première classe, contenant les voyages *amusans, comiques & critiques.*" A careful reading of Garnier's *avertissements* proves that these are errors; also they are corrected without comment in the "Liste des ouvrages" at the end of Vol. 3 of the *Supplément.*

subdivided the Logos into myth, legend, and *Märchen,* hastens to state that his "scheme is only a device enabling us to say of any particular Logos that at this or that point it is (on the whole) this or that kind of Story." [75] Later he adds that "it is possible to classify the Stories according to what seems the predominating characteristic of each, but . . . it is not possible to frame any categories of classification which shall be mutually exclusive. . . . At best we can but classify its aspects, and this is not in the scientific sense classification at all." [76] Nor did Garnier, who could have made a similar statement, lay any claims to a "scientific" arrangement of his *voyages imaginaires.*

Since no one (to my knowledge) has given in print any comprehensive consideration to Garnier's plan, it is necessary before a study of any aspect of the imaginary voyage can proceed beyond 1787 to pay it now some of that attention which it deserves. Garnier, by giving information about author and translator, by commenting on popularity and imitations, and by discussing the story and its comparative significance, fulfills the duties of an editor and presents all, presumably, of the information he himself possesses. That this knowledge is sometimes incomplete and even incorrect is to be expected, though he is cautious on doubtful points and ready to acknowledge his ignorance. Occasionally the inclusion of a translator's preface relieves him from extended comment of his own. Altogether, Garnier's own words in the thirty-six volumes constitute a body of critical introductions amounting to over 180 pages, of which 150 concern the imaginary voyages proper. Those parts of his *avertissements*

---

[75] *Op. cit.,* p. 21.

[76] *Ibid.,* p. 109; David Masson, *British Novelists and Their Styles: Being a Critical Sketch of the History of British Prose Fiction* (Boston, 1892), p. 234, calls Bulwer-Lytton's classification of novels into the familiar, the picturesque, and the intellectual "not a very scientific classification, but one which has an obvious meaning."

which are pertinent here are his conscious attempts to guide the reader from volume to volume and from one division to the next, by explanation of his choices, by comparisons, and by retrospective summaries. Before setting out to follow Garnier through these volumes one should have in mind a tabular reconstruction of his plan, particularly to show the relationship between his words *classe* and *division:*

Class I: Voyages imaginaires (vols. 1-30)
    Division 1: Romanesques (vols. 1-12)
    Division 2: Merveilleux (vols. 13-25)
    Division 3: Allégoriques (vols. 26-27)
    Division 4: Amusans, Comiques & Critiques (vols. 28-30)
Class II: Songes & Visions (vols. 31-32)
Class III: Romans Cabalistiques (vols. 33-36)

The first division of the first class, the *Voyages imaginaires romanesques,* begins with *Robinson Crusoe* in three volumes, for the sufficient reason "[qu'il] tient par-tout le premier rang parmi ce genre de roman," and the translation is Saint Hyacinthe's "parce qu'elle est la plus conforme au texte original." [77] Garnier logically follows this with what is in

---

[77] I, 7 f. Cf. the sentence concerning *Robinson* from the *Bibliothèque universelle des romans* quoted on p. 26 above. Garnier does not mention Justus van Effen, who seems to have done most of the translating; see W. J. B. Pienaar, *English Influences in Dutch Literature and Justus van Effen as Intermediary* . . . (Cambridge, 1929), p. 246. In the words of the preface the translation "n'est pas scrupuleusement littérale, & l'on a fait de son mieux pour y applanir un peu le style raboteux, qui dans l'original sent un peu trop le matelot, pour satisfaire à la délicatesse françoise. . . . On a eu soin . . . d'abréger les répétitions de mêmes pensées, ou de les déguiser par le changement des termes" (I, 16). For critical discussion of this translation see W. E. Mann, *Robinson Crusoé en France* (Paris, 1916), pp. 40-71. On the tendency of contemporary translators to "improve" English style see Joseph Texte, *Jean-Jacques Rousseau and the Cosmopolitan Spirit in Literature* . . . , tr. J. W. Matthews (London and New York, 1899), p. 146. But *Robinson* was also improved at home: "It is the conjecture of Professor William P. Trent that in 1722, certainly by 1726, the text of *Robinson Crusoe* was gone over by some one, and the style made

his opinion the best of imitations: "Le sort des romans
célèbres a toujours été de donner naissance à des suites ou à
des imitations; & l'on remarque ordinairement que ces productions médiocres figurent très-mal à côté de leurs modèles.
Il ne faut cependant pas penser ainsi des *Aventures de
Philippe Quarll;* . . . Il est rare, recherché, & mérite d'être
distingué de beaucoup d'autres imitations de Robinson" (IV,
[vii]). If the simple statement made about the *Histoire des
Sévarambes* is just, nothing further need be urged in its
favor: it "tient un rang distingué parmi les voyages imaginaires: le plan en est sagement conçu; & cet ouvrage, qui
réunit le triple avantage d'instruire, d'amuser, & d'intéresser,
ne pouvoit manquer d'avoir un succès complet: en effet, on
[le] place . . . parmi nos meilleurs romans philosophiques
& moraux." [78] These three works created no editorial problems. The fourth choice, however, *Gaudentio di Lucca,*
could raise doubts which the editor must allay. No matter
how many classifications of fiction might cover it, it relates
the discovery of a people unknown to the whole world, and
"C'est cette histoire, qui est la partie la plus considérable &
la plus essentielle du roman, qui le range parmi les *voyages*

---

more elegant. The eliminating, or the more frequent alteration of homely
expressions, resulted in a marked increase in the sophistication of the style
in the Seventh Edition of 1726."—Henry C. Hutchins, *Robinson Crusoe
and Its Printing 1719-1731: a Bibliographical Study* (New York, 1925), p.
119 n. 4. It may be observed here that the *Supplément* (III, 105-24) contains the "Délaissement d'un matelot ecossois, nommé Alexandre Selkirk,
dans l'Isle de Juan-Fernandés . . . ," with accompanying footnotes but no
mention of or cross reference to *Robinson Crusoe*.

[78] V, [vii]. Garnier's edition of *Sévarambes* is "much reduced in volume."—Geoffroy Atkinson, *The Extraordinary Voyage in French Literature before 1700* (New York, 1920), p. 92 n. 14 and p. 135. For the fullest
published study of this work see Emanuel Von der Mühll, *Denis Veiras
et son histoire des Sévarambes 1677-1679* (Paris, 1938). He gives reasons,
p. 9, for preferring the spelling *Veiras*. See also Thomas E. Lavender,
"The *Histoire des Sévarambes* of Denis Veiras," [*Harvard*] *Summaries of
Theses . . . 1937* (Cambridge, 1938), pp. 302-5.

imaginaires; &, comme les mœurs, les loix, le gouvernement & les habitudes de ce peuple, quoiqu'extraordinaires, ne passent pas les limites de la vraisemblance, l'ouvrage doit être mis dans la classe des voyages purement romanesque" (VI, [vii] f.; the information revealed in the final part of this sentence Garnier amplifies in other places). Certain unlikely suppositions must be made about the climate, soil fertility, and antiquity of the people discovered, he concedes, but "il faudroit être de mauvaise humeur pour critiquer cette supposition du romancier, & y attacher quelques idées suspectes. . . . Laissons donc les Mezzoraniens jouir d'un printems éternel au milieu des feux de la zone torride; laissons-les se vanter d'une antiquité beaucoup plus haute que celle que nos livres saints donnent à la création du monde: l'une & l'autre fiction est également permise au romancier, & n'attaque ni la religion, ni la physique" (VI, ix f.).

One other work, Grivel's *Isle inconnue* (1783), fills three volumes, placed at the beginning of the second half, as *Robinson* was of the first half, of the twelve volumes in the *romanesque* division. Furthermore, it has to Defoe's narrative a relationship which Garnier discusses at length. Being unwilling to include poor imitations, he must explain away the unfavorable criticism which Grivel's book had received, although it had several editions and "un grand nombre de contrefaçons" in evidence of its popularity.

[Its hero, Gastines,] jeté par un naufrage sur une isle déserte, comme Robinson, réduit aux mêmes besoins, exposé aux mêmes dangers, fait nécessairement beaucoup de choses semblables. . . . Mais nous osons croire qu'on n'eût point hasardé ces critiques, si l'on eût bien examiné le but & la marche des deux ouvrages.

Que s'est-on proposé dans Robinson? De nous faire voir ce qu'un homme, séparé de toute société, entouré de tous les besoins, & luttant contre la nécessité, peut trouver de ressources en lui-même. . . . Que se propose l'auteur de l'Isle inconnue? De nous faire connoître l'origine & la formation de la société, de présenter l'histoire de la civilisation des peuples, ou de la fondation des empires.

Pour remplir cet objet, l'auteur, obligé d'isoler son héros, étoit forcé de prendre pour théâtre une isle ou un désert quelconque. Tous les philosophes qui ont cherché l'origine de la société, sont partis de la même idée; elle naît de la chose.

Whereas Robinson needed to be alone, Gastines needs "une compagne qui le rendît père d'une nombreuse postérité, laquelle, toujours croissante, . . . pût devenir un peuple civilisé. . . ." Therefore, though the two may be alike at the beginning, one may observe that "tout le reste . . . diffère essentiellement . . . ; enfin que le but des deux auteurs étant absolument contraire, leur marche & les événemens qu'ils rapportent ne sauroient être plus dissemblables." Also, Robinson evokes pity and sadness through vicarious suffering, but Gastines turns the initial hardship into the consolations of touching domestic happiness. After this comparison Garnier seeks complete vindication:

Nous ne nous sommes permis cette courte analyse & cette comparaison, que pour les convaincre qu'en insérant l'*isle inconnue* dans notre collection, nous ne manquons pas à l'engagement que nous avons pris de n'y point présenter d'idées rebattues, de fades copies, ni de répétitions inutiles.[79]

After Grivel's thousand-page romance, the tenth volume provides a sort of relief with its seven titles, the last of which, the *Voyages of Boyle and Castleman,* continues throughout the next volume. In the remarks on his choices Garnier emphasizes the entertainment in store for his readers. Mar-

[79] VII, [vii]-xii. Garnier's analysis follows closely a comparison in "Copie d'une lettre" printed with the Paris, 1784, edition of *Gastines,* I, xx-xxxii. In quoting from Garnier here and occasionally later I combine without indication some of his paragraphs. I have not normalized his spelling, accentuation, capitalization, or italicizing.

tigny's *Alcimédon* (1751) presents an island inhabited by people whose only occupation is love, "mais d'un amour épuré, qui élève l'ame, l'ennoblit, & n'est nullement maîtrisé par les sens"; Moutonnet de Clairfons's *Isles fortunées* (1778), a story of wise and virtuous ancient Greek shepherds, is one of the few imitations of *Sévarambes* not too "froide & fastidieuse" to be included; and as for the *Histoire des troglodites* (from the *Lettres persanes,* 1721): "Nommer l'illustre Montesquieu, c'est faire le plus bel éloge du morceau que nous imprimons. . . . On verra que cet épisode tenoit trop intimement à notre plan, pour que nous ne nous empressassions pas de l'adopter." The account of Robert Boyle is so varied, pleasing, and interesting that "nous n'anticiperons pas sur le plaisir que feront à nos lecteurs ces . . . épisodes, en leur en donnant ici un extrait. Nous croyons qu'on y trouvera de quoi satisfaire à tous les goûts" [vii]-xiii).

With one volume to go Garnier has not forgotten that he promised to wring the hearts of his poor readers with narratives more relentless than *Robinson Crusoe.*

Ce volume est consacré à un choix d'histoires qui ne peut manquer d'intéresser vivement les ames sensibles. Il nous paroît terminer heureusement notre première classe des voyages purement romanesques. On y trouvera toutes les infortunes que peut essuyer un malheureux voyageur, & des tableaux fidèles de tout ce que peuvent lui faire éprouver de plus cruel, l'inconstance de la mer & la malice des hommes. (XII, 1)

So eager is the editor to exceed the tormenting hardships of the *Aventures d'un Espagnol* (extracted from the anonymous *Mémoires de Don Varasque de Figueroas,* 1738) and the misfortunes "encore plus cruelles" of the *Naufrage d'un vaisseau hollandois* (1675)[80] that he includes an apparently

---

[80] Ironically, this is also apparently true, but Garnier evidently took it for fiction. It is translated from Frans van der Heiden and Willem Kunst,

true narrative, Dubois-Fontanelle's *Naufrage de M. Pierre Viaud* (1769).[81] If Garnier held it to be true, its inclusion in his collection of imaginary voyages is perhaps a mistake

---

Vervaarlyke Schipbreuk van 't Oostindiesch Jacht ter Schelling. See Staverman, *op. cit.,* pp. 56 f., and Henry C. Hutchins, *Journal of English and Germanic Philology,* XXVIII (1929), 449.

[81] No satisfactory study of this work has clarified its uncertain status. Mann, *op. cit.,* pp. 136-38, discusses it and says that it appeared in 1769 "puisque le *Journal encyclopédique* de janvier 1770 donne la date 1769 et l'*Année littéraire* du 10 novembre 1769 consacre un long article à ce livre. . . ." Staverman, *op. cit.,* p. 61, quotes a review in *Boekzaal,* which called it "een groote verdienste, dat het geen 'roman,' maar ware historie is." Several collections of true voyages have included it, e.g., James S. Clarke, *Naufragia or Historical Memoirs of Shipwrecks* . . . (London, 1805-6), I, 199-258; Cyrus Redding, *A History of Shipwrecks and Disasters at Sea, from the Most Authentic Sources* (London, 1833), II, [141]-182; and Ferdinand Denis and Victor Chauvin, *Les Vrais Robinsons: naufrages, solitude, voyages* (Paris, 1863), [165]-180. Clarke writes (II, viii): "There are certainly many events narrated by Monsieur Viaud, which tend to render his Story as a true narrative of Facts, very dubious. Some persons have, in consequence, declared the whole to be a Fiction; and even the French themselves have lately given it a place . . . among their *Voyages Imaginaires.* But if the whole of every French Narrative must be assigned to the regions of Fairy Land, because . . . *It is given to lying;* I should imagine that the *tomes* of the *Voyages Imaginaires* would be prodigiously increased. . . ." Hermann Ullrich, *Robinson und Robinsonaden* . . . (Weimar, 1898), pp. 170 f., though recognizing its basis in truth, includes it as fiction, and so does Daniel Mornet in his edition of *La Nouvelle Héloïse* (Paris, 1925), I, 382. Thomas Washington-Metcalfe's *Captain Viaud and Madame La Couture* . . . (London, 1935), is an uncritical retelling of the narrative; a review in the London *Times Literary Supplement,* October 10, 1935, p. 625, expresses the belief "that Captain Viaud is telling the truth about his ordeal so far as his sufferings allow him to recall it." The solution to this confusion turns on the relationship between Viaud and Dubois-Fontanelle as writers. If the original is true, there are still revisions and adaptations to be considered. I have not yet felt justified in including it in my check list of imaginary voyages.

Another work by Dubois-Fontanelle, *Les Effets des passions ou mémoires de M. de Floricourt* (1768) has no connection with the Viaud story though sometimes confused with it. It is not an imaginary voyage, although a few pages of an inner story show the influence of *Robinson* (*Effects of the Passions* . . . , London, 1788, II, 193-97).

in judgment, except that he does not deceive his readers; instead he explains:

Quelques personnes seront surprises de trouver cette relation dans un recueil destiné à de pures fictions; cependant on doit nous savoir gré de l'y avoir employée, & nous croyons quelle y trouve naturellement sa place.

Nous ne pensons nullement à révoquer en doute l'existence de M. Viaud, non plus que la réalité des aventures douloureuses dont il nous a transmis le récit, quoique ces aventures soient accompagnées de circonstances si extraordinaires, qu'elles sembleroient avoir été imaginées à plaisir.

Le but principal que l'on se propose, est d'amuser, d'instruire & d'*intéresser*. Les aventures de M. Viaud ont complettement la dernière qualité: ce ne seroit cependant pas une raison pour sortir du genre que nous nous sommes prescrit; mais nous n'en sortons point. (XII, 3 f.)

Not being able to find in fiction a work to complete all the possible experiences which a well-rounded collection should present in order, Garnier is willing to draw upon nonfiction.[82] Robinson, Quarll, and Gastines were cast away and driven to wrest sustenance from nature, but no storyteller had imagined that nature might not respond. Possibly Garnier has in mind J. H. Campe's objection that Robinson had too much help from the salvaged products of civilization. Campe's *Robinson der Jüngere* (1779-80) shipwrecks the hero without any utensils so that he must rely solely on hands and brain. Though Garnier does not mention Campe's adaptation, he undoubtedly knew it, for it had at least four

---

[82] Editors of true voyages have for similar reasons turned knowingly to fiction; e.g., Stanley R. H. Rogers, *Crusoes and Castaways* (London, [1932]) in his collection of "Crusoes of fact" enters Chetwood's *Falconer,* "a work whose authenticity cannot be vouched for, but which, nevertheless, is too rare and diverting to be omitted on that score" (p. 58).

French editions by 1785.[83] Anyway, his next hero will be more severely tried than Campe's Robinson:

Il falloit qu'il fût jeté dans une île non-seulement déserte, mais stérile, sur un sol sec & ingrat, & sous le ciel le plus rigoureux. Il falloit qu'il s'y trouvâ transporté sans habits, sans armes, sans instrumens d'aucune espèce; c'étoit alors qu'en proie aux tourmens les plus affreux, il pouvoit peindre les nuances qui conduisent au plus grand désespoir; c'est ce que présentent les aventures de M. Viaud, & sous ce point de vue, elles étoient nécessaires à notre recueil. (XII, 5)

Such reasoning carries its own justification. What reader could have objected? An editor is obliged to please his readers more than his critics.

There is no reason to believe that Garnier is indulging in the pretensions to authenticity and genuineness common to authors of imaginary voyages. Nowhere does he attempt to strengthen such claims of an author; the very title of the collection argues against it, although it must be recognized that his method of excusing the inclusion of a "true" narrative would be particularly effective, if he knew it to be fictitious, especially as preparation for the next narrative, about the truth of which there could be no possible doubt but which is introduced without excuses simply as "une relation de naufrage plus récente & non moins intéressante que celle de M. Viaud. . . . Tableau également touchant & fait pour accompagner ceux qui précèdent" (XII, 5 f.). This is the *Relation du naufrage de Madame Godin,* in the form of a letter from her husband to La Condamine in 1773. A few years earlier she had displayed such fortitude in adversity that Prince Charles Bonaparte later honored her by naming a South American bird *Chamæpelia Godinæ.*

---

[83] Mann, *op. cit.,* p. 86 n. 1.

Garnier finds in a sentence in the original letter all the reasons necessary for including in his collection her experiences, "qu'elle n'eut, dit on, qu'une seule fois la force de raconter elle-même":[84]

Si vous lisiez dans un roman qu'une femme délicate, accoutumée à jouir de toutes les commodités de la vie, précipiteé dans une riviere, retirée à demi-noyée, s'enfonce dans un bois elle huitieme, sans route, & y marche plusieurs semaines, se perd; souffre la faim, la soif, la fatigue, jusqu'à l'épuisement, voit expirer ses deux freres beaucoup plus robustes qu'elle, un neveu à peine sorti de l'enfance, trois jeunes femmes, ses domestiques, un jeune valet du médecin qui avoit pris les devants; qu'elle survit à cette catastrophe; que restée [i.e., qu'elle reste] seule deux jours & deux nuits entre ces cadavres, dans des cantons où abondent les tigres & beaucoup de serpents très-dangereux, sans avoir jamais rencontré un seul de ces animaux; qu'elle se releve, se remet en chemin couverte de lambeaux, errante dans un bois sans route, jusqu'au huitieme jour qu'elle se retrouva sur le bord du Bobonosa; vous accuseriez l'auteur du roman de manquer à la vraisemblance; mais un historien ne doit à son lecteur que la simple vérité.[85]

Godin knew what any competent critic knows: as Maupassant succinctly restates a long-acknowledged critical axiom, "le vrai peut quelque-fois n'être pas vraisemblable." When a true narrative surpasses the inventions of artistic imagination, it may with some reason be included in a collection of

[84] Michaud, *op. cit.,* article "Mme. Isabelle Godin des Odonais."
[85] Charles de La Condamine, *Relation abrégée d'un voyage . . . augmentée d'une lettre de . . . M. Godin des Odonais, contenant la relation du voyage de Madame Godin, son Epouse* (Maestricht, 1778), pp. 355 ff. Also in Garnier, XII, 405 f., with minor alterations; also in the *Supplément,* III, 391 f. See my note 70 (4). Deperthes clearly follows the text in La Condamine's publication instead of Garnier's text, which apparently comes from the *Recueil amusant de voyages,* III, 235 f. This, as well as the inclusion of this work twice, is further evidence of lack of editorial connection between the *Collection* and the *Supplément.*

romances; only the strict literary classifier can pronounce *ex cathedra* that Garnier's selection of the adventures of Madame Godin des Odonais is illogical.

It is interesting to note that Garnier's borrowings from the realm of truth are supported a few years later in the *Nouvelle Bibliothèque universelle des romans* by similar but more ingenious reasoning, applied also to the narrative of Viaud's experiences. In a preface to a forty-page résumé the editors explain:

> Quelques personnes s'étonneront peut être de nous voir placer au rang des voyages romanesques le naufrage de M. Viaud. Nous pourrions d'abord nous étayer de l'opinion des éditeurs du recueil des Voyages imaginaires . . . ; mais une simple réflexion suffit pour nous justifier. De l'aveu de toutes les personnes sensées . . . les circonstances de son naufrage . . . sont si extraordinaires, qu'elles peuvent être regardées comme miraculeuses, ou comme romanesques. Dans cette double alternative, c'est à la dernière que nous nous en tenons. En deux mots, le voyage de M. Viaud est vrai ou controuvé; s'il est chimérique, il nous appartïent; s'il est vrai, il n'est pas vraisemblable: et sous cet aspect, il est encore à nous.[86]

What Garnier means by *romanesque* should be clear by now, although it is today a word of confusing connotation. In 1787 *romantic* may have been a proper English equivalent, but *romantique,* though found in the seventeenth century, was not fashionable until after Garnier's time and was not to be admitted to the *Dictionnaire de l'Académie française* until 1798. In the same decade the *Encyclopédie méthodique* specifically states that the two adjectives are not synonyms: "Le *romanesque* est ce qui appartient au roman, le *romantique* est ce qui lui convient ou qui a l'air de lui appartenir," and adds that "Le mot *romantique* appartient à la langue Angloise: plusieurs écrivains françois en ont fait

---

[86] Paris, 1800, seconde année, I, [47] f.

usage, & comme il n'a point d'équivalent dans notre langue, il mérite d'y être adopté." [87] Translators either avoided the English word signifying the response to waste, solitary places, and wild nature or rendered it by *romanesque* or *pittoresque*.[88] For Addison's well-known sentence in his *Remarks on Several Parts of Italy,* "It is so romantic a scene, that it has always probably given occasion to such chimerical Relations," the translator in 1722 used *romanesque*.[89] In 1776 Letourneur in a discourse prefixed to his translation of Shakespere explained his use of *romantique* by noting that neither *romanesque* nor *pittoresque* suggested to him both the physical and the moral connotation of *romantique:*

[*Romanesque*] très souvent pris en mauvaise part, est alors synonyme de chimérique et de fabuleux: il signifie à la lettre, un objet de Roman, qui n'existe que dans le pays de la féerie, dans les rêves bizarres de l'imagination, et ne se trouve point dans la nature. . . . Mais s'il est *Romantique,* on désire de s'y reposer, l'œil se plaît à le regarder et bientôt l'imagination attendrie le peuple de scènes intéressantes: elle oublie le vallon pour se complaire dans les idées, dans les images qu'il lui a inspirées.[90]

Rousseau is often credited with establishing the word *romantique* in his fifth *Rêverie du promeneur solitaire,* published in 1782, where he writes "Les rives du lac de Bienne sont plus sauvages et plus *romantiques* que celles du lac de

[87] Paris, 1791, LX (Beaux Arts, ii), 271.

[88] See Logan P. Smith, "Four Words," *Society for Pure English Tract No. XVII* ([Oxford], 1924), pp. 10-14, F[rederick] C. Green, *French Novelists from the Revolution to Proust* (London and Toronto, [1931]), p. 92, and Servais Étienne, *Le Genre romanesque en France depuis l'apparition de la "Nouvelle Héloïse" jusqu'aux approches de la Révolution* (Paris, 1922), p. 290.

[89] *Remarques sur divers endroits de l'Italie par Mons. Addison, pour servir au voyage de Mons. Misson* (Utrecht, 1722), p. 2, as quoted in Alexis François, "Romantique," *Annales de la société Jean-Jacques Rousseau,* V (1909), 205 n. 1.

[90] François, *loc. cit.,* pp. 211 f.

Genève," but it is not so often pointed out that in the same passage he speaks of "les *romanesques* rivages" of the same lake.[91]

Perhaps, had Garnier been writing a few decades later, he would have called his first division *voyages imaginaires romantiques* instead of *romanesques*. But the two words have always been synonymous in *some* meanings.[92] Garnier does not mean *romanesque* in Letourneur's sense, for his *avertissements* emphasize *vraisemblance*. All fifteen voyages in this division are realistic in the sense that they could have happened to any man, in the sense that their authors do not resort to preternaturalism, in the sense that they are possibilities, whether probable or improbable. This realistic quality makes neither *romanesque* the wrong word nor *romantique* the right word and argues against the substitu-

[91] The significance of Rousseau's apparent uncertainty about *romantique* is pointed out by E. Bourciez, *Revue critique d'histoire et de littérature,* LVI (1903), 277, to whom François refers, *loc. cit.,* pp. [199] f. The history of these words may be found principally in this article by François (pp. [199]-236), supplemented by F[ernand] Baldensperger, *Revue de philologie française et de littérature,* XXV (1911), 53-55; L. Delaruelle, "Encore 'romantique,'" *Revue d'histoire littéraire de la France,* XVIII (1911), 940; André Morize, "'Romantique,'" *ibid.,* p. 440; D[aniel] Mornet, *ibid.,* XVII (1910), 876-77; Alexis François, "De 'Romantique' à 'Romantisme,'" *Bibliothèque universelle et revue suisse,* XCI (1918), [225]-233; [365]-376; and L. P. Smith, *loc. cit.* Since these remarks and citations were prepared, a valuable list of usage has been published by Baldensperger, "'Romantique,' ses analogues et ses équivalents: tableau synoptique de 1650 à 1810," *Harvard Studies and Notes in Philology and Literature,* XIX (1937), [13]-105. None of these studies cites Garnier's use of *romanesque.*

[92] See Littré, *Dictionnaire de la langue française* (1873), Hatzfeld et Darmesteter, *Dictionnaire général,* 8e éd. (1926), and *Dictionnaire de l'Académie française,* 8e éd. (1932). Also Albert Sorel in *Madame de Staël* (1890): "Le mot *romantique* . . . s'employait comme synonyme de romanesque"—quoted in Eugène Ritter, *Les Quatres Dictionnaires français* (Genève, 1905), p. 216; and François: "Aussi arrivera-t-il encore fréquemment . . . que l'on confonde romantique et *romanesque,* tout comme Rousseau," *Annales,* p. 230.

tion of *idéalistique.*[93] It means merely that Garnier is restricting *romanesque* to the natural, the possible according
to the laws of nature, but nature in an exotic setting, often
wild and elemental, sometimes desolate and solitary, and
sometimes peopled by strange *human* beings in far-away or
inaccessible places. Perhaps a reader would not wish to go
on these voyages, much less remain in the realms discovered,
but his imagination should be captivated by the contempla-
tion stimulated by the narration of the voyages. Even *merveilleux* and *chimérique,* two common synonyms for *romanesque,* do not necessarily denote that which is unnatural.
But Garnier sets up *romanesque* and *merveilleux* as mutually
exclusive. As he proceeds to the division containing *voyages
imaginaires merveilleux,* he is specific enough to leave no
doubt about the difference and about the restricted senses in
which he employs the terms:

Les fictions que nous avons données jusqu'à présent à nos lecteurs, ont été resserrées dans les bornes de la vraisemblance. Il
n'a manqué aux terres où nous les avons fait voyager, que d'ob-
tenir une place sur nos cartes géographiques. Il n'en sera pas de
même de celles que nous allons leur faire parcourir. Ici l'imagination rompt tous ses liens, & prend un libre essor; rien ne l'arrête
dans sa course; il semble que l'univers ne soit point assez vaste
pour ses entreprises; elle le pénètre dans tous les sens.

Si elle prend son vol, c'est pour fendre les airs avec rapidité, &
visiter, sans obstacles, toutes les planetes; aucune n'échappe à ses
recherches; elle ne craint pas les torrens de flammes dont le
soleil est enveloppé, & sa marche n'est pas rallentie par les glaces
de Jupiter & de Saturne.

---

[93] F. C. Green, *French Novelists Manners & Ideas from the Renaissance
to the Revolution* (London and Toronto, 1928), pp. 1 f., seeking a term for
the early novel, points out that the French language "differentiates between
the *roman romanesque* and the *roman romantique,* the product of that
nineteenth-century literary movement which we call Romanticism. A better
though not wholly acceptable adjective for the novel which makes no
attempt to adhere to the facts of real life would be 'idealistic.' "

La même rapidité qui l'a élevée audessus de nos têtes, & l'a fait voyager dans les astres, lui fait percer notre globe jusqu'au centre, & lui fait rechercher curieusement ce qui s'y passe.

Quelquefois elle s'amuse à planer dans les airs; enfin, il n'est pas jusqu'au séjour des ombres, où elle ne porte un œil curieux, & où elle ne se promène à son gré.

Des découvertes curieuses & surprenantes devoient nécessairement être le fruit de courses aussi extraordinaires: pour s'en convaincre, il suffira de jetter un coup d'œil sur chacun des ouvrages qui composent cette division, destinée aux *voyages merveilleux.*[94]

Merveilleux indicates the kind of selections intended more definitely than did *romanesque,* but it presents problems for the editor to solve. Chronological order does not often superimpose itself easily upon Garnier's plan, but in the first three volumes of this division the progression from Lucian through Cyrano de Bergerac to Swift and Desfontaines's *Nouveau Gulliver* (1730) brings an expected arrangement into agreement with chronology, except that D'Ablancourt's seventeenth-century continuation of the *True History* falls into the place where it belongs, after Lucian.[95] Garnier is not deaf, as was Paradis de Moncrif, to the universal acclaim merited by Swift: "De tous les ouvrages dont cette classe est composée, nous ne croyons pas en présenter un qui mérite mieux les suffrages de nos lecteurs, que les voyages du capitaine Lemuel Gulliver" (XIV, [vii]). For the *Nouveau Gulliver* Garnier elaborates on Desfontaines's own explanatory preface. There follows the *Voyages récreatifs du Chevalier de Quévédo,* with no significant comment.

[94] XIII, [v] f.

[95] Eddy, *op. cit.,* pp. 55 and 205, and also in "A Source for Gulliver's Travels," *Modern Language Notes,* XXXVI (1921), 419-22, states that Nicolas Perrot d'Ablancourt (1606-64) wrote the continuation; he translated Lucian, but the continuation was the work of his nephew, Jean Jacobé de Frémont d'Ablancourt (1621-96). See J. Balteau, *Dictionnaire de biographie française.*

The *Relation du monde de Mercure* (1750) forces Garnier into an explanation:

Nous aurions pu insérer cet ouvrage dans la classe des romans de magie & de sortilège, puisqu'il est question d'un cabaliste qui, à l'aide d'une lunette magique, fait voir à l'auteur toutes les merveilles du monde de Mercure; mais, comme il s'agit d'un peuple nouveau dont on décrit les mœurs & le gouvernement; comme l'on y donne le tableau de la terre qu'il habite, & des différentes productions qu'elle renferme dans son sein, cet ouvrage nous a paru se rapprocher plus près des voyages imaginaires que de tout autre, & nous avons cru que sa place naturelle se trouvoit au milieu des relations qui nous peignent les habitans du soleil, de la lune & des autres planettes. (XVI, x f.)

Of the thirteen volumes in this division the first six, ending with Mme Robert's *Voyages de Milord Céton dans les sept planèttes* (1765), bring the reader to a temporary stopping point at which Garnier turns from planetary voyaging (although the planets have not been the setting in all and will appear again) to three accounts of subterranean travel. The *Voyage de Nicolas Klimius* leads into "les entrailles de la terre, où ils [nos lecteurs] seront agréalement [*sic*] surpris de se trouver dans un nouveau monde" (XIX, [vii]). "L'ouvrage qui suit plaira par sa singularité: c'est un *voyage du Pole Arctique au Pole Antarctique par le centre du Monde* [1721]. Le Voyageur traverse encore l'intérieur du globe, & donne la plus grande carrière à son imagination. Ces deux voyages ont assez d'analogie pour qu'on se plaise à les voir rassemblés" (XIX, xiii). The third is the chevalier de Mouhy's *Lamekis* (1735):

Nous promenons encore nos lecteurs dans l'intérieur de la terre; mais ce n'est point un nouveau monde que nous y parcourrons; nous y découvrons seulement une retraite de sages, ou, pour mieux dire, de zélés sectateurs de Sérapis, qui pour célébrer tranquillement leurs mystères, avoient cherché à se dérober aux yeux du reste des hommes. Il ne se passe pas moins de choses extraordinaires dans cette partie secrète de notre globe, & la féconde imagination de l'auteur de ce roman s'est exercée à son aise dans les différentes aventures qu'elle y fait naître, & les merveilles qu'elle décrit. (XX, [vii] f.)

Particularly in the realm of the marvelous an author's imagination is likely to keep no sharp distinction between literary types. Material which Garnier had been considering for the forty-one volumes of the *Cabinet des fées* must have constantly sought admission to the later collection, for a voyage of some marvelous sort is a prevalent element in fairy tales. The inclusion of Aunillon's *Azor ou le Prince Enchanté* (1750) and a few later pieces can be thus explained without charging the editor with being confused. "Cet ingénieux ouvrage," he himself knows, "est en même tems féerie & voyage imaginaire; nous croyons pourtant qu'il appartient plus particulièrement à la dernière classe" (XXI, [1]). The English savant Popinjay, to whom the abbé Aunillon attributed the authorship of *Azor,* takes his reader to a land of parrots, which tends further to align this story with those about unfamiliar nations of strange people.

More human but still marvelously strange are the flying men and women created by Robert Paltock. "Depuis que l'on est parvenu à s'élever dans les airs & à y faire des courses assez longues pour être regardées comme de véritables voyages, les *Hommes Volans* ne doivent plus être rangés au nombre des merveilles. Mais ce que nous devons à l'art, les *Glums* en sont redevables à la nature." [96] After giving a careful description of the wings and the method of using them, Garnier, as he often does skillfully in a few sentences,

[96] XXII, [vii]. The journals of the 1780s carry numerous accounts of balloon ascensions, particularly in France.

reveals enough about the setting to provoke a desire to get into the story:

Avec des dons si distingués, l'espèce des Glums paroît particulièrement favorisée de la nature, & s'élever beaucoup au-dessus de l'espèce commune des mortels, qu'elle a condamnés à ramper sur la terre; cependant ces richesses apparentes couvrent une véritable indigence; ces peuples vivent dans une nuit éternelle; la lumière du jour blesse leur vue trop foible pour la soutenir; les arts & les sciences sont inconnus parmi eux, & l'industrie est une chose qui leur est tout-à-fait étrangère, & dont ils n'ont même aucune idée. Tout ce qu'ils ont, ils le tiennent de la nature; &, contens de ses libéralités, ils ne cherchent point ailleurs de nouvelles jouissances. Nous ne nous étendrons pas davantage sur cette singulière & intéressante production: nous ne voulons pas anticiper sur le plaisir que l'on aura à la lire. On y trouvera des leçons d'une morale douce & saine, & les agrémens d'une fiction ingénieuse. (XXII, viii f.)

Legrand's *Aventures du voyageur aérien* (1724) "contient encore une relation des voyages faits dans les airs. Mais le Voyageur ne découvre pas des peuples nouveaux: son secret ne lui sert qu'à parcourir rapidement notre globe. . . . les courses aériennes de notre Voyageur ne servent que de cadre au roman, & donnent à l'auteur le moyen d'y réunir plusieurs morceaux, dont les uns sont des histoires intéressantes, . . . les autres des romans comiques & merveilleux, . . . & enfin des critiques . . ." (XXIII, [vii]). This is a good illustration of how a narrative form can be changed. With the usual characteristics of an imaginary voyage through the air, a story may land its hero for the purpose of a picaresque adventure, a euphuistic conversation, or a feigned true history of a European court.

One more work concludes this kind of air travel: *Micromégas;* "c'est un géant échappé de l'étoile Sirius, qui se promène de planètes en planètes, avec autant de facilité que nous allons d'un village à un autre. . . . & il faut convenir qu'après la hardiesse de celle-ci, il est difficile d'en entreprendre de nouvelles" (XXIII, viii). Whether true or not, this last statement should leave the readers assured that the editor has given them the best and that he can now turn to another kind of marvelous imaginary voyage. He has yet to fulfill his promise to conduct them into the world of the dead. This is where Fielding is called upon to contribute *Julien l'Apostat.* A universal pilot must include route-directions for the Champs-Élisées, but one example suffices, and the reader is led into the *Terres australes* in Foigny's *Aventures de Jacques Sadeur.* These lands, "inaccessibles aux voyageurs les plus intrépides, ne le sont pas à nos romanciers; c'est-là qu'ils font leurs découvertes les plus curieuses" (XXIV, 6).

Volume XXV

termine la classe nombreuse & intéressante des voyages merveilleux, & nous en aurions porté la collection à un nombre de volumes bien plus considérable, si nous eussions voulu n'offrir à nos lecteurs que des fictions ingénieuses, dignes d'occuper leurs loisirs.

Les deux ouvrages qui composent ce volume [Henri Pajon's *Histoire du Prince Soly* (1740) and Christoforo Armeno's *Voyage des trois princes de Sarendip*], approchent du genre de la féerie, par la nature des fictions qu'ils renferment, par le merveilleux qui y règne; ils appartiennent néanmoins aux voyages imaginaires. (XXV, vii f.)

Two volumes only are devoted to the nine *voyages imaginaires allégoriques,* which is the third division of the first class. The transition from division to division is not abrupt:

Nous commençons cette division par un ouvrage [G. H. Bougeant's *Voyage merveilleux du Prince Fan-Férédin dans la romancie*] qui est en même tems voyage merveilleux & voyage allégorique, & qui, en conséquence, forme naturellement la nuance des deux divisions: nous l'attribuons néanmoins à celle des allégories à laquelle il appartient plus particulièrement. (XXVI, [vii])

Allégorique opens upon as wide a field as *merveilleux,* but the choices are to be confined not only to voyages but to voyages to new worlds. "Nous ne donnons point ici un recueil ni un choix de toutes les Allégories ou Romans, Contes & Nouvelles allégoriques, mais de celles seulement qui ayant pour objet la description d'un peuple imaginaire, rentrent sous ce point de vue dans notre plan" (XXVII, [v]). Even more unity can be discerned in the fact that most of these imaginary people are discovered on islands. The map contains an *isle imaginaire,* an *isle d'amour,* an *isle de portraiture,* an *isle enchantée,* an *isle de la félicité,* an *isle taciturne,* and an *isle enjouée.* The allegories may be *critique, satyre, pastoral,* or *sentencieux,* and be so listed by other classifiers, but they are for this collection also imaginary voyages.

That this third division of the first class fills only two volumes and that the fourth division fills only three imply that both these last divisions, together occupying only five volumes out of thirty, are minor groups of works that might have been called "other miscellaneous imaginary voyages," *voyages imaginaires divers* perhaps. This is particularly true of those under the fourth heading, *amusans, comiques & critiques.* They are not to be considered as modifying seriously the genre. Garnier's own comments are as usual enlightening. After warping into line, almost as if he were conceding to the expected demands of his readers, Sterne's "ouvrage charmant . . . des observations philosophiques, critiques & morales faites par un voyageur qui ne parcourt le monde que pour étudier les hommes" (and the *Sentimental Journey* has defied more than one classifier), Garnier explains his succeeding choices:

Nous nous sommes bornés à un très-petit nombre de *voyages amusans*. Ce genre d'ouvrages ne pouvoit être exclus de notre recueil, mais d'un autre côté il ne devoit point y occuper trop de place; c'est une sorte de poésie fugitive qui ne tient que foiblement aux voyages imaginaires.

Nous ne donnerons donc que sept de ces voyages, dont le nombre est d'ailleurs considérable; mais en nous prescrivant des bornes aussi étroites, nous avons mis d'autant plus de sévérité dans notre choix. Il n'est aucune des pièces que nous employons, qui ne soit un vrai chef-d'œuvre. (XXVIII, 2 f.)

A reading of these seven voyages will show the pointlessness of arguing that a voyage may be both marvelous and amusing, or allegorical and amusing, and that therefore Garnier is illogical.[97] *Amusans* is used as a specialized critical term, not carefully defined because the voyages speak for themselves. Again one must look into the voyages instead of jumping to conclusions about the terms. None of these voyages is over fifty pages long; all except the last, which is only a fragment, are in the form of letters in both prose and verse. The tone and aim can be perceived in a few sentences from them. The *Voyage curieux, historique et galant de Chapelle & Bachaumont* (1680) by Claude Lhuillier and François le Coigneux de Bachaumont, which Garnier considers the best of them all, concludes with a promise to continue the account of their journey later:

Si nous allions tout vous déduire,
Nous n'aurions plus rien à vous dire;
Et vous saurez qu'il est plus doux
De causer, buvant avec vous,
Qu'en voyageant, de vous écrire. (XXVIII, 260)

The authors strive with affectation to avoid taking them-

[97] Compare Eddy, *op. cit.*, p. 12.

selves seriously. Lefranc de Pompignon in his *Voyage de Languedoc & de Provence* (1740) writes:

. . . croyez aussi que jamais parole ne fut plus légérement engagée. Je suis sûr
    Que toute homme sensé rira
    D'une entreprise si fallote;
    Que personne ne nous lira,
    Ou que celui qui le fera,
    A coup sûr très-fort s'ennuira,
    Que vers & prose on sifflera:
    Et que, sur cette preuve-là,
    Le régiment de la Calotte
    Pour ses voyageurs nous prendra. . . (XXVIII, [301] f.)

and the chevalier Antoine de Bertin apparently mocks his own efforts by a precious metaphor in the opening lines of his *Voyages de Bourgoyne* (1777):

Commençons par tremper notre plume légère
Dans les flots écumeux d'un nectar pétillant . . . . (XXVIII, 356)

One piece, Arnaud Berquin's *Voyage de Didier de Lormeuil* (c.1780), is a correspondence between a brother and a sister, who in her "dernière réponse" rallies him on his letters:

J'avois toujours ouï dire que rien ne servoit, comme les voyages, à former l'esprit: ta relation vient de m'en donner une preuve, à laquelle j'étois bien loin de m'attendre. Qui jamais eût pensé qu'un petit écolier de rhétorique, comme toi, se crût déjà philosophe, pour avoir fait six lieues! (XXVIII, 433)

As might be expected, some light is thrown on Garnier's use of the term *amusans* by observing how some of his contemporaries employed the word. Only a few years earlier (1783) had appeared the first four volumes of the *Recueil amusant de voyages, en vers et en prose,* edited by Laurent P.

Bérenger and Martin Couret de Villeneuve; two more volumes followed in the next year, and the last three in 1787,
just a year before Garnier's twenty-eighth volume. The facts
that this collection contains all the pieces included by
Garnier as *amusans* and that the texts correspond in all es-
sentials are convincing evidence that it served as the immediate source from which he made his limited selection. Its
preliminary explanation, therefore, becomes an important
guide to the interpretation of *amusans*. In dedicating the
Recueil amusant to his sister, Couret de Villeneuve flatter-
ingly but rather enigmatically states that it "ressemble à
votre esprit: il présente les fleurs les plus riantes de notre
Parnasse, à côté des fruits de la plus douce Philosophie." He
continues:

Ce mélange piquant d'idées, de tableaux, de réflexions & de
badinages, cette prodigieuse variété de langage, de tant de formes
& de cadres, me paroît fait pour amuser à la fois & pour instruire, & doit plaire à tous les esprits. C'est-là, si je ne me trompe,
le seul Livre qui conviendra désormais à ces Voyageurs intéressans, que le désir de voir conduit dans l'intérieur de nos Provinces
& vers nos Côtes méridionales. Ils verront, dans les Paysages
Poétiques que j'ai pris soin de rassembler, une aussi grande
diversité d'objets, que celle qui passera rapidement sous leurs
yeux: ils compareront la Nature avec son image, & ce ne sera
pas sans plaisir. Les Jeunes Gens y apprendront à décrire ce
qu'ils voient, avec la grace, le naturel & la facilité des Auteurs
aimables que je leur donne pour Compagnons de voyage. Mon
plus grand plaisir, à moi, seroit de parcourir avec vous quelques-
uns des Pays qu'ont chantés Chapelle & Bachaumont, & de vous
entendre lire leurs Vers. (I, [v]-[vi])

Among several other eighteenth-century collections with
some derivative of the verb *amuser* may be cited the
*Bibliothèque amusante et instructive, contenant des anecdotes
interessantes & des histoires curieuses tirées des meilleurs*

auteurs, edited by J. P. Niceron and F. J. Duporte-Dutertre
(Paris, 1753); the six-volume *Bibliothèque choisie et amusante* (Amsterdam, 1748-52); and the eighteen-volume
*Bibliothèque de campagne ou amusemens de l'esprit et du
cœur,* edited by Étienne Philippe de Prétot in a new edition
(La Haye et Geneve, 1749). The first of these in its *avertissement* stresses the knowledge of foreign manners and
customs to be conveyed to the reader "sans être obligé de
courir le monde, ou, ce qui est presque aussi fatigant, de lire
toutes les Relations des Voyageurs" and thereby proposes to
please and to instruct. The second includes one of the pieces
in Garnier, Louis Balthazar Néel's *Voyage de St. Cloud par
mer et par terre,* and the third includes the *Voyage de
Chapelle et Bachaumont.* When, therefore, an editor brought
out at Geneva in 1782 the *Voyage de Chapelle et de Bachaumont, suivi de quelques autres voyages dans le même genre,*
it is clear that the genre was *voyages amusans,* already established before the collection of Garnier.[98] The quarrel with
Garnier centers not on the word *amusans* but on the term
imaginaires, for some of these voyages seem to be elaborated
accounts of real itineraries.[99]

The *avertissement* to the next volume of Garnier's collection contains the editor's valedictory to the first class, the
voyages imaginaires. He is looking back beyond the immediately preceding *voyages amusans* to the earlier divisions and
preparing for the last two volumes of this class:

Après avoir fait parcourir à nos lecteurs des régions imaginaires &
merveilleuses, nous allons leur offrir de simples promenades,
uniquement propres à leur servir de délassemens. . . .

---

[98] Among the other voyages in the last-named book is Lefranc de
Pompignon's *Voyage de Languedoc,* pp. [59]-113, also in Garnier. Néel's
piece is in V, [183]-216 of the *Bibliothèque choisie.* I do not have the
date of the first edition of Philippe de Prétot's collection; there was a
Supplément, 7 vols. (Genève, 1761).
[99] See further on the *kleine Reiseromane,* pp. 173-74 below.

Ce ne sont plus de régions imaginaires que nous allons parcourir; cependant les ouvrages que nous donnons n'en sont pas moins des romans, & même des romans merveilleux, analogues au genre que nous avons adopté, & faisant essentiellement partie d'un recueil de voyages imaginaires. Les héros de ces romans sont des voyageurs qui, sans traverser les mers, ni errer dans des terres éloignées & inconnues, n'en ont pas moins des aventures dignes de piquer la curiosité, ou par des situations touchantes qui intéressent le cœur, ou par un badinage agréable qui amuse l'esprit.

La liste des voyages de ce genre est longue; mais le nombre de ceux que nous employerons sera resserré dans des bornes très-étroites: nous y consacrons ce volume & le suivant; ils termineront les voyages imaginaires.[100]

First in this volume is Mme de Murat's *Voyage de campagne* (1699), which "ne sert que de cadre à plusieurs contes & historiettes. . . . Quelques-uns . . . sont intéressans, d'autres sont gais & amusans, enfin il en est de merveilleux; car on y trouve aussi des contes de fées, des aventures de revenans & des sortilèges" (XXIX, ix). So, too, do some of the other works cut across lines of definite classification. L'Affichard's *Voyage interrompu* (1737), with its tone "comique, & quelquefois bouffon . . . est mélangé d'historiettes agréables"; and Marivaux's *Voiture embourbée* (1714), made "sur le même cadre . . . est d'abord un roman héroïque, ensuite un conte de fée, & enfin une facétie" (XXX, vii,ix). These critical remarks, instead of complicating, clarify Garnier's intentions. The *badinage qui amuse l'esprit* may turn into the comic, and good comedy is always critical. It is not difficult to establish the appropriateness of Garnier's classification, *amusans, comiques & critiques*.

Even though my subject is the imaginary voyage, one who

[100] XXIX, [vii] ff. See my note 74 on the errors on the title page of this volume and the following volume.

has followed Garnier so carefully through thirty volumes would be doing him an injustice not to look into the final six to discover his reasons for the other two classes, the *songes et visions* and the *romans cabalistiques,* and to comprehend once for all the total conception of the work. This can be accomplished by reading two *avertissements,* which reveal that, although he has left the class of the *voyages imaginaires* behind, a thread of voyaging and meeting strange peoples is woven into the plan of the whole collection. His distinction between different kinds of dreams shows relevant consideration of the terms to be employed:

Les songes & les visions ont un rapport sensible avec les voyages imaginaires; la seule chose qui y mette de la différence, c'est que dans les songes, le corps est supposé dans un plein repos, goûter même les douceurs du sommeil, tandis que l'esprit se promène & parcourt seul des mondes nouveaux, inconnus & chimériques.

Les *songes* sont aussi plus voisins du mer-veilleux que les voyages fictifs, & tiennent ainsi de plus près à la seconde division que nous avons indiquée des voyages imaginaires merveilleux. Comme ils sont une imitation des songes réels, & que ceux-ci ne connoissent point les loix de la vraisemblance. Le songe fictif doit représenter des choses extraordinaires. Enfin les songes sont circonscrits dans un espace de tems plus court, & la fiction imite encore ici la réalité. Les songes réels sont des enfans du sommeil, qui disparoissent avec celui qui leur a donné naissance: ils ne peuvent donc durer que quelques heures; les songes fictifs sont donc des sortes de pièces fugitives, qui ne doivent décrire que ce qui a pu se passer dans l'espace d'une nuit.

Nous ne distinguons pas les *rêves* des songes; ces deux dénominations nous ont paru synonymes & données indifféremment par les auteurs; cependant nous croyons avoir observé que l'on attribue plus particulièrement le nom de rêves à ceux qui rassemblent le plus d'idées disparates, extravagantes & singulières & que l'on conserve le nom de songes à ceux qui ont un ton plus sérieux, moins déraisonnable, & qui contiennent le plus de critique, de morale & de philosophie.

Les *visions* diffèrent essentiellement des songes. Elles sont enfantées par une imagination exaltée ou blessée, & approchent du délire; mais les visions fictives ont le même but & le même caractère que les songes, & il nous a paru inutile de les distinguer.

Cette classe sera la moins étendue du recueil; les ouvrages qu'elle renferme sont courts, le cadre en est uniforme; il ne se trouve de la variété que dans les détails. Nous avons cru devoir la resserrer encore plus que les autres. Le choix que nous y avons mis nous assure que nos lecteurs n'y trouveront pas moins d'agrément que dans ce qui a précédé. (XXXI, [vii] ff.)

The other *avertissement* is more to the point, for it reviews the progress of the whole work. It is an eloquent conclusion:

Jusqu'a présent nous n'avons cessé non-seulement de faire errer nos lecteurs dans des terres inconnues, mais nous leur avons encore fait franchir l'espace immense qui les sépare des planètes, & nous les leur avons fait parcourir les unes après les autres. Nous les avons ensuite ramenés sur notre globe pour les conduire jusques dans ses entrailles, & par-tout nous leur avons fait voir des merveilles dignes de piquer leur curiosité. Les voyageurs dont nous avons suivi les pas, ont été le jouet de la fortune, & exposés aux aventures les plus bizarres: géans chez les Lilliputiens, nains chez les peuples de Brobdingnag, bêtes de somme dans le pays des Houynhmms, esprits légers & superficiels auprès des Hommes-Plantes chez lesquels a voyagé Klimius, esprits lourds & paresseux dans la région des Hommes-Volans . . . il est peu de formes sous lesquelles ils ne se soient montrés.

Après ces courses étranges, nous leur avons procuré d'agréables promenades qui n'ont pas été néanmoins stériles pour leur imagination; nous les avons entretenus, pendant leur séjour à la campagne, de contes, d'historiettes & de nouvelles qui ont dû les délasser·de leur fatigues; & si en les berçant de ces charmantes bagatelles, ils se sont laissé aller au sommeil, nous leur avons envoyé des songes qui ne leur ont pas permis de regretter le tems de leur réveil.

Nous allons les tirer de cet état, pour leur procurer un nouveau spectacle & leur faire connoître des peuples nouveaux; mais nous nous y prendrons d'une autre manière pour leur faire faire ce voyage. Ces découvertes n'exigent point que nos lecteurs quittent leurs foyers; il nous suffira de désiller leurs yeux, & soudain ils seront entourés d'une multitude d'êtres dont ils ne soupçonnoient pas l'existence. Leurs regards perceront les entrailles de la terre, & iront y découvrir les Gnomes; il verront l'air rempli de Sylphes; du milieu des flammes, ils apercevront s'élever les Salamandres, & le sein des eaux ne cachera plus pour eux les Ondins & les Nymphes. Ce n'est pas tout; l'avare Acheron laissera échapper sa proie, les morts sortiront de leurs tombeaux, leurs ames viendront converser avec nous, & nous dévoiler des mystères qui semblent hors de la portée des foibles mortels.

Tel est le reste de la tâche que nous avons à remplir. Les romans cabalistiques & de magie que nous allons donner, tiennent de très-près aux Voyages imaginaires, & se trouvent naturellement à leur suite.

Ce ne sont pas les traités que l'on a faits sérieusement sur ces matieres que nous donnerons à nos lecteurs, rien ne seroit plus étranger à notre plan; nous leur présenterons seulement un choix de romans où l'on suppose l'existence des magiciens, des enchanteurs, des lutins, des revenans & du peuple élémentaire. (XXXIII, [1]-5)

Garnier's divisions of the imaginary voyage are certainly not coördinate; they are in an arrangement that may be called descending. Perhaps no wrong will be committed by supposing his process of reasoning (assuming in the absence of contrary evidence that he himself formulated the divisions): All fictitious voyages may be divided into two principal groups, the possible (*romanesque*) and the impossible (*merveilleux*). But not all impossibilities are marvelous; for example, allegories—impossibilities by definition—have a

special characteristic which separates them from the marvelous as long as the allegory dominates. Sometimes, however,
the allegory becomes subsidiary to the story, and then purpose gives way to narrative for its own sake. Good story-
telling is always more important than form or ulterior motive. The same is true of the satiric, the facetious, the purely
amusing; these can be put into one of the first two classes
if the emphasis is on the voyage first, if the voyage is made
to seem real, like an actual experience, whether possible or
impossible. But if the voyage is only a vehicle which becomes
lost, forgotten by the author, subordinated, then the work
belongs in a special subordinate class.

Thus might Garnier have reasoned. Decisions about the
validity of this reasoning must be postponed until presentation of the expressed opinions of later historians and critics
of fiction allows comparison. Garnier, it may be said now,
pretended to be neither a historian nor a critic but an editor;
as editorial accomplishment his work is entitled to approval.
If I have relied heavily on quotation from Garnier, the reason is that he has himself been able to prove the points which
I have wished to establish—points extracted not by inferen-
tial interpretation but by examination of what is inherent in
the work itself. If I have spent much time urging what may
(by now, I hope) seem simple and obvious, the reason is
only that for 150 years Garnier's work as an early collector
and classifier of one kind of fiction has been, when not
neglected entirely, misunderstood, misrepresented, and condemned as chaotic. Every subsequent critic who has had occasion to mention imaginary voyages singly or generically
could have profited by giving some study to Garnier's thirty-
six volumes.[101]

[101] I may further emphasize that I have been trying to see the problem of
a collection of imaginary voyages from Garnier's eighteenth-century point
of view. That later I eliminate from my check list several of his inclusions

B. THE NINETEENTH CENTURY

In English, as far as I can discover, no recognition or discussion of the imaginary voyage as a literary type appeared before the nineteenth century. Perhaps Clara Reeve just missed it in 1785 in the *Progress of Romance* where she decides that *Robinson Crusoe* and *Gaudentio di Lucca* "partake of the nature of both [romances and novels], but I consider them as of a different species from either. . . . I shall have occasion to place some later works under this class." [102] This promise turns out unsatisfactorily, when she reads her "list of Novels and Stories Original and uncommon," which includes, besides the two above, *Don Quixote, Pilgrim's Progress, Gulliver, John Buncle, Peter Wilkins, Tristram Shandy,* and the *Castle of Otranto.* The spark of recognition of any classification more definite than "originals" goes out when she adds "I shall next introduce another species of the same Genus of writing," which proves to be "Tales and Fables ancient and modern" (II, 53-56).

At Edinburgh in 1812 appeared a volume entitled *Popular Romances: Consisting of Imaginary Voyages and Travels.* In it in double columns of small type are reprinted four English narratives and one translation, all of the eighteenth century, named on the half titles as follows:

Travels into Several Remote Nations of the World by Lemuel
 Gulliver (pp. [3]-114)
A Journey to the World Underground by Nicholas Klimius
 (pp. [117]-200)
The Life and Adventures of Peter Wilkins . . . by R.S. . . .
 (pp. [203]-348)

cannot (I believe) be taken to be contradictory. Now that this examination is completed I readily acknowledge that at the time of first skimming his volumes I despaired of ever untangling the apparent confusion.

[102] Ed. Esther M. McGill (New York, 1930), I, 127.

The Life and Adventures of Robinson Crusoe by Daniel Defoe (pp. [351]-582)

The Capacity and Extent of the Human Understanding; Exemplified in the Extraordinary Case of Automathes . . . (pp. [585]-638)

Prefixed is a twenty-six-page "introductory dissertation" by Henry William Weber (1783-1818), editor of plays and romances and, in Lockhart's words, "half-starved amanuensis" to Sir Walter Scott, who characterized him as "a man of very superior attainments, an excellent linguist and geographer, and a remarkable antiquary." [103] This praise, however, was bestowed eight years after Weber's tragic death in insanity, and beside it should be read Scott's words in a letter to Ellis in 1808: "little Weber may be very useful upon antiquarian subjects, in the way of collecting information and making remarks; only, you or I must re-write his lucubrations. I use him often as a pair of eyes in consulting books and collating, and as a pair of hands in making extracts" (II, 98).

Weber followed in a small way the steps of Garnier. In the same year he edited three volumes of oriental tales which he compared "to the large and valuable French collection in forty-one volumes, entitled *Le Cabinet des Fées,*" [104] but he seems not to have known that Garnier was one of the editors. Similarly he refers in his *Popular Romances* to "an extensive collection of these classes of romantic voyages, combined with the more celebrated dreams, visions, and cabalistic romances . . . published at Amsterdam, in 35 [*sic*] volumes, in 1787

---

[103] John G. Lockhart, *Memoirs of the Life of Sir Walter Scott,* Cambridge ed. (Boston and New York, 1902), I, 401, and IV, 507.

[104] *Tales of the East: Comprising the Most Popular Romances of Oriental Origin; and the Best Imitations by European Authors* . . . (Edinburgh, 1812), I, lxii.

. . . [which] has become a standard work." [105] Despite the fact that Weber's publishers, the Ballantynes, spoke of his "gigantic scheme" for a collection of oriental tales,[106] his total of four volumes for the two publications, considered beside Garnier's seventy-seven, makes any further comparison between the two men as editors unfair.

To this opportunity for setting before English readers for the first time a critical discussion of the imaginary voyage Weber responded with only a general and discursive essay, written in pleasing manner but not much to the point. His first paragraph, as well as the title, will show how he digressed into remarks on popular medieval romances:

Perhaps the most legitimate and useful subject for a preface to a collection of this kind, is to trace the history of the works contained in it; but there are so few materials for such a purpose, that the reader must rest content with a very meagre detail of such facts as have come within our knowledge. As the history of what the French term *Voyages Imaginaires,* is so minutely connected with that of the belles lettres in general, and romance in particular, it seems reasonable to prefix a few hasty remarks on that subject, in order to enable the reader to obtain a more accurate view of what has appeared to have produced that comparatively modern species of romance. . . . (p. [xvii])

Thoughts on the period of chivalry come round to "the universal inclination for the marvellous, which . . . pervaded almost every department of literature and science." Theology, medicine, law, chemistry, astronomy, and geography, the lives of saints and martyrs, the most popular sermons, and trials by ordeal—all are mentioned as evidence.

---

[105] *Popular Romances,* p. xxii. He says that "it has been reprinted since," but I do not know of the reprinting to which he refers. Cf. my note 65.

[106] Samuel Smiles, *A Publisher and His Friends* . . . (London, 1911), p. 70. This was in 1809, three years before publication; the original plan may have been reduced.

This led to a similar style in the relations of travellers, and the descriptions of remote countries. A simple and true narrative of Sir John Mandeville's peregrinations would not have obtained very extensive popularity; it required the addition of marvellous incidents, descriptions of wonderful nations, . . . magnetic mountains, and almost superhuman works of art . . . (p. xix).

Nor did public belief in extravagant reports diminish much by the curiosity of the learned in the discoveries of the sixteenth century.

The points which Weber then proceeds to elaborate in many hundreds of words may be reduced to a few simple statements: "the transmission from travels and voyages actually performed . . . to such as were merely performed in the author's study, was easy"; the creation of an imaginary adventurer was the obvious result of the imagination's ranging from real travels to fancied realms; the discovery of "this ready mode of diverting and instructing" came surprisingly late, even though "the moral use which such a work might be made the vehicle of, was too obvious to escape observation"; the imaginary voyage is therefore "eminently qualified for the perusal of youth" as an antidote for vanity and absurd prejudices and as an illustration of the ideals of good government, "the necessity of self-control, and a due confidence in the real powers inherent in our bodily frame"; and the mature reader can be both instructed by the display of the philosophy of the human mind and pleased by the talents of the author in shadowing forth this philosophy under airy disguise.

All these observations are elementary; some are unsound. Although Weber knew of Garnier's collection, he makes no profitable use of his *avertissements*. Once, in a comparatively short paragraph, he implies a classification of imaginary voyages as possible and impossible or marvelous:

Setting aside the humorous work of Lucian . . . as well as the

fabulous voyages of Mandeville, together with those of Sinbad
. . . as not being strictly comprehended under the title of 'Imaginary Voyages and Travels,' the most ancient works of the kind
are the 'State of the Sun and Moon,' written by Cyrano de Bergerac . . . and the 'History of the Sevarambes'. . . . But though
France preceded in point of antiquity, the merit of having produced the most excellent and universally popular works, in the
two classes into which these productions of fancy naturally separate, indubitably appertains to the English. Of all those which
belong to the marvellous class, unconfined by the laws of probability or actual experience, 'Gulliver's Travels' bears away the
palm; and the same eminent distinction is due to 'Robinson
Crusoe,' among those which do not exceed the bounds of possibility. The noise which these two romances occasioned throughout Europe, produced a great bustle among the literati to emulate
their excellency, and equal the fame which they bestowed on the
authors. They met, as may be naturally inferred, with various
degrees of success, but none equalled that of their illustrious
prototypes. (pp. xxi f.)

Fifteen years after Weber's death another edition of *Popular Romances* was brought out in two volumes but so changed
that the plan of the first edition disappears. All three parts
of *Robinson Crusoe,* John Howell's *Life and Adventures of
Alexander Selkirk,* which had appeared meanwhile in 1829,
and *Automathes* fill these volumes. Although *Gulliver,
Nicolas Klimius,* and *Peter Wilkins* are omitted, the original
introduction with its discussion of these three works is retained.[107] The slight importance that may be attached to
Weber's book rests on priority and on a few ideas that he

[107] Edinburgh; Published for the Proprietors by W. & R. Chambers
. . . W. Orr, London, and W. Curry, Jun. & Co., Dublin, 1838 (The British
Library). In the Yale copy of Vol. I a publisher's slip pasted in the front
announces that Vol. II will contain *Klimius,* but Vol. II contains no explanation of the changes; on the final page is the line "End of Vol. II."
Possibly more volumes were planned, or issued, but I have found no trace
of them.

contributed to the work of a much more important literary historian.

Two years after the first edition of Weber, John Colin Dunlop (1785-1842) published in two volumes his *History of Fiction: Being a Critical Account of the Most Celebrated Prose Works of Fiction, from the Earliest Greek Romances to the Novels of the Present Day* (1814). Though condemned by a typically vituperative review in the *Quarterly* and commended only with reservations in the *Edinburgh Review*,[108] it has remained the most important early work in English on fiction. Dunlop devotes his penultimate chapter to seventeenth- and eighteenth-century French novels "reduced into four classes": those founded on a basis of historical events; those in which the incidents, whether serious or comical, are altogether imaginary; those of a moral or satirical tendency, where foreigners are feigned to travel through the different states of Europe, describing the manners of its inhabitants; and fairy tales, to which may be associated the French imitations of the oriental tales and *voyages imaginaires*.[109] The kind of "association" remains indefinite when the author comes to discuss his fourth class (happily the confusion in the four classes as a group is of no concern here) and says: "To the class of fairy and oriental tales may be referred that species of composition which in France was known under the title of Voyages Imaginaires" (II, 518). In view of his quadripartition of French novels Dunlop seems to be presenting the imaginary voyage as a special and subordinate kind of fairy tale. The chapter heading, however, reads "French Novels—Fairy Tales—Voyages Imaginaires." This tripartite arrangement corresponds more accurately to his actual method of discus-

[108] *Quarterly Review*, XIII (1815), 384-408; *Edinburgh Review*, XXIV (1814-15), 38-58.
[109] Edition cited (my note 17), II, [447].

sion throughout the chapter, with the novels subdivided into three and with the fairy tale and *voyage imaginaire* making two separate divisions. This then leaves Dunlop free to "associate" with the imaginary voyage *songes et visions* and *romans cabalistiques,* "the last species of this division of fiction, which it will be necessary to mention" (II, 540).

Dunlop is following the plan of Garnier. In fact, had Garnier's collection not existed, it is apparent that Dunlop would have given little attention at all to the imaginary voyages as a type. Besides mentioning the *necessity* of including the *romans cabalistiques,* Dunlop says that "in an historical account of fictitious writing, it would not be proper altogether to neglect" the imaginary voyages (II, 518). As one of the reviewers wrote of the work as a whole, "Dunlop seems to be somewhat ashamed of the companions whom he introduces, and in order to ward off from himself the ridicule of those who are perhaps incapable of appreciating their real worth, he is anxious to be the first to sneer at the society which he has chosen." [110] Such a perfunctory and apologetic attitude toward the imaginary voyage explains in part why Dunlop, with Garnier open before him, follows him from Volume One through Volume Thirty-Six, pausing occasionally to elaborate or to give a plot résumé, omitting much, but never once mentioning either the French collection or its editor.[111] Furthermore, Dunlop includes Weber's introduction among his unmentioned sources. The evidence is open to any one who cares to compare in detail the texts; charges against Dunlop are here only incidental to an evaluation of his discussion of the imaginary voyage. Echoes of

[110] *Quarterly Review,* XIII (1815), 408.

[111] My Dunlop references are to the revised edition (1896 [1888]) of Henry Wilson, who does refer to Garnier at least twice: in "Some Works Relating to the Subject" (I, x) and in a note on *Lamekis* (II, 537 n. 3), but these are not Dunlop's references.

both Garnier and Weber can be heard in the quotation that follows:

These productions bear the same relation to real voyages and travels as the common novel or romance to history and biography. They have been written with different views, but are generally intended to exhibit descriptions, events, and subjects of instruction, which are not furnished by the scenes of manners of the real world. In some cases, as in Robinson Crusoe, mankind are led to appreciate their own exertions by seeing what their species is capable of when in perfect solitude, and abandoned to its own resources. In l'Isle Inconnue they are shown what they may attain when confined to domestic society, and excluded from all intercourse with the rest of the world. Sometimes the imaginary traveller is received among nations of perfect and ideal wisdom. At others, the author, seizing the advantages presented by shipwrecks and pirates, throws his characters on some inhospitable shore, the fancied distance of which entitles him to people it with all sorts of prodigies and monsters. The planets, too, and centre of the earth were made the theatres of these chimerical expeditions, which, even in their most common form, are entertaining; and in their more improved state have sometimes become, as in the case of the celebrated work of Swift, the vehicle of the keenest satire, and even of philosophical research.[112]

After attributing the origin of "this species of fiction" to Lucian and the "remote original of this sort of fabling" to Homer, Dunlop summarizes in a paragraph the *True History* and then jumps to the Middle Ages by the easy means of observing that

the spirit of those extravagant relations satirized by Lucian never was extinguished, and fictitious embellishments were mingled

---

[112] II, 518 f. Cf. the first sentence with Henry Fielding, *Journal of a Voyage to Lisbon,* edition cited, X, 192: "But in reality, the Odyssey, the Telemachus, and all of that kind, are to the voyage-writing I here intend, what romance is to true history. . . ."

even with genuine narrative. The inclination for the marvellous
. . . pervaded every department of literature and science. This
led to a similar style in the relations of those travellers, who
described remote countries. Such productions would have been
little attractive to their readers, unless filled with wonders of
nature and superhuman productions of art. (II, 521)

To Weber's Mandeville, Dunlop adds Benjamin of Tudela
and Marco Polo, and he follows with long accounts of Ebn
Tophail's *Hai Ebn Yokdhan*,[113] which Garnier does not mention, and Cyrano de Bergerac's *Histoire comique*. It is these
long résumés throughout the *History of Fiction* for which
the work is today most valuable. The Cyrano passage, for
example, runs to over ten pages. Dunlop continues his discussion as follows:

Connected with these wonderful expeditions, there is a species
of allegorical travels into imaginary countries, feigned to be the
particular residence of some peculiar passion or folly. . . .
    To the above-mentioned classes of Voyages Imaginaires, may
be associated works resembling the Sentimental Journey, where
the country is real, but the incidents of the journey imaginary. . . .
    The class of Songes et Visions resembles the Voyages Imagi-
naires, and only differs from them in this, that the body is in
repose while the mind ranges through the whole chimerical
world. These productions are of a more fugitive nature, as their
duration is limited, than the Voyages Imaginaires, but they are

---

[113] Three important references on this book are Léon Gauthier, *Ibn
Thofaïl: sa vie, ses œuvres* (Paris, 1909 [Publications de l'École des lettres
d'Alger, XLII]); A[lexander] S. Fulton, ed., *The History of Hayy Ibn
Yaqzan by Abu Bakr Ibn Tufail*, tr. Simon Ockley (London, 1929; the
Treasure House of Eastern Story, ed. Sir E. Denison Ross); and Antonio
Pastor, *The Idea of Robinson Crusoe* (Watford, 1930), Vol. I. *The Life
and Surprizing Adventures of Don Juliani de Trezz; Who Was Educated
and Lived Forty-five Years in the Island of Malpa, an Uninhabited Island
in the East-Indies* (London, [c.1722]) is an abridged translation, reissued
in 1761 and 1766 under the title, *The Life and Surprizing Adventures of
Don Antonio de Trezzanio*, etc.

also less unnatural, since nothing is too extravagant to be presented to the imagination, when the eye of reason is closed with
that of the body. (II, 538 f.)

The three paragraphs from which these introductory sentences are taken are completed by a few statements about
examples which, with one exception, are all in Garnier. The
same is true of the section on the cabalistic romances. I do
not imply that Dunlop did not know at first hand the works
he mentions, and there is no reason to doubt H. R. Tedder's
statement that "in most instances he had carefully read the
works he describes." [114] He brought to his study a wider
background of reading than any other historian of fiction up
to his time, and yet of the many possible additions he could
have made to Garnier's list, even after taking over Garnier's
order of classification, he mentions only two, *Hai Ebn
Yokdhan* and Kircher's *Mundus Subterraneus.*
 Mention of English imaginary voyages Dunlop reserves
for his next and final chapter, "Sketch of the Origin and
Progress of the English Novel." "In the class of Fairy and
Oriental Tales, we are . . . deficient; but in that of the
Voyages Imaginaires, no nation of Europe has produced
three performances of equal merit with Robinson Crusoe,
Gulliver's Travels, and Gaudentio di Lucca" (II, 587 f.).
After setting forth their merits he names three imitations
of *Robinson Crusoe,* the first two of which Garnier does not
include: *Travels and Adventures of William Bingfield*
(1753), *Life and Adventures of John Daniel* (1751), and
Peter Wilkins.

As in Robinson Crusoe, Peter Wilkins is a mariner, who, after
undergoing various calamities at sea, is thrown on a distant uninhabited shore. He is furnished with stores, utensils, and provisions, from the wreck of the ship in which he had sailed. De Foe,

---

[114] *Dictionary of National Biography,* article "Dunlop."

however, confines himself to incidents within the sphere of possibility, while the author of Peter Wilkins has related many
supernatural adventures—he has also created a new species of
beings, which are amongst the most beautiful offsprings of
imagination. . . . (II, 591)

This is the only passage in which Dunlop suggests a division of the imaginary voyage into possible and impossible,
but the words are not his; they are almost verbatim from
Weber.[115] Dunlop's treatment of the imaginary voyage accomplished little more. than definite recognition in English
of a genre recognized in France long before, and became the
probable source of nearly every subsequent employment of
the term in English. Compared further with Garnier, it has
no bibliographical importance, for altogether Dunlop mentions only twenty-four titles, to only eight of which he gives
more than a passing reference, and only six of which are
not in Garnier. Of the eight discussed at length only one is
not discussed in Garnier.[116]

The first English attempt at an extensive bibliography of
the imaginary voyage was begun in the columns of *Notes &*

[115] *Popular Romances,* p. xxxii. "In both, the heroes are sailors, who
after undergoing various calamities at sea, are thrown upon distant uninhabited shores; in both, they are furnished with stores, utensils, and provisions from the wreck of the ships in which they had sailed; but the subsequent parts of these delightful compositions are very different. De Foe
confines himself to what is within the reach of possibility; while the
author of 'Peter Wilkins' created a new species of beings in his own
imagination. . . ." The reviewer in the *Quarterly, loc. cit.,* implied that
Dunlop borrowed ideas from Southey, but Dunlop in his "Advertisement
to the Second Edition" (1816, as reprinted in the Philadelphia, 1842, edition) successfully pointed out the injustice of the charge. However, when
Dunlop published in 1838 *Selections from the Latin Anthology, Blackwood's Magazine,* XLIII (1838), 526 ff., brought charges of plagiarism by
printing parallel passages.

[116] Eddy, *op. cit.,* p. 12 n. 7: "Criticism of *Imaginary Voyage* literature
began with, and must always be dependent upon, Dunlop's excellent review of a few of the most significant *Voyages.*"

Queries in 1873 by James T. Presley (1835-1921), librarian of the old Cheltenham Subscription Library. His contributions have been undeservedly neglected.[117] Although possibly a suggestion for the undertaking came from an enquiry of a few years before for information about works similar to More's *Utopia,* to which "Ignatius" replied with a list of ten titles and a postscript reference to Garnier's collection, Presley acknowledges that his interest was "excited by noticing the list inserted in Sydney Whiting's *Heliondé.*"[118] This fiction recounts that the hero, after taking a water cure, falls asleep and is "drunk up" by the sun. At the end he awakes from a dream, writes a successful book, and wins a wife, and in a conversation between them she asks:

"But tell me, have there been any imaginary voyages to other worlds written?"

"Yes, a great number. Shall I give you a list of them? for I have taken some trouble to hunt them out."

"No, thank you," she replies and thus reduces him to a footnote, where he sets down twenty-five titles which, together with the list by "Ignatius," form Presley's starting point.[119] His subsequent list approaches the imaginary voy-

[117] I am indirectly indebted to his daughter, Miss Ethel Presley of Cheltenham, for biographic information kindly sent to me by Mr. D. W. Herdman, F.L.A., librarian and curator of the Public Library, Art Gallery and Museum, Cheltenham. Since published information about him is apparently confined to an obituary in a local newspaper, I give some of the details. James Thomas Presley was born at Wotton-under-Edge, Glos., Sept. 29, 1835, was educated at the old Borough-road College, London, and became a teacher at Newcastle-upon-Tyne. Appointed librarian to the old Cheltenham Subscription Library, at 5, Royal Crescent ("a position congenial to his temperament, for he was a well-read man, and a true lover of books"), he continued in office for 42 years until the contents of the library were turned over to the Municipal Library. He died at Cheltenham on July 31, 1921.

[118] *Notes & Queries,* 3S.IX (1866), 372 and 440; and 4S.XII (1873), 41.

[119] *Heliondé; or, Adventures in the Sun* (London, 1855), p. 416 and note.

age largely from the point of view of utopian fiction, as his introductory classification shows:

Many (both great and little) wits have, from ancient times to the present, produced works of imagination, which may conveniently be grouped together and denominated, for want of a better title, *Utopian.* They, however, if regard be had to the purpose for which they were severally written, may be roughly divided into four classes, although some of them may partake of the nature of more than one, and others may not readily fit into either, of these divisions.

I. "Utopias" proper; works which describe an ideal state of society, according to the notions which the author may entertain of what political and social conditions it is probable or desirable that the human race should hereafter attain to.

II. Those which satirize, under feigned names, the manners, customs, pursuits, and follies of the age or nation in which the writer lives.

III. Those which pretend to give a somewhat reasonable account of the possible or probable future state of society or course of historical events, either near at hand or in remote ages.

IV. Those which, merely for the sake of amusement, or sometimes for the purpose of travestying the wonderful adventures related by actual travellers in remote regions, profess to recount travels or adventures in imaginary countries or inaccessible worlds, in which generally the most extravagant fancy runs riot. . . .

I shall not, however, attempt such a classification of the Utopian literature . . . , for with many of the works mentioned I am acquainted only by name. In drawing up such a catalogue, too, it is difficult to lay down a definite line of inclusion and exclusion. There are, no doubt, some other works of imagination nearly allied in character to those cited, which might be supposed entitled to a place in the list; but they have been omitted, from their wanting what I take to be the necessary elements of such romances,—namely, *satire, allegory, anticipation, extravagance of incident or description,* or some combination of these.

One class of books, in particular, I may mention as not falling within my plan; I mean such mere literary deceptions as the pretended travels of Fernan Mendez Pinto, George Psalmanazar, Christian Damberger, and Jean Baptiste Douville, put forth, and, in some cases, long credited as records of genuine travel.[120]

Beginning with Plato's *Republic* Presley appends a list which reached, in six installments in four years, ninety-seven titles, accompanied by occasional brief comments.[121] To this others contributed thirty-five more.[122] The principal objector was Sir Charles W. Dilke, then proprietor of *Notes & Queries,* who wondered why Mandeville's *Fable of the Bees,* Fénelon's *Télémaque,* Brandt's *Ship of Fools,* and several others were not included. If Harrington's *Oceana* be included, he asks, "why not include Hume's 'idea of a perfect commonwealth,' which much resembles it? . . . why [not] all the other biblical-political writers of the seventeenth century? . . . There is plenty of 'allegory' in them all. So there is in Swedenborg's *New Jerusalem.* . . ."[123] This criticism revealed to Presley some obvious faults in his classification, which he admitted and corrected in a reply:

I should perhaps have stated that I considered a narrative form of composition, not a mere disquisition, as essential, and therefore

---

[120] 4S.XI (1873), 519.

[121] *Ibid.,* pp. 519-21; XII, 2-3, 22-23; 5S.II (1874), 252; VI (1876), 38; VII (1877), 458.

[122] 4S.XII, 41, 62, 153; 5S.I (1874), 78, 237; VI, 118; VIII (1877), 13; 6S.IX (1884), 84.

[123] 4S.XII, 41. Incidentally, Presley was himself a Swedenborgian. For a better edition of the *Oceana* than Toland's or Morley's see S[ven] B. Liljegren, ed., *James Harrington's Oceana* (Heidelberg, 1924; Skrifter Utgivna av Vetenskaps-Societeten i Lund, 4). See further *idem,* "Some Notes on the Name of James Harrington's *Oceana," Probleme der englischen Sprache und Kultur: Festschrift für Johannes Hoops* (Heidelberg, 1925), pp. 231-49, and H. F. Russell Smith, *Harrington and His Oceana: a Study of a 17th Century Utopia and Its Influence in America* (Cambridge, 1914).

I freely acknowledge that Plato's *Republic* was, by inadvertence, wrongly included. . . . Mere satires (as such) were not within my scheme, and allegories I meant to include only so far as they possessed a political or social import, thereby excluding all the numerous theological allegories, after the style of Bunyan. . . .[124]

The validity of Presley's classification can be tested only by trying to fit the titles into his four divisions. Since he himself avoided the task, the precise interpretation of his intentions must remain in doubt. It is clear, however, that Presley's and Garnier's classifications conflict, for even after Presley confines his requirements to narrative, his plan admits works which have no voyages. Only seventeen works are common to both lists; Presley had the work of almost a hundred years more to choose from, during which thirty-nine of his ninety-seven titles were written. The correspondence would have been higher had he been a more thorough bibliographer. He desired to make his list as complete as he could,[125] but although he entered the title of Garnier's collection, he seems not to have known thoroughly its contents. Proof of this statement lies in the fact that his list contains in succession five works "of which I can discover neither the date nor authorship, and [I] place them at a guess between the seventeenth and eighteenth centuries," [126] though Garnier includes every one of these five and gives for each either the name of the author or the date. That none of the nine contributors to Presley's list furnished this missing information —he specifically asked for corrections and additions—indicates that Garnier's work had not emerged from obscurity in England, even among the antiquarian readers of *Notes &*

[124] 4S.XII, 91.

[125] *Ibid.*, p. 22.

[126] *Ibid.*, p. 3; on p. 22 he asks if any correspondent can furnish a table of contents of Garnier. Presley may have taken these five titles from Whiting.

Queries. From Presley's list one general principle can be drawn, the same principle that Garnier discovered: given divisions not mutually exclusive, the allocation of a work must often be decided arbitrarily according to various elements predominating either in the work itself or in the classifier's interest in the work. How much influence Presley had upon subsequent notice of imaginary voyages is difficult to determine accurately. Though he grouped them with utopias, the coincidence of the two is so frequent that similar bibliographic grouping by no means indicates dependence upon him. Besides, many subsequent classifiers were obviously ignorant of Presley's list.

In 1878 the Danish scholar, Julius Paludan (1843-1926), stating that no one had thoroughly shown the place of *Nicolas Klimius* in the particular genre to which it belongs, the fictitious and marvelous voyage, published a study of Holberg's book with particular consideration of previous satires in the same form (*Om Holbergs Niels Klim, med saerligt Hensyn til tidligere Satirir i Form af opdigtede og vidunderlige Reiser*). Within its limits this book contains more critical information and a wider outlook on the imaginary voyage and its background than any book written before or since; yet no other literary historian discussed in my book has used it or (so far as I can recollect) even referred to its existence.[127] This neglect has particular significance for the study of Swift; ever since Seyer Olrog's translation of *Gul-*

[127] København. This positive assertion must be qualified, for otherwise, not having had a knowledge of this book from the beginning, I should have to recheck every volume I have used against the possibility of some obscure note that may have escaped me; such a note would not seriously alter the assertion. Scandinavian literary histories, of course, cite Paludan; e.g., Fredrik Böök, *Romanens och prosaberättelsens Historia i Sverige intil 1809* (Stockholm, 1907), in discussing "fantastiska reseberättelsen," pp. 256-70, and Hakon Stangerup, *Romanen i Danmark i det Attende Aarhundrede: en komparativ Undersøgelse* (København, 1936), pp. 76-80. See also my check list under Holberg, 1741.

liver in 1768 Danish scholars, interested in their greatest
literary figure of the eighteenth century, have investigated
the sources of *Klimius* and of *Gulliver,* and especially the
relations between the two, so that there exists a body of information which has been unknown to students of *Gulliver.*
Paludan's study completes a century of such scholarship. Its
limits are suggested by the title: the author is concerned with
satire, and consequently his treatment in general stresses the
satirical element in the *opdigtede og vidunderlige Reiser*
rather than the genre itself.

But the first chapter, filling nearly half the book, traces
the genre from antiquity down to the imitators of Swift.
Paludan shows a development from the mythical geographic
sagas and sea stories through fabulous tales of Alexander to
the chivalric romances of the Middle Ages, closely allied to
journeys to the Holy Land and to the travels of Marco Polo
and Mandeville. Real voyages in the sixteenth century influenced the vogue of geographic *Reiseromaner* and in the
next two centuries provided the locale (particularly Aus-
tralia, the arctic regions, and inner Africa) for utopian romances. The last stage includes the wonderful voyages to
the planets or regions within the earth (*Astronomiske
Reiseromaner*). With *Robinson* and *Gulliver* the whole
genre became didactic and satiric, later degenerating into
trivial allegory and revolutionary propaganda, only to re-
vive in the next century with Jules Verne.[128] After the middle part of the book, covering a detailed examination of
Klimius with copious references to other works, Paludan
gives a brief chapter on imitations in Denmark, Germany,
and France. All these stages are illustrated by examples, not
by definition.

Two briefer contributions to this critical history of the

[128] So sketched on pp. 9 f., and so developed in the remainder of the
chapter to p. 164.

imaginary voyage came in the last decade of the nineteenth century. Thomas Seccombe (1866-1923) in his introduction to the *Surprising Adventures of Baron Munchausen* suggests a fourfold classification of imaginary voyages:

It is a curious fact that of that class of literature to which Munchausen belongs, that namely of *Voyages Imaginaires,* the three great types should have all been created in England. Utopia, Robinson Crusoe, and Gulliver, illustrating respectively the philosophical, the edifying, and the satirical type of fictitious travel, were all written in England, and at the end of the eighteenth century a fourth type, the fantastically mendacious, was evolved in this country. Of this type Munchausen was the modern original, and remains the classical example.[129]

When he considers the continuations that appeared with the third edition, he states vaguely that "Prototypes of the majority of the stories may either be found in Lucian or in the twenty volumes of *Voyages Imaginaires,* published at Paris in 1787" (p. xxix). The other contribution is the catalogue of a German bookdealer, Franz Teubner, who offered for sale 515 works under the following title: *Robinson-Litteratur: reichhaltige Sammlung seltener Robinsonaden Fahrten und Abenteuer Avanturiers aelterer Reisewerke u. Atlanten: nebst einem Anhange: Utopien und Staatsromane phantastische Reisen (Voyages imaginaires).*[130] These he divided roughly into three groups, the first dealing with *Robinson Crusoe,* the second and largest containing imitations and adventures including *merkwürdige Schiffbrüche,* and the third containing the appendix indicated in the title. This last group presents 102 titles arranged alphabetically. The whole offering does represent a rich collection which includes many

[129] New York, 1895, p. v.
[130] Antiquariats-Katalog Nr. 69, Düsseldorf [c.1897]; I base the date on a reference to it in "Antiquariatsmarkt," *Zeitschrift für Bücherfreunde,* I (1897-98), i, 113.

imaginary voyages, both in the appendix and in the second group, but since a bookdealer's justifiable basis for inclusion is relevance rather than genre, the catalogue is principally significant (to me) for the translation of the term *voyages imaginaires,* even in the limited sense of *phantastische Reisen,* and for the bibliographic information contained therein.[131]

C. BEGLEY TO R. E. TIEJE

In 1902 Walter Begley (1845-1905) appended to his translation of Samuel Gott's *Nova Solyma* a "Bibliography of Romance from the Renaissance to the End of the Seventeenth Century." [132] Objecting to the omission from the then latest edition of the *Encyclopedia Britannica*[133] of whole classes of romance, especially those of ideal states and the *Voyages imaginaires,* he divides "modern romance" up to 1700 into nine groups, of which one is "Fictitious Travels (Voyages Imaginaires)." Here belong seven works not including translations and adaptations: Hall's *Mundus alter et*

---

[131] Mixed with "Robinson-Litteratur" are true voyages, historical and geographic works, atlases, and dissertations as well as imitations of *Don Quixote* and *Gil Blas.* The catalogue seems to be tolerably reliable for places and dates of publication. An earlier bookseller's catalogue, probably containing many of the same works, is J. J. Schwabe, *Catalogus bibliothecae* . . . (Lipsiae, 1785), referred to in Ullrich, *Robinson und Robinsonaden* . . . , p. xv. Stangerup, *op. cit.,* p. 131 and *passim,* mentions several booksellers who issued similar lists earlier in the eighteenth century.

[132] *Nova Solyma the Ideal City; or Jerusalem Regained: an Anonymous Romance . . . Now First Drawn from Obscurity, and Attributed to the Illustrious John Milton* (London, 1902), II, 355-400. That the author was not Milton but Samuel Gott is proved by Stephen K. Jones, "The Authorship of 'Nova Solyma,' " *The Library,* 3S.I (1910), [225]-238.

[133] From Begley's remarks this is clearly the article on "Romance" by H. R. Tedder and Michael Kerney in the 9th ed., 1875, which out of 57 columns devotes 54 to Greek, Latin, and medieval romances and only two to "Modern Romance." This article was superseded in the 11th ed., 1910, by two articles, "Romance" by George Saintsbury and "Novel" by Edmund Gosse.

idem, Godwin's *Man in the Moon* (the only one originally in English), Cyrano de Bergerac, Zacharie de Lisieux's *Relation du pays de Jansénie,* Foigny, the continuation of Grimmelshausen's *Simplicissimus,* and Happel's *Insularische Mandovelt,* the last two being robinsonades before *Robinson Crusoe.* This list, except for incompleteness and the inclusion of *Jansenia,* presents no problems, but Begley gives as his other eight divisions the pastoral, the picaresque, the heroical, the utopian, the political, the allegorical (chiefly religious), and the social romances as well as the modern Latin romance of elegant satire. Such a classification confuses, especially since the social romance carries the parenthetical explanation "satirical and didactic; romans des mœurs." He rightly says that "the branch of prose fiction which is entitled Romance is much more extensive and full of variety than is generally supposed" (II,357), but the effort to establish and to try to keep separate nine such classes between Sannazzaro's *Arcadia* in 1504 and Fénelon's *Télémaque* in 1699 involves difficulties which few bibliographers would undertake to solve and about which Begley himself expresses introductory uncertainty. Had he known Presley's list and Garnier's collection, where together he would have found about twenty-five titles before 1700 not recorded by him, the confusion must have been greater than it is. Knowledge of either of these earlier works would have complicated his treatment of the relationship between utopian romances and imaginary voyages.

As introduction to a comparison of the works of Cyrano, Swift, and Rabelais, Pietro Toldo (1860-1926) surveys *voyages merveilleux* from Homer to Jules Verne and finds three kinds:

En laissant de côté les nouvelles proprement dites et les traditions populaires, on peut diviser les récits d'aventures et de voyages merveilleux en trois groupes: le premier (dont le représentant le plus remarquable, dans l'antiquité, est l'Odyssée) n'a d'autre but que celui d'amuser par des contes extraordinaires; il suppose un public dont le sens critique est rudimentaire, dont la religion n'est qu'un tissu de mythes naïfs, dont les connaissances géographiques et ethnologiques sont confuses et incertaines, et dont enfin l'imagination domine les autres qualités de l'esprit et se substitue à la recherche diligente de la vérité. Pour ce qui est du fond, la légende remplace l'histoire, c'est-à-dire que nous nous trouvons en présence de fictions poétiques où paraît le souvenir d'exploits nationaux et individuels. . . . Sous l'influence d'une autre civilisation, toujours aussi passionnée pour le merveilleux, on vit grandir la légende,—qui reçut plus tard un habit philosophique,—des états imaginaires, des peuples hyperboréens, des îles merveilleuses perdues dans l'Océan. . . .

Le deuxième groupe ou cycle est plus rapproché de nous, et on pourrait le dire issu de la civilisation de la Renaissance, si en Syrie, au commencement de l'empire d'Adrien, il ne s'était trouvé un esprit éclairé qui en eût déjà conçu le plan général et dessiné les traits caractéristiques. Le jour où, dans les états évolués de l'Europe (surtout en Italie et en France), l'artiste reprit les anciens sujets de voyages merveilleux et marcha à la découverte de pays chimériques, il était animé par le désir de se moquer de la superstition des temps passés aussi bien que par le besoin de faire la satire de la société humaine et de bâtir pour elle un nouvel édifice social. . . .

A ce cycle, dominé par le chef-d'œuvre de Rabelais, appartiennent les voyages de Cyrano et de Swift. . . . L'histoire des voyages merveilleux et des inspirations tirées de Rabelais reste encore à faire. . . .

Un troisième cycle, que l'on peut considérer comme contemporain . . . [est produit par] L'esprit moderne, ou mieux contemporain, [qui] ne saurait plus se contenter des fantaisies de Lucien, de Rabelais, de Cyrano et de Swift. Il veut que les voyages merveilleux eux-mêmes aient une apparence de possibilité scientifique et qu'ils soient fondés sur la réflexion et l'étude.[134]

---

[134] "Les Voyages merveilleux de Cyrano de Bergerac et de Swift, et

This analysis goes deeper in some respects than simple classification but covers too wide a range to apply beyond those works with which Toldo is primarily concerned. His division, like Paludan's, is based upon chronology rather than definition.

Begley's finely drawn divisions do not survive in Professor Robert P. Utter's *Studies in the Origins of the English Novel,* an unpublished Harvard dissertation of 1906. Under his sectional heading "Utopias and Imaginary Voyages" appear seventy-seven titles, those up to 1700 being drawn from Begley (to whom he refers) with the addition of only eleven. Works from seven of Begley's nine classes—all except the picaresque and the allegorical—contribute to Utter's list of utopias and imaginary voyages. Omissions make clear that he did not use the work of Garnier, Weber, and Presley. Even so he puts into the list for the first time sixteen titles.

Similar breaking-down of Begley's classification is effected by Professor Charlotte E. Morgan in the *Rise of the Novel of Manners: a Study of English Prose Fiction between 1600 and 1740.* Her discussion of romances includes the divisional heading "Political and Allegorical Romances" under which come "ideal commonwealths (of which the 'voyage imaginaire' is a variety) and allegories." [135] In just what respects the imaginary voyage is a variety she does not explain, probably because the point is too minute for her larger purpose of examining early fiction not as fiction but as material contributing to the novel. It is probably this point of view which leads her into saying that all the political and allegorical romances are unimportant to the historian of literary fiction, "since they mark the adoption of the romance form for purposes of satire and propaganda rather

---

leurs rapports avec l'œuvre de Rabelais," *Revue des études rabelaisiennes,* IV (1906), 296-99.

[135] New York, 1911, p. 19.

than any legitimate development" (p. 18). Thus to banish from the province of important literary history a body of literature produced by writers of all degrees of ability in nearly every decade since the invention of printing and thus to pass upon the *legitimate* development of romance should need no extensive refutation. *Gulliver's Travels* is "so permeated by a satiric and unromantic spirit, and in the method of presentation it is so closely affiliated with the realistic pseudo-voyages that it can scarcely be regarded as a representative ideal commonwealth" (p. 21); it is nevertheless "the culmination of the satirical 'voyage imaginaire'" (p. 23). But, the author adds, as a class the political and allegorical romances "were not without an influence on later fiction," for besides making "the element of actuality important . . . they were instrumental in the perfecting of two important devices, the 'voyage imaginaire' and the foreign observer" (p. 27). From these remarks one obtains no clear conception of what the imaginary voyage is or what is its relation to other forms. Furthermore, "in her references to the 'voyage imaginaire' as a development of the 'ideal commonwealth,' Miss Morgan fails to give due credit to long and respected—if not respectable—ancestry, omitting all mention of Lucian and Rabelais, and apparently not taking into account the immense vogue of their satire and its imitations in this period."[136]

Nearly a hundred pages at the end of Miss Morgan's book are taken up with a "Chronological List of the Prose Fiction First Printed in England between 1600 and 1740." This contains over 650 main entries (the largest list published up to 1911), but the absence of seven eligible titles in Presley's list and the omission of any reference to Presley indicate

[136] A. H. Upham, "The Rise of the Novel of Manners," *Modern Language Notes,* XXVII (1912), 221.

oversight of the work of this English predecessor.[137] Except
for the fact that this list is arranged chronologically and
therefore still valuable, it was somewhat superseded in the
following year by the alphabetical *List of English Tales and
Prose Romances Printed before 1740* by Mr. Esdaile.[138] The
value and limitations of his work are too well known to
students of fiction for comment here; bibliographic mention
is given for the first time to several imaginary voyages,
though not as such, for Esdaile does not undertake classification into types. But several titles are missing from his
list.

Another attempt at classifying fiction was made in the
same year by Dr. A. J. Tieje in *The Expressed Theory of
European Prose Fiction before 1740,* an unpublished doctoral
dissertation at the University of Illinois, chapters of which
later appeared separately. The scheme is much more elaborate than Presley's and has the advantage of being presented
in a critical manner, that is, with explanations of purpose
and scope. From it emerges the earliest definition that I
have found of the imaginary voyage: "By the *voyage imaginaire* is meant a rather unified narrative, aiming specifically
at literary criticism, at amusement through the introduction
of the wildly fantastic, or at social improvement of the
human race, and invariably carrying the reader into unexplored regions."[139] The most significant aspect of this
definition is that utopian fiction becomes therein a sub-

[137] It is only fair to add that Miss Morgan says with disarming diffi-
dence: "Neither the essay nor the bibliography makes any pretence to completeness. This study is, so to speak, but a clearing of the ground in a
field where little has been done and much remains to be accomplished"
(p. ix). Her book was a commendable predecessor of the subsequent detailed study which she knew was certain to supersede it.

[138] London, 1912.

[139] Arthur J. Tieje, "The Expressed Aim of the Long Prose Fiction,"
Journal of English and Germanic Philology, XI (1912), 405.

sidiary form of the imaginary voyage, in fact, as Tieje later says (p. 145), a "disintegrating influence" upon it. Otherwise, the definition, lifted from its context, is somewhat too vague to be useful.

In another publication Tieje himself amplifies his conception of the imaginary voyage and fully establishes the difficulties of classifying it with respect to fiction in general:

. . . its history is usually that of a sub-variety in one or another school [of fictional types]—with the result that the *voyage imaginaire* may have either coherent or incoherent structure, either nicely localized or wildly impossible setting, and either definitely realistic or hopelessly incredible characters. The aims, too, are naturally so diverse as almost to defy enumeration. For instance, the *voyage imaginaire* may outdo the nightmares of chivalric romance and the frame-work *conte de fée* . . . ; it may divulge scandal . . . ; it may explain philosophic or scientific dogma . . . ; it may satirize . . . fads . . . ; or it may be . . . reformative and Utopian. . . . If neither main aim nor structure nor characterization, then, made the pre-Richardsonians consider the *voyage imaginaire* a *genre,* what did? It was a subordinate purpose, that of carrying the reader into uncharted lands where might *possibly* be found the marvels determined by the controlling motive of the individual volume.[140]

No such recognition of the wide range and possibilities of the imaginary voyage as a literary form had been expressed since 1787 when Garnier had exemplified a similar range by his *avertissements* and his collection.

According to Tieje's study of the aims expressed by pre-Richardsonian fictionists themselves, the imaginary voyage is one of the six main types of fiction before 1740; the others are romance (subdivided into chivalric, pastoral, allegorical,

[140] A. J. Tieje, *The Theory of Characterization in Prose Fiction Prior to 1740,* University of Minnesota Studies in Language and Literature No. 5 (Minneapolis, 1916), p. 64.

religious, heroico-historical, informational-conversational, satirical), realistic narrative (subdivided into picaresque, novel of manners, historical-psychological novel, psychological novel proper), letter-novel (either romantic or realistic), *chronique scandaleuse* (real or fictitious), and framework *conte de fée*.[141] The apology for this somewhat cumbersome classification lies in disavowal of responsibility: "That the forms are not quite mutually exclusive is not my fault, but the authors' ";[142] the scheme is only a convenience having "the merit of being true to the development of fiction." [143] Clearly, had the imaginary voyage not been recognized by the authors themselves as a separate type, it would have been buried inextricably among the other five. Tieje's definition and analysis neatly present a solution to a problem that has apparently baffled most critics of the imaginary voyage: how to classify a form long recognized as a separate genre, a form that "cannot be classified as either romantic or realistic," [144] a form unclassifiable according to many of the usual critical terms denoting structure or aim. An additional condition should be made: denial of the right to begin all over again with a new set of critical terms. The problem does not bother the student of only the one type so much as it

---

[141] It will be noticed that this term has sometimes been used with *des*. On this point Rémy de Gourmont has written: "Nous disons bien aujourd'-hui *Contes de Fées*, mais est-ce ainsi qu'il faut dire? Tous les livres anciens portent invariablement *Contes des Fées*, ce qui est bien différent. La première formule signifie: contes où il y a des fées; la seconde: contes contés par les fées. Il y a de cela une preuve; c'est le titre même du grand recueil intitulé: le *Cabinet des Fées;* ce recueil porte, en effet, en sous-titre: *contenant tous leurs ouvrages en neuf volumes*. On donnait donc autrefois ces contes comme étant l'œuvre même des fées."—*Promenades littéraires* [1 sér.], 17e éd. (Paris, Mercvre de France, 1929), p. [248].

[142] "The Expressed Aim," p. 404 n. 5.

[143] *Ibid.*, p. 403; he himself uses the phrase "somewhat cumbersome" in his *Theory*, p. 2.

[144] *Theory*, p. 45. Cf. also pp. 49 and [74].

does the student of several types within the larger field of fiction.

Under "Voyages Imaginaires" Tieje lists in his bibliography sixty-nine titles, of which twenty-three are English.[145] But some titles in Morgan and Esdaile he has missed, besides being apparently unaware of Presley. He adds to the list of English titles only two. He has taken the trouble to look into Garnier's collection with the result that many non-English titles appear in a list of imaginary voyages for the first time since 1787. He relies on Garnier somewhat uncritically, for his list contains the *Naufrage de Mme Godin,* a true account of a real voyage written long after 1740.

Though Tieje gives to the imaginary voyage considerable attention incidental to his studies on the theory of prose fiction in general, it remained for his brother, Professor Ralph E. Tieje, to be the first to make a scholarly study concerned exclusively with the imaginary voyage as such. In 1917 he completed *The Prose Voyage Imaginaire before 1800,* a University of Illinois dissertation unpublished and apparently unconsulted by any of the scholars whom I mention later.[146] Finding that this long-existent type has been "undeservedly neglected" by classifiers, that it "has usually been assumed to be a sub-variety of some other species" (partly because "in the course of its development [it] dealt with a variety of purposes and has not always treated its material in the same way"), and that "the term has had very little real and exact signification," he states in the first chapter the main purpose of his study: "not alone to establish the *voyage imaginaire* in its rightful place as an important type

[145] *Ibid.,* pp. 127-29; "the bibliography makes no pretensions to completeness"—p. [115].

[146] Although I knew of the existence of this thesis early in my work, I completed my own study before making any inquiries about it. As soon as I wrote to Dr. Tieje, he was kind enough to take the trouble to send me his own copy, for which I am deeply grateful.

of prose fiction, but also to give the term a meaningful and workable definition, and at the same time to trace, as far as possible, the relation of the individual *voyages* to each other and in some measure to the development of prose fiction as a whole." In order to cut through the difficulties and arrive at a definition, he stresses two points that must be remembered:

The first is that, in and of themselves, the voyages, the ship-wrecks, the imaginary countries and beings (except where amusement is the author's sole design) have only a minor importance and a subsidiary interest in the story. The author seeks (except again where amusement is the sole design) to instruct, reform, or edify the reader by presenting the government or manners of an imaginary people. The second thing to be remembered is that the word "imaginary" in this term applies only to the non-existent; not only must no actual journey have been made, but the nation or country visited must also be one which has no real being. A *voyage imaginaire* is, then, a narrative, usually auto-biographic, of a supposed journey into an imaginary country written either for the pleasure or for the profit of the reader, or for both. (chap. i)

Tieje believes that the application of these qualifications is not difficult when an author's aim is clearly recognized to be instruction or reform but more difficult when the aim is amusement, especially through the relation of marvelous and improbable adventures in an imaginary country.

To avoid confusion [he explains] both the imaginary character of the country and the improbability of the adventures must be kept in mind. For if a fictitious hero having fictitious adventures during a fictitious journey in an "unexplored region" were all that is necessary . . . , then neither any romance of the sea nor any travel story can be distinguished from the class. But many of these are realistic, as, for example, Defoe's work. The fictitious alone, therefore, is not a sufficient qualification. Likewise, improbability alone is not a sufficient qualification. For if it were, then a host of improbable fictions with realistic settings, such as *Treasure Island* . . . , would intrude into the *genre*. In either case the lines of division become too vague and shifting for the term *voyage imaginaire* to have any special meaning and significance. (chap. i)

Thus by restricted conditions Tieje succeeds in making a meaningful definition, one for which he "must find justification in the historical survey" of those works which he has selected to examine. His bibliography consists of sixty-one imaginary voyages from ancient times to 1800 plus nineteen kindred works which intrude into the genre, such as *Robinson Crusoe* and *Captain Singleton,* both excluded by the definition. However workable he finds his definition in considering those sixty-one works, there are many other works which may perhaps justly have a place among the imaginary voyages.[147] Had Tieje's work been published, it would have been obligatory for all subsequent writers on the subject to refer to it as a basic secondary source whether or not they could agree with his point of view, his method, or his conclusions. However, because of several later independent and detailed studies his work is out of date.[148]

[147] Of his 61, 30 are eighteenth century, and of these 30, 14 I have not included in my check list. Six, however, in his list of kindred works do appear in my list so that the two lists have 22 works in common. It will be later apparent that our conceptions of what should be called imaginary voyages differ in several respects.

[148] Since Tieje's study is unpublished, I give here a brief account of some of his conclusions unsupported, it should be remembered, by his evidence, in order to show more clearly the scope of his work.

Chap. i—"The Definition of *Voyage Imaginaire*" (16 manuscript pages); summarized above.

Chap. ii—"The *Voyage Imaginaire* before More's *Utopia* (1516)" (41 pp.): Although he finds that the type did not become established until after More, Tieje traces many of its fundamental ideas from earlier works. From Herodotus authors "may have gained the suggestion of including descriptions of manners, morals, customs, governments, and religions; and

D. ATKINSON AND EDDY TO WIJNGAARDEN

The first of these more recent detailed contributions are

from him also they may have borrowed some of the marvels which they tell of in their works. But his greatest contribution to the development of prose fiction was the method of gaining verisimilitude by simple assertion on the author's part or by the testimony of a third party. To Lucian later authors are indebted for giving to the *voyage imaginaire* a satirical character by the introduction of extravagant exaggeration. Plato's influence is, perhaps, the greatest and most direct of all. . . . Plutarch's *Lycurgus* exerted an influence not dissimilar to that of the *Republic;* but it may, in addition, have suggested giving to the ideal state a practical and local application. Mandeville displays no essential characteristics not found in Herodotus; but in attempting to gain verisimilitude he appended to his book a lengthy testimonial given by a reliable and historic person, which may have suggested to some of his successors the elaborate prefaces that they employ for the same purpose."

Chap. iii—"The *Voyage Imaginaire* from More to Gott (1516-1648)" (77 pp.): "The development of the *voyage imaginaire* in this period shows many interesting changes in its subject-matter, aim, and form. In 1516 it was a wonderbook, but More grafted upon it the branch of the utopia which flourished and bore fruit. Almost one hundred years later Hall developed another off-shoot—social satire—which, while it did not at once mature, later waxed and grew strong. The *voyage* has, in other words, now become purposive literature, and such it remained until 1750. . . . The dialog which was borrowed from Plato, along with the conception of an ideal state, did not thrive. Only Campanella and Hartlib preserve it intact; More made the narrative a sort of lecture; and Hall, Andreae, and Gott emphasize the story form, until, with the latter, it becomes a full-fledged romance. . . . The effort to gain verisimilitude, however, did not develop. More was the only one who made an extended effort to 'force belief,' but his seed fell upon barren ground, and the labor of evolving the elaborate preface was left to Vairasse and his followers. But from the *Utopia* onward all except a few authors felt called upon to give a more or less exact location to their imaginary states. Characterization, too, has made little headway; and only in the *Nova Solyma* do we find more than faint suggestions of it." But this last-named work is "more of a romance than an imaginary voyage or a utopia."

Chap. iv—"The *Voyage Imaginaire* from Montpensier to Tyssot (1652-1710)" (55 pp.): To Cyrano de Bergerac "later authors owe suggestions for making the *voyage imaginaire* satiric of philosophical ideas and of man's conception of himself; and to him also is owing a revival of interest in carrying the traveller into places not of this earth. . . . Vairasse made

Professor Geoffroy Atkinson's two valuable and substantial studies of the French imaginary voyage up to 1720, under

---

a still more original contribution. . . . His utopian ideas are not essentially different from those of his predecessors, but he first made the Robinsonade element an integral part of those *voyages imaginaires* which dealt with the sea. His *Preface*, moreover, is the first to present an elaborate and carefully worked-out scheme for the purpose of creating verisimilitude. Foigny's influence was along similar lines. . . . All three of these men helped . . . to make the *voyage* more of a story, and to give the hero something of a personality. . . . They also introduce into the story for the first time love episodes which have a more or less vital connection with the main thread of the narrative. . . . In general, then, it is clear that the *voyage imaginaire* has established itself as a medium not only for the presentation of utopian ideas, but for those of any other kind as well; that it has become true fiction with something of character portrayal, love interest, and narrative suspense; and that authors of the type have seen the necessity for a careful effort to force belief and have supplied it."

Chap. v—"The *Voyage Imaginaire* from Swift to Walker (1726-1799)" (53 pp.): "When the second quarter of the eighteenth century opened, the *voyage imaginaire* had already become a story, and this character it maintained throughout the whole of the new period. Pure story forms appeared although as yet they did not become numerous; for the 'ulterior purpose' which the narrative had always had was still retained—the famous *voyages* of the century, Swift's, Desfontaines', and Holberg's, being satires. The utopias, however, were less numerous and often less serious. The Robinsonade element, too, now became yet more important than it had been in the previous half-century, practically every *voyage* making use of this device. . . ." By "1800 the development of the *voyage imaginaire* was complete. Its authors had learned how to make it a story and how to lend it verisimilitude. They had adapted it to the portrayal of utopian conditions and to the purposes of moral, political, and philosophic satire. All its possibilities had been developed. Later authors could but continue the tradition of the imaginary state and add to the effort of Robert Paltock the element of a more probable, but still fanciful, science."

Chap. vi—"The Artistic Theory and Development of the *Voyage Imaginaire*" (14 pp.): "Standing usually upon the border-line between fiction and some other field of intellectual endeavor—politics, education, philosophy, or social criticism—the *voyage imaginaire* was naturally affected by these practices and theories [in the development of prose fiction]; but being more often the product of men who were not professional romancers or novelists, it, as naturally, expresses in itself but little of fictional theory." Primarily the *voyage imaginaire* concerned itself, as did most

the title *The Extraordinary Voyage,* the earlier on the
seventeenth century and the subsequent one on the first two

---

fiction, with edification and instruction rather than amusement. "This
moral aim also affected other portions of theory as applied to the *voyage
imaginaire.* In the utopias, for instance, character could not receive attention. Interest being centered in the nature of the state and its practice,
men, except *en bloc,* were of little interest; and seldom do we learn anything of individuals, national character alone being portrayed." Even
"histories" of lovers are never mere digressions; rather they "seek to shed
light upon the practice of the nation under discussion or to add point to
the satire." Since "the *voyage imaginaire* has never in its pure types been
weaned away from the first person in its narrative," omniscience being
"necessary both as a means of explaining how the author came by his
knowledge and as a means of gaining verisimilitude," "long discussions
over the relative values of first and third person never affected it." Description "always retained its place" as a necessary means of presenting
strange places, but writers of the *voyage imaginaire,* being "exempted from
the limits naturally imposed upon those who dealt with the known world,"
contributed nothing to the development of description in the sense of
accurate setting. However, they had "to make an especial effort to secure
belief" not only through such tricks as pretended manuscripts but also
through attempting "accuracy of detail and directness of style." The first
led to exploitation of geographical setting and the second to a simplicity
resulting from the implication that the narrator was a seaman or a man
of little education. The problem of the unities did not affect the *voyage
imaginaire,* for they are largely impossible in a travel book; and so too
the "genealogical beginning" usually prevailed over all temptation to begin
in medias res. "Thus far it is clear that in the development of fictional
theory the *voyage imaginaire* has followed as often as it has led, reflected
as often as it has been reflected. Only in the effort to force belief has this
type contributed much to general practice. But in spite of its apparent
imitation in theory, the *voyage imaginaire* has made an important contribution to prose fiction. . . . If these authors had not transported their
heroes or themselves into far off lands, the description of the ideal state
must have remained forever the abstract philosophical treatise of Plato.
. . . To satire also the *voyage imaginaire* lent a power not otherwise
inherent in that sort of writing. Without the right to describe imaginary
lands, satirists would have found themselves limited in scope; and without
the additional privilege of transporting a hero into those lands, satire, like
the utopia, would have found even the imaginary country of no great
advantage, for the concreteness necessary to effective composition would
have been denied. . . . Finally, the *voyage imaginaire* has made the story

decades of the eighteenth century.[149] Definition of the term and its relation to the larger imaginary voyage may be best presented in the author's own words:

The term *Extraordinary Voyage* is used to designate a novel of the following type: A fictitious narrative, purporting to be the veritable account of a real voyage made by one or more Europeans to an existent but little known country—or to several such countries—together with a description of the happy condition of society there found, and a supplementary account of the traveler's return to Europe.

The *Extraordinary Voyage,* as defined, is a particular type of *Imaginary Voyage.* Another recognized type of *Imaginary Voyage* is the *Fantastic* or *Marvelous,* in which dreams, witchcraft, or other supernatural agencies preclude any serious attempt at realistic authentication. A third type is the *Extra-terrestrial Voyage,* of which Cyrano de Bergerac's travels to the sun and moon are perhaps the best known. A fourth type of *Imaginary Voyage* is the *Satirical* or *Allegorical,* in which the hero travels to a frankly imaginary Land of the Jansenists, to the Land of Love, or to the Utopia of Dogs. A fifth type, far older than Jules Verne's story, is the *Subterranean Voyage.* (It is necessary to exclude from consideration [these other types, as well as] accounts of travel by land only, of travel in familiar European countries, . . . [and, by definition,] of voyages actually made, although these [last] accounts may contain many or all of the characteris-

_____

of extravagant adventure possible. As long as such fiction had to confine itself within the bounds of the known world, so long did it run the danger of becoming ridiculous. . . . Exotic plants, strange beasts, unknown lands and peoples march through its pages. . . . They need the soft and transforming magic of the glow which is given off only by the *voyage imaginaire.* In this theatre of the imaginary voyage a veritable wonder house is displayed. Imagination is once more free, and the incredible becomes the real."
Bibliography (5 pp.)
[149] *The Extraordinary Voyage in French Literature before 1700* (New York, 1920) and *The Extraordinary Voyage in French Literature from 1700 to 1720* (Paris, 1922).

tics of the *Extraordinary Voyage* barring that of a voyage made in the imagination rather than in reality.)

The distinguishing feature of the *Extraordinary Voyage* is its geographic realism. Authors of *Extraordinary Voyages* try to authenticate their stories in order that they may be mistaken for true accounts.

In addition to travel and adventure, the novel of *Extraordinary Voyage* always has a philosophical or utopian content.[150]

This commendable precision enables a reader to go through these two volumes with complete understanding of the author's reasons for choosing the works discussed. These are principally Foigny's *Terre australe connue,* Veiras's *Sévarambes,* and Fénelon's *Télémaque* before 1700 and Gilbert's *Calejava,* Misson's *Leguat,*[151] and Tyssot de Patot's *Jacques Massé* and *Voyage de Groenland* after 1700, examined both as fiction, with emphasis upon the use of real voyages for authenticated realism of setting, and as criticism, religious, social, and political. Furthermore, certain excluded works are mentioned briefly in an appendix with a summarized restatement of purpose, in which occurs a significant phrase:

In classifying Imaginary Voyages, there are two general divisions: (1) Those which might, *by a stretch of the imagination,* be true, (2) Those which are admitted, even by their authors, to be false. The novel of Extraordinary Voyage . . . falls within the first class, being a sincere and somewhat authenticated type

---

[150] . . . *from 1700 to 1720,* pp. 7 f. The parenthetical sentence is adapted from a similar explanation in *Before 1700,* p. ix. I could have quoted from either volume, but the second is more specific about the types other than extraordinary. The opening definition of *extraordinary voyage* is, of course, the same in both volumes. Cf. also his *Relations de voyages . . . ,* p. [v]: ". . . les *Voyages Extraordinaires,* qui sont des Voyages Imaginaires dans des cadres géographiques."

[151] The inclusion of the *Voyages et aventures de François Leguat, et ses compagnons, en deux isles désertes des Indes orientales . . .* (London, 1708; i.e., 1707 postdated) is of particular interest; see my check list under 1707.

8

of story. Imaginary Voyages which are fantastic and purely satirical fall naturally in the second group of novels which are professedly insincere and totally unauthenticated.[152]

This classification rests in part upon the answer to an unanswerable question: how far can the critical and noncredulous imagination stretch before it shifts a voyage from the extraordinary type to the fantastic or marvelous? The question requires no specific answer; it is framed merely to show that in so far as it is unanswerable the divisions will be controversial, depending as they do partly on the reader, with respect to the knowledge of his age and his understanding of it as well as to the elasticity of his imagination, and partly on the author, with respect to his purpose and to his ability in the application of a realistic technique to fictitious material. Here are variables allowing many permutations.

As already indicated, Atkinson has by definition worked out the problem for a specialized group of French voyages within a restricted period. He has specifically eliminated as fantastic or marvelous the voyages of Laurent Bordelon, Guillaume Bougeant, and Pierre Lesconvel for their utter lack of geographic realism. The impossible and therefore marvelous animals and peoples in his group of extraordinary voyages are considered incidental to the authenticated realism in the narratives. It should be remembered that Atkinson is interested in these works primarily for their rationalistic contribution to the movement of ideas in the seventeenth and early eighteenth centuries rather than for considerations of literary form. The present critical examination of his terms is almost totally apart from the scholarly achievement of his main purpose. The immediate object is to determine how far his classification and definition may be extended to the imaginary voyage of other languages and other times.

---

[152] . . . from 1700 to 1720, p. [111]; italics mine.

Professor Chinard, for example, expresses doubts even about the later eighteenth-century French fiction:

De la masse considérable de récits de voyages plus ou moins authentiques, de voyages purement imaginaires et fantastiques, de romans utopiques à tendances philosophiques ou déjà socialistes qui ont paru au dix-septième siècle, M. Atkinson a détaché et choisi pour sujet de son étude un groupe d'ouvrages auxquels il applique le terme de "voyages extraordinaires". Bien que M. Atkinson ait emprunté cette appellation à M. Lanson, il est bon de remarquer qu'il prend le mot voyage au sens strictement anglais de voyage par mer et qu'il exclut "les relations de voyages dans les autres planètes [etc.] . . . ." Il y a quelque danger à prendre ainsi dans une acception purement anglaise un terme qui existe en français avec un sens beaucoup plus compréhensif, surtout quand il s'agit d'étudier un groupe d'ouvrages purement français. Si M. Atkinson poursuit son étude à travers le dix-huitième siècle, . . . il se trouvera plus d'une fois embarrassé et sera forcé d'exclure des œuvres importantes qui ne répondent que de très loin à sa définition. Ces réserves faites, on peut à la rigueur classer sous le titre de voyages extraordinaires ¡une combinaison du roman d'aventures et du roman utopique opérée vers la fin du dix-septième siècle sous l'influence des relations authentiques de voyages.[153]

The connotation of the word *extraordinary* in its connection with voyages has a curious history. Quotations from Garnier have already shown the meanings that he attached to it. That it would be questioned Atkinson is aware:

The term *Extraordinary Voyage* is then merely a label, convenient for purposes of classification. It implies, not of itself, but because it has been so defined here, the limitations which have

---

[153] Gilbert Chinard, *Modern Language Notes,* XXXVII (1922), 491, in a review of both volumes together, which are "indispensable à qui veut étudier les premières manifestations de l'esprit philosophique en France à la fin du dix-huitième siècle" (p. 495).

been arbitrarily assigned to it. It is perhaps unfortunate that the terminology of literary history does not furnish a word which would imply the limitations above defined. The fact remains that there is no fitting term at present in use, so that limitation by definition becomes necessary. The reason for choosing the word "extraordinary" rather than any other is that the title *Voyages extraordinaires* has already been applied to this category by M. Gustave Lanson in designating the group of novels whose treatment is undertaken here.[154]

The reference is to the *Manuel bibliographique de la littérature française moderne* where in the section on "Le Roman de 1660 à 1715" under the heading "Voyages extraordinaires" appear the voyages of Foigny, Veiras, Gilbert, Fénelon, Lesconvel, Misson, Bordelon, and Tyssot de Patot, that is, works both included and excluded by Atkinson. Furthermore, Lanson under "Collections" gives in part the contents of Garnier's volumes, using Garnier's divisions but inexplicably altering *voyages imaginaires romanesques* to *voyages extraordinaires romanesques*.[155] However, nothing would be accomplished by arguing that Lanson once thought of *extraordinaire* as roughly synonymous with *imaginaire*, for Atkinson's studies were undertaken at his suggestion and apparently completed with his approval.[156]

One eighteenth-century fiction significantly employs the word in its title: *Lamekis, ou les voyages extraordinaires d'un Égyptien dans la terre intérieure avec la découverte de l'Île*

[154] . . . *before 1700*, pp. ix f.

[155] Gustave Lanson, *op. cit.*, nouv. éd. (Paris, 1921), Nos. 7175-93 and No. 496. Atkinson's reference is to the 1914 ed. In . . . *1700 to 1720*, pp. [111] f., he mentions that he is deliberately excluding works sometimes listed (as in Lanson) as extraordinary voyages.

[156] See Atkinson's prefaces. For further less restricted use of the term by Lanson see his "Origines et premières manifestations de l'esprit philosophique," *Revue des cours et conférences*, 17e an., 1 sér. (1908), pp. 219 and [259], and his "Formation et développement de l'esprit philosophique," *ibid.*, p. 505.

des Silphides (1735), by the chevalier de Mouhy, wherein *extraordinary* applies to an utterly impossible subterranean voyage. Though beginning realistically, as the most fantastic voyages often do, it turns into what Professor Green calls "a perfect phantasmagoria introducing the inevitable island inhabited by people colored blue and pink and such monsters as barnyard fowls with cats' heads!"[157] It is no surprise, therefore, that a translator made *die wunderbaren Reisen* the equivalent of *les voyages extraordinaires*.[158] On the other hand, Chinard in one of his admirable volumes on exoticism writes, "Jusqu'ici, les aventures de [Foigny's] Sadeur sont presque vraisemblables, nous allons maintenant entrer dans l'extraordinaire. . . . au roman chimérique va maintenant succéder le roman social."[159] This stresses a distinction even more restricting than Atkinson's definition. A decade after Atkinson's books Professor Van Tieghem refers to *voyages extraordinaires* as "ces récits d'aventures merveilleuses et ces descriptions de pays imaginaires."[160] It should also be recalled that Jules Verne's numerous fictions known as *romans scientifiques* were published in a series as *les voyages extraordinaires*. Considering the varying meanings which have been attached to the word in French litera-

[157] F. C. Green, "The Chevalier de Mouhy, an Eighteenth-Century French Novelist," *Modern Philology*, XXII (1924-25), 229.

[158] *Lamekis, oder die wunderbaren Reisen eines Egypters in dem Innern der Erde* . . . 1 Theil (Liegnitz und Leipzig, 1789), as reviewed in *Allgemeine deutsche Bibliothek*, XCVI (1790), ii, 446-48. A relevant earlier use of *extraordinary* but without similar significance occurs in the introduction to *Sevarambes* (1675). Veiras writes, "I examin'd them with great Care, and found them [the manuscript notes] to contain Things so extraordinary, and marvellous, that I could not be at rest till I had reduc'd them into order" (1738 ed., p. ix). The French and German texts are literal equivalents: "si extraordinaire & si merveilleuse" (in Garnier, V, xix) and "so auszerordentlich und wunderwürdig" (Göttingen, 1783, p. 14).

[159] *L'Amérique et le rêve exotique* . . . , p. 197.

[160] Paul van Tieghem, *La Littérature comparée* (Paris, 1931), p. 75.

ture, it seems wise not to try to extend its use for purposes
of classification to English, particularly since it has not been
so used. Dr. William A. Eddy in his study of *Gulliver's
Travels,* expressing much indebtedness to Atkinson, might
have used it, but instead he dismisses it as unfortunate. "The
connexion made by Atkinson between his *Extraordinary
Voyages* and contemporary rationalism, renders the term un-
suitable for a more inclusive classification, even were it a
desirable one." [161]

Eddy's *Critical Study* begins with a discussion of those
voyages which are related to *Gulliver's Travels* and with the
expressed intention of presenting "a consistent division
[which] will bring order out of the chaos in which *Imaginary Voyages* have been allowed to remain" (p. 12). Unfortunately this intention has not, in my opinion, been
completely accomplished, at least not to the extent of being
"exhaustive" and "indisputable" although such a competent
critic as Professor Émile Pons has high praise for Eddy's
classification: "La multiplicité des faits est éclairée par une
présentation logique et nette, par une classification 'scientifique' longuement méditée—et réalisée pour la première
fois—des divers genres de voyages imaginaires." [162]

[161] William A. Eddy, *op. cit.,* p. 13.

[162] *Revue de littérature comparée,* IV (1924), [149]. M. Pons is en-
thusiastic. He says also: ". . . cette étude continue, complète et couronne
les travaux récemment entrepris sur les voyages imaginaires à l'époque
classique, en particulier ceux d'Atkinson. . . . [Elle] contient énormément
de nouveautés ou de faits anciens rajeunis, et elle mérite, à une ou deux
réserves près, au moins en ce qui concerne l'étude des sources, l'épithète
d' 'exhaustive.' " I am not now concerned with the unquestionable value
of Eddy's book (though without an index) as a source-study or as
Swiftiana. The imaginary voyage studied exclusively from the point of
view of *Gulliver* (see especially pp. 3, 13, 14) is likely to become somewhat
distorted as fiction; a specific minor example may be seen in Eddy's
résumé of Lucian's *True History,* where the voyager is called "Lucian's
'Gulliver' " (p. 16); however, Walter Besant, *The French Humorists from
the Twelfth to the Nineteenth Century* (Boston, 1877), p. 129, uses the

To Eddy the term *imaginary voyage* means "a voyage that never had any existence outside . . . the writer's imagination." It may be divided into the *philosophic voyage* and the *non-philosophic* or *romantic* voyage.[163] "The term *Philosophic Voyage* is employed . . . to designate a didactic treatise in which the author's criticism of society is set forth in the parable form of an *Imaginary Voyage* made by one or more Europeans to a non-existent or little-known country, including an account of the traveler's journey and adventures, together with a description of the imaginary society visited." According to the *Oxford English Dictionary* the word *treatise* to designate a narrative became obsolete in the early seventeenth century; since it now means invariably a "methodical discussion or exposition of the principles of the subject," its application to a classification "made on the basis of narrative forms" may be infelicitous. Likewise confusing is the phrase *parable form,* which perhaps ought to restrict the philosophic voyage to a "short fictitious narrative of something which might really occur in life or nature" (Webster). No wholly satisfactory reason can be made for requiring that all such voyagers be Europeans; in this restriction Eddy has followed Atkinson, who does have a reason for the same restriction. If it is hypercritical to point out that Lucian, whose *True History* is the "earliest known *Philosophic Voyage*," was not a European, certainly *Wasob-*

---

same phrase and Alfred J. Church published *The Greek Gulliver: Stories from Lucian* (London, 1905). Cf. Robert Schönborn, *Der griechische Münchhausen oder die wahre Geschichte von Lukians wundersamer Reise* . . . (Halle, 1868).

[163] Pages [8]-15. Eddy nowhere states specifically the terms for such a bipartition, but such is the implication: "It may be that some *Voyages* will elude classification as *Philosophic* or *Romantic*" (p. 11); "These same narrative forms exist . . . in *Voyages* that are purely romantic and fictional, as well as in those that are didactic [i.e., philosophic]" (p. 10); and "The *Odyssey* is . . . of the non-philosophic variety" (p. 14).

yoe, a Japanese work published in 1774 and considered without qualification a philosophic voyage,[164] falls outside the definition.

Both the philosophic and the nonphilosophic are divided into the fantastic and the realistic:

The phrase *Fantastic Voyage* is employed . . . to designate a narrative of a chimerical voyage made by one or more Europeans to a fabulous country, in which the marvelous or supernatural elements are sufficiently prominent to make the account obviously unreal.

The fundamental distinction of *Fantastic Voyages* is their admittedly marvelous character, the fact that they are not credible and not intended to be accepted by readers as authentic. . . .

Fantastic Voyages may be sub-divided for convenience as follows:

(1) *Extra-terrestrial.* Example, Cyrano de Bergerac's *Histoire comique de la lune.*

(2) *Sub-terrestrial.* Example, Holberg's *Journey of Klimius to the World Underground.*

(3) *Terrestrial.* Example, *Gulliver's Travels.*

The phrase *Realistic Voyage* is employed . . . to designate a fictitious narrative purporting to be the veritable account of a voyage made by one or more Europeans to an existent country, or one that might easily exist, in which the mode of travel and the adventures are restricted to the possibilities of an actual voyage. . . .

The above classification of *Imaginary Voyages* into *Fantastic* and *Realistic,*[165] with convenient sub-divisions, will . . . cover

---

[164] Pages 68-71; 131-33; 169-70; 206. Translated in part by Basil H. Chamberlain, *Transactions of the Asiatic Society of Japan,* VII (1879), 285-308; 311-12.

[165] Since *imaginary* is divided into *philosophic* and *nonphilosophic,* under both of which *fantastic* and *realistic* become subdivisions, the jump from *imaginary* to the secondary subdivisions is not perhaps so confusing as it seems at first. Before this the statement is made that "all *Voyages* hereafter mentioned in the text are *Philosophic,* unless it is otherwise stated" (p. 10 n. 4).

every *Imaginary Voyage,* not alone those of didactic content. The *Voyages of Sindbad the Sailor,* Jules Verne, and Baron Munchausen are *Fantastic;* Sterne's *Sentimental Journey* [to a *well-known* country!], and Defoe's matchless imitations of real travel, are *Realistic.* The classification is made on the basis of form and is therefore indisputable. Readers may differ about the purpose for which a book is written, but there can be no question about the form in which it is published.

If this classification *were* based throughout on form, it might be indisputable. But the primary division between philosophic and nonphilosophic seems to be based partly on purpose, as further indicated in various places by such remarks as these:

The *Philosophic Voyage* is wholly fictitious and primarily didactic. (p. [8])

[It is] written primarily to expound a philosophical position, . . . in which the narrative is simply a vehicle for instruction. (p. 9)

The *Philosophic Voyage* is a form of novel, analogous to the modern novel of propaganda, that deals with a social "Problem"; analogous also to the dramatized sermons of Bernard Shaw. So *Gulliver's Travels,* and all *Philosophic Voyages,* are critical works disguised as fiction. . . . (p. 9)

[They are] primarily works of criticism rather than works of fiction. (p. 11)

Didacticism and criticism are unquestionably qualities denoting purpose about which "readers may differ." The critical or didactic or romantic or satiric or allegoric qualities of fictitious narrative are, *as far as form goes,* secondary qualities.

With regard to the subdivision into fantastic and realistic, the definitions contain phrases implying purpose and making a clear and strict distinction between the two impossible.

In a sentence amplifying the definition of the fantastic voyage, Eddy says, "Realistic strokes may abound, as they do in *Gulliver's Travels,* but if so they are only a part of the narrator's art, calculated to insure the reader's interest rather than to impose upon his credulity." This statement is the first of many to demonstrate that the definitions given are too narrow for the work to the study of which this classification is an introduction. Eddy's own words substantiate this:

. . . *Gulliver's Travels* belongs to the type of *Philosophic Voyage* which I have defined as Fantastic, though as I shall show in the next chapter it is something else as well. (p. 27)

This *Realistic* type of narrative ["actual travel, distinguished by the standard, invariable experiences of an ordinary seaman"] is important, because it is the narrative form of *Gulliver's Travels,* in substance a *Fantastic Voyage* [although earlier he has stated that "the classification here used . . . is made on the basis of narrative forms"]. (p. 29)

However much the countries visited [by Gulliver], or the adventures narrated, may find their analogues in the *Fantastic Voyages,* the form of the story is that of an authentic history. (p.31)

However much *Gulliver* may resemble the authentic narratives of men like Dampier, this difference remains, that the latter were written by real travellers, while *Gulliver* was composed by a clergyman in his study. Its realism, then, is only pseudo-realism, and the apparent truth nothing but a clever counterfeit [which is to say only that it is a fictitious narrative purporting to be the veritable account of a voyage]. The question arises, what precedent was there for this composition, with the aid of the imagination alone, of a *Realistic Voyage,* for which there was no basis in fact? (p. 33)

A rereading of the definitions will perhaps remove this confusion temporarily and reveal only that substance and method have been confused and that a voyage fantastic or nonrealistic in substance may be realistic in method. But a division into the coördinate classes of fantastic and realistic on any basis is of doubtful value if the classes must be immediately set aside so that on another basis the same terms become, if not actually reversed, at least subordinate to each other. The realistic-fantastic *Gulliver* is not the only example. There is the fantastic-realistic *Sadeur*.

Foigny's *Jacques Sadeur* is according to Eddy the earliest example of a realistic voyage. In the definition of this type occurs a sentence stating that "the adventures are restricted to the possibilities of an actual voyage." In amplification Eddy says: "In determining the 'possibilities of an actual voyage' the knowledge possessed by the author's contemporaries must be taken into account. A seventeenth century *Voyage* describing unicorns and hermaphrodites does not on that account fail to be a *Realistic Voyage,* however prodigious such features may seem to a modern scientist." This is a reasonable qualification, but one to be used only with extreme caution. In addition to the race of hermaphrodites, to the unicorns, and to the giant birds in *Sadeur,* one reads about web-footed fish like water spaniels, which jump into boats; other fish like huge eagles with over a twelve-foot wingspread; red, green, yellow, and blue sheep; winged horses with claws; bears with each foot as large as the whole animal; natives with striped legs indicating their ancestry of half-man, half-tigress; inventors who create birds and dogs from moistened dirt, who grow flowers from lifeless pieces of wood, and who make themselves invisible for two hours at a time; pigs which without an overseer plow fields in straight lines ready for planting; camels with cavities, instead of humps, large enough to hold two men; and so on throughout the book.[166] Checking these monstrosities with the knowledge of a modern scientist is beside the point;

[166] See the analysis of *Sadeur* in Atkinson, . . . *before 1700,* pp. 40-86.

among Foigny's contemporaries no one able to read could have swallowed enough of this fiction to bring it within the definition of a realistic voyage. The definite statement of one contemporary corroborates this opinion. Bayle in the 1697 edition of his *Dictionnaire* says: "La maniere dont il dit . . . qu'il vainquit les bêtes farouches qui le vouloient dechirer, & qu'il se retira enfin de ce païs-la . . . est quelque chose de si étrange, que je ne pense pas qu'il y ait des inventions plus grotesques ni dans l'Arioste, ni dans l'Amadis." [167] Sadeur was, as a twentieth-century commentator has called him, "the Mandeville, the Ferdinand Mendez Pinto, the very De Rougemont of the seventeenth century." [168]

Eddy in a brief résumé of *Sadeur* refers to some of the "remarkable adventures and shipwrecks, bordering on the fantastic" and admits that

as a narrative, *Sadeur* may seem to some a *Fantastic* rather than a *Realistic Voyage*. . . . On the other hand, there is a great deal of effective pseudo-realism in *Sadeur;* nearly one-fourth of the book is devoted to Sadeur's earlier voyages to less remote lands. Its importance for our study lies in the fact that the *Sadeur* is the earliest instance of a *Realistic Voyage* in which there is a balance

---

[167] *Ibid.*, p. 50 n. 14. Though actually 21 years after the first edition of *Sadeur*, the opinion is not therefore barred from being considered contemporary. Foigny's dates are 1640-1692; Bayle's, 1647-1702. Chinard, *Modern Language Notes*, XXXVII (1922), 493, applies to *Sadeur* a remark that "me semble avoir échappé à l'attention des chercheurs," made by Lesage in *La Valise trouvée* (1740): "Ce Livre étoit un amas de fictions extraordinaires & prodigieuses." It seems, however, that Lesage—the only edition I have seen is Maestricht, 1779, p. 33— is not necessarily referring to *Sadeur* but rather that he is inventing an anecdote for his immediate purpose. Every material fact mentioned by Lesage disagrees with those for *Sadeur*—title-wording, date, and place of publication.

[168] A. T. S. Goodrick, "Robinson Crusoe, Imposter," *Blackwood's Magazine*, CLXXXIII (1908), 680, where his "farrago of lies" is effectively emphasized. See Henri Louis Grin, *The Adventures of Louis de Rougemont as Told by Himself* (London, 1899).

between adventure and satire, absent in works of the *Utopia* type, but characteristic of *Gulliver* and of all typical *Philosophic Voyages.*[169]

This final comparison is a necessary recognition of the fact that both *Gulliver* and *Sadeur* are compounded of so many diverse elements that classification of them in rigid terms of *realistic* and *fantastic* cannot be mutually exclusive.[170]

This analysis of Eddy's approach to the imaginary voyage touches in no serious way the value of his study of Swift's work voyage by voyage. The interests of my book have made it necessary to decide whether Eddy has succeeded in his incidental intention of establishing a consistent classification, and particularly whether the same approach, which in his own words is not intended to be exhaustive, may be extended to the imaginary voyage as a genre of fiction apart from the point of view of any one period or work.

As Eddy's book was being completed, Dr. Sybil Goulding

[169] Page 38. This is not to understate the fantastic nature of *Gulliver*. Eddy (p. 29 n. 2-b) rightly challenges Dennis's remark that "If we once accept the scale on which the countries and their inhabitants are drawn, there is nothing in what follows to throw any strain on our credulity." Eddy's vigorous objections should be read in connection with the realistic-fantastic "issue": "A moment's reflection will expose the absurdity of this statement. If, for example, we accept the Lilliputian scale, then Gulliver becomes a prodigy, and his actions must be viewed, as they appeared to the Lilliputians, as monstrous. Accept the Brobdingnagian scale, if you will, and then try to account for the tiny dwarf Gulliver, who can be thrust into a marrow bone, without straining your credulity. The only escape from this dilemma would be through the simultaneous acceptance of both scales as normal, a feat that is beyond the powers of the human mind. Whether the reader bears in mind the point of view of the traveller, or that of the natives, he will find every adventure fantastic and incredible."

[170] Into this quibbling over terms I have not inserted the possible objections to considering *Gulliver* a terrestrial voyage. The aërial departure from Brobdingnag and the flying island of Laputa make *Gulliver* in part extraterrestrial. Eddy (p. 31) mentions these as violations of Swift's realistic method.

was preparing her *Swift en France;* so the two works, each of which might have profited from the other, are independent. Miss Goulding is less attentive than Eddy to the various kinds of imaginary voyages but shows that French readers were well prepared to accept the type of fiction that *Gulliver's Travels* is:

> Quant à la forme précise du récit de Gulliver, il n'y a rien, comme le remarque Desfontaines dans sa préface, de bien nouveau. . . . Profitant de la passion du public du xviie siècle pour les relations véridiques de voyages réels dans les pays inexplorés, les romanciers se sont mis à inventer des "voyages imaginaires" où se dessine de plus en plus nettement la satire sociale, et qui, il est important de le noter, deviennent de plus en plus fades et ennuyeux. En 1727, on est . . . assez près du xviie siècle pour être ravi d'entendre parler de la possibilité d'un roman du même genre, qui joindrait à la fiction fantaisiste et satirique l'intérêt d'un récit de véritable explorateur, cet intérêt qu'on a dû beaucoup gouter dans une fiction récente, . . . le *Robinson Crusoë.* . . .[171]

After discussing the editions of *Gulliver* in the eighteenth century, she turns to "une autre preuve plus subtile de son emprise sur l'imagination populaire," that of imitation. The next twenty-five pages constitute a brief contribution to the history of the imaginary voyage in France, with the following introductory passage:

> . . . bien qu'on reconnaisse que la forme de l'ouvrage de Swift n'est pas nouvelle, que des mondes merveilleux, utopiques ou

---

[171] *Swift en France: essai sur la fortune et l'influence de Swift en France au XVIIIe siècle, suivi d'un aperçu sur la fortune de Swift en France au cours du XIXe siècle* (Paris, 1924), p. 74. Cf. a statement by Wijngaarden: "Si . . . *Le Nouveau Gulliver* . . . n'a pas eu le succès qu'a remporté *l'Histoire des Sévarambes,* c'est qu'il a été publié à une époque où l'on n'a plus recours aux allusions, aux allégories, où l'on dit la vérité sans fard" (p. 157).

non, ont déjà été découverts par d'intrépides Européens, il faut convenir en même temps que la façon dont Swift traite son sujet est entièrement originale et infiniment supérieure à tout ce qui existe déjà dans le même genre. Swift démontre qu'il est possible en 1726 de créer une fiction merveilleuse, un conte de fées, propre à se faire goûter par ses qualités intrinsèques de lecteurs très sérieux, très exigeants, aussi bien que d'autres plus frivoles. Ainsi, à considérer le goût inné du merveilleux dans la nature humaine de tout temps, sans même tenir compte des tendances satiriques si prononcées à cette époque, il n'est pas déraisonnable de s'attendre à voir *Gulliver* donner une grande impulsion à son propre genre littéraire. En effet, en rendant vraisemblable l'impossible, Swift stimule bien des imaginations d'ordre très médiocre, qui, selon toute probabilité, auraient autrement rejeté comme ridicule l'idée de la possibilité de faire quelque chose de nouveau et de réussi sur le modèle d'un *Voyage aux Etats de la Lune* ou d'une *Histoire des Sevarambes.* Dans cette poussée vers le roman des voyages imaginaires, *Robinson Crusoë,* comme Gulliver loin d'être le premier, mais incontestablement le chef-d'œuvre du genre, joue bien entendu un rôle important, mais il est intéressant de noter que c'est *Gulliver,* postérieur pourtant de six ans à *Robinson,* qui déclanche l'influence de celui-ci. Dans les débuts, *Robinson* n'a pas eu en France un succès comparable à celui de *Gulliver,* et il semble qu'il ait fallu le succès fou de ce dernier pour attirer l'attention du public sur la possibilité d'utiliser l'histoire de l'île solitaire. Alors les influences de ces deux contes anglais, entrelacées et souvent impossibles à démêler, commencent à traverser ensemble le siècle.

Il serait, on le comprend bien, aussi ridicule d'affirmer que tous les pays utopiques visités par des voyageurs imaginaires postérieurs à Lemuel Gulliver, sont des souvenirs du pays des Houyhnhnms, ou de voir dans chaque critique satirique l'ombre du roi de Brobdingnag, que de reconnaître dans chaque île celle de Robinson. On se demande, cependant, ce qui aurait existé de toute cette littérature de "roman-voyage" sans l'impulsion de ces deux œuvres. Bonne, mauvaise ou médiocre, la voilà toute cette production, s'amoncelant en tas énormes à travers soixante ans. . . . Il est impossible de croire que la "voyage imaginaire," sans lequel il est difficile de se figurer le xviiie siècle, se serait revêtu d'une pareille importance sans *Gulliver* et plus tard *Robinson*. (pp. 88 f.)

One does not need now to take sides on the relative importance of the two stories. Usually it varies directly with whether one is principally interested in Defoe or in Swift, but whereas a large body of critical history attests the influence of *Robinson,* as will be shown later, the studies of *Gulliver* as a type are less numerous, and (fortunately) the conception of a *gulliveriad* as a genre is practically nonexistent. With a few exceptions, such as Desfontaines's *Nouveau Gulliver, Gulliver Revived* (the third edition of *Munchausen,* 1786), and *Modern Gulliver's Travels* (1796), the word *Gulliver* was not used indiscriminately in titles as was *Robinson,* and consequently literary historians have not had the complications of such a genre forced upon them, although its absence creates its own tantalizing problem: why did hack writers not see possibilities in a French Gulliver or a German Gulliver, in a Family Gulliver, and especially in a Female Gulliver? [172]

Miss Goulding discusses twenty-one works of the eighteenth century, all French except three, *Niels Klim, Peter Wilkins,* and *Munchausen.* "On pourrait dire que dans toute cette littérature postérieure à *Gulliver* et qui lui ressemble en quelque façon, il n'y aurait rien qui présenterait le moindre intérêt durable, si elle ne contenait une exception éclatante à la règle de médiocrité générale" (p. 100). The exception is the satirical romances of Voltaire, particularly the one most like *Gulliver, Micromégas* (1752).

---

[172] There were others than the three cited, but most of them were in the nineteenth century and were adaptations of the original for children, such as *Le Gulliver des enfants* (1843), *Le Petit Gulliver* (1869), and *Le Gulliver de la jeunesse* (1876). See Goulding, p. 153.

In 1925 Professor Daniel Mornet brought out his four-volume critical edition of *La Nouvelle Héloïse,* of which the first volume is devoted to an exhaustive introduction concerning not only Rousseau's novel but also the state of French fiction from 1741 to 1780. Mornet separates these years into two equal periods and proceeds to number and classify those "romans, nouvelles et contes" which he has been able to read or examine. The first twenty years saw over 800 editions or reëditions, which he lists under fourteen classifications, of which one is *voyages imaginaires.* The class contains seven titles published eleven times. During the years 1761-80 there were ten titles published eighteen times in the same class, one of twenty-four different kinds in this period, published in over 900 editions or reëditions. These figures are, however, somewhat misleading, as far as the imaginary voyage is concerned, because of inconsistencies and errors. In the first period, translations of *Gaudentio di Lucca* (attributed to Berkeley) and of *Nicolas Klimius* are *voyages imaginaires,* whereas translations of *Robinson Crusoe* and of *Gulliver's Travels* are *traductions;* but in the second period *Robinson* (in Feutry's version) has become a *voyage imaginaire* along with the translation of *Peter Wilkins,* listed twice, once as anonymous and once by Puisieux, and *Gulliver* remains a *traduction.*[173] Béthune's *Relation du monde*

---

[173] *J.-J. Rousseau: La Nouvelle Héloïse: nouvelle édition publiée d'après les manuscrits et les éditions originales avec des variantes, une introduction, des notices et des notes* (Paris, Librarie Hachette, 1925), I, 335-85. No system of classification of fiction is more certain to cause trouble than that which includes translations as a separate class. Mornet's list has been partly superseded by Silas P. Jones, *A List of French Prose Fiction from 1700 to 1750* . . . (New York, 1939), but for the period 1751-80 it is still a valuable contribution, even though his classifications are confusing in themselves and further complicated by the absence of any index: to make certain whether a given title is included, one must examine 48 separate alphabetical lists. To imaginary voyages which he lists under other classes I make no references, for the reason already made clear in

de Mercure appears under both *contes fantaisistes et galants* and *voyages imaginaires;* although this work may be put in either group, under Mornet's system it should not be in both.

Mornet in his discussion of fiction as a background for *La Nouvelle Héloïse* gives only a passing glance at the imaginary voyage and makes no suggestion that its popularity may have influenced Rousseau to send Saint-Preux around the world with Commodore Anson. This speculation is strengthened by Rousseau's well-known veneration for *Robinson Crusoe;* even so, the vogue of real voyage-literature is probably sufficient suggestion for Saint-Preux's voyage, which, furthermore, is not related in the manner of the voyagers but in the outline form of a few separated sentences contained within eight paragraphs.[174]

---

this book that one work may often be classified several ways. Also Mornet himself says (I, 336): "Il va de soi qu'il y a dans ce classement une part irréductible d'arbitraire et que tel roman, selon l'impression du lecteur, pourrait passer de la catégorie *roman sentimental* à celle du *roman d'intrigue sentimental* ou inversement." The lists under *voyages imaginaires* in I, 350 and 382, should be compared with the two charts on pp. 303 and 304 f., listing year by year from 1741 to 1780 the "nombre de romans édités ou réédités." The charts do not always agree with the lists. For an important review of Mornet's study of fiction see S[ervais] Étienne, "La Méthode en histoire littéraire à propos d'une publication récente sur le roman français au XVIIIe siècle," *Revue belge de philologie et d'histoire,* V (1926), [351]-380.

[174] 4e pte., lettre iii; *ibid.,* III, 142-52: "J'ai passé quatre fois la ligne; j'ai parcouru les deux hémisphères; j'ai vu les quatres parties du monde. . . . Je suis trop pressé de vous envoyer cette Lettre pour vous faire à présent un détail de mon voyage. J'ose espérer d'en avoir bientôt une occasion plus comode. Je me contente ici de vous en donner une légère idée, plus pour exciter que pour satisfaire votre curiosité. J'ai mis près de quatre ans au trajet immense dont je viens de vous parler. . . . J'ai vu d'abord l'Amérique méridionale. . . . J'ai séjourné trois mois dans une Isle déserte et délicieuse. . . . J'ai surgi dans une seconde Isle déserte plus inconnue, plus charmante encore que la première. . . ." This brief sketch does not make *La Nouvelle Héloïse* an imaginary voyage even in part.

Mornet has investigated the relation between the novel and Richard Walters's account of Anson's voyage, in "Une Source d'une lettre de la

Mornet's critical estimate is brief:

Les voyages imaginaires mêlaient le goût du romanesque et du merveilleux à celui de la satire et de la philosophie. C'est par lui, pour une part, que le libertinage de l'esprit avait risqué ses premières audaces dans les romans de Denis Veiras et de Tyssot de Patot. On publie, de 1741 à 1760, une dizaine d'éditions de ces voyages. On en publie 18 de 1761 à 1780. Mais le genre s'affadit. Les philosophes ont maintenant des armes mieux aiguisées. Ils veulent autre chose que des utopies. Par le conte et la nouvelle ils atteignent mieux les "abus" et les "préjugés," quand ils ne les dénoncent pas directement dans les traités en forme. Ainsi le voyage imaginaire se réduit à n'être plus qu'une fantaisie d'imagination. La grande collection [de Garnier] . . . n'est plus qu'une assez anodine compilation pour les grands et petits enfants, où l'on doute qu'il y ait eu dans l'*Histoire des Sévarambes* des impiétés, mais où l'on supprime, par précaution, les passages qui inquiétèrent les âmes pieuses. (I, 300)

Nouvelle Héloïse," *Revue universitaire,* XII, ii (1903), 146-51, which he summarizes and continues in his critical edition, III, 142-47 n. 1; in part: "Il choisit dans ses souvenirs à sa guise pour ne retenir que ce qui confirme ses idées philosophiques sur la bonté de l'état de nature et le bonheur d'une vie libre des liens sociaux. Il transforme le récit du voyageur anglais parce que c'est lui qui le raconte et l'imagine, et qu'ainsi les choses prennent une couleur nouvelle comme les événements une signification plus haute. La lettre de Saint-Preux n'est pas un résumé; elle est animée de l'âme de l'auteur et de la vie du roman." With regard to what influenced him: "Si Rousseau fait voyager Saint-Preux autour du monde c'est sans doute parce qu'il avait rêvé autrefois lui-même d'un pareil voyage," as evidenced in his notes to the *Discours sur l'inégalité.* On the background of this see Gilbert Chinard, "Influence des récits de voyages sur la philosophie de J. J. Rousseau," *Publications of the Modern Language Association,* XXVI (1911), 476-95; also his *Amérique et le rêve exotique,* pp. [341]-365. Rousseau was the author also of *Le Nouveau Dédale,* an imaginative exposition on the possibilities of flying, written supposedly in 1742; it is included in Pierre P. Plan, "Jean-Jacques Rousseau aviateur," *Mercvre de France,* LXXXVII (1910), [577]-597. Paul Nourrisson, *Jean-Jacques Rousseau et Robinson Crusoé* (Paris, 1931), makes a thorough study of "l'influence qu'a exercée sur Rousseau l'idée fixe de la solitude" but uses *Robinson* only as a starting point.

Mornet, from the point of view of Rousseau-study, finds it easy to relegate the imaginary voyage to "grands et petits enfants." But, as has been recently stated: "Si nous connaissions mieux les goûts du public du XVIIe siècle, il n'y aurait rien d'étonnant à constater que ces utopies et voyages fantaisistes, un peu puériles, aient été lus et goûtés des mêmes lecteurs qui faisaient leur délices de Boileau, de Bourdaloue et de la *Princesse de Clèves.*"[175] Although this caution is applied to the seventeenth century, there is no reason why, *mutatis mutandis,* it cannot be applied similarly to the age of Rousseau. Another French scholar, Professor Pons, guided by his interest in Swift, carefully works out what he calls an "Esquisse rapide de l'histoire du 'Voyage imaginaire' du XVIe au XVIIIe siècle," a genre definitely established in the Renaissance in the works of More, Rabelais, Thomas Artus (*Les Hermaphrodites,* 1605), Campanella, and Bacon, in which appear its two fundamental characteristics:

1. Le récit de voyage est tout à fait imaginaire (bien que le degré de ressemblance ou d'invraisemblance varie à l'infini, depuis la manière sérieuse qui prétend donner le change au lecteur, jusqu'à la plus folle extravagance).

2. Il décrit, en même temps que des voyages, périples, explorations, etc. des pays et cités, imaginaires aussi, qui sont de nature *utopique,* c'est-à-dire qui sont systématiquement idéalisés, afin que leurs perfections fassent apparaître par contraste les défauts et vices des institutions politiques et des mœurs des nations civilisées et, plus particulièrement, de celle à laquelle appartient l'auteur.

L'élément satirique est ainsi lié au caractère utopique du livre; il est lié aussi au caractère imaginaire du récit, qui permet à l'auteur de donner sans crainte libre cours à sa verve.

Mais par ces deux traits distinctifs, le voyage imaginaire de la Renaissance se rattache à toute une série d'œuvres, antérieures

---

[175] Henri Peyre, *Romanic Review,* XXX (1939), 304.

appartenant soit à l'antiquité—classique et de basse époque—soit au moyen âge.[176]

From this background Pons traces three elements or themes, the ideological (Plato), the imaginative (chiefly Homer and Lucian), and the oriental (exemplified in *Sindbad*). "Au XVIIe siècle, ces divers éléments achèvent de s'amalgamer, de se fondre en une tradition littéraire. . . . Les 'Voyages' les plus divers sortiront de ce pillage de la matière exotique par les imaginations avides. Il y aura d'abord des œuvres mixtes ou bâtardes, à la fois relations historiques de voyages réels et commentaires idéologiques, utopistes ou satiriques. . . ." These seventeenth-century "voyages philosophiques," as he calls them, "annoncent déjà et expliquent par maints côtés—à la fois au point de vue de la forme et au point de vue de la pensée, les romans philosophiques d'une valeur littéraire beaucoup plus grande qui seront les œuvres capitales du XVIIIe siècle: Gulliver, Candide, Micromégas, etc.—et même Robinson—quelque grandes que soient la nouveauté et l'originalité de ceux-ci." *Gulliver,* he decides, links more closely with this genre than *Robinson,* which "s'écarte du type normal et courant de voyage imaginaire à la fois parce qu'il prétend à une vraisemblance absolue et qu'il est d'un autre lignage. . . ." [177] Pons's analysis, admittedly a sketch full of unexplained generalities, unfortunately goes no further, for it shows an excellent grasp of the subject and makes clear suggestions for its study. Pons himself slightly amplifies his remarks in the introduction to his school edition of *Gulliver*.[178]

In 1932 Dr. Nicolaas van Wijngaarden published a study of twenty-one French imaginary voyages under the title,

[176] Émile Pons, "Le 'Voyage' genre littéraire au XVIIIe siècle," *Bulletin de la faculté des lettres de Strasbourg,* IV (1925-26), 99 f.

[177] Pages 100 f., 144, and 201.

[178] Paris, [1927], pp. lxxvii-lxxxix.

Les Odyssées philosophiques en France entre 1616 et 1789.[179]
Fully aware that many of these works have been utilized
by such predecessors as Lichtenberger, Chinard, Lanson, Atkinson, and Lachèvre[180] in their studies of the development
of ideas, he makes clear his own approach:

> . . . j'ose aborder une nouvelle étude de ces voyages imaginaires
> . . . non seulement pour ajouter quelques titres de romans incon-
> nus et pourtant fort curieux à leurs listes d'odyssées philoso-
> phiques, mais aussi pour faire ressortir que toute cette littérature
> de second ordre est née des conditions politiques et économiques
> sous lesquelles ont vécu ses auteurs, qu'elle n'est qu'une réaction
> contre le système gouvernemental en vigueur du vivant des
> écrivains . . . (p. 15).

This he can show by carefully limiting the imaginary voyages to a special kind, a kind to which will apply his statement that "on verra le nombre des voyages imaginaires se
multiplier à mesure que les conditions sociales et économiques deviennent plus mauvaises" (p. 77). The *odyssées
philosophiques* include, then,

> les relations à base politique et économique dont l'auteur, pour
> authentiquer son récit, place l'action dans un cadre réaliste, savoir
> la description d'un voyage qui eût pu se faire dans un pays nou-
> vellement découvert, chez des peuples inconnus dont le gouverne-

---

[179] Haarlem, 1932. One of the works is *Gaudentio di Lucca*, translated
from the English but so changed and augmented in the Dupuy-Demportes
edition that Wijngaarden regards it as "un véritable roman français"
(p. 182); cf. my note 71. In summarizing, however, he says that "comme
ce roman est une adaptation d'une utopie anglaise, il vaut mieux l'éliminer
de notre classement" (p. 240 n. 424).

[180] "Malgré les travaux de M. Lachèvre et l'esquisse donnée par M.
Lanson sur les Origines de l'Esprit philosophique . . . , on peut dire que
le travail reste presque tout entier à faire. On ne pourra connaître et
juger le xviiie siècle que le jour où il aura été fait." This was written in
the preceding year by Chinard in his edition of Lahontan's *Dialogues
curieux* . . . (Baltimore), p. 71. Cf. my note 153.

ment, la religion et les mœurs rendent jaloux tous ceux qui ne connaissent que les conditions politiques et économiques de l'Europe. (pp. 236 f.)

As a type the *odyssée philosophique* lends itself easily to full and coherent analysis of economic and political ideas, as long as any work under discussion falls within the definition. But authors do not usually suppress deliberately whatever ability they possess to narrate well, even when they employ narrative only as a disguise or sugar-coating for didacticism: should they be blamed if the thesis sometimes becomes subsidiary or even lost?

Of Rustaing de Saint-Jory's *Femmes militaires* (1735) Wijngaarden writes: "c'est un roman, il est amusant pour les lecteurs du XVIIIe siècle qui aiment les plaisanteries d'un goût douteux; il est sage mais incomplet puisqu'on n'y trouve ni les idées de l'auteur sur la foi ni celles concernant le commerce." [181] To trace ideas so zealously that a fiction can be condemned for omitting the discussion of ideas looked for is a startling kind of literary criticism. Speaking of Grivel's *Ile inconnue,* Wijngaarden wonders "pourquoi l'auteur a donné son œuvre à un public qui cherche dans les relations de voyage la description de quelque cité idéale" (p. 227), which seems to argue that an author who neglects to use the imaginary voyage for utopian purposes really has no reason for writing. A critic who sets out to trace the utopian content may rightly concentrate on the one chapter in six volumes which expounds the socialistic laws of an unknown people, but he cannot logically consider all the other chapters wholly superfluous and a cause for wondering

---

[181] Page 181. The wording is based on a review of *Les Femmes militaires,* which appeared in the *Journal litéraire,* XXIV (1737), 193: "C'est un roman. Il est sage, il est amusant, il y a du naturel et du merveilleux, il y a du vieux, du neuf . . . ," as quoted in Wijngaarden, p. 172.

why the author wrote it or the public read it. *Sethos* (1731) by the abbé Terrasson is considered unimportant because its influence "a été nulle: un peuple à la veille d'une révolution ne s'occupe pas d'idylles pastorales, où le roi absolu, bon père de famille, est 'le délice de ses peuples'" (p. 172). This reasoning makes it difficult for one to understand the popularity of many imaginary voyages, as well as hundreds of the other romances in Mornet's bibliography, from 1731 on; it is judging an imaginary voyage solely by the significance of its utopian content.

Considering together the *Histoire du grand et admirable royaume d'Antangil* (1616), "la première utopie écrite par un Français en langue française,"[182] and the two works of Foigny and Veiras, which "appartiennent au groupe des utopies à cadre exotique" (p. 77), Wijngaarden sees a basis for generalizing upon the development in the type:

Les premières odyssées philosophiques étaient toutes d'une même affabulation: la description du naufrage du héros, son sauvetage miraculeux, suivis de quelques chapitres consacrés à la religion, à l'éducation, au gouvernement et aux mœurs du peuple nouvellement découvert. Au XVIIIe siècle au contraire l'auteur se plaît à imaginer une suite d'aventures périlleuses, de rencontres imprévues, quitte à disséminer dans ce fatras d'anecdotes, de digressions et de dissertations quelques rares observations philosophiques ou morales; après la mort du roi [Louis XIV] on ne publie que "ces recueils puérils de voyages où le vrai est sacrifié au merveilleux, l'utile à l'agréable, où l'on nous apprend tout ce que nous pourrions ignorer sans inconvénient et presque rien de ce qu'il importe de savoir. (pp. 204 f.)

Here emerges one probable clue to Wijngaarden's point of

[182] Page 17. Wijngaarden argues that the author was Joachim du Moulin, but this attribution is disputed by Frédéric Lachèvre, "Un Double Problème bibliographique et littéraire," *Bulletin du bibliophile et du bibliothécaire*, n.s. XII (1933), [58]-65 and [109]-115. See Lachèvre's edition (Paris, 1933).

view: the inner quotation comes from the *Dictionnaire universel des sciences morale, économique, politique et diplomatique ou bibliothèque de l'homme d'état et du citoyen,* published in the year 1777; the implied test for the quality of an imaginary voyage is that of a philosophic dictionary of twelve years before the Revolution. Unquestionably the *philosophes* sought in the voyages the description of some ideal city; what the fiction-reading public sought and enjoyed was a good story based on the narrative technique by which it should be judged.

These examples show the danger of adopting as a definite subdivision of the imaginary voyage the *odyssée philosophique* as defined; having served its purpose for an approach to the study of prerevolutionary France, its independent existence as a literary form ceases. This is, in fact, what happens at the end of Wijngaarden's book: "Groupons d'abord nos auteurs en deux catégories diamétralement opposées, c.-à-d. en adhérents de la communauté des biens, du communisme intégral, et en défenseurs de la propriété individuelle, du commerce international" (p. 240); and: "A côté de ce classement-ci, je voudrais en proposer un autre, la distinction en odyssées philosophiques et en relations morales" (p. 241).

Particular interest on the part of Wijngaarden centers on five works which have "échappés à l'attention des grands-maîtres de la critique," [183] in fulfillment of his promise at

---

[183] Page 237. The only one of these which I have not found mentioned elsewhere is the third, of which Wijngaarden says (p. 189): "Cette relation rarissime, inconnue jusqu'ici, ignorée de Barbier même, se trouve à la Bibliothèque Municipale d'Aix-en-Provence." Of the work by Varennes de Mondasse he says (p. 145 n. 54): "Nulle part on ne mentionne cette relation curieuse dont un exemplaire . . . se trouve à la Bibliothèque Municipale de Dijon." It is, however, mentioned in Lenglet du Fresnoy, *op. cit.,* II, 340, and reviewed in *L'Esprit de l'Abbé Desfontaines,* edition cited, IV, 305.

the beginning: Varennes de Mondasse's *Découverte de l'empire de Cantahar* (1730), *Les Femmes militaires,* the *Voyage curieux d'un Philadelphe* (1755), the *Histoire d'un peuple nouveau* (1756), and the *Voyage de Robertson aux terres australes* (1766). The examination of these little-known imaginary voyages constitutes the most valuable contribution of Wijngaarden's book.[184]

v. The Robinsonade

Robinson Crusoe was hardly allowed to dry before it was imitated. The *Adventures of James Dubourdieu* and the *Adventures of Alexander Vendchurch* appeared only a few days after the second volume of *Robinson.* Though Theophilus Cibber had some basis for believing that "for some time after its publication, it was judged by most people to be a true story," [185] critics throughout Europe recognized it at once as fiction,[186] and writers of fiction, when not actu-

[184] I have mentioned in the text ten and in note 179 one of the twenty-one works discussed. The others are *Télémaque,* Gilbert's *Calejava* (1700), the *Voyages* and the *Suplement* of the Baron Lahontan (1703), Lesconvel's *Montberaud* (1703), Tyssot de Patot's *Jacques Massé* and *Groënland,* De Lassay's *Royaume des feliciens* (1727), Desfontaines's *Nouveau Gulliver,* and *La République des philosophes* (1768). For comment on Wijngaarden's interpretations see a review by Daniel Mornet, *Revue d'histoire littéraire de la France,* XL (1933), 128-30; Von der Mühll, *op. cit.,* p. 253 n. 43; and the introductory material in Lachèvre's edition of *Antangil.*

[185] *Lives of the Poets of Great Britain and Ireland* (London, 1753), IV, 322.

[186] See, e.g., *Journal des Sçavans,* LXVIII (1720), 387-94; *Nouvelles littéraires* for December, 1719, as referred to by Mann, *op. cit.,* p. 14: "Le correspondant londonien . . . trouve cet ouvrage dans le goût de l'*Histoire des Sévarambes* et de *Jacques Sadeur,* qu'il est 'assez grossièrement imaginé et qu'on y pèche plus d'une fois contre la vraisemblance' "; *Neue Zeitungen von gelehrten Sachen* of 13 Juni, 1720, p. 373: "Das wunderbahre ist darinn überall so sehr gesucht, dasz an einigen Orthen kaum einige Wahrscheinlichkeit mehr übrig ist"; and Benjamin Hoadley in the *London Journal* for September 4, 1725: a *"most palpable Lye, from Beginning to End,"* as quoted in *The Library of Literary Criticism of English and American Authors,* ed. Charles W. Moulton (Buffalo, 1902), III, 32.

ally imitating it, soon tried to deflect some of its popularity toward their own writings. Penelope Aubin introduces her *Strange Adventures of Count de Vinevil* (1721) with the plea that "since *Robinson Cruso* has been so well received, which is more improbable, I know no Reason why this should be thought a Fiction," [187] and a translation of Tyssot de Patot's *Vie de Pierre de Mesange* (1720) appeared in the following year as *Des Robinson Crusoe dritter und vierter Theil.* If the interpretation of a recent critic is at all valid, the irony of Defoe's position begins to appear. Robinson may be looked upon as a sinner who ran away to sea against his parents' will and whom Providence punished:

Though *Robinson Crusoe* was thus made into a history of a conversion, its composition caused trouble to Defoe's conscience. Though he deceived many readers, he could not hide from himself the fact that it was not an autobiography as it purported to be. . . . Most of the little stones he used in the composition of his mosaic were empirical facts. But the whole was fiction nevertheless, perilously near to a kind of literature he thoroughly abhorred in theory. He made many attempts to explain for his own and his readers' benefit why the kind of story he wrote was good and useful, whereas the chimney-corner romances and inventions of other men were deceitful and dangerous lies.[188]

As the influence of *Robinson* spread, Defoe was to become responsible for a larger development in "deceitful lying" than he could possibly have anticipated. In 1722 came two anonymous imitations, *Der teutsche Robinson oder Bernhard Creutz* and *Der sächsische Robinson oder Wilhelm*

---

[187] "Preface," in *A Collection of Entertaining Histories and Novels* (London, 1739), II, [iii]. Although this preface is not signed and may have been written by the publisher, the wording and sentiment seem to me to be the author's. The storms and shipwrecks of this romance are confined to the Mediterranean.

[188] Rudolf G. Stamm, "Daniel Defoe: an Artist in the Puritan Tradition," *Philological Quarterly,* XV (1936), 244.

Retchirs Reisen. The "Avertissment" to the latter indicates what is happening:

Ist aber *Robinson Crusoe* ein Gedichte, warum hat man denn gegenwärtige wahrhaffte Historie mit dem Namen *Robinson* belegt, da doch derjenige, von welchem diese Geschichte handelt, nicht *Robinson,* sondern Wilhelm heisset? Man antwortet darauf: Das Wort *Robinson* hat seit einiger Zeit bey Uns Teutschen eben die Bedeutung angenommen, die sonsten das Frantzösische Wort *Avanturier* hat, welches einen Menschen anzeiget, der in der Welt allerhand ausserordentlichen Glücks- und Unglücks-Fällen unterworffen gewesen. Und in diesem Verstande überlieffere ich auch hier dem *Publico* die Beschreibung meiner 28. jahrigen Reisen, auch zu Land und Wasser mir zugestossenen Glücks- und Unglücks-Fälle unter dem Titul des Sächsischen *Robinsons.*
. . .[189]

These two are the first of the Robinson progeny. When authors could not supply the demand, publishers did not hesitate to rechristen fictitious heroes already flourishing. Thus, among a score, *Gil Blas* (1715) became *Der spanische Robinson* (1726), *Krinke Kesmes* (1708) became *Der holländische Robinson* (1721), and *François Leguat* (1707) became *Der französische Robinson* (1723).[190] Even supposedly

[189] 2 Auf. (Leipzig, 1723), pp. iii f. Retchir's experiences are Mediterranean and European.

[190] This rechristening process was not confined to the decade after *Robinson* or even as is sometimes supposed to the eighteenth century. J. F. Cooper's *Crater* (1847) became in his *Œuvres complètes*, tr. Émile de La Bédollière (Paris, 1851-54), *Le Robinson américain,* and Mayne Reid's *Desert Home* (1851) became *Der Robinson der Wildnisz* (1852) and *Le Robinson des prairies* (1854). As for new Robinsons, they too multiplied long into the nineteenth century. Neither La Bédollière's *Dernier Robinson* (1860) nor Montgomery Gibbs's *Six Hundred Robinson Crusoes* (1877) could stem the tide. One confusing result of the rechristening is that whereas the student of French robinsonades does not have to consider *Gil Blas,* the student of German robinsonades has not only to discuss it but to call it a French robinsonade; and so on for several other originals and their renamed translations.

true voyage-accounts were not exempt: Antonio Zucchelli's *Relazioni del viaggio e missione di Congo* (1712) became *Der geistliche Robinson* (1723). By 1731 so many Robinsons had arisen—most of them new—that Johann Gottfried Schnabel in the "Vorrede" to his *Insel Felsenburg* bestowed upon them a name: "Allein, ich höre leider schon manchen, der nur einen Blick darauf schieszen lassen, also raisonieren und fragen: Wie hält's, Landsmann, kann man sich auch darauf verlassen, dasz deine Geschichte keine bloszen Gedichte, Luzianische Spaszstreiche, zusammengeraspelte Robinsonadenspäne und dergleichen sind?"[191] Subsequently, imitations of *Robinson* have been known usually as *Robinsonaden* or *robinsonades* (only rarely as robinsoniads), and similar works published before 1719 as *prerobinsonades*.

The hundreds of volumes that constitute this kind of fiction have been studied, the most important ones with considerable thoroughness, and it is outside my purpose to go over the same material in the same way. It is, however, relevant to sketch chronologically the history of the criticism of this fiction in order to demonstrate how the conception of the robinsonade as a type has grown up, how it has been variously defined, and how it is related to the imaginary voyage.

In 1778 Heinrich A. O. Reichard (1751-1828) devoted part of a chapter in his *Bibliothek der Romane* to "Robinsone," which

machen einen besondern und sehr ansehnlichen Zweig der deutschen Romane aus. . . . England blieb bey Einem Robinson, aber Deutschland erhielt ihrer hundert. . . . Seit 1760 hat sich diese Seuche ziemlich gelegt, aber die unbewohnten Inseln sind noch immer Mode. . . . Eylande . . . kommen haufenweise in

---

[191] Ed. F[ritz] Brüggemann, in *Vorboten der bürgerlichen Kultur* . . . (Leipzig, 1931), p. 20. Schnabel's "Vorrede" has a claim to being the earliest critical commentary on the type.

diesen Romanen vor, deren Einflusz auf die Sitten vieler Stände sehr merklich war, und mit aller der Stärke wirkte, mir der ein Lieblings-Roman . . . auf seine Leser zu wirken pflegt.[192]

After remarking upon the popularity of Turkish slavery as a constituent of the German robinsonades he examines *Robinson* itself and then divides the imitations into two conflicting classes: "die Robinsons mit dem Titel Robinson," and "die unbewohnten Inseln," represented by a list of forty and of two respectively. The main significance of this early analysis lies in the fact that Reichard stresses the desert island motive.

Following Reichard in some respects, but adding a brief introductory section entitled "Vorläufer der Robinsonnaden," Erduin Julius Koch (1764-1834) in his *Grundriss einer Geschichte der Sprache und Literatur der Deutschen von den ältesten Zeiten bis auf Lessings Tod* (1798) listed fifty-two titles in two groups, those with and those without the word *Robinson*.[193] Some of Reichard's titles he omits for no apparent reason except that he calls his list "die bekanntesten dieser Nachahmungen."

In the last decade of the eighteenth century three abortive attempts were made to do for the robinsonade what Garnier

---

[192] Berlin, II, [147]f. A list of 15 robinsonades may be found earlier in Theophilus Georgi, *Allgemeines europäisches Bücher-Lexicon* . . . (Leipzig, 1742), III, 308, but these are under the alphabetical catchword *Robinson,* not under the classificatory term *robinsonade.*

[193] Berlin, II, 254-72. Called also *Compendium der deutschen Literatur-Geschichte* . . . from the preliminary title page. He refers to Reichard on p. 274. Actually he lists 53 titles, but one is repeated. According to Ullrich, *Robinson und Robinsonaden,* p. xv, there was a careless bibliography of robinsonades between Reichard and Koch in J. G. Meusel's notes to *Biographien grosser und berühmter Männer aus der neueren brittischen Geschichte* (Züllichau, 1794), which I have not seen. This is a translation, apparently with additions, of Thomas Mortimer's *British Plutarch* which in the editions of London (1762), Dublin (1793), and Perth (1795), has no list of robinsonades. The *Traduction du Plutarque anglois* (Paris, 1785) omits the life of Defoe.

had just completed for the imaginary voyage. The only one to show unmistakably by title that the *Voyages imaginaires, songes, visions, et romans cabalistiques* was in the mind of the editor is *Die Rothe Bibliothek, enthaltend Robinsonaden, Visionen und cabalistische Erzählungen* (1792). Since Volume One contains a translation of *Quarll*, which is the first inclusion in Garnier after the three volumes taken up by *Robinson*, perhaps the editor intended to translate the French collection entire, but he never went beyond the first volume.[194] The other two are *Sammlung der vorzüglichsten Robinsons und Abentheurer* (1792), edited by K. Hammerdörfer, and *Robinsonaden neu erzählt* by August Wilhelm Meyer (1800), both of which stopped with the first volume; in fact, in the latter the adaptation of *Die gesuchte Perlen-Insul* (1735) breaks off in the middle.[195]

With more success Johann C. L. Haken (1767-1835) began in 1805 his *Bibliothek der Robinsone in zweckmäszigen Auszügen,* which ran to five volumes by 1808.[196] It differs from Garnier's collection so much that there is no reason

[194] Leipzig. I have been unable to find a copy of this work, which is cited by Ullrich, *Robinson und Robinsònaden*, p. 122. The University of Michigan has a volume which I take to be the same, but it contains no reference to *Die rothe Bibliothek;* perhaps a preliminary title page or announcement is wanting.

[195] Both Leipzig. I have been unable to find either; see Ullrich, *Robinson und Robinsonaden*, pp. 111 and 157, and *Zeitschrift für Bücherfreunde*, N.F., XII (1920), Beiblatt, 62.

[196] *Vom Verfasser der grauen Mappe.* Berlin. Two years after he completed the *Bibliothek der Robinsone* Haken himself published a robinsonade, *Die Inquiraner*, a retelling of J. F. Bachstrom's *Land der Inquiraner* (1736), a work not included in his *Bibliothek*. Haken undertook a *Bibliothek der Abentheur* (Magdeburg, 1810), which ceased after the first volume, devoted entirely to one work, *Der abentheurliches Simplicissimus* (1669). On this last see Otto Roquette, "Ueber den Simplicissimus und seine literarische Familie," *Westermans Jahrbuch der illustrirten deutschen Monatshelfte*, VII (1859), [434]-447, and Kenneth C. Hayens, *Grimmelshausen* (London [etc.], 1932; St. Andrews University Publication No. XXXIV).

for supposing any influence, yet, like Garnier's, it remains up to the present the only successful undertaking of its kind.[197] The principal difference has been already indicated in the title. Altogether Haken treats thirty-four works —*Robinson* plus six adaptations of it and twenty-six robinsonades plus an adaptation of *Insel Felsenburg*—some by a comment of only a few sentences, others by critical résumés, and still others by abridgments running to as many as 355 pages for *Robinson* and 518 for *Insel Felsenburg*. Only nine works, not counting the adaptations—those of *Robinson* take up the whole second volume—receive enough attention to give a reader more than a mere sketch. Of the total, twenty-six are German originals; the others are translations from French (three), English (two), Italian (two), and Dutch (one); and all but the adaptations and four others were written before 1732, five of them before 1719.[198] The results

[197] In 1916 began a series announced for ten volumes entitled *Robinsonaden: eine Sammlung von Abenteurergeschichten früherer Jahrhunderte,* bearbeitet und herausgegeben von Maximilian Lehnert (Berlin, n.d.). Vol. V, the only one I have seen, carries the imprint Charlottenburg, Raben-Verlag [1920]. According to a review of the first four volumes by Ullrich, *Zeitschrift für Bücherfreunde,* N.F. XII (1920), Beiblatt, 61-63, the collection is a sorry publishing venture of poor selections by editors ignorant of what constitutes a robinsonade. There has also been published an unimportant book of fifty pages entitled *Robinsonaden: neues Bilder- und Lesebuch für die Jugend* (Nürnberg, n.d.); it gives less than eight pages to *Robinson* and eleven to *Insel Felsenburg.*

[198] These figures consider *Wahrhaffte und merckwürdige Lebens-Beschreibung Joris Pines* . . . (1726) a German original so greatly enlarged from Henry Neville's *Isle of Pines* (1668) that it cannot even be called an adaptation. Schnabel writes (ed. Brüggemann, pp. 20 f.): "Die Geschicht von Joris oder Georg Pines hat seit ao. 1667 einen ziemlichen Geburts- und Beglaubigungsbrief erhalten, nachdem aber ein *Anonymus* dieselbe aus dem Englischen übersetzt haben will und im Teutschen als ein Gerichte Sauerkraut mit Stachelbeeren vermischt, aufgewärmet hat, ist eine solche *Ollebutterie* daraus worden, dasz man kaum die ganz zu Matsche gekochten Brocken der Wahrheit noch auf dem Grunde der lange Titsche finden kann." On Neville's work see especially Max Hippe,

do not form a representative cross section of the whole group of robinsonades.

A nineteen-page preface reveals that Haken's interest was that of the literary historian rather than of the editor. Finding these once-popular romances so scarce that some seemed known in his day only by hearsay, he wished to preserve a record of them, accompanied by some analysis of the type:

> . . . was es denn eigentlich war, das dieser Dichtungsart so viel Liebe gewann und erhielt? Denn allerdings doch muszte die *Ursache* der *Wirkung* einigermaaszen entsprechen; und volle achtig Jahre lang kann ein ganzes Publikum unmöglich aus so verschrobenen Köpfen bestehen, dasz man, um diese Erscheinung zu erklären, seine Zuflucht zu einer beispiellosen Idiosynkrasie zu nehmen genöthigt wäre.
>
> Abgesehen von allen Ausstattungen des Styls, der poetischen Mahlerei, der tiefgeschöpften Menschenkenntnisz oder der philosophischen Reflexion, kann ein romantisches Werk sich durch das blosze Uebergewicht einer feurigen und leicht beweglichen Phantasie, oder einer glücklich aufgefaszten und verfolgten Grund-Idee, den sichern Anspruch auf die Theilnahme des Lesers erwerben. Gerade dies aber scheint mir das Verdienst Defoe's und seiner deutschen Nachahmer ["gebohrnen Imitatoren ihrer Nachbaren" (p. ii)] zu seyn, und ihnen jenen, auf den ersten Blick so sehr befremdenden Erfolg gesichert zu haben. Robinsons Geschichte ist die Geschichte des Menschen und seiner fortschreitenden Kultur im Kleinen. (I, v f.)

An amplification of this last observation, long since a familiar part of almost every discussion of *Robinson,* leads to the obvious conclusion that the imitations, dealing with the same theme, have more or less the same appeal. "Sollte

---

"Eine vor-Defoe'sche englische Robinsonade," *Englische Studien,* XIX (1894), 66-104; Worthington C. Ford, *The Isle of Pines, 1668: an Essay in Bibliography* (Boston, 1920); and J. H. Scholte, "Die Insel der Fruchtbarkeit," *Zeitschrift für Bücherfreunde,* N.F. XXII (1930), 49-55.

10

es denn nun der Mühe nicht werth seyn, eine Revision an-
zustellen, *bis in wie weit* es unsern Romantikern damit
gelungen ist, und *was* sie zur Bereicherung dieses Gemähldes
wirklich geleistet haben?" (I, viii f.). Having thus stated
his purpose, he shows that the notoriety associated with this
kind of fiction proceeds from the addition of ingredients
not found in *Robinson*. These he can overlook, but even
the remaining similarities and dissimilarities require some
kind of logical arrangement; he attributes the failure of
Meyer's undertaking to absence of a well-considered plan
(I, xvi f.). In the following remarks he displays considerable comprehension of his problem and attempts to distinguish six kinds of robinsonades (this is the earliest extensive
classification):

Eben dadurch aber wird auch dem Bibliothekar der Robinsone,
insonderheit bei dieser ersten Klasse seines zu musternden
Heeres, *den eigentlichen Robinsonen,* die Pflicht auserlegt, seine
Leser, so wie mit allen, nicht in irgend einer andern Beziehung
interessanten Nebenverzierungen, Episoden, Auswüchsen und
Schnörkeln seiner Originale, so insonderheit auch mit jenen, eben
erst denunciirten Vorstöszen gegen den *Commonsense* sorgfäl-
tigst zu verschonen. . . . Bei dem groszen Haufen des Makula-
turs in dieser Gattung aber wird es genügen, bald eine kurzge-
drängte Inhaltsanzeige in diese Bibliothek niedergelegt,—bald
durch blosze Einregistrirung des Titels, zum Behuf des Litera-
tors, eine Abfindung getroffen zu haben.

In dieses trockne Namenregister werden sich vorzüglich alle
die Machwerke mit Bequemlichkeit einschichten lassen, aus
denen eine *zweite* Klasse dieser Bibliothek besteht, und die, durch
eine, von Haus aus unglückliche Fröhnung des Zeitgeschmacks,
den Namen "Robinson" zwar an der Stirne tragen, allein denselben lediglich zu einem Aushängeschild benutzen, um Leser
herbeizulocken, und dadurch blosz beweisen, mit welchem
Heiszhunger das Publikum dieserlei Speise zu fordern nicht

müde ward. Von Abentheuern jeder Art . . . ist in denselben die Rede. . . .

Dagegen haben mehrere deutsche Schriftsteller Defoe's Grund-Idee, und oft nicht ohne Glück, aufgefaszt und weiter ausgesponnen, ohne sich sofort schon auf dem Titel als seine sklavischen Nachahmer anzukündigen. *Diese* durften in einer Bibliothek der Robinsone noch weniger als jene, sich vermissen lassen, und werden als *dritte* Klasse, auch in gehöriger Reihe ihre Stelle in derselben finden. Es sind die Entdecker und Bevölkerer wüster Inseln und Länder, bei welchen jedoch mehr die rohen Anfänge und stufenweisen Fortschritte des gesellschaftlichen Zustandes, als das einsame Bewohnen von Inseln und Ländern, das Wesentliche des Stoffes ausmachen. . . .

Auf entferntere Weise reihen sich an sie, in der *vierten* Klasse, die Entdecker unbekannter Südländer, welche jedoch es mehr damit zu thun haben, die Sitten und politischen sowohl als bürgerlichen Institute der dort geträumten Völker, in Gemählde von meistens nicht sonderlichem Werthe zu bringen.

Wiederum häuft eine *fünfte* Klasse, ohne sich namentlich als *Robinsone* anzukündigen, in der That auch eigentlich nur eine Masse von Abentheuern zu Wasser und zu Lande auf einander; und das einsame Inselleben ihrer Helden ist mehr eine gelegentliche Zuthat der Nothdurft, oder der Kaprice des Autors, als wesentliches Erfordernisz des, von ihm angelegten Planes.

Näher aber, als dieses ganze Heer von Bastarden des, von uns eingemarkten, ächten Robinsonismus, steht demselben eine kleinere Anzahl von Schriften, welche sich mit dem, seiner Natur nach so anziehenden Thema beschäftigen, die psychologischen Erscheinungen während der allmähligen Geistes-Entwickelung eines, vom frühesten Kindesalter aus der Gesellschaft mit seines gleichen entrückten Menschen darzustellen. Ungerne würde man sie in einer Sammlung von der Tendenz der gegenwärtigen vermissen; und auch *sie* sollen, als eine *sechste* Klasse, in einem Anhange gebührend beigebracht werden.

Und zu einem gleichen Supplement scheinen denn endlich auch einige literarische Produkte berechtigt, welche—lange Zeit vor Robinson Crusoe's Erscheinung—ihren Lesern bereits wüste Inseln und einsame Bewohner derselben auftischen. . . . Ohne alle diese angegebne Klassen zu willkührlich durcheinander zu werfen, wird der Herausgeber sich bei Vorführung derselben weniger von diesem Schema, als von der chronologischen Folge seiner Materialien, so wie von der Verwandtschaft ihrer Ideen, leiten lassen. . . . (I, x-xvi)

Haken as both literary historian and bibliographer and Reichard and Koch as bibliographers became standard references for all treatment of robinsonades for the next half-century, during which time were made no significant contributions beyond the addition of a few titles.[199] In 1854 Hermann J. T. Hettner (1821-82) published a study entitled *Robinson und die Robinsonaden,* which when incorporated in 1865 in his standard *Literaturgeschichte des achtzehnten Jahrhunderts* became widely known. In the volume devoted to English literature from 1660 to 1770 he divides robinsonades into two groups, *pädagogischen* and *fabuliren-den:* "Die einen halten sich vorwiegend an die lehrhaften, die anderen an die erzählenden Bestandtheile ihres Vorbildes." [200] Of the latter he writes:

Sie haben alles Ideelle und Gedankenmäszige im Robinson abgestreift. Sie halten sich nur an das Ueberraschende und Auszergewöhnliche der Schicksale und Begebenheiten, die dem

---

[199] See, e.g., Franz Horn, *Die schöne Litteratur Deutschlands, während des achtzehnten Jahrhunderts* (Berlin und Stettin, 1812-13), II, 180-84; Rasmus Nyerup, *Almindelig Morskabslaesning i Danmark og Norge igjennem Aarhundreder* (Kjøbenhavn, 1816), pp. 218-26, where "Robinsonader" is the last of seven classes of popular fiction; Friedrich Bouterwek, *Geschichte der Poesie und Beredsamkeit seit dem Ende des dreizehnten Jahrhunderts* (Göttingen), X (1817), 387 f.; Johann S. Ersch, *Handbuch der deutschen Literatur* . . . , neue Ausg. (Leipzig), II (1840), Abth. 2, Sp. 387-89, 1276-78; and O. L. B. Wolff, *Allgemeine Geschichte des Romans, von dessen Ursprung bis zur neuesten Zeit,* 2 Ausg. (Jena, 1850), pp. 235-44.

[200] 5 Auf. (Braunschweig, 1894), I, 283.

Helden zustoszen. Das Wundersame steigern sie zum Wunderbaren und Fabelhaften, das Mögliche und Naturwahre zum Unmöglichen und Phantastischen. Es ist nicht mehr die einfache Scenerie des Robinson, die hier festgehalten wird, es ist die Phantasmagorie des Shakespeare'schen Sturm oder vielmehr, da es unzulässig ist, hier an ein so vollendetes Kunstwerk zu erinnern, die Phantasmagorie und Romantik den alten wundersüchtigen Reise- und Abenteurergeschichten, welche ursprünglich aus der Verwilderung der spanischen Schelmenromane hervorgegangen waren. (I, 284)

He is thinking chiefly of English imitations such as *Peter Wilkins* and *John Daniel.* "Bei den Franzosen lassen sich die Einwirkungen weniger deutlich wahrnehmen, weil diese schon an und für sich eine weitschichtige Literatur von *Voyages imaginaires* hatten"; and Germany "bildete sich ein eigener Zweig der Literatur, die Literatur der sogennanten Aventuriers . . . und Freibeuter" (I, 285). When he turns to discuss German literature from 1648 to 1740, he divides robinsonades this time into three classes: *satirische Lehrgeschichten, Abenteurerromane,* and *romanhafte Reiseschilderungen* (called *Robinsonaden im engeren Sinne* in the index).[201] Of the second he says:

Ursprung und Wesen derselben offenbart sich unzweideutig, wenn wir sehen, dasz 1726 der Gilblas von Lesage unter dem Namen des spanischen Robinson übersetzt wird. Einige dieser Geschichten nennen sich Robinsonaden, andere Aventürierromane. Doch ist dies nur ein Unterschied des Namens, nicht ein Unterschied der Sache; beide Titel sollen in gleicher Weise das Seltsame, Wunderbare und Abenteuerliche hervorheben.[202]

The third class he apparently thinks of as the equivalent of

[201] 4 Auf. (1893), III, 296. My references use the numbering system of the index, which regards the whole as in six volumes and by which III is the first half of the second bound volume.

[202] III, 296 f. Cf. his reference to *Gil Blas,* I, 285.

the *fabulirenden Robinsonaden* among the English imitations.

The discussions of Haken and Hettner demonstrate that the conception of robinsonades as a type has become enlarged to include much more than imitations of Defoe's original. The confusion results partly from the indiscriminate use of the word *Robinson* in titles and partly from the critics' inevitable recognition of similarities in other types. An early attempt to distinguish between the robinsonade and the imaginary voyage appears in a short article by W. Stricker:

> Die fingirten Reisen hängen aufs engste mit den Robinsonaden zusammen; sie haben von *Lucian* an bis zur Gegenwart den verschiedensten Zwecken gedient. Bald waren sie satyrisch, wie *Lucian* selbst, wie Gulliver's Reisen . . . , bald dienten sie der Neugierde und Wundersucht, wie die Reiseabenteuer *Ernst's von Schwaben,* wo dieselben Motive sich finden, wie in Sindbad dem Seefahrer der Orientalen; bald sind sie ein Gefäss für Unterbringung aller möglichen Realien, bald endlich dienen sie zur Darlegung gefährlicher Lehren über Staat und Kirche.[203]

Paludan also, in his *Om Holbergs Niels Klim,* traces briefly the development of the robinsonade because it is closely related to fictitious and marvelous voyages; that is, in stories of voyages and shipwrecks it has from the beginning been a supporting element, plays a more and more prominent role, but does not, like the imaginary voyages he cites in connection with *Klimius* and *Gulliver,* tend to be satiric.[204]

Attempts to restrict the robinsonade as a type began with

[203] "Ueber Robinsonaden und fingirte Reisen," *Jahres-Bericht des frankfurter Vereins für Geographie und Statistik,* XXXV (1870-71), 30.
[204] Chap. ii, sect. 4, especially pp. 271 f. He coördinates with *satiric* the word *utopian* ("Tendensen er ikke egentlig satirisk eller utopisk"), but he later qualifies that by showing utopian elements in some robinsonades.

a series of more specialized studies in the influence of *Robinson* on Continental literature; the first of these is Hermann F. Wagner's *Robinson in Oesterreich* (1886). This is too thin and too much under the influence of Hettner to receive more than passing mention. More important is the examination of forty robinsonades in August Kippenberg's *Robinson in Deutschland bis zur Insel Felsenburg* (1892), in which the *robinsonmotiv* is defined as "die Darstellung des Lebens einer oder mehrerer Personen auf einer weltabgelegenen, leeren Insel."[205] In his bibliography he retains the broad categories of robinsonades with and robinsonades without the word *Robinson* in the title, but in the text itself he divides them less artificially into "rein abenteuerlichen Robinsonaden" and "eine zweite Gattung deutscher Robinsonaden, die sich mit der Bevölkerung leerer Eilande und Darstellung utopischer Inselstaaten beschäftigt."[206] The first kind often draws into the narrative such favorite themes of the previous century as the Turkish war, corsairs, pagan imprisonment, and sea-battles.[207] The German imitators developed two principal ingredients of the robinsonade: the existence, before the hero is wrecked, of an earlier island solitary who either may have died and left records behind him or may still be living; and the introduction of women in the "solitary" existence.[208] Kippenberg is not primarily interested in analyzing the robinsonade into separate classes; he is pointing to his final chapter on the *Insel Felsenburg,* which is the best example of the second class and which at the same time, through its numerous inner-narratives, takes

[205] Hannover, p. 1.

[206] Pages 44 and 121. Cf. p. 95: "Zum Idealstaat wird die Robinsonade erst bei Schnabel ausgebildet, und eine *zweite Gattung der deutschen Robinsonaden* hebt mit ihm an."

[207] See pp. 71 f.

[208] Pages 55 f. As Kippenberg himself points out, the second of these may be traced to the second part of *Robinson.*

over the best of the robinson-motives and lifts the type out of the low repute into which it had fallen.[209] It is a sort of fusion of the two classes with elimination of the excrescences.

After seven years of preparation Hermann Ullrich published in 1898 his *Robinson und Robinsonaden,* the first and only careful and extensive bibliography.[210] First listing 196 English editions of *Robinson,* 110 translations, and 115 revisions (*Bearbeitungen*), he comes to 277 imitations.[211] Here

[209] See pp. 83 f. and 104.

[210] . . . *Bibliographie, Geschichte, Kritik: ein Beitrag zur vergleichenden Litteraturgeschichte, im Besonderen zur Geschichte des Romans und zur Geschichte der Jugendlitteratur. Teil I. Bibliographie* (Weimar; Litterarhistorische Forschungen, VII Heft). As the full title indicates, this volume he planned as an indispensable beginning for a complete study of the subject. Volume II, however, was never written; cf. p. 148 below. Between Hettner and Ullrich five contributors of lists of robinsonades should be cited to continue those in my note 199: Jean G. T. Graesse, *Trésor de livres rares et précieux* . . . (Dresde [etc.], 1861), II, 350 f.; William Lee, ed., *Robinson Crusoe* (London, [1869]), pp. xiv f.; W. Davenport Adams, *Famous Books: Sketches in the Highways and Byeways of English Literature* (New York, 1879), pp. 318-20—copying from Lee; Karl Goedeke, *Grundrisz zur Geschichte der deutschen Dichtung* . . . , 2 Auf. (Dresden, 1887), III, 262-64; and Joseph Sabin, *Dictionary of Books Relating to America* . . . (New York), XVII (1888), 413-15.

[211] He points out that a distinct line between translations and revisions cannot be easily drawn, and "Von einer Bearbeitung endlich zu einer Nachahmung bedarf es ebenso oft nur eines kleinen Schrittes" (p. [xx]); cf. his remarks on the same point in *Zeitschrift für Bücherfreunde,* N.F. XI (1919), i, 40. The figures given total 698, but his numbering system is misleading and faulty. Though new editions of the English original and of the translations are numbered serially, new editions and translations of the revisions and imitations, as well as revisions of the imitations, are entered alphabetically as a, b, c, etc. For example, No. 7 on p. 67 of the *Bearbeitungen* is J. H. Campe's *Robinson der Jüngere* (1779-80), but between that and No. 8 on p. 84 are 19 other editions, 67 translations, 72 *Bearbeitungen,* and 17 continuations, or a total of 175 unnumbered publications. Furthermore, each of the main divisions and of the two subdivisions under imitations begins with Number One, and there is no general index so that unless a user has foreknowledge he cannot always readily determine whether Ullrich has a given title or not. These blemish an otherwise excellent book. One other difficulty has no easy solution:

he casts out the long-standing illogical divisions into works
with and without the word *Robinson* in the title,

... denn sehr viele Bücher, die mit jenem Namen prunkten,
haben ... mit dem Robinsonmotiv nichts zu thun, sondern
bedienen sich jenes Namens nur als eines Aushängeschildes, in
der ausgesprochenen Absicht, dem Buche mehr Leser zuzufüh-
ren, als es ohne diesen Kniff zu erwarten hatte, oder aber in
unbefangener Naivität, weil ihre Verfasser zum Verständnis des
Grundgedankens von Defoe's Werk nicht durchgedrungen
waren (p. x).

Instead he divides them into *wirkliche Robinsonaden* and
pseudo-Robinsonaden, borrowing this latter phrase from
Haken,[212] and then proceeds to state clearly his basis for
decision:

Für die vierte Abteilung, die Robinsonaden, muss schon hier
bemerkt werden, dass für die Kriterien der Aufnahme oder Aus-
scheidung nur der erste Band des Defoe'schen Robinson massge-
bend war. Aufgenommen und als Robinsonaden vor mir bezeichnet sind demnach alle mir bekannt gewordenen Werke, die das
Hauptmotiv des Robinson, insularische Abgeschlossenheit von
der menschlichen Gesellschaft, zum Mittelpunkt der Erzählung
machen oder doch episodisch verwerten, mögen sie sich als Robinson oder Robinsonade bezeichnen oder nicht. Ausgeschlossen
und in einer besonderen Unterabteilung als Pseudorobinsonaden
von mir bezeichnet sind alle Werke, die sich als Robinson oder
Robinsonade geben, aber jenem Kriterium nicht Stich halten.

---

editions of all three parts of *Robinson* are made numerically coördinate
with editions of the first part only or of Parts One and Two only. Besides
a few inevitable and excusable errors in dating, some imitations are entered
anachronistically under the dates of the German translation instead of the
original, e.g., *Krinke Kesmes* under 1721; *Leguat,* 1723; and *Franz
Pelerin,* 1783. Ullrich himself added the most important supplement in
"Zur Bibliographie der Robinsonaden, Nachträge und Ergänzungen zu
meiner Robinson-Bibliographie," *Zeitschrift für Bücherfreunde,* XI (1907-
8), ii, 444-56; [489]-498.

[212] *Op. cit.,* III [i]: "Pseudo-Robinsonen."

Es lag sonach schlechterdings keine Veranlassung vor, Bücher aufzunehmen, die keine Robinsonaden sind und sich auch als solche nicht ausgeben. . . . Ebensowenig haben die blossen Utopien . . . einen Platz in meiner Arbeit zu beanspruchen.[213]

This important restriction of the robinsonade to only the first volume of Defoe's work Ullrich stresses again four years later in a fifty-page introduction to his edition of the first volume of *Insel Felsenburg* and adds there that this kind of fiction still awaits a more detailed investigation.[214]

The specialized studies began to multiply after Ullrich's bibliography furnished a basic starting point. In 1907 Professor Werner H. Staverman added *Robinson Crusoe in Nederland een bijdrage tot de geschiedenis van den roman in de XVIIIe eeuw,* with a modification of Ullrich's definition to include "alle werken, die òf den naam Robinson dragen, òf het hoofdmotief van den Robinson Crusoe, het leven van één of meer schipbreukelingen op een onbewoond eiland, meer of minder uitgebreid behandelen,"[215] thus refusing to outlaw the pseudo-robinsonades. Ullrich criticizes vigorously this return to the practice of the earlier bibliographers:

Unser Verf. meint, dass man im 18. Jahrh. unter Robinsonade oder Robinson einen Aventurier-Roman schlechthin verstanden habe. Darin hat er für einen grossen Teil des Jahrh. und einen beträchtlichen Teil der betr. Werke Recht, anderseits zeigt die immer mehr zunehmende Zahl der Werke, die eine mehr oder weniger gelungene Nachahmung des eigentlichen Robinson-motivs darstellten, faktisch einen Wechsel in jener Auffassung,

---

[213] Page xiv. It should be noted that works which Ullrich could not himself examine but which had titles suggesting that they might be robinsonades he put under the first division rather than under the pseudo-robinsonades. These number 92.

[214] Berlin, 1902 (Deutsche Litteraturdenkmale des 18. u. 19. Jahrhunderts, No. 108-120, N.F. No. 58-70), pp. iii f.

[215] Groningen, p. 5.

ich muss es daher für einen groben Missgriff halten, wenn ein Forscher sich jene schiefe Auffassung des Begriffs Robinsonade noch jetzt zu eigen macht. . . . Was *wir* unter Robinsonade zu verstehen haben, ist mit einigem Nachdenken nicht schwer zu finden. Man mache die Probe! Wer tritt auf das Stichwort Robinson aus den Kulissen unseres Gedächtnisses heraus, wenn wir das Buch seit längerer Zeit nicht gelesen haben? Etwa der brasilianische Pflanzer Robinson, oder der Sklave in Saleh oder der in grosser Gesellschaft die Pyrenäen übersteigende Reisende? Gewiss nicht, sondern der auf einer Insel vereinsamte Mensch.[216]

Furthermore, Ullrich argues, Defoe devoted about three-quarters of the original narrative to Robinson's island existence, in which the reader is principally interested—so much so that the story becomes less interesting when additional people arrive on the island.

To this criticism Staverman several years later makes a mild reply. Ullrich's division into robinsonades and pseudo-robinsonades he finds "unpractical and superfluous, as the border-line cannot be drawn between those works that contain the island-motif, however briefly, and those which contain it no longer. For the eighteenth-century mind there was no difference." [217] In *Robinson Crusoe in Nederland* Staverman studies, in addition to translations and adaptations of *Robinson*, twenty-five imitations translated into Dutch and twelve Dutch originals,[218] shows that the Dutch imitators

[216] "Zur Robinson-Literatur," *Literaturblatt für germanische und romanische Philologie,* XXXIII (1912), 106 f.

[217] "Robinson Crusoe in Holland: on the Two Hundredth Anniversary of the Death of Daniel Defoe," *English Studies,* XIII (1931), 55 n. 1. Cf. Staverman, *Museum: Maandblad voor Philologie en Geschiedenis,* XXXII (1924-25), 304: "Prakties maakt het echter geen verschil, want men kan òf de avonturiersroman met de naam 'Robinson' onder de Robinsonades rekenen, òf men kan ze uitschakelen, doch is dan verplicht, ze als pseudo-robinsonades weer in te halen, gelijk Ullrich in zijn bibliographie ook doet."

[218] In the bibliographic groupings "Vertaalde Navolgingen," "Niet Ver-

took the word *Robinson* to mean, in their language, "Avonturier," and explains that, despite special robinson-motives to be looked for in the robinsonade, *Robinson Crusoe* itself is an adventure-romance.[219] Thus he would by anticipation try to meet Ullrich's objection.

This problem of the relationship between the adventure-romance and the robinsonade is approached in the same year by Berthold W. Mildebrath in *Die deutschen "Aventuriers" des achtzehnten Jahrhunderts.* Finding in authors' apparent and expressed opinions a similarity in the two terms, except that the former does not imply insularity, he shows "dasz eine solche Auffassung im groszen und ganzen nicht berechtigt ist." [220] He arrives at a definition of *Avanturier* in the literary sense as:

ein Mensch, der häufig wie ein picaro eine harte Jugend durchzumachen hat, sich aus den niedrigsten Schichten der Gesellschaft emporarbeitet, dabei keine Mittel scheut, mannigfache Abenteuer sucht und erlebt und endlich als seszhafter Bürger sein Leben beschlieszt. Doch wie sich die Eigenschaften der spanischen picaros auch nicht alle in einem Vertreter dieser Zunft vereinigen, so haben auch einige "Avanturiers" nur vereinzelte charakteristische Züge aufzuweisen. Bei ihnen überwiegt das Robinsonadenhafte; weite Seereisen mit mannigfachen Glücks- und Unglücksfällen bilden einen Hauptteil der Erzählung; die Helden geraten in türkische Gefangenschaft oder leben eine Zeitlang auf einsamen Inseln, auf denen einzelne auch

---

taalde Navolgingen" (called also "Oorspronkelijke nederlandsche Robinsonades," including "Robinsonades zonder 'Robinson' op den Titel"), and "Robinsonades vóór 1719."

[219] Pages 134-36. Cf. Henry C. Hutchins, *Journal of English and Germanic Philology*, XXVIII (1929), 447, and my quotation from *Der sächsische Robinson* on p. 124.

[220] Gräfenhainichen, 1907, p. 1. German titles of the eighteenth century use *Avanturier, Aventurier,* and *Avanturieur; Mildebrath,* except in his title, consistently employs the first spelling. *Avonturier* is the Dutch equivalent.

neue Staatswesen gründen. Noch andere "Avanturiers" endlich
bedienen sich ihres Titels überhaupt mit Unrecht; hier ist das
Wort nichts als ein Aushängeschild berechnender Verfasser oder
Buchhändler.

So ergibt sich eine Teilung in zwei Hauptgruppen, "Avanturiers" und "Pseudoavanturiers," von denen die erste wieder in
zwei Unterabteilungen zu zerlegen ist. Die eine umfaszt diejeni-
gen Werke, die das Gepräge des Schelmen- oder Landstreicher-
romans mehr oder weniger deutlich zeigen, während der andern
einige Werke angehören, die den Robinsonaden näherstehen.
(pp. 9 f.)

After finding twenty *Avanturiers* to examine under this
classification Mildebrath tries to clarify what he means by
näherstehen:

Aber diese Beziehungen berechtigen nicht dazu, beide Gattung-
en gleichzustellen oder gar zu verschmelzen. Zugegeben, dasz
der gröszte Teil der "Avanturiers" sein Entstehen dem unge-
heueren Erfolge der Robinsonerzählungen zuschreiben kann, so
ist doch der Verlauf eines Avanturierlebens so verschieden von
dem Leben eines echten Robinsons dasz eine "Avanturier" Erzählung nie eine Robinsonade genannt werden kann. Vielmehr hat
man in den "Avanturiers" die letzten Ausläufer des deutschen
Schelmenromans zu sehen. Ihre Zahl wäre eine gröszere, wenn
die Verfasser von "Pseudorobinsonaden" und von "Robinsonaden," in die das Robinsonmotiv nur äuszerlich hineingebracht
ist, weniger unter dem Banne des Titels "Robinson" gestanden
hätten. (pp. 136 f.)

Mildebrath might have wished further that authors intend-
ing to write a robinsonade could have been prevented from
using the word *Avanturier* in their titles, for he feels com-
pelled to classify five of his *Avanturiers* as robinsonades. To
draw the line as strictly as he does, though it simplifies his
own study, is to fail to recognize that the two types do fuse,
especially if Ullrich's inclusion of the *episodic* robinson-

motive be accepted. Walther Brecht in a review of Mildebrath's book would avoid the difficulty by stricter definition:

> ich möchte noch weiter gehn und aus seiner [Ullrichs] defini-
> tion der Robinsonade die möglichkeit der bloss *episodischen*
> verwertung des R.-motivs ausscheiden; denn hierdurch wird die
> so nötige abgrenzung wider illusorisch gemacht, und ob in
> einem werke der mischgattung das Avanturier- oder das speci-
> fisch Robinsonmässige überwigt, wird sich in jedem falle ausma-
> chen lassen. ein Avanturier, der ua. eine Robinsonepisode erlebt,
> bleibt deswegen doch ein Avanturier.[221]

But these attempts to separate the two types are based on
only those German romances which employ *Avanturier* in
their titles; Mildebrath is not studying the adventure-
romance at all. That is why he finds only twenty in the
whole eighteenth century. He has not met the problem
fairly or logically and has not provided for criticizing a
relevant work which has neither *Avanturier* nor *Robinson*
in its title.[222] All reasonable examination of the robinsonade
reveals that it cannot be cut off from the adventure-romance.

The first critic to present a formal study of the English
robinsonade as a type after 1719, Zora Prica in *Daniel Defoe's
Robinson Crusoe und Robert Paltock's Peter Wilkins* (1909),
makes the following classification:

> Mann kann die englischen Nachahmungen in drei Klassen
> teilen: die einen machen die insulare Abgeschlossenheit von der
> menschlichen Gesellschaft zum Mittelpunkt der Darstellung; die
> anderen führen uns in höhere Regionen und schildern das
> insulare Leben auf einer exotischen in der Luft schwebenden
> Insel; zur dritten Klasse rechne ich diejenigen, welche sich vor-

---

[221] *Anzeiger für deutsches Altertum und deutsche Litteratur*, XXXIV
(1910), 175.
[222] Compare Ullrich, *Euphorion Zeitschrift für Literaturgeschichte*, 9.
Ergänzungsheft (1911), 21-23.

wiegend den abenteuerlichen Reisebeschreibungen nähern und das Robinsonmotiv nur episodenhaft verwerten.²²³

Though *Nachahmungen* happens to be the word in this passage, she constantly speaks of the eighteen included works as *Robinsonaden*. For example:

Abgesehen von Trueman's Bearbeitung bewirkte "Peter Wilkins" eine zweite Gruppe von Robinsonaden. Der charakteristische Zug dieser Nachahmungen zeigt sich vorwiegend in der grossen Vorliebe zum Abenteuerlichen. Die Erlebnisse der Helden fallen hauptsächlich in das Gebiet des Wunderbaren. Der Aufenthalt auf einer einsamen Insel erscheint den Autoren zu einfach. Meistens kommen die Abenteurer durch mirakulöse Expeditionen in eine andere, uns fremde Welt. Die Lust, eine Zeitlang auf Himmelskörpern zu verweilen, mag auch durch französischen Einfluss gekommen sein in Folge der Nachahmung von Cyrano de Bergerac. (p. [48])

And of the third class she writes:

Diese abenteuerlichen Reisebeschreibungen bilden einen besonderen Zweig der englischen Robinsonaden. Sie sind blosse Nachahmungen der verschiedenen authentischen Reisebeschreibungen in der unterhaltenden Form des Robinsonmotivs. Solche Erzählungen würden gewiss die Leser nicht sehr angezogen haben, wenn sie nicht fesselnde Berichte von fremden Ländern enthalten hätten.²²⁴

²²³ Budapest, p. [8]. Several informal references to these English imitations had been made earlier in literary histories and articles on Defoe. Cf. my note 210, and see especially A. T. S. Goodrick, "Robinson Crusoe, Impostor," *Blackwood's Magazine,* CLXXXIII (1908), 672-85.

²²⁴ Page 17. One of her robinsonades in this class is Shelvocke's *Voyage round the World by Way of the Great South Sea.* The source of this erroneous inclusion probably lies in a misreading of Lee's introduction to *Robinson Crusoe.* After mentioning the popularity of imitations of *Robinson,* Lee says (p. xv): "I may also notice, in order of date, while passing, that on the 20th of January, 1726, was published 'A Voyage Round the World . . . By Captain George Shelvocke.'"

In their striving for sensational and phantastic experiences she finds that the English robinsonades introduce "eine neue, eine politisch-satirische Richtung. . . . Sie machen Utopien und denken sich in diese hinein, erlöst von Übel der Zeit" (p. 54). Her robinsonade, then, is no longer Ullrich's; it designates an uncertain category of mixed motives, which her book is too superficial to clarify. But it becomes apparent that the influence of *Robinson* on English fiction cannot easily be traced as a single line after 1726, for thereafter the influence combines with that of *Gulliver,* just as, to a similar extent, the influence of *Robinson* on German fiction combines after 1731 with that of *Insel Felsenburg.*

How this work changed the robinsonade appears best in an excellently thorough analysis by Fritz Brüggemann, *Utopie und Robinsonade: Untersuchungen zu Schnabels Insel Felsenburg* (1914). "Die 'Insel Felsenburg' erscheint uns nun nicht mehr nur im Rahmen jener Literaturgattung, die uns unter dem Namen der Robinsonaden bekannt ist, sondern gleichzeitig auch im Rahmen einer ganz anderen Literaturgattung, eben der der Utopien." [225] Its three essential motives indicate

1. dasz die Insel den Bewohnern kein *Exil* ist, sondern ein *Asyl;* und zwar ein Asyl vor der Nachstellung, der Kabale, die auf dem Mangel an sozialem Gefühl in der europäischen Welt beruht; 2. dasz der asylhafte Charakter des Eilandes zu einem systematischen und keineswegs nur unfreiwilligen *Abschlusz* gegen die Auszenwelt führt, besonders gegen die europäische Kulturwelt des sogenannten politischen Menschen; und schlieszlich 3. dasz dieser Abschlusz keinerlei Durchbrechung erführe, wenn nicht ein *geschlechtliches Moment* dazu zwänge. (p. 85)

---

[225] Weimar; Forschungen zur neueren Literaturgeschichte . . . XLVI, p. 5. This book renders two earlier studies relatively unimportant: Franz K. Becker, *Die Romane Johann Gottfried Schnabels* (Bonn, 1911), and Karl Schröder, *J. G. Schnabels "Insel Felsenburg"* (Marburg, 1912).

The influence of *Insel Felsenburg* may be determined by analysis of subsequent robinsonades to discover how closely they employ these three motives. "Müssen die Robinsonaden daher einesteils erst aus der allgemeinen Literatur der Reiseromane gesucht werden, so musz anderenteils die verhältnismäszig noch gar nicht so sehr grosze Zahl echter Robinsonaden aus dem Wust angeblicher Robinsonaden ausgesondert und mit den ersteren zusammengestellt werden." The necessary division into the genuine and the pseudo-robinsonades has been made by Ullrich, but "Interessant ist es, dasz allerdings einzelne der Schriften, die Kippenberg noch berücksichtigt hatte, von Ullrich aber ausgeschieden sind, bei uns hernach in der Betrachtung der utopistischen Literatur wieder auftauchen werden" (p. 105). This observation is more than interesting; it illustrates significantly how the type changes with a change in point of view, determined by the characteristics of the work under examination. Brüggemann looks to the motives in *Insel Felsenburg* to point the difference between his conception of the robinsonade and Ullrich's:

Wir werden deshalb aber auch zu dem Schlusz kommen, dasz der Begriff des Exils für die Robinsonaden charakteristisch und erforderlich ist, dasz jedenfalls der Begriff des Asyls auf einem Hineintragen eines der Robinsonade im Grunde fremden Elements beruht. Demnach wird sich die *Definition der reinen Robinsonade* gegenüber der Forderung Ullrichs noch dahin einschränken lassen, dasz für sie *auszer dem insularen Charakter des Landes noch der exilhafte Charakter für den Aufenthalt der Helden verlangt werden musz* in dem Sinne, dasz dieser Aufenthalt für die Verschlagenen die Bedeutung einer unfreiwilligen Gefangenschaft annimmt und die lebhafte Sehnsucht nach Aufhebung dieser Gefangenschaft in ihnen erzeugt. . . . mit der "Insel Felsenburg" beginnt keine zweite Gattung der deutschen Robinsonaden, wie Kippenberg meint, sondern es entsteht eine ganz neue Romangattung durch die Verbindung

11

der Robinsonade mit einem ihr im Grunde geradezu widerstre-
benden Element.[226]

Though the robinsonade has been primarily a German
literary phenomenon as far as formal criticism is concerned,
several French works require the special study begun by William E. Mann in *Robinson Crusoé en France, étude sur l'influence de cette œuvre dans la littérature française* (1916).
After the initial chapters on the original, on translations,
and on adaptations, chapter four treats " 'Robinson Crusoé'
et le Roman du xviiie siècle." Here Mann does not wish to
establish any specific definition; he traces *Robinson's* influence in romances "où il est question d'un séjour sur une île
déserte ou d'une existence solitaire quelconque" [227] and
shows that these motives are found in *romans d'aventures,
romans sentimentaux,* and *romans utopiques.* Of the thirteen works which he discusses at length, most depart in some
significant respect from Robinson and from Ullrich's definition of the robinsonade; these differences Mann does not
have to reconcile or fit into subdivisions, for he prefers consistently to employ the word *imitation* rather than *robinsonade.* Many of these imitations are listed, however, in Ullrich's bibliography.

Another French study of *Robinson* goes over some of this
ground without becoming entangled in precise or exclusive
definitions. Paul Dottin in *Daniel De Foe et ses romans*
(1924) [228] employs *robinsonade* freely; he states that "l'origi-

---

[226] Pages 187 f. To prevent misunderstanding, one must complement this
quotation by Brüggemann's next paragraph, which I quote on pp. 160 f.
[227] Paris, p. 112 n. 4.
[228] Paris; in three parts: "La Vie et les aventures étranges de Daniel
De Foe," "Robinson Crusoë: étude historique et critique," and "Les
Romans secondaires de Daniel De Foe." A peculiar interest attaches to
Dottin's study of *Robinson,* for he had never read it until he chose Defoe
as subject for his doctoral dissertation; see his "Defoe et la France,"
English Studies, XIII (1931), 74. One result is absence of the nostalgic

nalité de De Foe a consisté, non pas à créer un genre nouveau, mais à concilier deux genres qui existaient déjà: le livre pieux et la relation de voyages" (p. 327). Robinson's English posterity—"des bâtards ou des dégénérés" (p. 387)—underwent some changes, but "après deux siècles de vie, Robinson trône seul en son pays: père dénaturé, il a réussi à dévorer un à un tous ses descendants" (p. 394).

Les succès de l'*Ermite* [*Quarll*], venant quelques mois après le succès, plus retentissant encore, des *Voyages de Gulliver,* orienta la robinsonnade dans une direction nouvelle; le réalisme des petits détails pratiques et terre-à-terre fut abandonné, et, avec lui, le souci de se rapprocher le plus possible de la vie. Deux tendances se manifestèrent. D'abord, l'introduction de doctrines philosophiques plus ou moins utopiques, que l'on amalgama avec le thème habituel des robinsonnades. . . .

La seconde tendance qui se manifesta dans la robinsonnade fut l'introduction, non plus d'un élément philosophique, mais d'un élément féérique destiné à plaire à la foule. (p. 391)

This type Dottin calls the *robinsonnade gullivérienne,* a union contrary to the distinctive characteristics of each component but particularly popular in English fiction. In his remarks on the French imitations he mentions the "robinsonnade de la famille" and the "robinsonnade de l'enfant"

---

sentimentalism which often clutters critical remarks on this novel. The translation by Louise Ragan, *The Life and Strange and Surprising Adventures of Daniel De Foe* (New York, [1929]) misrepresents itself as a translation of *Daniel DeFoe et ses romans.* Actually it is a free translation of only a third with the insertion of a chapter of 29 pages, entitled "Defoe's Novels," which is allowed to stand for 505 pages of the original, yet the translator gives no hint of this difference. Though the bibliography is brought up to date in some respects, it is much shorter than that in the original and carries over without correction misprints and errors. Consequently the value of Dottin's contribution to the study of Defoe's romances cannot be recognized by readers and reviewers ignorant of the original. However, Dottin himself approved the translation in this abridged form.

(p. 415) of the latter part of the eighteenth century without
implying that these are classificatory terms, and when he
turns to Germany he speaks of the "genre des *Robinsonaden*" (p. 439) almost as if this were a critical term different
from his word *robinsonnade*.

This sketch of the scholarly treatment of the robinsonade
has been leading up to a book that was never written. When
Ullrich in 1898 published his bibliography, he called it Volume One. Through a long series of publications he had
become at the time of his death in 1932 the world's leading
student of *Robinson* and its influence, but the only volume
to crown his lifelong interest is a little book of a hundred-
odd pages entitled *Defoes Robinson Crusoe: die Geschichte
eines Weltbuches* (1924), offered somewhat reluctantly and
regretfully: "Und so empfehle ich denn mein Buch als eine
Abschlagszahlung auf das schwierige Thema der Teilnahme
der Gebildeten wie auch dem sachkundigen Urteil der Fach-
genossen." [229] His extensive collection of robinsonades had
been sold,[230] and pressure of other duties prevented him from

[229] Leipzig, p. vi; i.e., this is not Volume II, the "noch zu schreibende
Geschichte des Robinsonbuches" (p. [v]) which he had planned. For
his publications on Defoe see "Hermann Ullrich: a Bibliography," *English
Studies*, XIII (1931) 87-89, and for brief obituary see W. H. S[taverman],
ibid., XIV (1932), 219.

[230] *Geschichte eines Weltbuches*, p. vi; cf. his "Zum Robinsonproblem,"
Englische Studien, LV (1921), 236 n. 1: "Die Robinsonaden nebst Zubehör
sind von der Firma Otto Harrassowitz zu hohem Preise nach Holland
verkauft worden und so für die deutsche Forschung so gut wie verloren."
These books were sold to Mr. N. Posthumus, bookseller, in The Hague
and subsequently purchased by the late Lucius L. Hubbard, who donated
them to the University of Michigan. I am indebted to Professors R. W.
Zandvoort and W. H. Staverman for information about Ullrich's library.
The Hubbard Collection of Imaginary Voyages in the Rare Book Room
of the University of Michigan contains about 2,500 volumes, including
1,680 narratives, of which 730 are editions of *Robinson* and 325 are editions of *Gulliver*. Also included is Ullrich's personal copy of his *Robinson
und Robinsonaden*, in which he made numerous manuscript corrections.

completing the great work which he many times insisted ought to be written on the subject. Though his last book only outlines the possibilities, it contains a clear restatement of the importance he attaches to the island motive as the unifying thread of the robinsonade:

> Mit der Zentralidee des "Robinson," dem *Inselmotiv,* war aber ein Thema angeschlagen, das hier zum erstenmale in der Welt-literatur in voller Breite der Behandlung auftritt. In voller Breite der Behandlung, sagten wir, denn neu war es nicht, son-dern man kann im Gegenteil *a priori* behaupten, dasz es so alt sein wird wie die Geschichte der Schiffahrt. Solange es eine Schiffahrt gibt, wird es vorgekommen sein, dasz ein Schiffsin-sasse oder mehrere infolge Scheiterns seines Schiffes oder infolge Aussetzens, vielleicht auch aus freier Wahl, auf einer Insel, getrennt von der übrigen Menschheit und ihrer Zivilisation, für kürzere oder längere Zeit, sein Leben zu fristen gezwungen oder veranlaszt worden ist, um schlieszlich erlöst zu werden oder aber seinem Elend zu erliegen oder auf seiner Insel eines natürlichen Todes zu sterben. Vor dem Entdeckungszeitalter sind uns aber nur wenige derartige Fälle durch die Literatur überliefert wor-den, die aber doch als Beleg für das Gesagte dienen können. (p. 46)

Though Ullrich insists that island existence is more im-portant in the robinsonade than voyages to foreign lands or slavery, he adds: "Das Entscheidende des Motivs ist aber nicht der Aufenthalt eines einzelnen Menschen gerade auf einer Insel, sondern nur eine von der menschlichen Gesell-schaft und ihrer Zivilisation abgeschlossene, insularische (=gleichwie auf einer Insel), isolierte Existenz (man wolle im Auge behalten, dasz das Wort isolieren von *insula* ab-geleitet ist)" (p. 80). Isolation may be attained in the woods or on top of a mountain (but not properly speaking in a prison). It may last a long or short time. An individual may be isolated by himself or in company with others. Even the solitary, like Robinson, has his childhood memories, his Bible, his salvage, and even his language,[231] so that society exerts a distant influence upon him. Because these considerations are relative and philosophic, they do not establish a practicable test for the robinsonade. Ullrich, however, has a test:

Um das Vorhandensein eines Robinsonlebens festzustellen, müssen wir uns jedesmal die Frage vorlegen: Sind die Schwierigkeiten einer Existenzfristung nicht vielleicht so grosz, dasz ein einzelner ihnen von vornherein in kürzester Zeit erliegen müszte, und ist es daher dem Verfasser eines solchen Robinsonlebens nicht von vornherein gestattet, die Überwindung dieser Schwierigkeiten auf mehrere Personen zu verteilen und auf einen kürzeren Zeitraum zu beschränken? . . . Unter einer Robinsonade verstehen wir also eine mehr oder weniger kunstvoll komponierte Erzählung, die uns die Erlebnisse von einer Person oder mehreren in insularischer Abgeschlossenheit, d.h. von der menschlichen Gesellschaft und ihren Zivilisationsmitteln isolierter Lage, die nicht das Ergebnis einer sentimentalen Weltflucht ist, als Hauptmotiv oder doch als gröszere Episode vorführt. Die Abgrenzung gegen den mit dem Robinsonmotiv blosz tändelnden Aventurierroman wird eine schärfere, wenn man die blosz episodische Verwendung des Motivs nicht mehr als Robinsonade gelten läszt.[232]

Ullrich's analysis completes the account of the robinsonade as a critical term from the time that Schnabel first used it up to the present. It has been identified with or allied to several different kinds of fiction and retained within definite limits only with considerable difficulty. One result of this rigorous insistence on a particular interpretation seems to

[231] Compare Fr[édéric] Bastiat, *Harmonies économiques* (Bruxelles [etc.], 1850), pp. 99 f.
[232] Pages 81 f. Another vigorous insistence on the significance of the Robinson-motive Ullrich gives in "Der zweihundertste Geburtstag von Defoes Robinson," *Zeitschrift für Bücherfreunde,* N.F. XI (1919), i, 36.

me the demonstration that the simplest, commonest definition is untenable: the robinsonade is not an imitation of
Robinson Crusoe. One book has so dominated the type to
which it most nearly belongs that critics have taken *some*
of the characteristics of that one book for characteristics of
the type and have measured less important works by the
closeness with which they adhere to the arbitrarily selected
characteristics of the one dominating book. This approach
results in deeper understanding of the partial significance of
Defoe's masterpiece but obscures the fact that island solitude
is generic in relation to the specific island solitude of *Robinson Crusoe.* This book, being in its entirety much more
than a story of island solitude, having in fact a universality
that makes any narrow classification of it impracticable,[233]
is larger than the robinsonade, and elements in it which do
not directly concern island solitude exist apart from those
which make it a robinsonade. The solution to this apparent
contradiction lies in my conclusion that the robinsonade as
defined simply names a theme or motive for the development of which authors before Defoe but principally after
him employed the imaginary voyage as vehicle, and the
trail of critical discussion which I have followed has been,
though nominally unified under the heading of robinsonades, actually an approach to a specialized branch of the
imaginary voyage.

Staverman in a review of Dottin's book on Defoe writes:

For the present, research into Defoe's life and into *Robinson*
may be allowed to rest. The first great work that must be done

---

[233] Eugène M. de Vogüé, "Le Livre anglais: Robinson Crusoé," *Revue
des deux mondes,* CXXXI (1 oct. 1895), 667, writes: "Il y a dans la
littérature séculière deux récits qui échappent à toute classification, à toute
comparaison, parce que leur universalité les place hors de pair: le *Don
Quichotte* et le *Robinson Crusoé."* Robinson is one of the ten characters
in J. Calvet, *Les Types universels dans les littératures étrangères* (Paris
[1932]), pp. 171-[192].

is that which we should have liked to see Ullrich achieve, which the latter in his *Defoes Robinson Crusoe* and Dottin in his second volume have done cursorily: an enquiry into the significance of *Robinson Crusoe* and the development of the *Robinsonade* in the 18th and 19th centuries. May we hope that Dottin will take this task upon him? [234]

Whoever undertakes this work, which has been anticipated now for several decades, must decide unequivocally whether he wishes to study the development of a theme or the technique of fiction, and his success will depend in part on keeping the two separate. To trace fully the theme of island solitude will be to study a philosophic idea wherever it manifests itself—in fiction, in poetry, in essay, or in biography.[235] Even Ullrich's definition excludes none of these, and the influence of *Robinson* has reached as far as to bring into existence in the terminology of editors and critics a large group of true robinsonades.[236] The robinsonade in fiction co-

[234] *English Studies*, VIII (1926), 193.

[235] Two noteworthy volumes have been written from this point of view of solitude: Antonio Pastor, *The Idea of Robinson Crusoe* (Watford, 1930), and Walter de la Mare, *Desert Islands and Robinson Crusoe* (New York, 1930). The latter pleasantly rambles through a book full of odds and ends of information and allusion to solitude and universal interest in desert islands; see two excellent and encomiastic reviews—Clennell Wilkinson, *London Mercury*, XXII (1930), 140-46, and Mario Praz, *Criterion*, X (1930-31), 195-97. A third book of some apparent importance I have not read (although I have looked into it): Yrjö Hirn, *Ön I Världshavet* (Stockholm, [1928]); see Ullrich's review, *Literaturblatt für germanische und romanische Philologie*, L (1929), [321]-323. See also a pertinent passage on solitude in Van Meter Ames, *Aesthetics of the Novel* (Chicago, [1928]), pp. 111 f., and Walter Leisering, *Das Motiv des Einsiedlers in der englischen Literatur des 18. Jahrhunderts und der Hochromantik* (Halle, 1935).

[236] In addition to references in the works already cited, see the following (arranged chronologically): F. C. Boll, "Der erste Robinson," *Morgenblatt für gebildete Stände*, V (1811), [617]-619; Victor Chauvin, "Les Vrais Robinsons," *Revue des cours littéraires* . . . , II (1864-65), 294-96; Ferdinand Denis and Victor Chauvin, *Les Vrais Robinsons: naufrages*,

ordinates with prerevolutionary ideas or exoticism or political and social satire. This is not to say that the robinsonade is necessarily propagandist fiction. Although all great fiction must mirror significant life—is likely to be in some sense philosophic, as Baker has pointed out[237]—it nevertheless remains a literary form: if the robinsonade is to be studied as narrative technique, it must be fitted into the larger background of the imaginary voyage before it can be seen in proper perspective in relation to the still larger field of fiction. This perspective has been consistently lost by many of its historians, particularly Ullrich and his followers. Though fully aware that the robinsonade developed out of the voyage-adventure-picaresque literature and changed until it became associated with other motives,[238] Ullrich nevertheless tried to isolate it from both its origins and its later development. To approach this fiction from the point of view of the imaginary voyage is to regard it as a more significant and a

solitude, voyages (Paris, 1863); Charles Russell, abridged translation of the preceding (Boston and New York, 1871); Peter G. Laurie, *"Robinson Crusoe" Collett: a Tale of Shipwreck and a Desert Island: a Family Memoir* (Brentwood, 1900); Maurice Muret, "Pedro Serrano, le vrai Robinson Crusoé," *Journal des débats*, XV (1908), ii, 595-96; Hermann Ullrich, "Zu den Quellen des 'Robinson,'" *Literarische Echo*, XI (1908-9), 154; Max Günther, *Entstehungsgeschichte von Defoe's Robinson Crusoe* (Greifswald, 1909); Arthur W. Secord, *Studies in the Narrative Method of Defoe* (Urbana, 1924); Paul Schneider, *Erlebte Robinsonaden abenteuerliche Fahrten und Schicksale aus den Zeiten der Entdeckungsreisen, nach Originalberichten* (Berlin, [c. 1925]); Pedro de Peralta Terrerôs y Guevara, *El Robinsón español manuscrito de fines del siglo XVIII . . .* , ed. Augusto Genin (Madrid [etc.], 1927); Stanley R. H. Rogers, *Crusoes and Castaways* (London, [etc., 1932]); and *Life on Desolate Islands; or, Real Robinson Crusoes . . .* (London, Religious Tract Society, n.d.). I can see little point, however, in writing a history of true robinsonades, for it would be only an artificially classified division of the history of shipwrecks and castaways.

[237] *Op. cit.*, II, 264.
[238] See especially his "Der zweihundertste Geburtstag von Defoes Robinson," *Zeitschrift für Bücherfreunde*, N.F. XI (1919), i, 40.

more living form. The only objection is that the influence of Defoe is not thus so much the main point, but this from the point of view of the development of fiction is an improvement rather than a loss. Dr. Hutchins has the perspective which I have been stressing:

> If, in attempting to define the term "Robinsonade," one emphasizes particularly solitary isolation from man's companionship . . . , then this genre is not large. Include, however, more than one person, and the growing colony of Crusoe easily becomes a Utopia. Transfer the realistic oceans, ships, islands, and cannibals of Defoe to the realm of the unreal, the simple scenery of *Robinson Crusoe* becoming the romance of the old wonder-filled travel and adventure stories, and one may be permitted to include under the heading of "Robinsonades" the flying "Gawreys" of Robert Paltock's *Peter Wilkins,* and giant roosters of *A Voyage to Cacklogallinia. . . .* Heroes far removed from the simple-hearted, hard-working Englishman of Defoe's novel, though still bearing his name, accustom themselves to living in the moon, or deep down under the ocean in the dwelling of some fabulous sea monster.

Then, finally, the elements of shipwreck, and of living alone on an uninhabited island somewhere, disappear altogether, and the name "Robinson" occurs in the titles of what are nothing more than picaresque adventure stories. These, later still, were made to point a moral, and the semblance of reality was given by a vast number of historical incidents.[239]

vi. The Relation of the Imaginary Voyage to Other Kinds of Prose Fiction

In this survey of critical and bibliographic consideration of the imaginary voyage and the robinsonade, what was obvious at the beginning has been consistently and persistently

[239] [Henry C. Hutchins], "Robinson Crusoe at Yale," *Yale University Library Gazette,* XI (1936-37), 32 f.

confirmed: the imaginary voyage closely relates to several other kinds of fiction. Any attempt to chart these relationships by interlocking circles necessitates the same dubious distinctions among unsatisfactorily defined and sometimes undefinable subdivisions into which earlier classifiers have been drawn. A critic soon finds that almost any work of fiction often cuts across his type-boundaries, that his types themselves are generally not mutually exclusive, and that classification frequently, as has been pointed out, depends on the point of view of the classifier. No sooner does he distinguish sharply between two contemporary types than he traces their origins only to find the types joined in part by their sources. If he does not trace origins, he loses historical perspective. Thus the fictions of More, Rabelais, Cyrano, Veiras, Defoe, Swift, Schnabel, and Holberg have all been called by one critic or another both prototypes and culminations of various genres. Kirchenheim's observation is not so ingenuous as it may first seem: "il y a une filiation que pourrait poursuivre celui qui voudrait écrire une histoire du roman." [240]

To identify, then, a certain work with a literary type does not preclude the possibility that at some one or several of its points of development it may coincide with a work in another category. No theory or argument is necessary to substantiate such an obvious statement. A moment's reflection will reveal, also, that a work may be in two or more categories. But here lies the source of trouble for many classifiers. To maintain order in their classifications they must decide which type predominates and classify a work accordingly. The next step is to imply or maintain that a work does not belong in a certain type because the characteristics of that type do not predominate. This tendency has been the

[240] Arthur von Kirchenheim, *L'Eternelle Utopie: étude du socialisme à travers les ages,* ed. A. Chazaud des Granges (Paris, 1897), p. 251.

principal cause of confusion and dispute in separating these related types of fiction which often coincide.

That type of fiction which coincides more often than any other with the imaginary voyage is, if the robinsonade be now excepted, the utopia, as already indicated by the number of times it has been mentioned. It would take a long chapter to outline the numerous attempts to define and analyze this type of literature, but such a survey would be irrelevant here, for the differences of opinion lie primarily in political and social science, not fiction; "a Utopia is born whenever a man adds to his dissatisfaction with the terms of his life a formulated proposal of what he would accept as a satisfactory sort of existence." [241] Whenever the utopist presents that proposal in narrative instead of expository form, the result is utopian fiction. Brüggemann suggests the issues when he asks

Was ist ein utopistischer Roman oder, wie der Staatswissenschaftler lieber sagt, ein Staatsroman? Hierüber aber gehen die Meinungen auseinander. Sind die Staatswissenschaftler schon unter sich über diese Frage nicht einig, so werden sie sich darüber noch viel weniger mit dem Literarhistoriker einigen, der mit ganz anderen Bedingungen an dasselbe Material herantritt wie jene. Es ist denn gleich charakteristisch, dasz die "Insel Felsenburg," die doch von Stern, Strauch, Kippenberg, Ullrich, Becker u.a. ohne weiteres als Utopie angesprochen wird, in keiner der Darstellungen der Staatswissenschaftler auch nur erwähnt wird, auszer in der Mohls: und dieser lehnt sie als "Staatsroman" ab. Wir sehen daraus bereits, dasz der Literarhistoriker und der Kulturhistoriker einen viel weiteren Begriff mit den utopistischen Romanen verbinden müssen als der Staatswissenschaftler, und dasz die "Staatsromane," die dieser

---

[241] Frances T. Russell, *Touring Utopia, the Realm of Constructive Humanism* (New York, 1932), p. 44.

gelten läszt, nur einen Teil der Literaturgattung ausmachen, die jene in Rücksicht zu ziehen haben.[242]

Hence, one reason for the variety of definitions. Brügge-mann's own is simple: "Ein utopistischer Roman ist jede Darstellung eines idealen Gemeinwesens in Romanform, ob dessen Ideal nun in staatlichen Einrichtungen oder dem sittlichen Verhalten der Einwohner zum Ausdruck ge-langt." [243] This defines utopian romance, but in fact most definitions of the utopia itself consider it "a species of prose fiction" before continuing in some such terms as these:

. . . setting forth the ways of a society. It is a graphic presenta-tion of a nation where perfect social relations prevail and where human beings, living under a faultless government, enjoy a happy existence free from turmoil, harassing cares, and endless worries of actual life. Utopias are a variety of propaganda fic-tion, their matter presented to set a goal toward which a people may work, or to draw a contrast with or to criticize existing conditions. On the whole the pattern is set by "the father of English utopias," Sir Thomas More's *Utopia.*[244]

But the fiction which gave its name to the type is not an

[242] *Op. cit.,* pp. 6 f. For Kippenberg, Ullrich, and Becker see my bibliog-raphy; Brüggemann's other three references in this paragraph are as fol-lows: Adolf Stern, "Der Dichter der 'Insel Felsenburg,'" *Historisches Taschenbuch,* 5 F. X (1880), [319]-366; Philipp Strauch, "Eine deutsche Robinsonade (Insel Felsenburg)," *Deutsche Rundschau,* LVI (1888), [379]-399; and Robert von Mohl, *Die Geschichte und Literatur der Staatswissen-schaften* (Erlangen, 1855-58), I, [167]-214.

[243] Page 12. This definition he accompanies with a chart divided into (1) "Archistische Utopien," i.e., "rein politische Utopien" like Campanella, and (2) "Anarchistische Utopien," i.e., (a) "politisch-kulturelle Utopien mit radikalen Nebengedanken" like Foigny and (b) "rein kulturelle Utopien ohne jeden politischen Nebengedanken" like Schnabel. The "Staatsromane im engeren Sinne" comes under (1); the "Staatsromane oder sozial. Utopien im weiteren Sinne" comes under (1) and (2a); and the "Utopistische Romane in unserem Sinne" under both (1) and (2).

[244] Victor Solberg, "A Source Book of English and American Utopias," *Ohio State University Abstracts of Doctors' Dissertations,* X (1933), 298.

imaginary voyage, for the existence of the island is reported as fact, not discovered by narration. It is precisely at this point that a distinction can easily be made. When the utopist chooses to discover his nonexistent civilization by narrating the account of a voyage, he produces both a utopia and an imaginary voyage. Storm and shipwreck generally occur as devices for drawing the discoverer off into unknown realms. Rarely does an author gather together a group of malcontents and send them off over a known course with the deliberate intention of joining an already-known utopian people, or even of establishing a utopia, as does James Burgh in his utopian *Account of the Cessares* (1764). The elements of strangeness, adventure, and accidental discovery are more appealing. Professor Frances Russell has well summarized the possibilities:

It is obvious that every Utopia must be at some remoteness, whether great or small, in either space or time; partly to lend enchantment but more to borrow credibility. It is clear also why the earlier productions should specialize on the spatial contrivance, and the later on the temporal. In the days when geography was still in the making and imaginary voyages unhampered by knowledge, Utopians might roam the globe in magic exploration, fancy free. Then the peerless roaming place was the ocean. . . .

. . . And when the surface of the globe was all used up, there remained the spacious interior. . . .

In rarer instances the basement of Neptune's domain has been colonized, but it is harder for us to become aquatic, even in imagination. And for some of the most expansive imaginations this little planet, inside or out, is too restricted. These take us on journeys to the moon, to Mars, to Mercury, to a world out beyond Sirius.

That about exhausts the choices of space and forces us to change to the time-machine for transportation. (pp. 47 ff.)

The imaginary voyage frequently offers a double opportunity to the utopist. The voyager's native guide—the con-
ventional figure who teaches him the language and explains
the customs—usually relates the story of the founding of his
commonwealth; if the people are descended from Europeans,
then their origins involve an earlier voyage and shipwreck.
So the utopist, perhaps not artistically interested in writing
fiction at all, finds in the imaginary voyage the readiest
vehicle, especially in the seventeenth and eighteenth centuries, for his optimism and his enjoyment of vicarious
justice.

Some students of this fiction have often been too ready to
contemn it as propaganda or applied art. They set themselves a dilemma:

Si nous disions que ce sont de mauvais romans, on pourrait
aisément nous répondre que, d'abord, ce ne sont pas des romans,
mais des ouvrages de science politique qui ont pour but unique
d'exposer les questions ardues sous une forme légère. . . . Si
nous faisions la critique des idées, nous nous trouverions encore
dans une situation difficile, car on nous objecterait alors que ce
ne sont pas là des ouvrages scientifiques, mais de pures fictions![245]

However, the weakness in many of these romances is to be
attributed not so often to the fact that their content is utopian
as to the fact that they are products of writers who are far
from competent in narrative ability; that their narrative
presentation of an ideal commonwealth should be inchoate
follows inevitably. On the other hand, the utopian content
itself was often only imperfectly developed. As André Lichtenberger has clearly suggested:

Les idées, comme les peuples, traversent avant la période historique une période héroïque, légendaire, où elles sont en for-

---

[245] Kirchenheim, *op. cit.*, p. 328.

mation. . . . Leur [xviiie siècle] socialisme est, si l'on peut dire, moins "social" que sentimental et moral. . . . Il se plaît à esquisser des sociétés imaginaires où il n'y aura ni malheureux ni méchants, puisqu'on aura supprimé la propriété qui les divise et les rend mauvais. C'est un socialisme idéal de rêveurs et de sentimentaux, un *socialisme utopique.*[246]

This seems to me a proper attitude toward the eighteenth-century utopia; the disparaging phrase "propagandist fiction" misses the mark. There is no reason to assume that utopian society should not serve as aptly for a fictional study of human nature as any other society, provided only that the narrative technique of the utopist is sufficiently competent.

Ullrich, having excluded from his bibliography of robinsonades "alle blossen Utopieen," is faced with the question of whether or not *Robinson Crusoe* is a utopia. "Nein und abermals nein," for, he explains, Robinson's colony bears none of the characteristics of an ideal state.[247] The colony, however, lies outside that part of the book on which the definition of the robinsonade is based. The best analysis of the precise relationship between the utopia and the robinsonade is made by Brüggemann in his conclusion:

Wir müssen uns aber auch klar machen, dasz es mit der Verbindung von Utopie und Robinsonade eine eigene Sache bleibt. Wenn für die Robinsonade der Begriff des Exils unerläszlich und für die Utopie derselbe Begriff des Exils im Grunde ausgeschlossen erscheint, so dürfen wir gegenüber den Betrachtungen in unserer Einleitung jetzt wohl sagen, dasz Utopie und Robinsonade nur in den äuszeren Voraussetzungen (Inselcharakter des Landes und zwangsweiser oder freiwilliger Abschlusz von der übrigen menschlichen Gesellschaft) ähnlich sind, und dasz *nur diese Äuszerlichkeiten* zu einer Verbindung von Utopie und

[246] *Le Socialisme utopique* . . . (Paris, 1898), pp. 4 f.
[247] See "Einleitung" to his edition of *Die Insel Felsenburg,* pp. x-xii.

Robinsonade auffordern, während sich diese ihrem inneren Wesen nach vielmehr einander vollkommen ausschlieszen.[248]

The difference between seclusion and solitude, even externally, necessitates a fine distinction, recognizable by critics whenever it exists but seldom premeditated by authors. Brüggemann himself has written that "das Motiv der Abgeschlossenheit ein typisches Motiv der utopistischen Romane ist." [249] The author's motive, however, may be simply adventure growing out of the discovery of a mysterious island, a theme older than Sir Thomas More, older than Plato.

La raison en est simple. L'aventure s'identifie en quelque sorte avec la mer. La mer d'eau ou la mer de soleil et de sables, le fluide, le mystérieux, l'illimité, voilà le milieu, la matière passive ou la matrice de l'aventure. Le roman d'aventures s'épanouira naturellement chez un peuple de marins, Grecs, Anglais, Arabes de la mer Rouge, et les repos et les découvertes et les fleurs de la mer ce sont ses îles. . . .

De sorte que réellement, tout roman d'aventures tend à cristalliser sous la forme de Robinson et de l'île de Robinson. . . . L'aventure de Robinson est la plus extraordinaire qu'un homme puisse vivre, et en même temps on la voit à la portée de chacun. Tout coin de terre où nous sommes peut nous devenir l'île de Robinson.[250]

This return to *Robinson* reveals an approach to the imaginary voyage through another kind of literature to which it is closely related, already suggested, particularly by Mildebrath's book. In fact, the utopia itself does not lie outside the boundaries of the romance of adventure, itself by no means

---

[248] *Op. cit.*, p. 188. Cf. Friedrich Wackwitz, *Entstehungsgeschichte von D. Defoes "Robinson Crusoe"* [Berlin, 1909], pp. 44-47.

[249] *Ibid.*, p. 186.

[250] Albert Thibaudet, ". . . Le Roman de l'aventure," *Nouvelle Revue française*, XIII (1919), 610 f.

a fixed form; one critic points out that by seventeenth-century fictionists even "le mot *mœurs,* littérairement parlant, était pris dans le sens du mot *aventure*." [251] Thibaudet mentions three kinds, the active (English), the romanesque (French), and "le roman de l'aventure intellectuelle, le motif de l'aventure lié de façon ironique et symbolique à un certain romanesque de l'intelligence libre." [252] As examples of this third kind he cites the works of More, Cyrano, and Swift. All imaginary voyages are adventure stories in the broad sense, and though the reverse is not true, such specialized kinds of adventure as the heroic romance and the picaresque often coincide with the imaginary voyage.

Allen Aventuriers [writes Ullrich], mit ganz wenigen Ausnahmen, ist der häufige Wechsel des Schauplatzes gemeinsam. Dieser beschränkt sich nicht auf Europa, auch Asien, Afrika, Amerika kommen häufiger vor; von den rein pikarischen Produkten gilt diese Ausdehnung des Schauplatzes indessen nicht; dieser beschränkt sich vielmehr auf die gröszeren Städte Frankreichs, Hollands, Spaniens, Dänemarks, ist aber doch noch ausgedehnter als der der spanischen Vorbilder. So sinkt diese Romangattung daher vielfach in den alten Reiseroman zurück. [253]

Relationship between types does not necessarily indicate that one has influenced the other. Professor Secord rightly insists that "The narratives of travel had been sending their heroes to foreign lands for hundreds of years before the 'English Rogue' was written," [254] but it is not always easy, however advisable, to draw the line that Professor Chandler insists on: "Since the rogue moves from master to master, he is often a traveler, yet that fact offers no excuse for con-

[251] Eugène Maron, "Le Roman de mœurs au dix-septième siècle," *Revue indépendante,* 2S. XIII (1848), 264.

[252] *Loc. cit.,* pp. 608 f.

[253] *Euphorion,* 9 Ergänzungsheft (1911), p. 23.

[254] *Studies in the Narrative Method of Defoe,* p. 74.

founding the picaresque novel with the novel of mere adventure." [255] The lad who cheated his master and ran off to the next town might remain a rogue, but the lad who ran away to sea and practiced his cleverness on pirates, savages, strange peoples, mutinous crews, or overbearing officers could rise to heroic proportions. What was picaresque in Europe often underwent a sea-change in *terra incognita,* and the distinction has no particular value in the study of the imaginary voyage beyond showing the frequent inextricableness of its elements.

Dibelius says of Defoe's novels as a group:

Da finden sich nun die altbeliebten . . . Motive des heroisch-galanten Romans: Kampf, Gefangenschaft, Schiffbruch, Leben in der Ferne unter fremden Völkerstämmen, Seeraub usw., nur alles nicht heroisch, sondern bürgerlich-realistisch dargestellt; statt übernatürlicher Kämpfe tritt an den Helden das Problem heran, wie er draussen auf einsamer Insel sich vor Hunger und Kälte schützt; er erlebt seine Abenteuer nicht auf der Ritterfahrt zu einer berühmten Prinzessin, sondern als Kaufmann wie Robinson, als Seeräuber wie Singleton. . . .[256]

The middle-class hero in the imaginary voyage, questing for material gain through trade or plunder—often undistinguishable means to the same end—struggles to better his standing in a hostile world, from which he partly escapes temporarily by voyaging, and he may manifest an unscrupulous antisocial attitude much the same as that found in picaresque fiction:

L'étude des romans picaresques démontre que plus essentiel

---

[255] Frank W. Chandler, *The Literature of Roguery* (Boston and New York, 1907), I, 5.

[256] Wilhelm Dibelius, *Englische Romankunst: die Technik des englischen Romans im achtzehnten und zu Anfang des neunzehnten Jahrhunderts,* 2 Auf. (Berlin and Leipzig, 1922), I (Palaestra XCII), 34. Arguments for not relying too heavily on Dibelius are set forth by A. J. Tieje, *Journal of English and Germanic Philology,* XI (1912), 626-35.

que la coquinerie des protagonistes est leur désir de démasquer leurs semblables; bien que répudiés, ils se proclament cousins germains des hommes les plus respectés. Victimes eux-mêmes de l'ordre social, ils offrent aux opprimés toute la sympathie dont ils sont capables tandis que les grands et les fortunés sont en butte à une ironie inquisitoriale. . . . L'esprit picaresque, comme l'esprit réaliste, est inspiré par la réaction contre une fausse conception de la vie; tous deux sont des défis à l'imposture ou à ce qu'ils considèrent comme tel. Par picaresque donc, nous entendons le désir d'enlever le masque aux hommes, surtout aux grands, et à la société. Au fond, ce n'est que le désir de séparer l'apparence de l'essence. C'est en un mot le cartésianisme social, le cartésianisme destructeur du xviiie siècle.[257]

Such an attitude, when present, reveals itself sometimes by implication only but more often by either satire or the didacticism of the utopist. Thus can be detected an affiliation between such apparently different types as the utopia and the picaresque, both forms of the adventure romance and both occasionally coinciding with the imaginary voyage.

Two statements made about the picaresque by critics just quoted reveal another point of view and another classificatory term for consideration:

In construction most of the novels of Captain Frederick Marryat are allied to the romance of roguery; for they chronicle the

---

[257] Benjamin M. Woodbridge, *Gatien de Courtilz Sieur du Verger: étude sur un précurseur du roman réaliste en France* (Baltimore and Paris, 1925), p. x. Since important novelists in Germany in the late seventeenth and early eighteenth centuries were Grimmelshausen, Weise, Reuter, and Schnabel, the merging of the picaresque in the imaginary voyage is a usual theme of histories of the early German novel; see, e.g., Hellmuth Mielke, *Geschichte des deutschen Romans* (Leipzig, 1904), Hubert Rausse, *Geschichte des deutschen Romans bis 1800* (Kempton and München, 1914), and *idem*, "Der Abenteurerromane des 17. und 18. Jahrhunderts," *Die Kultur Viertel-Jahrschrift f. Wissenschaft Literatur und Kunst*, XV (1914), [218]-226.

progress of a not over-scrupulous hero from obscurity to com-
fortable or distinguished position.[258]

Eine Spezialuntersuchung über Defoe würde unter seinen
Romanen mindestens zwei Gruppen unterscheiden müssen, die
Seeromane und die Schelmenromane, deren literarische Herkunft
wahrscheinlich nicht ganz dieselbe ist. Für die Wirkung auf die
Folgezeit ist diese Unterscheidung belanglos, da der spätere
Seeroman (Smollett, Marryat) eine deutliche Abzweigung aus
der grösseren Gattung des Abenteuerromans darstellt. Und für
alle Punkte der typischen englischen Romantechnik verhalten
sich die beiden Gruppen gleich, so dass sie in dieser Betrachtung
wohl als eine einzige gefasst werden dürfen.[259]

The problem here is not a difficult one. Marryat wrote sea
novels. Clearly the sea novel comes into being only with or
after the novel itself and is therefore largely a product of
the nineteenth century, with forerunners like Smollett and
Defoe. A good definition comes from one of the earliest
studies of this type:

Wir wollen unter Seeroman die Gattung des Romans verstehen,
deren Hauptschauplatz das Meer ist mit seinen Stimmungen und
Schönheiten, von der friedlichen Windstille bis zum tobenden
Orkane, und dessen. Hauptpersonen die Seeleute sind mit allen
ihren Seltsamkeiten und mit der ihnen eigentümlichen Den-
kungsart. Was wir also in diesen Romanen suchen dürfen, ist
eine lebenswahre Schilderung aller Angehörigen der Marine vom
einfachen Schiffsjungen bis zum Admiral, von ihrem Thun und
Treiben, von ihren Arbeiten und ihren Vergnügungen, ferner
eine naturgetreue Darstellung aller Verhältnisse und Einrichtungen an Bord des Schiffes, mit denen also ein Autor von See-
romanen vollständig vertraut sein muss.[260]

---

[258] Chandler, *op. cit.*, II, 397.

[259] Dibelius, *op. cit.*, I, 33.

[260] Arno Schneider, *Die Entwickelung des Seeromans in England im
17. und 18. Jahrhundert* (Leipzig, 1901), pp. 4 f. This dissertation was

This *Seeroman* differs from Dibelius's *Seeroman* in the same way that the novel differs from the romance. This difference Schneider recognizes by putting Defoe's *New Voyage round the World* in "die Klasse der Reisebeschreibungen" and by calling *Captain Singleton* a "typischen Vertreter der Seeschilderungen (im weitesten Sinne des Worts)," a "Vorläufer des Seeromans . . . ein Mittelding zwischen Seeroman und Abenteurerroman," that is, a "Seeabenteuerroman": "Von einem liebevollen Eingehen auf die Natur des Meeres mit all seinen Schönheiten findet sich bei Defoe noch nichts." [261] The sea that forms the background for the *Odyssey,* for the Greek romances, for *Polexandre* ("chose rare sinon unique au xviie siècle, un roman maritime" [262]) is the same sea that furnishes the setting for the imaginary voy-

complemented by Karl Richter, *Die Entwicklung des Seeromans in England im 19. Jahrhundert* (Leipzig, 1906). Richter's condensed definition (p. 11) is: "Wir verstehen natürlich unter Seeroman den engeren Roman, der sich nur mit der See beschäftigt, dessen hauptsächlichstes Moment für uns die Schilderungen des Seelebens und des bunt bewegten Treibens auf dem Schiffe sind." Except for chapters in biographies and criticisms of individual authors, adequately full study of the sea novel, especially in comparative literature, is almost wholly lacking. Three introductory studies are Ernest C. Ross, *The Development of the English Sea Novel from Defoe to Conrad* (Ann Arbor, [192-]); Nathan C. Starr, *The Sea in the English Novel from Defoe to Melville,* unpublished Harvard dissertation, 1928; and Harold F. Watson, *The Sailor in English Fiction and Drama 1550-1800* (New York, 1931). See also chapters in histories of the nineteenth-century novel, e.g. especially Georgette Bosset, *Fenimore Cooper et le roman d'aventure en France vers 1830* (Paris, [1928]), pp. [97]-217, and M[arion] G. Devonshire, *The English Novel in France 1830-1870* ([London], 1929), pp. 243-54.

[261] Pages 15, 16, and 26.

[262] Chinard, *L'Amérique et le rêve exotique* . . . , p. 69; for special discussion of *Polexandre* as a *roman maritime* and for Gomberville as a romancer who "avait le goût des relations de voyages," see Louis de Loménie, ". . . Le Roman sous Louis XIII," *Revue des deux mondes,* 2e pér. XXXVII (1 fév. 1862), 733-47. Bosset, *op. cit.,* p. [117], calls Eugène Sue's *Kernok le pirate* (1830) "le premier roman maritime français."

age and for the sea novel. It relates these types but does not make them one. The sea novel does not supplant the imaginary voyage; it distinguishes itself from the imaginary voyage by the presence of those qualities, however they be defined, which constitute the novel. Their absence means that an author is dealing in the matter not of novels but of travels. In fact, extensive use of a voyage in an intended sea novel may break down the unity which a well-constructed novel is supposed to have, for, as Dibelius has pointed out,

Es [das Motiv der Reise] hat geringe konstruktive Kraft; denn auf einer Reise kann dem Helden alles begegnen. Der Vorzug des Motivs besteht darin, dass es sich leicht für das Studium des Milieus, für ständische Satire und ethnographische Wirkungen fruchtbar machen lässt; hier und da haben Seitenschösslinge des Romans (von Cyrano de Bergerac und Swift bis zu Jules Verne und Wells) es auch zu philosophischer Satire und wissenschaftlicher Spekulation verwendet. . . .[263]

Though *Seitenschösslinge* is ambiguous, this specific mention of four authors of imaginary voyages in a passage discussing the sea novel points significantly both the similarities and dissimilarities. Both could be brought under one larger term sometimes used, *geographical romance,* which has the advantage of not suggesting confinement to any one period in the development of fiction. Hettner speaks of a seventeenth-century *Geographieroman* (Happel's *Insularische Mandorell,* 1682); Kingsley calls *Captain Singleton* "certainly the best geographical romance which has ever been written"; Lichtenberger writes of other eighteenth-century *romans à cadre géographique,* and Roustan says that Ullrich's bibliography is necessary for the history of the *roman de la géographie.*[264]

[263] *Op. cit.,* II (Palaestra XCVIII), 341.
[264] Hettner, *op. cit.,* III, 299; Henry Kingsley, Globe ed., *Robinson Crusoe* (London, 1868), p. xxx; Lichtenberger, *Socialisme au XVIIIe*

Two other similar terms are sometimes employed, but both seem to me less useful than *geographical romance*. *Fictitious travel* is, in the words of one who has himself used the term,

not altogether felicitous. It really covers two quite different types of stories. There is the type of which the Odyssey may be taken as a primitive sample, the story which professes to be nothing else but fiction, in which travel plays a more or less prominent part. More recent types will suggest themselves in the Defoe stories, in Munchausen, and in the marvellous series of creations of Jules Verne. Of stories of travel which are actually meant to deceive, which are pure fiction from beginning to end, passed off as fact, happily there are not many examples. But there are various modifications of the type, legends mostly founded on a little nucleus of fact, which have evolved into formidable dimensions in the course of the centuries. The Phantom Lands referred to in the title of this paper are, to a large extent, the creation of the *voyages imaginaires*.[265]

The other is *apocryphal voyage*, a highly restricted term, applicable only to those deceptions which historians of voyages have to expose with prefatory remarks like these:

Es giebt viele Bücher, welche, nach ihrem Titel, und nach der Anordnung ihres Inhalts, Reisebeschreibungen zu seyn scheinen, und doch nichts weiter als Erzählungen solcher Reisen sind, welche die Verfasser entweder gänzlich erdichtet, oder ganz oder zum Theil aus andern Reisebeschreibungen und Topographien

---

siècle, p. 41; L. Roustan, *Revue critique* . . . , N.S. XLVIII (1899), 134-35. Cf. J. Hetzel as quoted in Charles Lemire, *Jules Verne 1828-1905: l'homme, l'écrivain, le voyageur, le citoyen: son œuvre, sa mémoire, ses monuments* (Paris [etc.], 1908), p. 68: "Jules Verne, on le sait, est le créateur du *roman scientifique* et du *roman géographique*"; i.e., neither *roman géographique* nor *roman maritime* (see my note 262) is a fixed term.

[265] J. Scott Keltie, "Fictitious Travel and Phantom Lands," *Harper's Monthly Magazine*, CXV (1907), [186].

zusammengeschrieben haben. Alle diese gehören viel mehr in die Klasse der Romane, als hieher.[266]

No matter how strongly one insists that Defoe intended to deceive his readers, the fact remains that no living Captain Singleton, no living Robinson Crusoe, was appearing among his contemporaries to say "these are my voyages" and to elaborate or supplement various incidents. E. A. Baker, for example, explains that Defoe's fictions are "not honestly addressed to the imagination as works of art" (I, 12); nevertheless, his realism and his devices for obtaining authenticity are artistic in the sense that, by the device of pseudonymity, he created voyagers whom no one ever knew in the flesh. Even presumably competent judges might be fooled by the written word,[267] but "inartistic" realism came from living men concerned not with the art of fiction but with the practice of it, men who lived the lie of convincing navigators, geographers, and ministers of state, as well as the public, that their imaginary voyages were true, men to whom such fiction was a means to their livelihood or to some ulterior reward. As soon as the historian of voyages pronounces them

[266] Johann Beckmann, *Litteratur der älteren Reisebeschreibungen. Nachrichten von ihren Verfassern, von ihrem Inhalte, von ihren Ausgaben und Uebersetzungen* . . . (Göttingen, 1807-10), I, 673.

[267] A particularly interesting example occurs in a review by James M'Queen (F.R.G.S. and author of a *Geographical Survey of Africa*) entitled "Captain Speke's Discovery of the Source of the Nile" printed as Part ii of Richard F. Burton, *The Nile Basin* (London, 1864). M'Queen writes (pp. 184 f.): "Before coming to a conclusion, we must notice a work, published at Edinburgh in 1810, by De Foe. Extracts [an account of Captain Singleton's journey across Africa] from it have been sent to us by the Secretary of the Asiatic Society of Bombay. . . . We have not ourselves seen this book, but the author of it seems to have written it with some knowledge of this portion of Africa. Here is, therefore, another claimant for the honour of the discovery of the sources of the White Nile." As surprising as this is, I cannot see any reason for supposing that irony is intended.

apocryphal, the historian of imaginary voyages must include them for careful study.

As usual, however, borderline cases complicate decisions. Returned voyagers sometimes fall into the hands of editors.[268] As long as an editor confines himself to improving the diction and style, to filling in the background with unimportant but probable details, and to rearranging in order to heighten mildly the dramatic situations, that is, as long as he preserves the essential truth, then the voyage does not encroach upon the domain of the imaginary. But sometimes an editor "romanticizes" the basic materials by the addition of incidents grown solely out of his own imagination, by unscrupulously altering important facts, and by distorting in order to advance his own ideas particularly about ethnology, political science, or natural history. Then, though the voyager actually sailed on a certain boat, at a certain time, over a certain course, the narrative becomes in its significance and implications imaginary.

Another borderline case comes from the voyager who is honest by intention but untrustworthy as a reporter. I do not refer to conflicting accounts written separately by two persons on the same voyage; both may be authentic if not absolutely true. Except for deliberate falsehoods a reader can make allowances for the limitations of human witnesses and reporters and for the tricks that memory often plays. This merely exemplifies concretely the usual difficulties in determining the truth. I refer rather to the credulous, the incautious, and the predetermined voyagers. The first believes and retells what natives or fellow travelers report to him, and he may neglect to state that he himself was not an eye-

[268] Compare David Bone, "The Sea Ghosts of Bohemia," *Saturday Review of Literature*, VIII (1931-32), [469], 472. Captain Cook's introduction to his second voyage contains a declaration of independence from editors somewhat comparable to Dr. Johnson's famous letter to the Earl of Chesterfield.

witness. The incautious jump to conclusions without adequate observation or background knowledge. By far the most troublesome, from the point of view of distinguishing between the authentic and the fictitious, is the voyager with a head so full of preconceptions that he deceives himself. As Pons writes,

C'est ainsi que non seulement les auteurs des voyages imaginaires mettent à contribution les relations des voyageurs et explorateurs, mais que, chose plus curieuse, les voyageurs se laissent maintes fois influencer par les écrivains utopistes et découvrent ou croient découvrir dans les pays nouveaux qu'ils ont sous les yeux les républiques idéales dont leur mémoire est emplie.[269]

Such deviations from the truth do not necessarily turn real voyages into imaginary voyages, but they show that the same elements may sometimes be found in both. Pons, after making in another work an observation similar to the one just quoted, adds: "Les deux domaines, en apparence inconciliables, du réel et de l'irréel, du vrai et du faux, ont donc entre eux des points de contact plus nombreux qu'on ne serait disposé à le croire." [270]

Another point of contact is suggested by an anecdote about John Bell's true *Travels from St. Petersburg in Russia to Various Parts of Asia* (1763). He sought advice from the Scottish historian William Robertson, who said, "Take Gulliver's Travels for your model, and you cannot go wrong." This Bell did and produced what has been called "the best model perhaps for travel-writing in the English language." [271] However much Swift's style may have been af-

---

[269] "Le 'Voyage' genre littéraire . . . ," p. 98. He refers to the fuller discussion of this relationship in Atkinson, *Les Relations de voyages . . .*, chap. iii.

[270] His edition of *Gulliver's Travels*, p. lxxix.

[271] *Quarterly Review*, XVII (1817), 464 and n†. Cf. review of Bell's *Travels* in the *Critical Review*, LVIII (1789), 175-83.

fected by his reading of true voyages, he demonstrates the simple, direct style so perfectly and with such convincing probability that his fiction could in turn teach a profitable lesson to the writers of true voyages.[272] But not all travelers were so concerned with style as Bell was, and hence some imaginary voyages, for example *Munchausen,* grasped the opportunity to burlesque the turgid, unconvincing style of some of the true voyagers. Thus the relationship between the imaginary and the real voyage becomes further complicated in both style and substance.

The external relationships between real and imaginary voyages—those implicit in the very term *imaginary voyage*—are so obvious on the surface that not sufficiently careful study has been made of them for any considerable period. Some of the books I have cited, especially those by Chinard, Atkinson, Secord, and Von der Mühll, and Bonner's *Captain William Dampier Buccaneer-Author,* treat special aspects of the subject. Pons uses the large term *voyage genre,* under which rubric "sont assemblés . . . des ouvrages de caractère radicalement différent":

Si *Robinson Crusoe* et les *Voyages de Gulliver* peuvent assez bien aller ensemble, ils s'apparient mal au *Sentimental Journey* de Sterne. Les deux premiers de ces ouvrages sont des voyages imaginaires, le troisième se range parmi les récits authentiques

---

[272] Compare Lord Monboddo, *Of the Origin and Progress of Language,* 2d ed. (London), III (1786), 367 f.: "I would therefore advise our compilers of history, if they will not study the models of the historic style which the antients have left us, at least to imitate the simplicity of Dean Swift's style in his Gulliver's Travels, and to endeavour to give as much the appearance of credibility to what truth they relate as he has given to his monstrous fictions; not that I would be understood to recommend the style of those travels as a pattern for history, for which it never was intended, being indeed an excellent imitation of the narrative of a sailor, but wanting that gravity, dignity, and ornament which the historical style requires."

et plus exactement encore parmi ceux qui contiennent essentiellement des *impressions* de voyage.[273]

As different as these two groups may be, the words *imaginary* and *authentic* do not keep them apart. Without the
necessity of deciding how much fiction there is in the *Sentimental Journey,* the fact remains that the *impressions de
voyage* may be sometimes partly imaginary. Garnier, it will
be recalled, included some of them under his general heading of *voyages imaginaires,* and Fritz Neubert has made a
special study under the revealing title, *Die französischen
Versprosa-Reisebrieferzählungen und der kleine Reiseroman
des 17. und 18. Jahrhunderts: ein Beitrag zur Geschichte der
französischen Rokoko-Literatur.* He explains:

> Die Aufgabe, die ich mir nun hier gestellt habe, ist die: die
> *Entstehung* und *Entwicklung* einer bestimmten kleinen Gattung
> der Erzählungsliteratur zu zeigen, die man kaum anders als im
> Roman unterbringen kann, und die, wie so manche andere, ihren
> Ausgang im 17. Jahrhundert nimmt, um im 18. Jahrhundert zu
> einem beliebten Genre zu werden. Es handelt sich um das Genre,
> das ich kurz als *"Reisebrieferzählung"* und *"kleinen Reiseroman"*
> bezeichnen will.[274]

This merely recognizes that in the same way that *grands
voyages* are complemented by *petits voyages,* so *Reiseromane*

[273] "Le 'Voyage' genre littéraire . . . ," p. 97.
[274] Jena und Leipzig, 1923 (*Zeitschrift für französische Sprache und
Litteratur,* Supplementheft XI), p. 2. For further study of this type of
literature, both true and fictitious, see such works as Albert Babeau, *Les
Voyageurs en France depuis la Renaissance jusqu'à la Révolution* (Paris,
1885); Kurt Müller, *Über den Einfluss der klassischen Literatur auf die
Reiseschilderungen* (Crimmitschau, 1905); Thomas Seccombe, "A Short
List of Works, Mainly on Travel in France and Italy during the Eighteenth Century . . . ," *Smollett's Travels through France and Italy* (London [etc., 1907]; World's Classics XC), Appendix A; and Fritz Neubert,
"Französische Rokoko-Probleme," in *Hauptfragen der Romanistik: Festschrift für Philipp August Becker* (Heideiberg, 1922), pp. 256-79.

are complemented by *kleine Reiseromane*. The "little voyages," from London to Paris, from France to Italy, or up the Rhine, even if largely fictitious, do not require more than passing mention in a study of the imaginary voyage; they are more properly (in English equivalents) journeys or trips. They could, however, be included under a larger category of geographical narrative.

As soon as an author removes his imaginary voyager from the surface of the earth and sends him into the air (before the age of balloons and airships) or to the center of the earth, he breaks his relationship with real voyages and enters into a realm of fantasy. His style he may owe to the real voyages, but his subject matter draws upon all kinds of fiction of the past. Closely allied to the imaginary voyages of this kind is the fairy tale. Goulding definitely calls *Gulliver* "une fiction merveilleuse, un conte de fées," and Dottin puts Peter Wilkins in a group of "robinsonnades féériques." [275] Fürst in his *Vorläufer der modernen Novelle im 18. Jahrhundert* discusses oriental tales, imaginary voyages, and *Feenmärchen* as a group, implying that the imaginary voyage is a special kind of fairy tale or that fairy tales could be also imaginary voyages. The *conte* became in the eighteenth century one of the *formes fixes*. Lanson says, "On peut ranger dans cette catégorie toutes les narrations de choses imaginaires et impossibles, voyages fantastiques, contes orientaux, contes de fées . . . et tant d'autres récits où l'idée s'exprime, voilée et pourtant claire, dans d'étranges ou extravagantes formes," [276] and includes among his examples two imaginary voyages, *Micromégas* and *Sévarambes*.

Because of such multifarious relationships between the

[275] Goulding, *op. cit.*, p. 88, and Dottin, *op. cit.*, p. 392.

[276] Gustave Lanson, *L'Art de la prose* (Paris, 1909), pp. 181 f. For a good discussion of the *conte* as a genre distinct from the *roman* see Dorothy M. McGhee, *Voltairian Narrative Devices as Considered in the Author's Contes Philosophiques* (Menasha, 1933).

imaginary voyage and other types of fiction as those mentioned in this section, no final *inclusive and exclusive* definition of the imaginary voyage is possible. It has been a living, shifting, and combining form, analogous, for example, to the essay, which is definable only with respect to a few main characteristics; yet one who knows something of the attempts to define the essay and some of the critical discussions of it can recognize it as a literary form. In a similar way knowledge of the criticism sketched in this book is a better guide for recognizing the imaginary voyage than any single definition could possibly be. Whatever working, tentative definition one adopts, it needs to be interpreted by a knowledge of this background rather than applied literally. Furthermore, the interpretation cannot be wholly free from arbitrary decisions.

In the check list which follows, a conception of the imaginary voyage as a narrative of a voyage performed in the imagination needs to be amplified and interpreted in the light of several qualifications. Length in days or miles cannot be quantitatively specified. The terrestrial voyage should be preferably oceanic, not coastal or thalassic. The geography may be principally authentic (as in Defoe's *New Voyage*) or fictitious (as in *Gulliver*), but it must be geography, not simply an abstract *carte de Tendre* (as in the *Relation du voyage mysterieux de l'Isle de la Vertue*, 1711). I have arbitrarily discarded all imaginary voyaging which confines itself to the Mediterranean Sea (as in Jane Barker's *Exilius*, 1715, or Penelope Aubin's *Strange Adventures of the Count de Vinevil*, 1721); which confines itself to historical naval battles and expeditions (as in *Roderick Random*); and which proceeds directly as intended from one known port to another known port (even though across the ocean) merely for the sake of moving fictitious characters to another country (as in *Moll Flanders*, or George Walker's *Vagabond*,

1799). No stated proportion between the space given to the actual voyage and the length of the whole book is applicable; the account of the voyage must be a part of the action of the story, not simply a one- or two-paragraph summary stating that a voyage has taken place (as in *La Nouvelle Héloïse,* or George Psalmanazar's *Description of Formosa,* 1704). But it must be remembered that the word *voyage* generally includes, by connotation and use, discovery and that therefore the voyage-account continues after the characters have landed. I have also here excluded voyages in verse (such as Dr. Kirkpatrick's *Sea-Piece,* 1750, in five cantos), brief, uncontinued narrative essays in periodicals (as in *The Female Spectator,* bk. xviii, 1745, or the *Gray's-Inn Journal,* No. 102, 1754), and pieces like Horace Walpole's *Account of the Giants Lately Discovered* (1766) and the abbé Coyer's *Letter to Dr. Maty* (1767).

Extraterrestrial and subterranean voyages must be conducted by existent or imagined physical means, whether possible or impossible; that is, I have excluded voyages in dreams[277] (as in Francis Gentleman's *Trip to the Moon by Humphrey Lunatic,* 1764, or in Daniel de Villeneuve's *Vo-*

[277] The qualification about dreams is one of the most difficult to apply; for example, Martigny's *Voyage de Alcimédon* carries an "avertissement de l'Auteur" in which is stated that "tout ce qui est arrivé d'étrange à Alcimédon, n'est dû qu'à une trop forte dose de syrop de diacode. . . . Il dormit . . . quarante-huit heures de suite, pendant lesquelles il fit le voyage que l'on va lire" (Garnier, X, [xv]). However, in the narrative itself he does not go to sleep at the beginning nor does he awake at the end. Without the foreword attributed to the author, no one would have to call this a dream, though it has the vagueness and unreality often present in romances. It is, then, as much an imaginary voyage as *Gulliver* would still be had Swift been so inartistic as to state in a prefatory note that Captain Lemuel had dreamed his experiences. A working test for such fictions might be stated as follows: after removing the prefatory remarks, the as-I-fell-asleep first paragraph, and the then-I-awoke final paragraph, one should try to decide whether the narrative is free enough from the dream atmosphere to justify calling it an imaginary voyage.

yageur philosophe dans un pais inconnu, 1761), voyages by
means of familiar, cabalistic, or Rosicrucian spirits or demons
(as in William Thomson's *Man in the Moon*, 1783; the
chevalier de Mouhy's *Lamekis*, 1735; or Le Sage's *Diable
boiteux*, 1707), and voyages by magic or metamorphosis (as
in the abbé Bordelon's *Gomgam*, 1711, or Mme Marie de
Roumier Robert's *Voyages de milord Céton*, 1765). In general, I have eliminated voyages solely to the land of the dead
(as in Fielding's *Journey from This World to the Next*).
But episodic appearance of any of these situations in a voyage chiefly free from them should not be basis for auto-
matic exclusion.[278]

Aside from implying a subdivision into terrestrial, extra-
terrestrial, and subterranean, which are by no means mutually exclusive categories, I have not attempted any classification of imaginary voyages. Such terms as *romanesque,
marvelous, fantastic, satiric, philosophical, allegorical, realistic,* and *extraordinary,* as employed by Garnier, Atkinson,
Eddy, and others, are useful in critical discussion of style
and content but cannot be logically applied for purposes of
list-making to the whole body of imaginary voyages without

[278] I believe many of these exclusions will appear obvious from common
sense or from necessity of avoiding confusion. Some of them deserve and
get treatment in separate studies of exoticism, orientalism, magic, etc. The
Mediterranean voyages generally involve encounters with and temporary
subjection to the pagans of northern Africa and Asia Minor and derive
strong influences from the Greek Romances; they should be treated in
studies that will carry on the excellent book of Samuel C. Chew, *The
Crescent and the Rose: Islam and England during the Renaissance* (New
York, 1937), or extend backwards such books as Charles Tailliart, *L'Al-
gérie dans la littérature française*, 2 vols. (Paris, 1925) and apparently
(for I have not seen it) Roland Lebel, *Les Voyageurs français du Maroc
. . .* (Paris, 1936). Two probably relevant unpublished dissertations I
have also not seen: Warner G. Rice, *Turk, Moor, and Persian in English
Literature from 1550 to 1660* (Harvard, 1927), and Wallace C. Brown,
*The Near East as Theme and Background in English Literature, 1775-
1825* (Michigan, 1935).

13

utter confusion and futile involution. Even cautious attempts
to employ these terms after arbitrarily defining them have
invariably resulted in trouble whenever the objective has
been categorical classification. Instead of breaking up the
imaginary voyage into various kinds I have thought of it as
itself a division within a more comprehensive category, under which it combines with some of its related types. This
category may be called geographical fiction, comparable in
scope to historical fiction. The student of seventeenth- and
eighteenth-century fiction, by keeping before him a few
broad categories to which smaller groups of fiction contribute instead of continually dividing and subdividing into
smaller types, may achieve a broader synthesis.[279] He need
not abandon the critical terms in common use, for they will
always serve as shorthand means of identifying individual
works and of emphasizing detail. There can be no synthesis
without analysis, and synthesis carried to extremes is useless.
But a list of imaginary voyages without subdivisions should
be more useful to the study of them as a kind of fiction than
a list with many subdivisions so dubious that they foster
interminable dispute.

[279] Compare W. H. Staverman, "Robinson Crusoe in Holland: on the
Two Hundredth Anniversary of the Death of Daniel Defoe," *English
Studies,* XIII (1931), 57. See an interesting list of nearly 400 "novelistic
types well-established in European criticism" in Seldon L. Whitcomb,
The Study of a Novel (Boston, 1905).

PART TWO

Annotated Check List of
Two Hundred and Fifteen Imaginary
Voyages from 1700 to 1800

Annotated Check List of Two Hundred and Fifteen Imaginary Voyages from 1700 to 1800 » » » »

In the preceding pages I have discussed the basis for including the imaginary voyages that appear in this check list. I have included no work on the sole evidence of its title, titles often being thoroughly misleading, or of its inclusion in an earlier list of imaginary voyages. Whenever I have been unable to examine a work itself in some one of its editions, I have required in secondary sources enough information about its contents to enable me to decide whether or not it is apparently an imaginary voyage; lacking this information I have omitted. I cannot be certain that I have always interpreted secondary evidence correctly.

Editions which I have examined are all marked with a "tp" (title page) preceding the abbreviation for the library in which they are held, and for these volumes I assume the responsibility for evidence that they exist under the titles and imprints indicated. I have followed the title pages in punctuation, accentuation, and spelling; in the capitalization of initial letters only; and in the use of Roman or Arabic numerals for dates. I have not indicated differences in fonts, line divisions, or the presence of colors, borders, and devices. I have included names of all the publishers and printers that appear on the title pages though usually omitting, as indicated by ellipses, their street addresses and shop names.

Editions which I have not examined fall into three classes: (1) those located in libraries in the United States: every title or imprint so designated by a library abbreviation not preceded by "tp" has been verified either by correspondence or deputy, and the existence of such editions may be deemed certain; (2) those located in Paris by means of printed catalogues: such information is reliable as far as it goes but is sometimes not specific enough to insure certainty; and (3) those based upon the authority of the bibliographers and literary historians whose names are cited: this kind of secondary evidence varies considerably, and dependence upon it means inevitably that some errors are unavoidable. Occasionally I have had to reconstruct a full title or imprint from two incomplete secondary sources. Fully aware of the dangers in such procedure I have exercised caution against perpetuating errors and against "creating" editions that do not exist. I have not relied on the sometimes-ambiguous terms "8vo," "12mo," etc., as evidence for two different editions, nor have I taken edition notes on title pages as evidence for the existence of an otherwise unknown edition; for example, I have never assumed a second edition on the sole authority of a title page which bears on it "the third edition," for such evidence has proved not always reliable.

I have tried to give the full title of the original edition and of the first translation in each of the other languages in which a book appeared. Thereafter I have indicated subsequent editions only by imprints, except when important changes in the title wording might cause confusion or when my title for an original is fragmentary. *The phrase "another edition" in brackets without specification of language always means in the language of the preceding entry;* otherwise, unbracketed words from the title page clearly indicate the language. The word *edition* is here used in a general (not a "critical") sense to include without distinction issues, reprintings, revisions, abridgments, chapbooks, etc., although I have sometimes noted such variations. Dates in brackets following the imprints, if not explained in the annotations, are the dates attributed by libraries or authorities cited.

I have adopted chronological order regardless of language in preference to the usual system of grouping editions linguistically. Eighteenth-century fiction has a much closer interlingual relationship than is always realized.[1] My system enables one at a glance both to determine the spread and diffusion of each work and to observe possible influences. This interlocking development one cannot ordinarily see under the usual system without reconstructing the chronology on a separate sheet of paper, whereas under my system the continuity in any one language is not sacrificed, for one can simply skip intervening editions in other languages. My system has one disadvantage that may lead to error: whenever editions of the same work in two or more languages are dated in the same year, an arbitrary priority must often be established.[2] Two or more different imaginary voyages published in the same year I have arranged alphabetically by authors' surnames (with anonymous works last), except when knowledge of monthly chronology dictates otherwise.

For some of the major works (*Sindbad, Aboulfaouaris, Robinson, Gulliver, Cleveland, Felsenburg, Klimius, Mi-*

[1] Compare Paul van Tieghem, "La Sensibilité et la passion dans le roman européen au XVIIIe siècle," *Revue de littérature comparée,* VI (1926), 429.
[2] Furthermore, this system works only for a check list or systematic bibliography, not for a critical bibliography—see Theodore Besterman, *The Beginnings of Systematic Bibliography* (London, 1935), p. 1—because if the title pages for Volumes II, III, etc., were to be given, the listing would be complicated whenever the subsequent volumes are dated in different years.

cromégas, Candide, and *Munchausen*) I have not given a
complete check list either because I am unable to add anything to a bibliography already existing in one place or
because the magnitude of the task requires separate study
and separate publication. The two hundred and fifteen
voyages appear in over one thousand editions, but no statis-
tical year-by-year table for the eighteenth century would be
valid now because of (a) the missing editions mentioned at
the beginning of this paragraph; (b) the absence of
eighteenth-century reëditions of imaginary voyages originally published before 1700; and (c) my conservative estimate that the total number of imaginary voyages in the
eighteenth century runs over three hundred. Even a linguistic analysis is at present inconclusive because of the
number of possible imaginary voyages, especially in foreign
languages, which has been unavailable to me for examination. However, the two hundred and fifteen imaginary
voyages may be grouped according to their original languages as follows:

English	67
French	65
German	59
Dutch	10
Danish	5
Swedish	5
Italian	2
Latin	1
Japanese	1

I have not attempted to balance the annotations; they are
long or short and are concerned with author, bibliography,
content, or criticism according to the issues connected with
each work, and some voyages have no comment at all because I have nothing significant to say beyond the fact of

ANNOTATED CHECK LIST 185

inclusion. Except in special instances I have omitted cross references to my text; discussion there should be added to that in the annotations by use of the index. Unless specifically stated otherwise, I have read and evaluated independently every one of the references cited, and all quotations are direct from the indicated sources.

The system of indicating libraries in America follows that of the Library of Congress as explained in *Key to Symbols Used in the Union Catalog,* revised edition by Ernest Kletsch (U.S. Government Printing Office, Washington, 1936).[3] References by abbreviation or by surname will become clear by consulting one of the following three places:

a—the annotation following each imaginary voyage; or
b—the bibliography at the end of this book; or
c—the following special list of check list abbreviations.

[3] A copy of this was given to my by the director, Mr. George A. Schwegmann, Jr., who has kindly helped me also in other ways. The basic plan is outlined by Malcolm G. Wyer, "Standardized Abbreviations for the Names of Libraries," *The Library Journal,* LII (1927), [802]-806, an article which, however, in many details is now made obsolete by the revised system. I urge wider adoption of this *Key to Symbols* in order to avoid the confusion that results from independently contrived systems; the advantages of widespread familiarity with one standard system should be self-evident.

Abbreviations Used in the Check List

ADB: Allgemeine deutsche Bibliothek.

Ars: Bibliothèque de l'Arsenal, Paris (locations based on Jones).

Barbier: Antoine A. Barbier, *Dictionnaire des ouvrages anonymes.* 3 éd., Paris, 1872-79. 4 vols.

Beckmann: Johann Beckmann, *Litteratur der älteren Reisebeschreibungen. Nachrichten von ihren Verfassern, von ihrem Inhalte, von ihren Ausgaben und Übersetzungen* . . . , Göttingen, 1807-10. 2. vols.

Blakey: Dorothy Blakey, *The Minerva Press 1790-1820,* London, Bibliographical Society, 1939.

Block: Andrew Block, *The English Novel 1740-1850: a Catalogue Including Prose Romances, Short Stories, and Translations of Foreign Fiction,* London, 1939.

BM: British Museum, London.

BN: Bibliothèque Nationale (Catalogue), Paris.

Bod: Bodleian Library, Oxford.

Bruun: Christian V. Bruun, *Bibliotheca danica: Systematisk Fortegnelse over den danske Literatur fra 1482 til 1830* . . . , Kjøbenhavn, 1877-1902. 4 vols.

CHEL: Cambridge History of English Literature, ed. by A. W. Ward and A. R. Waller, New York and Cambridge, 1907-33. 15 vols.

CLU: University of California at Los Angeles, Calif.

Cohen: Henri Cohen, *Guide de l'amateur de livres à gravures du XVIIIe siècle,* ed. by Seymour de Ricci, Paris, 1912.

CSmH: Henry Huntington Library, San Marino, Calif.

CtHi: Connecticut Historical Society, Hartford, Conn.

CtY: Yale University, New Haven, Conn.

DCU-H: Catholic University Library, Washington, D. C., Hyvernat Collection.

DL: Dealer's List (used sparingly and confined to a few dealers who publish consistently reliable lists).

DLC: Library of Congress, Washington, D. C.

DNB: Dictionary of National Biography, ed. by Leslie Stephen and Sidney Lee, New York, 1908-9. 22 vols.

Evans: Charles Evans, *American Bibliography: a Chronological Dictionary of All Books, Pamphlets and Periodical Publications Printed in the U. S. A. from . . . 1639 Down to . . . 1820,* Chicago, 1903-34. 12 vols.

GM: Gentleman's Magazine.

GPB: Gesamtkatalog der preussischen Bibliotheken . . . , Berlin, 1931-37. 10 vols.

Gumuchian: *Les Livres de l'enfance de XVe au XIXe siècle* [Catalogue XIII], Gumuchian et Cie., Paris, [1931]. 2 vols.: [I] Texte; [II] Planches.

Halkett and Laing: Samuel Halkett and John Laing, *Dictionary of Anonymous and Pseudonymous English Literature,* ed. by James Kennedy, W. A. Smith, and A. F. Johnson, Edinburgh [etc.], 1926-34. 7 vols.

Heilman: Robert B. Heilman, *America in English Fiction 1760: 1800; the Influences of the American Revolution,* Baton Rouge, Louisiana State University Press, 1937 (Louisiana State University Studies, No. 33).

ICJ: John Crerar Library, Chicago, Ill.

ICN: Newberry Library, Chicago, Ill.

ICU: University of Chicago Library, Chicago, Ill.

IU: University of Illinois Library, Urbana, Ill.

JEGP: Journal of English and Germanic Philology.

Jones: Silas P. Jones, *A List of French Prose Fiction from 1700 to 1750 with a Brief Introduction,* New York, 1939.

Longman: Charles J. Longman, *The House of Longman 1724-1800: a Bibliographical History with a List of Signs Used by Booksellers of That Period,* ed. by John E. Chandler, London [etc.], [1936].

188 *ABBREVIATIONS*

Loshe: Lille D. Loshe, *The Early American Novel*, New York, 1907.

MA: Amherst College, Amherst, Mass.

MB: Boston Public Library, Boston, Mass.

MdBG: Goucher College, Baltimore, Md.

MdBP: Peabody Institute, Baltimore, Md.

MH: Harvard University, Cambridge, Mass.

MiU: University of Michigan, Ann Arbor, Mich.

MiU-C: University of Michigan, William Clements Library.

MLN: Modern Language Notes.

MNF: Forbes Library, Northampton, Mass.

MnU: University of Minnesota, Minneapolis, Minn.

MP: Modern Philology.

MWA: American Antiquarian Society, Worcester, Mass.

NHi: New York Historical Society, New York, N. Y.

NjP: Princeton University, Princeton, N. J.

NN: New York Public Library, New York, N. Y.

NNC: Columbia University, New York, N. Y.

NNH: Hispanic Society, New York, N. Y.

NNS: New York Society Library, New York, N. Y.

NNU-H: New York University, University Heights Library, New York, N.Y.

N&Q: Notes & Queries.

OCl: Public Library, Cleveland, Ohio.

PBL: Lehigh University, Bethlehem, Pa.

Pigoreau: [Alexandre N. Pigoreau], *Petite Bibliographie bio-graphico-romancière, ou dictionnaire des romanciers, tant anciens que modernes, tant nationaux qu'étrangers* . . . , Paris, 1821.

PMLA: Publications of the Modern Language Association.

PPL: Library Company of Philadelphia, Philadelphia, Pa.

Price: Mary B. Price and Laurance M. Price, *The Publication of English Literature in Germany in the Eighteenth Century,* Berkeley, 1934 (University of California Publications in Modern Philology, XVII).

PU: University of Pennsylvania, Philadelphia, Pa.

RCC: Revue des cours et conférences.

RPB: Brown University (John Hay Library), Providence, R. I.

RPJCB: John Carter Brown Library, Providence, R. I.

Ry: John Rylands Library, Manchester.

S: Series.

Sabin: Joseph Sabin, Wilberforce Eames, and R. W. G. Vail, *A Dictionary of Books Relating to America, from Its Discovery to the Present Time,* New York, 1868-1936. 29 vols.

Stammhammer: Josef Stammhammer, *Bibliographie der Socialismus und Communismus,* Jena, 1893-1909. 3 vols.

Stuck: Gottlieb H. Stuck, *Verzeichnis von aeltern und neuern Land- und Reisebeschreibungen: ein Versuch eines Hauptstücks der geographischen Litteratur* . . . , ed. by M. I. E. Fabri and H. C. Weber, Halle, 1784-87. 2 vols.

Tay: Taylor Institution, Oxford.

Tchemerzine: Avenir Tchemerzine, *Bibliographie d'éditions originales et rares d'auteurs français des XVe, XVIe, XVIIe et XVIIIe siècles* . . . , Paris, 1927-33. 10 vols.

Teerink: H[erman] Teerink, *A Bibliography of the Writings in Prose and Verse of Jonathan Swift, D.D.,* The Hague, 1937.

TLS: London *Times Literary Supplement.*

tp: title page.

TxU: University of Texas, Austin, Texas.

ViU: University of Virginia, Charlottesville, Va.

YWES: Year's Work in English Studies.

Short Title Index to the Imaginary Voyages
Arranged Alphabetically by Authors

Author	Name	Date	Language
Anonymous	Aerostatic Spy	1785	English
	Americanische Robinson	1724	German
	Anna Blound	1756	Dutch
	Arabischen Weltweisen	1774	German
	Authentic Relation of a Dutch Sailor	1728	English
	Autonous	1736	English
	Berkeley Hall	1796	English
	Böhmische Robinson (Traunhold)	1796	German
	Chevalier de ***	1768	French
	Constantius and Pulchera	1795	English
	David Tompson	1756	French
	Découvertes dans le Mer du Sud	1798	French
	Diana Therezia	1731	Dutch
	Einiger neuer Seefahrer	1773	German
	Engelænder Berthold	1740	Danish
	Fletcher Christian	1796	English
	Fonseca	1708	English
	Franz Severin van Ditthefft	1756	German
	Glantzby	1729	French
	Gulliver Vol. III	1727	English

Author	*Name*	*Date*	*Language*
Anonymous (*Cont.*)	Gulliver's Narrative in Letters	1728	English
	Gustav Landcron	1724	German
	Haagsche Robinson	1758	Dutch
	Hartz-Robinson	1755	German
	Hollandsche Robinson	1743	Dutch
	Human Vicissitudes	1798	English
	Insul Charlotten-Burg	1753	German
	Jean Peter van Anterson	1740	German
	Jesuit auf dem Thron	1794	German
	Kidnapped Orphan	1767	English
	Leonhardus Mirificus	1751	German
	Maldivischen Philosophen Robine	1753	German
	Maria Kinkon	1759	Dutch
	Mother-in-Law	1757	English
	Nagzag (Christophe Rustaut)	1771	French
	Nieuwe Avanturier	1731	Dutch
	Nil Hammelmann	1747	German
	Nil Stair	1746	German
	Oude en Jongen Robinson	1753	Dutch
	Philadelphe	1755	French
	Piccartus	1755	German
	Pole Arctique	1721	French
	Reise auf dem Lufft-Schiff	1744	German
	Reise eines Europäers in den Mond	1745	German
	Reise eines Philosophen	1764	German
	Robertson aux terres australes	1766	French
	Robinson vom Berge Libonon	1755	German
	Sailor Boy	1800	English

Author	Name	Date	Language
Anonymous (*Cont.*)	Scots Heiress	1791	English
	Solitaire espagnol	1738	French
	Speelhofen der Jüngere	1800	German
	Steyerische Robinson (Joseph Müller)	1791	German
	Teutsche Robinson (Bernhard Creutz)	1722	German
	Thomas Jenkins and David Lowellin	1783	English
	Tyroler	1751	German
	Voyage to the Moon	1793	English
	Walchersche Robinson	1752	Dutch
	Wasobyoe	1774	Japanese
	Winterfield	1788	English
	World in the Centre of the Earth	1755	English
Argens	Législateur moderne (Meillcourt)	1739	French
	Memoires de St. ***	1747	French
Aubin	Charlotta du Pont	1723	English
	Noble Slaves	1722	English
Aunillon	Azor	1750	French
Bachstrom	Inquiraner	1736	German
Baculard d'Arnaud	Makin	1775	French
Balthazard	Isle des philosophes	1790	French
Bancroft	Charles Wentworth	1770	English
Bannac	Crusoe Richard Davis	1756	English
Barnard	Ashton's Memorial	1725	English
Bartholomäi	Gustav Moritz Franken	1769	German
Bawier	Merckwürdige Reise	1752	German
Beaurieu	Eleve de la Nature	1763	French
Belek	Um die ganze Welt	1755	German
Bellgrave	True History	1744	English
Bergeström	Indianiske Bref	1770	Swedish
	Nahkhanahamahhem	1771	Swedish
Berington	Gaudentio di Lucca	1737	English

Author	*Name*	*Date*	*Language*
Bickerstaffe	Ambrose Gwinett	1770	English
Bie	Fra Maanen hjem-komme Politicus	1772	Danish
Bingfield	Travels and Adventures	1753	English
Bordelon	Mital	1708	French
Bowman	Travels	1778	English
Brachfeld	Insul Jaketan	1739	German
Brunt	Cacklogallinia	1727	English
Casanova	Jcosameron	1788	French
Catalde	Paysan Gentilhomme	1737	French
Chetwood	Richard Falconer	1720	English
	Robert Boyle	1726	English
Chiari	Uomo d'un altro mondo	1768	Italian
Coyer	Frivola	1750	English
Daubenton	Zélie dans le désert	1786	French
Defoe	Captain Singleton	1720	English
	Consolidator	1705	English
	George Roberts	1726	English
	Madagascar (Robert Drury)	1729	English
	New Voyage	1724	English
	Robinson Crusoe	1719	English
Desfontaines	Nouveau Gulliver	1730	French
Dibdin	Hannah Hewit	1796	English
D'Orville	Lord Kilmarnoff	1766	French
Dralsé	Divers Voyages	1718	French
Dubois-Fontanelle	Aventures philoso-phiques	1766	French
Ducray-Duminil	Lolotte et Fanfan	1788	French
Duperron de Castera	Theatre des passions	1731	French
Duplessis	George Wollap	1787	French
Durret	Marseille à Lima	1720	French
Engelhardt	Karl Bruckmann	1798	German
Evans	James Dubourdieu	1719	English
Ewald	Ost- und Westindien-fahrer	1798	German

14

Author	*Name*	*Date*	*Language*
Fleischer	Dänische Robinson (Niels Bygaard)	1750	German
	Isländische Robinson (Gissur Isleif)	1755	German
	Nordische Robinson (Woldemar Ferdinand)	1741	German
Fontenelle	République des philosophes	1768	French
Gain de Montagnac	Chevalier de Kilpar	1768	French
Galland	Sindbad	1704	French
Geiger	Erdbewohner in den Mars	1790	German
Gilbert	Calejava	1700	French
Gildon	New Athens	1720	English
Gleich	Edwin und Blanka	1798	German
Gomez	Jeune Alcidiane	1733	French
Goodall	Capt. Greenland	1752	English
Grivel	Ile inconnue (Gastines)	1783	French
Hauffe	Kosakischen Standesperson	1766	German
	Pachterstochter	1776	German
	Verkehrte Welt	1769	German
Haywood	Fruitless Enquiry	1727	English
	Philidore and Placentia	1727	English
Hertel	Jonas Lostwater	1758	German
Holberg	Nicolai Klimius	1741	Latin
Holmesby	Voyages	1757	English
Jakobsen	Dänische Avanturier	1751	German
Jauffret	Rolando	1799	French
Joly	Mathurin Bonice	1783	French
Kersteman	Vrouwelyke Cartouche	1756	Dutch
Kimber	Joe Thompson	1750	English
	Neville Frowde	1758	English
Krook	Fonton Freemasson	1741	Swedish
Lassay	Royaume des féliciens	1727	French

Author	Name	Date	Language
Lesage	Robert Chevalier (Beauchêne)	1732	French
Lesconvel	Prince de Montberaud	1703	French
Lesuire	Grégoire Merveil	1782	French
Lilienstein	Weitbereiste Straszburger	1752	German
Longueville	Hermit (Philip Quarll)	1727	English
Löwenthal	Begebenheiten	1754	German
McDermot	Trip to the Moon	1728	English
Marivaux	Effets surprenans	1713	French
Martigny	Alcimédon	1751	French
Mauvillon	Soldat parvenu	1753	French
Meerheim	Indianischen Insuln	1753	German
Misson	François Leguat	1707	French
Momoro	Nouveau Voyage à la lune	1784	French
Morris, Drake	Travels	1754	English
Morris, Ralph	John Daniel	1751	English
Mouhy	Masque de fer	1747	French
Moutonnet de Clairfons	Iles Fortunées	1778	French
Navarre	Amusemens géographiques	1786	French
Northmore	Planetes	1795	English
Nyrén	Mappa geographica Scelestinae	1786	Swedish
Paltock	Peter Wilkins	1750	English
Pétis de la Croix	Aboulfaouaris	1712	French
Pfeiffer	Graziani Agricolae Auletis	1721	German
Philips	Voyages	1724	English
Pierot	Americanische Freybeuter	1742	German
Piroux	Art de voyager dans l'air	1784	French
Prahl	Lars Larsen (Aagerup)	1758	Danish
Prevost	Philosophe anglois (Cleveland)	1731	French

Author	Name	Date	Language
	Robert Lade	1744	French
Price	Life and Transactions	1752	English
Rabenius	Peter Sparre	1756	Swedish
Raspe	Munchausen	1785	English
Restif de la Bretonne	Découverte australe	1781	French
Reveep	Life and Adventures	1755	English
Robert	Voix de la nature	1763	French
Russen	Iter Lunare	1703	English
Rustaing de Saint-Jory	Femmes militaires	1735	French
Saunier de Beaumont	Innigo de Biervillas	1736	French
Schkolanus	Seltsame und merkwürdige Schicksale	1778	German
Schnabel	Alberti Julii (Insel Felsenburg)	1731	German
Searle	Wanderer	1766	English
Senzion	Schulmeisters Sohn	1760	German
Seriman	Enrico Wanton	1749	Italian
Sinhold von Schütz	Glückseeligste Insul	1723	German
Smeeks	Krinke Kesmes	1708	Dutch
Stanislaus I	Dumocala	1752	French
Stieff	Schlesischer Robinson	1723	German
Swift	Gulliver's Travels	1726	English
Symson	New Voyage to the East Indies	1715	English
Taurinius	See- und Landreisen	1799	German
Terrasson	Sethos	1731	French
Thielo	Charlotte	1757	Danish
	Matrosen	1759	Danish
Thomson	Mammuth	1789	English
Timlich	Österreichische Robinson (Andreas Geiszler)	1791	German
Timme	Wenzel von Erfurt	1784	German
Tiphaigne de la Roche	Galligènes	1765	French
Treby	Unfortunate Shipwreck	1720	English
Turpin	Ceilan	1770	French

Author	Name	Date	Language
Tyler	Algerine Captive	1797	English
Tyssot de Patot	Jaques Massé	1710	French
	Pierre de Mesange	1720	French
Varennes de Mondasse	Cantahar	1730	French
Verdion	Dreszdner Avanturieur	1755	German
	Elias Bendel	1770	German
	Martin Speelhoven	1763	German
	Peter Robert	1743	German
	Zweyer Schwaben	1753	German
Voltaire	Candide	1759	French
	Micromégas	1752	French
Wasse	Char Volant	1783	French
Wezel	Belphegor	1776	German
Whitmore	Modern Gulliver's Travels	1796	English
Willock	Voyages	1789	English
Winkfield	Female American	1767	English

Annotated Check List

1700

[Claude Gilbert (1652-1720)]
Histoire de Calejava ou de l'Isle des Hommes Raisonnables, avec le Paralelle de leur Morale et du Christianisme [Dijon, Jean Ressayre] M.DCC. BN
——— [MS in the Bibliothèque de Dijon.] Lachèvre p. x

On the authority of the abbé Philibert Papillon, *Bibliothèque des auteurs de Bourgogne,* Dijon, 1745, "un Avocat, qui avoit lû quelque chose de cet Ouvrage, dit à l'Imprimeur que s'il y mettoit son nom, il pourroit en être inquiété. Celui-ci remit toute l'Edition à l'Auteur, qui la brula entiérement, ainsi qu'il me l'a assuré plusieurs fois, avec serment, à la réserve d'un exemplaire." This one copy shows, according to Lachèvre, p. x n. 1, that it lacks six chapters or dialogues which Gilbert presumably suppressed before printing. The Dijon MS is a copy of the book. The work is discussed by Lanson, *RCC,* XVIIe an. (1908-9), 1 sér., pp. 219-23, by Atkinson,[b] chap. i, and by Wijngaarden, chap. iii, who, p.95 n.68, reasons that more copies than one exist. Lachèvre, pp. [215]-232, reprints two chapters and lists the titles of all the chapters.

1703

[Pierre de Lesconvel (1650?-1722)]
Ide'e D'Un Regne Doux Et Heureux, Ou Relation Du Voyage du Prince de Montberaud dans l'Ile de Naudely. Premier

Partie . . . A Caseres, Capitale de l'Ile de Naudely. Chez
Pierre Fortané . . . M.DCCIII.   tp DLC, tp BM
———— [Another edition, augmented] Relation du voyage du
prince de Montberaud . . . Merinde, P. Fortuné, 1705.   Ars
———— [Another edition] A Merinde, Chez Innocent De-
mocrite . . . M.DCCVI.   tp BM
———— [Another edition] Nouvelle Relation Du Voyage Du
Prince De Montberaud . . . A Merinde, Chez Innocent Démo-
crite . . . [1706?].   tp MH
———— [Another edition] Relation Historique Et Morale Du
Voyage Du Prince De Montberavd . . . Par l'Autheur des
avantures de Thelemaque . . . A Merinde. Chez Pierre For-
tuné . . . M.DCCIX.   tp NNC
———— [Another edition, first part only] Relation Du Voyage
. . . A Amsterdam, Chez Paul Maret. M.DCC.XXIX. tp MH

For the fictitious imprints read "Paris? or Liége?" Bibliographers have listed at least five other confusing variations in
title or imprint, but these should not be recorded as other editions
until copies are located; see full list in Jones, pp. 7 f., 10, and 16.
The preface of the 1709 edition states that "ce premier Volume
sera suivi, par consequent de plusieurs autres."
Lenglet du Fresnoy, II,276, refers briefly to this work "dans
lequel il prétendoit surpasser en beauté, en caracteres, en morale
& en politique le Telemaque. . . . Le Public, qui n'est pas ordinairement la dupe du médiocre, lui a rendu bonne & briéve
justice." But Mary E. Storer, *Un Épisode littéraire de la fin du
XVIIe siècle: la mode des contes de fées (1685-1700)*, Paris, Champion, 1928 (Bibliothèque de la revue de littérature comparée, t.48),
p.164 n.2, states that "On a cru à tort que Lesconvel y voulait imi-
ter le *Télémaque*. . . ." A long résumé occurs in Gourcuff, and
a discussion in Wijngaarden, chap. iii, who writes, p. 109: "Après
1706 pourtant, personne ne parle plus de sa fiction; à tort, ce
me semble, car l'œuvre de Lesconvel est le prototype de l'utopie
bourgeoise que nous allons rencontrer au moment où les philosophes n'ont plus besoin de fables et de pseudonymes pour la
publication de leurs œuvres." See also Schomann, pp. 69-71.

From the preface of the 1709 edition: "On croit qu'il seroit assez inutile de marquer ici en quelle partie du monde l'Ile de Naudely est située: par qui, & en quel tems la découverte en a été faite, &c. On a gardé là-dessus un profond silence, afin de laisser la liberté aux sçavans de faire sur ce sujet toutes les réfléxions qu'ils estimeront à propos. Ils la placeront, s'ils veulent, dans les espaces imaginaires."

1703

David Russen
Iter Lunare: Or, A Voyage To The Moon. Containing Some Considerations on the Nature of that Planet. The Possibility of getting thither. With other Pleasant Conceits about the Inhabitants, their Manners and Customs . . . By David Russen of Hythe. London, Printed for J. Nutt . . . 1703.

tp DLC, tp BM

————[Another edition] London, Printed for Robert Gosling . . . 1707.

tp MH, tp BM

Prefaces of both editions are signed "March 20, 1702 . . . David Russen." It contains "a detailed account and criticism of Cyrano Bergerac's 'Selenarchia' . . . in the English version by Thomas St. Sere," states G. LeG. N[orgate], *DNB,* where may be found a brief résumé of the plan of the book but no mention of the voyage.

1704

Antoine Galland (1646-1715), *translator*
Histoire de Sindbad le Marin [in *Les Mille & Une Nuit. Contes Arabes. Traduits en François par Mr Galland. Tome III.*] A Paris, Chez la Veuve de Claude Barbin, M.DCC.IV.

Macdonald p.390

Sound reasons might be presented for keeping in a compartment and in a book by itself the subject of oriental influence upon European fiction, but no thorough consideration of the imaginary voyage should overlook the fact that after the publication of Galland's third volume (equivalent to the first half of

Volume II in the later six-volume editions) the story of Sindbad
the Sailor spread rapidly through Europe. Galland had translated it from a MS never identified, had written about it with
mild enthusiasm to Bishop Huet early in 1701, and had later
learned that it was part of a larger collection, for which he sent
to Syria and into the translation of which he inserted the Sindbad voyages (see the dedicatory epistle to the marquise D'O;
Macdonald, p.390; and Zotenberg, p.170). There is also evidence that Pétis de la Croix had translated it in 1701 but never
published it (Chauvin, *Bibliographie*, VII,3). Thus it stands at
the very beginning of occidental knowledge of the *1001 Nights,*
which upon publication were reprinted immediately and pirated
widely. Macdonald's opinion, pp.405 f., on the uncertainty of
its first appearance in English is that a Grub Street hack turned
a La Haye pirated edition into English perhaps as early as 1706,
inventing for it the title *Arabian Nights' Entertainments* ("which
has stuck to the *Nights* in English ever since and was even
translated into Arabic for the Calcutta edition . . . of 1839-42"),
but the actual date is not known. The date of the first German
translation is also uncertain, but probably was about 1710, judging from a dated preface in a Leipzig 1730 edition (Kirby, p.469).

No approximately complete bibliography of editions has been
attempted. Most of the extant 18th-century sets are imperfect in
that they are mixtures of various issues; the edition notes on the
title pages are wholly unreliable. Consequently any attempt to
give here more than the Galland of 1704 would be out of place,
particularly since my concern is with *Sindbad* and not the *1001
Nights.* Of *Sindbad* there were at least seven 18th-century separate editions:

———— [Serially, beginning with the 4th voyage, in *The
Church-Man's Last Shift, Or, Loyalist's Weekly Journal*, Nos.
1-5, May 14; June 11; June 11 to June 18; June 18 to June 25;
and July (i.e., June) 25 to July 2] London: Printed and Sold by
T. Bickerton . . . [1720].   tp CtY, tp BM (incomplete)
———— Geschichte des Sindbad . . . Berlin 1770.
                                           Chauvin VII, 4

———— The Seven Voyages . . . Philadelphia: Printed And Sold By H. and P. Rice . . . 1794. tp MB

———— History of Sindbad . . . Boston: Printed and sold by S. Hall . . . 1795. Evans X,8

———— The Seven Voyages . . . Boston: Printed and sold by William Spotswood . . . 1795. Evans X,8

———— [Another edition] Salem [Mass.], Cushing & Carlton [c.1795]. *Constantius & Pulchera* (1795) p. [56]

———— The History of Sindbad . . . Gainsborough, H. and G. Mosley, 1798. Gumuchian I,387

I know of over forty separate editions since 1800, but this number is clearly so far from complete that there is no point in giving here the detailed list.

From the mass of references to the *1001 Nights,* I have selected those which are valuable to the study of *Sindbad* as an imaginary voyage; those with an asterisk are best:

*C. Raymond Beazley, *The Dawn of Modern Geography* . . . , London, 1897, I,235-39; 438-50.

Robert P. Blake, "Georgian Secular Literature . . . ," *Harvard Studies and Notes in Philology and Literature,* XV(1933), 40 ff.

Bozorg Fils de Chahriyâr de Râmhormoz, *Livre des merveilles de l'Inde* . . . tr. L. Marcel Devic, Leide, 1883-86.

Richard F. Burton, *A Plain and Literal Translation of the Arabian Nights' Entertainments,* Medina ed., n.p.,n.d., privately printed for the Burton Club. Vols. VI and X.

*Victor Chauvin, *Bibliographie des ouvrages arabes* . . . , Liége, Vaillant-Carmanne. Vols. IV (1900) and VII (1903).

———— "Homère et les mille et une nuits," *Musée belge,* III (1899), [6]-9.

Gabriel Ferrand, *Voyage du marchand arabe Sulaymân en Inde et en Chine* . . . , Paris, 1922 (Les Classiques de l'Orient, VII).

*M. J. De Goeje, "De Reizen van Sindebaad," *De Gids,* LIII (1889), iii, [278]-312.

*Richard Hole, *Remarks on the Arabian Nights' Entertainments; in Which the Origin of Sinbad's Voyages, and Other Oriental Fictions, Is Particularly Considered,* London, 1797.

W. F. Kirby, "Contributions to the Bibliography of the Thousand and One Nights, and Their Imitations," in Burton, X,465-531.
Edward W. Lane, *The Thousand and One Nights . . .* , ed. E. S. Poole, London, 1865. Vol. III.
L[ouis] M. Langlès, *Les Voyages de Sind-Bâd le marin . . . traduction littérale, accompagnée du texte de notes,* Paris, 1814. (The 1st ed., in Claude E. Savary, *Grammaire de la langue arabe,* Paris, 1813, lacks the notes.)
Duncan B. Macdonald, "A Bibliographical and Literary Study of the First Appearance of the *Arabian Nights* in Europe," *Library Quarterly,* II (1932), 387-420.
John Payne, *The Book of the Thousand Nights and One Night . . .* , London, 1884. Vol. IX.
E. Rehatsek, "A Few Analogies in the 'Thousand and One Nights' and in Latin Authors," *Journal of the Bombay Branch of the Royal Asiatic Society,* XIV (1878-80), 74-85.
J. G. H. Reinsch, *Die beiden Sindbad, oder Reiseabenteuer Sindbads des Seefahrers . . .* , Breslau, 1836.
O. Rescher, *J. Oestrups "Studien über 1001 Nacht" aus dem Dänischen (nebst einigen Zusätzen) übersetzt,* Stuttgart, 1925.
*Erwin Rohde, *Der griechische Roman und seine Vorläufer,* pp.179 ff., esp. p.180 n.1.
*Baron Walckenaer, "Analyse géographique des voyages de Sind-Bad le marin," *Nouvelles Annales des voyages et des sciences géographiques,* LIII (1832), [5]-26.
Henry Weber, *Metrical Romances of the Thirteenth, Fourteenth, and Fifteenth Centuries,* Edinburgh, 1810, III, 333-45.
H[ermann] Zotenberg, "Notice sur quelques manuscrits des Mille et Une Nuits et la traduction de Galland," *Notices et extraits des manuscrits de la Bibliothèque nationale,* XXVIII (1887), le pte., [167]-233 (reprinted separately, Paris, 1888).

That this "Arabian Odyssey" does not lack its geographical and historical sources is confirmed by the studies of orientalists. Hole, by arguing that it is no more incredible than many occidental tales, gives an early example of the scholarly study of folklore beliefs, although his 18th-century scholarship has sometimes been depreciated (e.g., Émile Galtier, "Fragments d'une étude sur les Mille et Une Nuits," ed. Émile Chassinat, *Mémoires . . . de l'Institut français d'archéologie orientale du Caire,* XXVII, 1912, [135] n. 2). Walckenaer, p. 11, has gone as far as to say, "Je ne trouve dans Sind-Bâd qu'une seule invraisemblance qui me paraisse trop forte; c'est qu'à la fin, il se corrige de la soif des richesses." Payne, IX, 308, believes that "whatever may have been the primitive derivation of the incidents . . . , it appears almost certain that it was suggested by and mainly composed of extracts and adaptations from the writings of well-known Arab geographers and cosmographers . . . ," and Burton, X, 152, brings it even closer to the imaginary voyage by stating that "In its actual condition 'Sindbad' is a fanciful compilation, like De Foe's 'Captain Singleton,' borrowed from travellers' tales of an immense variety . . . ," and by coupling it also with *Robinson Crusoe.* In this latter connection Ullrich[a], p.48, dismisses *Sindbad* because the Robinson-motif is "immer nur in dürftigster Weise behandelt und mit zum Teil uralten Märchenmotiven . . . verquickt." Chauvin, *Bibliographie,* VII, 92, speaks of the imitations as "peu nombreuses en Occident et les auteurs modernes de voyages merveilleux ont puisé à d'autres sources d'inspiration (Edg. Poë, J. Verne, Louis de Rougemont, H. G. Wells). Comme imitation, nous ne connaissons guère que le troisième des sept voyages de Huckaback, dans le Pacha of many Tales de Marryat. Par contre, on a souvent employé le nom de Sindbâd pour des titres mais sans, d'ailleurs, rien emprunter à ses aventures."

1705

[Daniel Defoe (1660?-1731)]
The Consolidator: Or, Memoirs Of Sundry Transactions From The World in the Moon. Translated from the Lunar Language, By the Author of The True-born English Man. London: Printed, and are to be Sold by Benj. Bragg . . . 1705 [26 March].   tp MH, tp BM
——— The Second Edition . . . London, Printed for B.

Bragge . . . [1705, 17 November].   tp MH
——— [Another edition] 1706.   Esdaile p.202
——— [In *Novels and Miscellaneous Works*, Vol. IX] Oxford: Printed By D. A. Talboys, For Thomas Tegg . . . London. 1840.   tp NNC, tp BM
——— [In *The Earlier Life And The Chief Earlier Works* of D.D., ed. Henry Morley. The Carisbrooke Library, Vol. III.] London George Routledge And Sons . . . Glasgow, Manchester, And New York 1889.   tp CtY, tp BM

Apparently no 18th-century editions after 1706 appeared. There were, however, numerous pamphlet extracts, imitations, and continuations (such as *A Journey to the World in the Moon,* 1705), some of which are undoubtedly by Defoe and, according to Thomas Wright, *Life of Daniel Defoe* (New York, 1894), p. 112, "may be regarded as appendices" to the *Consolidator.* I know of no attempt to gather these into one list. Cf. remarks by Marjorie Nicolson and Nora Mohler, *Annals of Science,* II (1937), 426 f., on the spurious *New Journey to the World in the Moon* . . . (London, 1741). Defoe's *Review,* VII, No. 15, for April 29, 1710 (ed. A. W. Secord, Facsimile Book 17, New York, 1938), contains a story allegedly omitted from the *Consolidator;* this was reprinted with some application to local affairs as *News from the Moon,* Boston, 1721. See full discussion by Andrew McF. Davis, "A Bibliographical Puzzle," *Publications of the Colonial Society of Massachusetts,* XIII (1912), 2-15, and Chester N. Greenough, "Defoe in Boston," *ibid.,* XXVIII (1935), 461-93, "an attempt at a partial solution" of the bibliographical puzzle. It has even further (though insignificant) associations with the imaginary voyage by being grouped by some bibliographers (e.g., Sabin, XIII, 322) with a series of contemporary colonial pamphlets dated from Robinson Crusoe's island and having to do with the currency disputes. See Davis, *Colonial Currency Reprints 1682-1751* (Boston, Prince Society, 1910-11), I,59, and II,109-37; and Thomas Hutchinson, *History of the Colony and Province of Massachusetts-Bay,* ed. L. S. Mayo (Cambridge, Harvard University Press, 1936), II, 184 ff.

Acknowledged sources in the *Consolidator* itself are Bishops Wilkins and Godwin. Eddy, pp.23 f., discusses it as a source for *Gulliver* but seems to be mistaken in stating (1923) that the work "is practically unknown, and has never been mentioned in connexion with *Gulliver's Travels.*" In the preface to Cadell's edition of *Robinson Crusoe* (1820) the editor writes that "it certainly contains the first hints of many of the ideas which Swift . . . embodied in Gulliver, particularly in his account of Laputa, the book-making machine, &c.&c," as quoted in Walter Wilson, *Memoirs of the Life and Times of Daniel De Foe* (London, 1830), II, 343 n.D. A contributor to the *Edinburgh Review*, LXXXII (1845), 268, speaks of it as "a prose satire remarkable for the hints it threw out to *Gulliver*," and William Chadwick, *Life and Times of Daniel De Foe* . . . (London, 1859), p. 258, calls it "the model upon which Swift moulded his *Gulliver's Travels.*" (Chadwick gives an extended discussion of the *Consolidator*, pp.251-66.) Hermile Reynald in his introduction to an edition of Borel's translation of *Robinson Crusoe* (printed also in *La Revue politique et littéraire*, 23 Nov., 1878, pp. 486-94) says in reference to the *Consolidator* and the *Voyage to the Moon:* "Swift peut y avoir puisé quelques-unes des idées qu'il developpa dans les *Voyages de Gulliver*," and Angelo de Gubernatis, *Storia universale della letteratura* (Milano, 1883), IX,356, says more definitely: "Swift, che tratta Daniele De Foe come un ignorante, ruba al *Consolidatore* . . . del povero Daniele, l'idea de'regni di Laputa e di Lilliput . . . ." A decade later (1894) Thomas Wright says, p.112: "Perhaps the chief interest of the 'Consolidator' to us lies in the fact that from it Swift got a good many of the ideas which he subsequently embodied in 'Gulliver.' " Finally, referring to Wright's statement, Hermann Ullrich, "Einführung in das Studium Daniel Defoes," *Zeitschrift für französischen und englischen Unterricht*, XIX(1920), 26, comments: "Dieser Hinweis ist von deutschen Forschern, die sich mit Swifts Quellen zum *Gulliver* beschäftigt haben, stets übersehen worden." For evidence that one of Defoe's sources is *A Tale of a Tub* see W. van Maanen, "Defoe and Swift," *English Studies*, III (1921), [65]-69. In November, 1937, Dr. John

F. Ross read before the Philological Association of the Pacific Coast an unpublished paper entitled "Swift's Debt to Defoe: Laputa and the 'Consolidator.'"

1707

[François Maximilien Misson (c.1650?-1722)]
Voyage Et Avantures De François Leguat, & de ses Compagnons, En Deux Isles Desertes Des Indes Orientales. Avec la Rélation des choses les plus remarquables qu'ils ont observées dans l'Isle Maurice, à Batavia, au Cap de Bonne-Esperance, dans l'Isle St. Helene, & en d'autres endroits de leur Route . . . A Londres, Chez David Mortier . . . MDCCVIII [postdated]. 2 vols. in 1.   tp NN, tp BM (2 vols.)
——— [Another edition] Amsterdam, J. L. deLorme, 1708.
2 vols. BN
——— A New Voyage To The East-Indies By Francis Leguat And His Companions. Containing their Adventures in two Desart Islands, And an Account of the most Remarkable Things in Maurice Island, Batavia, at the Cape of Good Hope, the Island of St. Helena, and other Places in their Way to and from the Desart Isles. . . . London: Printed for R. Bonwicke, W. Freeman, Tim. Goodwin, J. Walthoe, M. Wotton, S. Manship, J. Nicholson, B. Tooke, R. Parker, and R. Smith. MDCCVIII.   tp MH, tp BM
——— De gevaarlyke en zeldzame Reyzen Van Den Heere François Leguat Met zyn byhebbend Gezelschap Naar twee Onbewoonde Oostindische Eylanden. Gedaan zedert den jare 1690, tot 1698 toe. Behelzende een naukeurig verhaal van hunne scheepstocht; hun tweejaarig verblijf op het Eylandt Rodrigue, en hoe wonderlyk zy daar af gekomen zijn: Als meede De wreede mishandelingen door den Gouverneur van Mauritius; hun driejaarig bannissement op een Rots in Zee; en hoe zy door ordre der Compagnie t'Amsterdam, buyten verwagting, daar afgehaald en naar Batavia gevoerd wierden. Uyt het Frans in't Neerduyts overgebragt . . . Te Utrecht, By Willem Broedelet . . . 1708.   MiU, tp BM

———— Hn. Francisci Legvat, eines Frantzosen, und seiner Gefehrten Reisen und Wunderliche Begebenheiten nach zweyen unbewohnten Ost-Indischen Insuln. Nebst Einer Erzehlung der merckwürdigsten Dinge, die Sie auf der Insul Mauritii, zu Batavia, an dem Cap der guten hoffnung, auf der Insul S. Helena und andern Orthen, worauf Sie zukommen, angemercket haben . . . Franckfurth und Leipzig, Verlegts Michael Rohrlachs seel. Wittib und Erben, in Liegnitz. 1709. 2 vols. in 1.   MiU

———— [Another French edition] Londres, 1711.

De Richemond p. 3

———— [Another edition] A Londres [i.e., Rouen?], Chez David Mortier . . . MDCCXX. 2 vols.

tp MdBP, tp BM (2 vols. in 1)

———— [Another edition] A Londres, Chez David Mortier . . . M.DCC.XXI. 2 vols. in 1.   tp DLC

———— Der Frantzösische Robinson . . . Franckfurth und Leipzig, Verlegts Michael Rohrlachs sel. Wittib und Erben, in Lignitz 1723.   MiU

———— [Another edition by Friedrich Dürkheim] Leignitz, 1792.   Ullrich p. 116

———— [In *Bibliothèque d'aventures et de voyages*] Publiées Et Annotées Par Eugène Muller Paris Maurice Dreyfous . . . [1883].   tp BM

———— [Another English edition] Transcribed From The First English Edition. Edited and Annotated By Captain Pasfield Oliver. . . . London: Printed for the Hakluyt Society . . . [Vols. 82-83] M.DCCC.XCI.   tp NNC, tp BM

———— [In *Nouvelle Bibliothèque des voyages*] Publiés Par Jacques Boulenger Paris Libraire Plon Les Petits-Fils De Plon Et Nourrit . . . [1934].   tp MH, tp BM

Oliver states, I, xxii, that the MS was "printed and published in London, in French and English simultaneously." Even in the absence of a 1707 title page, evidence points to that year, which is given by Staverman, p. 57, without proof, and by Atkinson, particularly in "A French Desert Island Novel of 1708," *PMLA*,

XXXVI (1921), 511, where he cites two journals that noticed the work in 1707. The *Journal des Sçavans,* XXXVIII (1707), in the "Suplément" for Nov., pp. 394-406, gives a résumé of the edition "A Londres, chez David Mortier, & se trouve à Amsterdam, chez les Waesberge, 1708." Though this bound volume of the *Journal* has M.D.CCVIII on the title page, its 514 pages are numbered serially for the last three months in 1707, the monthly supplements following each month so that the November supplement had to be completed before the December reviews were prepared. Of all the books reviewed in this volume the *Leguat* is the only one dated 1708, though two books dated in that year are mentioned by title only, pp. 217 and 435, as new books. I can find no reasons for believing that these sections of the *Journal* were predated or regularly late. Eugène Hatin, *Histoire politique et littéraire de la presse en France* . . . (Paris, 1859), II, 163, says that the *Journal* from its beginning "continua à paraître ainsi, avec plus ou moins de régularité, le lundi de chaque semaine, jusqu' en 1724, donnant de temps à autre un supplément." The evidence of *Nouvelles de la république des lettres,* XLIII (Dec., 1707), 603-22, is not so convincing because this journal was published by David Mortier, who might easily have reviewed a book in preparation in his own shop. This review, however, deplores the fact that "une main étrangère ait ainsi défiguré" the *Voyage* by additions and false-hoods (p. 606).

Atkinson,[b] chap. iii and appendices ii and iii, and in the *PMLA* article already cited, devotes much care to a thorough investigation of the fictitiousness of this voyage. In the former, p. 138, he implies that there is no mention of Leguat in A. A. Bruzen de la Martinière, *Dictionnaire géographique,* as quoted by Oliver, I, xxvi. But in the preface to the Paris edition of 1768, I, viii, Bruzen puts it in the group of "voyages fabuleux . . . qui n'ont pas plus de réalité que les songes d'un fébricitant." The fact is important in establishing whether or not the voyage has always been considered authentic. Beckmann in his résumé, I,309-35 (and 552n. on Paul Bennelle) defends its authenticity, but says, p. 330, "Aber einige Jahre nachher [i.e., 1708] haben sie manche für eine Erdichtung und den Verf. für einen Betruger erklärt."

15

Haken includes it, III,221-95, with the explanation: "Wirklich stoszen wir hier auf keinen, von einem müszigen Kopfe aus-geheckten Roman, sondern auf eine buchstäblich wahre Robin-sonade." Résumés appear also in Denis and Chauvin, pp. [115]-130, in F. de Richemond, *Les Robinsons français 1690-1698: Paul Bennelle & François Leguat (1637-1735)* [La Rochelle, c.1885-1895?], and even as late as 1925 in Paul Schneider, pp. 47-[89]. British scientists named an extinct bird, once native to the island of Rodriguez, *Aphanapteryx Leguati*, and the *Report of the U. S. National Museum . . . 1893* (Washington, Government Printing Office, 1895), pp. 656 f., cites Leguat as an authority: "All that we know about the Solitaire has been gathered from the journal of Francois Leguat, who tells us. . . ." Atkinson's counterevidence has not, however, been accepted without dispute: see in *Revue de l'histoire des colonies françaises,* XX(1927), 630 f., comment on two articles (which I have not seen) by Cdt. J. Vivielle and Henri Dehérain in the *Bulletin du comité des travaux historiques et scientifiques, section de géographie,* XLVI (1926), 147-77, and also Tilley,[b] pp. 178 f., who states on the basis of secondary opinion that the narrative "does not belong to the category of Extraordinary Voyages." It is also discussed in Brüggemann, pp. 113-21. R. W. Frantz, "Gulliver's 'Cousin Sympson,'" *Huntington Library Quarterly,* I(1937-38), 332 f., n. 14, calls attention to the fact that Oliver in his edition of *Leguat,* II, 183 n. 2, and 284 f., n. 1, takes seriously the corrobora-tive evidence of a nonexistent Capt. Sympson. For information about Misson and his background see Georges Ascoli, "L'Affaire des prophètes français à Londres," *Revue du dix-huitième siècle,* III(1915-16), [8]-28, [85]-109; and Virgile Pinot, *La Chine et la formation de l'esprit philosophique en France (1640-1740)* (Paris, Geuthner, 1932), pp. 400-405.

1708

[Laurent Bordelon, *abbé* (1653-1730)]

Mital Ou Avantures Incroyables, Et toute-fois, & cætera. Ces Avantures contiennent quinze Relations d'un voyage rempli

d'un tres-grand nombre de differentes sortes de Prodiges, de Merveilles, d'Usages, de Coûtumes, d' Opinions, & de Divertissemens. A Paris, Chez Charles Le Clerc . . . M.DCCVIII. . . .   tp MH, tp BM
———— [Another edition] A Amsterdam, Chez Pierre Humbert. M.DCCVIII [imprint fictitious?].   tp DLC, tp BM

Bound with the Harvard copy is *Suite De Mital . . . Contenant, La Clef, deux Lettres, plusieurs Scenes, une Table Alphabetique des noms de plus de cent quatre-vingts Autheurs, citez sur ce qu'il y a de plus incroyable dans ces Avantures*, A Paris, Chez Charles Le Clerc . . . M.DCCVIII. This key, authenticating the incredible adventures, includes such names as Antonius Diogenes, Bacon, Mendez Pinto, LaHontan, Kircher, Mocquet, Odorico, Ramusio, Tavernier, Du Tertre, and Thevenot. Lenglet du Fresnoy, II, 340, calls the author "fort honnête homme & fort mauvais écrivain." Eddy, pp. 205 f., gives a brief résumé.

1708

[Henrik Smeeks (d. 1721)]
Beschryvinge Van het magtig Koningryk Krinke Kesmes. Zynde een groot, en veele kleindere Eilanden daar aan horende; Makende te zamen een gedeelte van het onbekende Zuidland. Gelegen onder den Tropicus Capricornus. Ontdekt door den Heer Juan De Posos, En uit deszelfs Schriften te zamen gestelt Door H. Smeeks. Te Amsterdam, By Nicolaas Ten Hoorn . . . 1708.   tp MH, tp BM
———— Tweden Druk. Te Amsterdam, By Nicolaas Ten Hoorn . . . 1721.   MiU
———— Beschreibung Des Mächtigen Königreichs Krinke Kesmes, Welches eine grosse Insul, nebst vielen dazu gehörigen kleinen Eylanden, in sich fasset, und zusammen Ein Theil Des Unbekannten Südlandes, So unter dem Tropico Capricorni gelegen ist, ausmachet, Worinnen Die seltsame Lebens-Historie Eines Holländers, So in dem 6. Cap. dieser Beschreibung wietläufftig enthalten, erzehlet, Und Nebst der Policey und Justiz,

Gottesdienst, Handelschafft, Auferziehung der Kinder, Sitten und Gewohnheiten der Einwohner, auch sehr vielen andern Merckwürdigkeiten beschrieben wirb Durch Den Herrn Juan de Posos. Darbey zugleich verschiedene curieuse Physicalische, Medicinische, Oeconomische, Politische, und insonderheit Moralische Materien abgehandelt werden, Wegen der ungemeinen Curiositat ins Teutsche übersetzet . . . Leipzig, 1721. Verlegts Georg Christoph Wintzer. . . .   tp NNC
[Between pp. 110 and 111 is a special title page: Der Hollandische Robinson Crusoe, oder Das merckwurdige Leben und Die besonders curieusen Avanturen Henrich Texels Eines Hollanders, *etc.* The running head throughout is: Curieuse Reise-Beschreibung.]
———— [Another Dutch edition] Te Amsterdam, By Samuel Lamsveld . . . 1732.   MiU
———— [Another edition] Te Deventer, By Marienes de Vries . . . [c.1740].   MiU
———— Des Herrn Juan de Posos Beschreibung des machtigen Königreichs Krinke Kesmes . . . Nebst dem Hollandischen Robinson, oder dem merckwürdigen Leben und den besonders curieusen Avanturen Heinrich Texels, eines Hollanders, Welcher auf derselben 30. Jahr lang auf eine hochst-wunderbare Weise in der Einsamkeit zugebracht, von ihm selbst beschrieben . . . in das Deutsche übersetzt . . . [zweyten Auflage] Delitzsch, bey J. C. E. Vogelgesang. 1748.   tp CtY
———— Dritte und verbesserte Auflage. Delitzsch, bey J. C. E. Vogelgesang, 1751.   tp BM
———— Vierte und verbesserte Auflage. Schweinfort und Leipzig, 1776.   MiU
———— [Another German edition] Delitzsch, 1776.   Ullrich p. 105
———— [Another Dutch edition] Te Amsterdam. Gedrukt voor Abram Cornelis . . . 1776.   Staverman p. 180
———— [Another German edition] Leipzig, Gräff, 1785.   Ullrich p. 105
———— [Extract translated by Max Lehnert in *Robinsonaden,*

Bd.5] Der Hollandisch Robinson. Charlottenburg, Raben-
Verlag, 1920. tp MiU

────── [Extract] A Dutch Source For Robinson Crusoe The
Narrative Of The El-Ho "Sjouke Gabbes" (Also Known As
Heinrich Texel) An Episode From The Description Of The
Mighty Kingdom Of Krinke Kesmes, Et Cetcra By Hendrik
Smeeks 1708 Translated From The Dutch And Compared
With The Story Of Robinson Crusoe By Lucius L Hubbard
. . . Ann Arbor, George Wahr, Publisher, 1921. tp NNC

────── [Dutch edition of the preceding] Een Nederlandsche
Bron Van Den Robinson Crusoe . . . Den Haag N. Posthumus . . . 1921. MB, tp BM

After 200 years of undistinguished existence this mighty kingdom arose to become the center of a major controversy among
students of Defoe. The indirect cause was the almost sudden
discovery that the *editio princeps* dates from 1708 instead of 1721,
two years *after* Defoe's masterpiece. The principal steps should
be followed chronologically:

1907–W. H. Staverman, *Robinson Crusoe in Nederland,* chap.
　　ii.

1909–G. J. Hoogewerff, "Een Nederlandsche Bron van den
　　Robinson Crusoe," *Onze Eeuw, Maandschrift voor
　　Staatkunde, Letteren* . . . IX, [360]-412.

　-J. G. Talen, "Holländischer Brief," *Das literarische Echo,*
　　XII, 276 f.

1910–S. P. L'Honoré Naber, "Nog eens de Nederlandsche Bron
　　van den Robinson Crusoe," *Onze Eeuw,* X,[427]-448.

　-Talen, *loc. cit.,* XII,1338.

1914–Léon Polak, "Vordefoesche Robinsonaden in den Nieder-
　　landen," *Germanisch-romanische Monatsschrift,* VI,
　　304-7.

　-Polak, "A Source of Defoe's 'Robinson Crusoe,' " *N&Q,*
　　11S. IX (June 20), 486.

1921–L. L. Hubbard, *op. cit.*

1922–"A Dutch Source for Robinson Crusoe," *TLS,* Aug. 3,
　　p. 501.

–J. W. Krutch, "Source of 'Crusoe'?" *Literary Review*, III, No. 1 (Sept. 9), 12.

1923–Hubbard, [reply to Krutch], *Literary Review*, III, No. 48 (July 28), 870.

  –Hermann Ullrich, [review of Hubbard's *Een nederlandsche Bron* . . .], *Literaturblatt für germanische und romanische Philologie*, XLIV, 18-22.

  –W. van Maanen, [review of Hubbard's *Dutch Source*], *English Studies*, V, 136-39.

  –Julius Goebel, "The Dutch Source of Robinson Crusoe," *JEGP*, XXII, 302-13.

1924–A. W. Secord, *Studies in the Narrative Method of Defoe*, pp. 96-106.

  –Paul Dottin, *Daniel De Foe et ses Romans*, pp. 321-22.

  –Ullrich, *Defoes Robinson Crusoe: die Geschichte eines Weltbuches*, pp. 58-64.

1925–Staverman, "Een Nederlandse Bron van de Robinson Crusoe," *Nieuwe Taalgids*, XIX, [16]-26.

1926–Leopold Brandl, "Krinke Kesmes und Defoes *Robinson*," *Neophilologus*, XI, 28-40.

1929–J. C. van Slee, "De Auteur van Krinke Kesmes," *Tijdschrift voor Geschiedenis*, XLIV, [40]-56.

Before Staverman's book in 1907 *Krinke Kesmes* (Enrikk Smeeks anagrammatized) was regarded as an imitation of *Robinson Crusoe* (e.g., Kippenberg, pp. 45-47), *despite* the fact that in 1898 Ullrich, p. 105, had said the German is "nur eine Uebersetzung, bez. Bearbeitung eines vor Defoe erschienenen Werkes" and had given the Dutch title of 1708 and that ten Brink[a] had discussed it, pp. 439 f., as a work of 1708. Staverman, however, considered it along with several other works both fictitious and true before 1719 and stated conservatively his conclusion that Defoe was not necessarily indebted to any of them. His words, p. 62, are important enough to quote in full: "Mogen we nu uit deze punten van overeenkomst de conclusie trekken, dat Defoe en zijn navolgers die oudere werken gekend hebben? Zeer zeker niet. De vermelde details als elementen in het verhaal van een

verblijf op een onbewoond eiland liggen zóó voor de hand, ze
volgen zóó onmiddellijk uit de omstandigheden, dat ze als
vanzelf den schrijver uit de pen moesten vloeien. Slechts in één
punt zijn, zooals later blijken zal, de reisbeschrijvingen van in-
vloed geweest: de stijl van de Robinsonades is aan haar ontleend.
Doch in dit opzicht dienden niet alleen de bovengenoemde ver-
halen tot voorbeeld, maar de reisbeschrijvingen in het algemeen."
But Hoogewerff, Naber, and Polak saw a certain source in *Krinke
Kesmes*. The two items by Talen are significant only in that they
again called the attention of German readers to the correct date,
as Polak's *N&Q* notice did for English readers. When Hubbard's
arguments appeared with a partial translation in parallel columns,
the storm broke. Van Maanen, Goebel, and the *TLS* agreed with
Hubbard. Krutch objected on principle, Ullrich (in his review)
was unconvinced, Secord made such a thorough study of Defoe's
sources that the case for Smeeks dissolves, and Brandl vigorously
and completely rejected one by one all Hubbard's parallels. The
result of the controversy seems to be exactly as Staverman stated
first in 1907 and again in 1925. For example, three leading Defoe
scholars arrived independently at these conclusions:

"The fairest conclusion possible . . . is that the episode of the
El-ho related by Smeeks has some general and a few specific
resemblances to "Robinson Crusoe"; that it is not at all certain
that Defoe either knew or used the Dutch story; and that, if he
did so, it was of far less service to him than Mr. Hubbard and
others have asserted, since most of the material contained therein
was available to Defoe in English works which we are certain
that he knew and used."—Secord, p. 106; this restrained fairness
conceals the author's evident belief that Defoe had never heard of
the work.

"... il ne s'ensuit pas que l'un des deux écrivains ait imité, ni
même connu, l'ouvrage de son confrère. . . . Nous ne pouvons
raisonnablement conclure que De Foe se soit inspiré de Smeeks.
. . ."—Dottin, pp. 321 f.

"Nach unserer Überzeugung besteht fast gar keine Ähnlichkeit.
Wo stofflich Gleiches vorliegt, ist es ganz verschieden behandelt,

oder das Gleiche ist die Folge der gleichen Situation, die sich bei
jedem Schiffbruch mehr oder weniger ahnlich wiederholen wird.
. . . Wir können diese Robinsonade unbefangen wegen ihrer
realistischen Treue und naiven Darstellung würdigen, auch ohne
in ihr eine Quelle des 'Robinson' zu erkennen."—Ullrich[a],
p. 63 f.

Investigation of whether or not Defoe knew Dutch has centered
in part on his use of the phrase "Den wild zee." That this is
ungrammatical led to ambiguous interpretations until it was discovered that Hoogewerff had explained away the difficulty by
stating that the phrase occurred regularly in contemporary log-
books. The weight of his authority increased so much that it is
necessary to return to his actual words, p. 380: " 'Den wild zee'
voor: 'de wilde zee' is hier geen fout door den vreemdeling
gemaakt, zooals men wellicht meenen zou, maar de uitdrukking
'den wild-zee' komt inderdaad in de XVIIe en XVIIIe eeuw
regelmatig als term in de scheepsjournalen voor." This one sentence without any proof (as Brandl pointed out, p. 30) is too
flimsy a basis for any sound conclusion; besides, no one seems to
have noticed that some (and perhaps all) of Defoe's translators
were so far ignorant of the alleged cant usage that they corrected
the error; see Staverman, p. 39. Heinrich Texel as a name for the
hero is not in the original (Staverman, p. 54 n. 3) and Sjouke
Gabbes is a name bestowed on him by Hubbard. Both are
anachronisms; on this point see Secord, p. 97 n. 330, and Brandl,
p. 29.

1708

Anonymous
　　A Voyage To The New Island Fonseca, Near Barbadoes.
With some Observations Made in a Cruize among the Leward
Islands. In Letters from Two Captains of Turkish Men of
War, driven thither in the Year 1707. Translated out of Turk-
ish and French. London, Printed in the Year 1708.　　tp MB

1710

[Simon Tyssot de Patot (1655-1727?)]
Voyages Et Avantures De Jaques Massé. A Bourdeaux [i.e., La Haye?], Chez Jaques L'Aveugle. M.DCC.X.
　　　　　　　　　　　　　　　　　tp NNC, tp BM
———— [Another edition] A Bordeaux, Chez Jaques L'Aveugle. M.DCC.X.　　　　　　　MiU, tp BM
———— [Another edition] A Cologne, Chez Jaques Kainkus. M.DCC.X.　　　　　　　tp MB, tp Bod
———— The Travels And Adventures Of James Massey. Translated [by Stephen Whatley] from the French. London: Printed for John Watts . . . MDCCXXXIII.　　tp MB, tp BM
———— [Another French edition] Rouen, 1734. Stuck I, 226.
———— Peter Martons, Eines gebohrnen Frantzosen Merck-würdige Lebens-Beschreibung Worinnen viele wunderliche Begebenheiten enthalten. Die ihm in seinem Leben und auf Reisen zugestossen alles von ihm selbst wohl aufgezeichnet und seines Werths halben In rein Deutsch aus dem Frantzösischen übersetzt von A. B. C. [Johann Friederich Bachstrom?] Leipzig und Görlitz, In der Marcheschen Buchhandlung 1737. MiU
———— [Another English edition] Translated from the Original French written by the Celebrated Monsieur Bayle. Being A General Criticism upon Religion, the several Arts and Sciences, Trade, Commerce, &c. The Second Edition: In which are inserted the Passages omitted in the First Edition. London: Printed for J. Watts: And Sold by B. Dod . . . MDCCXLIII.
　　　　　　　　　　　　　　　　　tp DLC, tp BM
———— [Another edition of Peter Marton] Görlitz, 1751.
　　　　　　　　　　　　　　　　　Beckman I,680
———— [Another French edition] L'Utopie [Germany?], chez Jacques l'Aveugle, M.DCC.LX.　　　Lachèvre p. [257]
———— [Chapbook] Printed and sold by J. Davenport . . . London. [176-?].　　　　　　　　　　MH
———— Jakob Massens Reisen in unbekannte länder und merkwürdige begebenheiten auf denselben. Von ihm selbst

beschrieben . . . Alexandrien [i.e., Ruppin] 1799. 2 vols. in 1.
                                                        ICU
——— [Chapbook, added to *Obi; or the History of Three-
Finger'd Jack*] Printed by M. Angus & Son, Newcastle [1820?].
                                                        tp BM

Lanson, who devotes several pages to this work in *RCC,* XVIIe
an.(1908-9), [259]-271, states without evidence that it was published "non pas à Bordeaux, mais en Hollande"; so van Slee,
p. 207 n. 6, and Lachèvre, p. x. The earliest authority I can find
on this point is Prosper Marchand, *Dictionnaire historique* . . .
(La Haye, 1758), I,318 n. 39 (article "Impostoribus"), who calls
it "Mauvais Ouvrage . . . par un Ecrivain très méprisable . . .
& imprimé, non à Bordeaux, mais à la Haie. . . ." The attribution to Bayle is groundless. It is not generally recognized that
Peter Marton is Jacques Massé; see Johann Beckmann, I, 673-80,
and Ullrich, *loc. cit. supra* p. 293, p. 321.

Among early literary historians to call attention to it LeBreton
laments provocatively, forgetting, perhaps, Defoe's ancestry:
"N'en serait-il pas un peu de notre littérature exotique comme de
nos colonies? Combien de contrées par le monde où le premier
qui ait mis le pied était un Français, où des Français ont eu toute
la peine de la conquête et de la colonisation première, où des
Anglais se sont installés ensuite et ont récolté ce que nous avions
semé! On l'a dit avec raison: à l'origine de presque toutes les
grandes découvertes modernes il y a un Français, et presque
toujours les profits en sont allés à d'autres, d'autres en ont eu
l'honneur. Non seulement nous nous laissons supplanter: il faut
encore que nous chantions les louanges de celui qui nous sup-
plante et perdions de vue nos titres de premiers occupants. Daniel
de Foe est devenu du jour au lendemain populaire en France et y
a été regardé comme un initiateur, tandis que le livre de Jacques
Massé disparaissait, au fond de nos bibliothèques, sous une
épaisse couche de poussière" (pp. 362 f.).

Chinard[b], pp. 210-15, discusses it ("réalisme, illuminisme, socialisme se heurtent dans une inexprimable confusion," p. 214);
also Tilley[b], pp. 179-83, and Wijngaarden, chap. iii. J. C. van Slee,

"Simon Tyssot de Patot: Professeur à l'École Illustre de Deventer (1690-1727) . . . ," *Revue du dix-huitième siècle* (1917), pp. [200]-219, is the fullest biographical essay; in it he quotes, p. 207, from F. Reinmannus, *Historia universi atheismi,* p. 588 (which I have not seen), the label "liber atheisticus et scandalosus." With reference to it as an imaginary voyage he writes, p. 216: "Ce roman doit-il être considéré comme l'une des Robinsonnades, antérieure à l'oeuvre de Daniel de Foé? Je déclinerai toute compétence sur la solution de cette question, encore qu'il me semble qu'il y ait bien quelque chose de cela. Mais les dissertations sur les sciences, la religion, la morale, y sont si fréquentes et si étendues, y ont une importance si prépondérante, qu'on ne peut laisser de penser que l'auteur a eu un tout autre but que d'écrire une simple relation de voyage. Il est infiniment plus plausible que Tyssot s'est avisé là d'un cadre commode pour y glisser ses réflexions les plus osées." Van Slee's article was published originally in Dutch in *Nieuw theologisch Tijdschrift,* V (1916), [26]-53.

Atkinson[b], in his full discussion in chap. iv, regards it, p. 70, as a landmark in the development of the French voyage novel, points out, pp. 88 ff., sources in both real and imaginary voyages, particularly Veiras and Foigny, and emphasizes, p. 74, three significant elements of realism: detailed description of relatively unimportant things; mention of a fact without elaboration and later return to this fact, already established, and then elaborating; human touches and natural dispute rather than lengthy argument. Valkhoff, despite his title and his calling it "een avonturenroman," is concerned primarily with philosophic significance, as indicated by his concluding sentence: "Zó dat hij, tijdens zijn leven onbekend, nù mag beschouwd worden als een belangrijke voorlooper van de 'Aufklärung'?"

A recent Johns Hopkins dissertation on Tyssot by David R. McKee I have not seen.

1712

François Pétis de la Croix (1653-1713), *translator*

Les Aventures Singulières d'Aboulfaouaris, surnommé le

Grand Voyageur [in *Les Mille et un Jour. Contes Persans, traduits en François par M. Pétis de la Croix . . . Tome IV*] A Paris, Chez Nicolas Gosselin . . . 1712.   Chauvin IV, 127

Aboulfaouaris belongs in any list that contains *Sindbad,* but the *Thousand and One Days* has no such record of annotated translations and studies as the *Nights,* nor has any complete bibliography of editions been prepared. Chauvin, *Bibliographie des ouvrages arabes,* IV, 127, 219; VII, 60-64, is an important source of information. The first volume appeared in 1710; the work was published in English twice in 1714, in translations by Ambrose Philips and by William King and others (see Duncan B. Macdonald, *Library Quarterly,* II, 1932, 415, and R. H. Griffith, "Persian Tales," *TLS,* Nov. 16, 1935, p. 752), and into German, Leipzig, 1745 (see Walter Schiller, "Über die Märchen von Tausend und ein Tag," *Zeitschrift für Bücherfreunde,* N.F. I, i (1909), [41]-63. On the disputed matter of Pétis de la Croix's source, Macdonald writes: "That he acted throughout in good faith and that he had a Persian manuscript such as he has described, with title *Thousand and one days,* I regard as certain. My assurance is based upon the three prefaces to Volumes I, II, and V, and upon some knowledge of, and experience in, such story literature. . . ."

1713

[Pierre Carlet de Chamblain de Marivaux (1688-1763)]
Les Aventures De * * * Ou Les Effets Surprenans De La Sympathie. A Paris, chez Pierre Prault . . . M.DCC.XIII [-XIV]. 5 vols.   Ars
———— [Another edition] Paris, chez P. Huet, 1714.   Ars
———— [Another edition] A Amsterdam, Pour La Compagnie. MDCCXV. 5 vols. in 2.   tp BM
———— [Another edition] 1719.   Ars
———— [in *Œuvres complettes* de M., Vols. V-VI] A Paris, Chez la Veuve Duchesne . . . M.DCC.LXXXI. . . .
                                    tp NNC, tp BM

"Le récit de Marivaux n'est qu'une naive esquisse de *Robinson*" says LeBreton, p. 359, perhaps following Ferdinand Brunetière, who earlier commented on this relationship, *Études critiques* . . . 3e sèr. (Paris, 1887), p. 177, and J. J. Jusserand, *Le Roman anglais et la réforme littéraire de Daniel Defoe* (Bruxelles, 1887), pp. 30-33. Both W. P. Trent, *CHEL,* IX, 476, and Dottin, pp. 397 f., refer to this as an anticipation of *Robinson Crusoe,* and Mann, p. 117, mentions its similarity to *Quarll.* Studies of Marivaux, concerned with his plays and *La Vie de Marianne,* generally confine comment on the *Aventures* to a few sentences but do recognize him as the author, e.g., Gustave Larroumet, *Marivaux, sa vie et ses œuvres* . . . nouv. éd. (Paris, 1894), pp. 296 f., although the work has been attributed to the chevalier de Mailly and to the abbé Bordelon (under whom the BN catalogues it). Jean Fleury, in his discussion of this work in *Marivaux et le Marivaudage* (Paris, 1881), pp. 13-18, refers to the fact that Marivaux's *Voiture embourbée* (1714) carries the information "par l'auteur des deux premiers volumes des *Effets de la Sympathie.*"

1715

William Symson, *pseudonym*
A New Voyage To The East-Indies: Viz. I. To Suratte, and the Coast of Arabia, containing a compleat Description of the Maldivy-Islands, their Product, Trade, &c. II. The Religion, Manners, and Customs of the Inhabitants, never before related by any English Author. III. Many curious Observations concerning Arabia and India, not to be found in any other Books of this Nature; with Directions for Travellers. By Capt. William Symson. To which is added, A particular Account of the French Factories in those Parts, and of the general Trade throughout all India. With many excellent Remarks by the Sieur Luillier . . . London, Printed by H. Meere, for A. Bettesworth . . . and E. Curll . . . 1715.   tp BM
———— The Second Edition. London, Printed for A. Bettesworth . . . and E. Curll . . . 1720.   tp ICU, tp BM

———— The Second Edition. London: Printed, and Sold by
J. Wilford . . . 1732.   MH

"The method employed was to change the name of Ovington's
ship, to move the date of the voyage into the early eighteenth
century, and to simplify and compress the narrative," writes R. W.
Frantz, "Gulliver's 'Cousin Sympson,'" *Huntington Library
Quarterly*, I(1937-38), 332 n.14, in establishing that the work is
in part a plagiarism from John Ovington's *Voyage to Suratt*
(1696) and that no Capt. William Symson existed. He points
out also other sources and shows that Swift undoubtedly used it
for *Gulliver*. In a *Key, Being Observations and Explanatory
Notes upon the Travels of Lemuel Gulliver* (London, 1726), p.
16n., Richard Sympson is identified by reference to "Capt. William Sympson [sic], his near Relation."

1718

Dralsé de Grandpierre, *supposed author*
  Relation De Divers Voyages Faits Dans L'Afrique, dans
  l'Amerique, & aux Indes Occidentales. La Description du
  Royaume de Juda, & quelques particularitez touchant la vie du
  Roy regnant. La Relation d'une Isle nouvellement habitée
  dans le détroit de Malaca en Asie, & l'Histoire de deux Princes
  de Golconde. Par le Sieur Dralse' De Grand-Pierre, ci-devant
  Officier de Marine. A Paris, Chez Claude Jombert . . .
  M.DCCXVIII. . . .   tp NN, tp BM
  ———— [Another edition, n.p.; device has motto, *Spes nostra
  Deus*] M.DCCXXVI.   tp BM

The *Neue Zeitungen von gelehrten Sachen*, 1718, p. 808, says
"Es ist ein Roman . . . viele Fabeln . . . übel geschrieben," and
in a later number, 1719, p. 306: "Man hat wenig Reisebeschreibungen die so angenehm sind, als diese. Der Autor hat keine
fremden Anreitzungen weder suchen kömmen noch sollen, um
sein Buch beliebt zu machen. Die Historien, oder Histörchen,
welche er in selbiges gebracht, die Gespräche, die Beschreibungen,
vergnügen, ergötzen, erwecken eine Hochachtung vor den sinn-

reichen Autorem, und geben eine gute Idee von seinem Hertzen. Seine Helden und Heldinnen sind freygebig und groszmüthig, und der Ausgang seiner Geschichte ist fast immer erbaulich. Aber darinn vorkommenden wunderbahren Zufälle bringen den Leser auf den Argwohn, dasz mehr erdichtetes als wahres darinne sey, und erwecken einen Zweifel an der Aufrichtigkeit des Autoris." Stuck, I,95, labels it "eine erdichtete Reise mit einigen wahren Nachrichten."

1719

[Daniel Defoe]
 The Life And Strange Surprizing Adventures Of Robinson Crusoe, Of York, Mariner: Who lived Eight and Twenty Years, all alone in an un-inhabited Island on the Coast of America, near the Mouth of the Great River of Oroonoque; Having been cast on Shore by Shipwreck, wherein all the Men perished but himself. With An Account how he was at last as strangely deliver'd by Pyrates. Written by Himself. London; Printed for W. Taylor . . . MDCCXIX[-XX] [April]. 3 vols.   CtY
 ———— La Vie Et Les Avantures Surprenantes De Robinson Crusoe, Contenant entre autres évenemens, le séjour qu'il a fait pendant vingt & huit ans dans une Isle déserte, située sur la Côte de l'Amerique, près de l'embouchure de la grande Riviere Oroonoque. Le tout écrit par lui-même. Traduit De L'Anglois [by Themiseul de Saint-Hyacinthe and Justus van Effen]. A Amsterdam, Chez L'Honnore' & Chatelain. MD CC XX[-XXI] [March]. 3 vols.   tp CtY
 ———— Het Leven En de wonderbaare Gevallen van Robinson Crusoe, Behelzende onder andere ongehoorde uitkomsten een verhaal van zyn agt en twintig jaarig verblyf op een onbe-woond Eiland, gelegen op de Kust van America by de mond van de Rivier Oronooque. Alles door hem zelfs be-schreven, Nu uit het Engels vertaald . . . t'Amsterdam, By de Jansoons van Waesberge. MDCCXX[-XXII]. 3 vols.
              Staverman p. 146

———— Das Leben und die gantz ungemeine Begebenheiten des berühmten Engelländers, Mr. Robinson Crusoe, welcher durch Sturm und Schiffbruch, (worinn alle seine Reise-Gefährten elendiglich ertruncken,) auf der Americanischen Küste, vorn an dem grossen Flusz Oroonoko auf ein unwohntes Eiland gerahten, Acht- und zwantzig Jahre lang darauf gelebet, und zuletzt durch See-Räuber wunderbahrer Weise davon befreyet worden. Göttlicher Providentz zum Preise, und curioser Gemuhter besonderem Vergnügen, nach der dritten Engelländis. Edition auf vornehmes Begehren ins Teutsche übergesetzet [by Ludwig Friedrich Vischer]. Hamburg, gedruckt bey sehl. Thomas von Wierings Erben . . . 1720 [Ostermesse]. 2 vols.   Deneke p. 3.

No attempt is made here to do more than give these first four important editions. The 18th century saw five more translations: Italian (1731), Swedish (1738), Danish (1744), Bohemian (1797), and Serbian (1799). Since then it has appeared in at least 45 languages and, if adaptations (particularly J. H. Campe's *Robinson der Jüngere*, 1779-80) be included, in over 1,000 editions. Ullrich's extensive work of 1898 is not complete enough to offset the need for a new and up-to-date bibliography; this statement may be confirmed by an examination of Ullrich[d]; Hippe; the BN *Catalogue* (1908); W. S. Lloyd, *Catalogue of Various Editions of Robinson Crusoe and Other Books by and Referring to Daniel Defoe* ([Germantown, Philadelphia, Pa., 1915]); Gumuchian; and the DLC and NN card files, to mention only some of the many sources of information. Of first importance for study of early editions is Henry C. Hutchins, *Robinson Crusoe and Its Printing, 1719-1731* . . . (New York, Columbia University Press, 1925); see further his three articles: "Two Hitherto Unrecorded Editions of *Robinson Crusoe*," *The Library*, 4S. VIII(1927), [58]-72; "The Yale *Robinson Crusoe*," *Yale University Library Gazette*, VIII (1933-34), [85]-94; and "Robinson Crusoe at Yale," *ibid.*, XI (1936-37), [17]-36; also Ullrich, "Zur Textgeschichte von Defoes Robinson Crusoe," *Archiv für das Studium der neueren Sprachen und Literaturen*, CXI (1903),

[93]-105, and his review of Hutchins, *Literaturblatt für germanische und romanische Philologie*, XLVII (1926), 281-85; Lucius L. Hubbard, "Text Changes in the Taylor Editions of Robinson Crusoe with Remarks on the Cox Edition," *Papers of the Bibliographical Society of America*, XX (1926), 1-76; Otto Deneke, *Robinson Crusoe in Deutschland: die Frühdrucke 1720-1780* (Göttingen, 1934; Göttingische Nebenstunden 11); and George S. Layard, "Robinson Crusoe and Its Illustrators," *Bibliographica*, II (1896), 181-203 (cf. Rümann).

Not repeated here are the listings of the many books and articles in my bibliography and footnotes which include consideration of *Robinson,* except that, of authors whose titles do not mention Defoe, four should be particularly noted: Dibelius for his chapter in Volume I; Brüggemann, pp. [87]-104; E. A. Baker, III,130-74 and 223-29; and Bonner, pp. 68-92 and *passim.* A few not mentioned elsewhere in my book should be added: Ullrich, "Der Robinson-Mythus," *Zeitschrift für Bücherfreunde,* VIII (1904-5), i, 1-10; Mark Jefferson, "Winds in *Robinson Crusoe,*" *Journal of Geography,* XI (1912-13), 23-25; Ullrich, "Einleitung," *Leben und Abenteuer des Robinson Crusoe,* neue Auf. (Berlin, Otto Hendel [1923]), pp. [v]-xvi; transliterated: M. P. Alekseyev, *Sibir v Romanye Defo* (Irkutsk, 1928), which supplements Secord's discussion of Robinson in Siberia; Hoxie N. Fairchild, *The Noble Savage: a Study in Romantic Naturalism* (New York, Columbia University Press, 1928), pp. 52-56; Charles E. Burch, "British Criticism of Defoe as a Novelist 1719-1860," *Englische Studien,* LXVII (1932-33), [178]-198 (cf. LXVIII, [410]-423); and Ch'en Shou-yi, "Daniel Defoe, China's Severe Critic," *Nankai Social & Economic Quarterly,* VIII (1935), [511]-550. Of innumerable essays in appreciation five seem to me excellent enough for special recommendation: A[lexandre] Vinet, "Robinson," *Revue suisse,* VII (1844), [10]-29; Leslie Stephen, "Defoe's Novels," *Hours in a Library* (New York, 1875), [I], [1]-46; Eugène M. de Vogüé, "Le Livre anglais: Robinson Crusoé," *Revue des deux mondes,* CXXXI (1 oct. 1895), [666]-681; Virginia Woolf, "Robinson Crusoe," *Nation and Athenaeum,* XXXVIII (1925-26), 642-43 (reprinted in her *Second Common*

Reader, New York, Harcourt [1932], pp. 50-58); and Virginia Harlan, "Defoe's Narrative Style," *JEGP*, XXX (1931), 55-73. References to many approaches to *Robinson* other than as an imaginary voyage are comparatively irrelevant; but even those studies which stress social, economic, and religious significance are not wholly irrelevant, for they often throw light directly upon the reasons for the book's popularity; see, e.g., Fr[édéric] Bastiat, *Harmonies économiques* (Bruxelles [etc.], 1850), pp. 99 f., 214 ff., 269; C[lement] L. Martzoeff, "Robinson Crusoe—a Study in the New Geography," *Journal of Geography*, X (1911-12), 295-97; and Henry E. Jackson, *Robinson Crusoe, Social Engineer* . . . (New York, Dutton, 1922). An extensive and fairly complete bibliography of critical material can be acquired by tracing all the references in a majority of the following eight places: Ullrich, "Einführung in das Studium Daniel Defoes," *Zeitschrift für französischen und englischen Unterricht*, XIX (1920), 6-28; Secord; Dottin; Ullrich[a]; Pons, pp. 201-7; Hermann M. Flasdieck, " 'Robinson Crusoe' im Lichte der neueren Forschung," *Deutsche Rundschau*, CCXIV (1928), 47-61; Ullrich, "Zwölf Jahre Defoeforschung (1916-1928)," *Germanisch-romanische Monatsschrift*, XVII (1929), 458-69; and Hans W. Häusermann, "Aspects of Life and Thought in *Robinson Crusoe*," *Review of English Studies*, XI (1935), 299-312, 439-56. (Volume XIII, 1931, of *English Studies* is a Defoe anniversary number.) It must be remembered, however, that there is considerable interdependence in these references and that there are many articles of varying importance still outside what amounts to an established canon of Defoe criticism.

1719

[Ambrose Evans, *supposed author*]

The Adventures, And Surprizing Deliverances, Of James Dubourdieu, And His Wife: Who were taken by Pyrates, and carried to the Uninhabited-Part of the Isle of Paradise. Containing A Description of that Country, its Laws, Religion, and Customs: Of Their being at last releas'd; and how they came to Paris, where they are still living. Also, The Adventures of Alexander Vendchurch, Whose Ship's Crew Rebelled against him, and set him on Shore on an Island in the South-Sea, where he liv'd five Years, five Months, and seven Days; and was at last providentially releas'd by a Jamaica Ship. Written by Himself. London: Printed by J. Bettenham for A. Bettesworth and T. Warner . . . C. Rivington . . . J. Brotherton and W. Meadows . . . A. Dodd . . . and W. Chetwood . . . 1719 [October].   M;U

Lucius L. Hubbard has made a brief study of this work (or, more accurately, these works) in *Notes on the Adventures . . . of James Dubourdieu . . . a Source for Gulliver . . .*, Ann Arbor [for private distribution], 1927. He states that the text is signed by "Ambrose Evans." Ullrich[a], p. 87, calls the Dubourdieu story the first robinsonade. That a real "Alexander Vendchurch" could have written autobiographically about island solitude in October, 1719, would be an incredible coincidence.

1720

[William Rufus Chetwood (d. 1766)]
The Voyages, Dangerous Adventures, And imminent Escapes Of Captain Richard Falconer: Containing The Laws, Customs, and Manners of the Indians in America; his Shipwrecks; his Marrying an Indian Wife; his narrow Escape from the Island of Dominico, &c. Intermix'd with The Voyages and Adventures of Thomas Randal, of Cork, Pilot; with his Shipwreck in the Baltick, being the only Man that escap'd: His being taken by the Indians of Virginia, &c. Written by Himself, now alive . . . London, Printed for W. Chetwood . . . T. Jauncy . . . A. Bettesworth . . . J. Brotherton, and W. Meadows . . . and J. Graves . . . 1720 [December, 1719?].
                                        tp NN, tp BM
———— The Second Edition Corrected. London: Printed for J. Marshal . . . W. Chetwood . . . N. Cox . . . and T. Edlin . . . MDCCXXIV.   ICN, tp BM

———— Third Edition. London, 1734.   Sabin VI,346
———— The Fourth Edition Corrected. To which is added, A
Great Deliverance at Sea, by William Johnson, D.D. . . . Lon-
don: Printed for J. Marshall . . . MDCCXXXIV.   tp NN
———— Richard Falconers Erstaunliche Seefahrten, seltsame
Begebenheiten und wunderbare Errettung deme beygefüget
Thomas Randals Schiffbruch, aus dem Englischen übersetzt
von Theodor Arnold. Leipzig, im Weidmannischen Buch-
laden, 1743.   Ullrich p. 102
———— The Fifth Edition Corrected. London: Printed for
G. Keith . . . 1764.   Ullrich p. [101]
———— The Sixth Edition, Corrected . . . London: Printed
for G. Keith . . . and F. Blyth . . . 1769.   tp DLC
———— Richard Falconers eines Englischen See-Hauptmanns
Erstaunliche Seefahrten . . . Frankfurt und Leipzig, bey Hein-
rich Ludwig Brönner, 1778.   tp MH
———— [Chapbook] Manchester: J. Imison, 1785. Sabin VI,346
———— [Another English edition] London: Printed and Sold
by S. Fisher . . . also sold by T. Hurst . . . and Wilmott and
Hill . . . [1801].   tp NN
———— Fifth Edition, Reprinted From That of 1734 London:
Edward Churton . . . MDCCCXXXVIII.   tp MNF
———— [Another edition] Thrilling Adventures of a Somerset-
shire Lad [Edinburgh?, 18-?]   De la Mare p. 226

Sir Walter Scott in a letter of November 10, 1814, to Daniel
Terry expresses much joy at receiving a copy of this work, on the
flyleaf of which, according to J. G. Lockhart, *Memoirs of the
Life of Sir Walter Scott* (Boston and New York, Houghton
Mifflin, 1902), III,8 n. 1, he wrote: "This book I read in early
youth. I am ignorant whether it is altogether fictitious and
written upon De Foe's plan, which it greatly resembles, or
whether it is only an exaggerated account of the adventures of
a real person. It is very scarce. . . . Yet Richard Falconer's adventures seem to have passed through several editions." It was
so much the delight of Scott that, according to De la Mare, he
reprinted it at his own expense under the title of the *Thrilling*

Adventures . . . , although he knew it in the fourth edition under its right name. Possibly a chapbook version is involved in the change.

A reading of it leaves no doubt of its fictitiousness. James S. Clarke in *Naufragia or Historical Memoirs of Shipwrecks* . . . (London, 1805-6) prints a long résumé, I,259-365, and states, II,xiv, that "it has never been considered as an authentic Narrative throughout; but as one, in which real Facts have been combined. . . ." Watson, p. 113, says that Esquemeling's *Buccaneers of America* is a principal source; Bonner, pp. 184-89, shows that Dampier was used generously; and Engel, p. 134, names Richard Ligon, *History of the Island of Barbadoes* (1657). It is sometimes, however, considered in histories of true voyages, as in Cyrus Redding, *A History of Shipwrecks, and Disasters at Sea, from the Most Authentic Sources* (London, 1835), IV, [1]-91, and in Rogers, pp. 58-75, where it is called "a work whose authenticity cannot be vouched for, but which, nevertheless, is too rare and diverting to be omitted on that score" (p. 58). I think there is no basis for his note on the same page: "This book is believed to have been printed prior to *Robinson Crusoe."* The preface of the first edition is dated at Canterbury, November 7, 1719. Prica, pp. 9-12, compares it sketchily with *Robinson.* A condensation may be found in Chambers's *Miscellany of Instructive & Entertaining Tracts,* ed. W. and R. Chambers, new ed. (London and Edinburgh [c.1870]), Vol. III, No. 45. See also Benjamin Bissell, *The American Indian in English Literature of the Eighteenth Century* (New Haven [etc.], Yale University Press, 1925), pp. 84-87. The addition in the fourth edition is a reprinting of *Deus nobiscum,* a sermon by a chaplain to Charles II.

1720

[Daniel Defoe]

The Life, Adventures, And Pyracies, Of the Famous Captain Singleton: Containing an Account of his being set on Shore in the Island of Madagascar, his Settlement there, with a Description of the Place and Inhabitants: Of his Passage from thence,

in a Paraguay, to the main Land of Africa, with an Account of
the Customs and Manners of the People: His great Deliverances
from the barbarous Natives and wild Beasts: Of his meeting
with an Englishman, a Citizen of London, among the Indians,
the great Riches he acquired, and his Voyage Home to England: As also Captain Singleton's Return to Sea, with an Account of his many Adventures and Pyracies with the famous
Captain Avery and others. London: Printed for J. Brotherton
. . . J. Graves . . . A. Dodd . . . and T. Warner . . . 1720
[June].   tp DLC, tp BM
———— [Serially in *The Post-master; Or, The Loyal Mercury*,
beginning in No. 15, Friday, Nov. 4] Exon, Printed by Andrew
Brice . . . 1720.   tp BM (incomplete)
———— [Another edition] London, Printed and sold by Na-
thaniel Mist, 1721.   Esdaile p. 206
———— The Second Edition. London: Printed for John King
. . . and Thomas King . . . 1737.   TxU, tp BM
———— Third Edition. London, 1754.   Sabin V, 311
———— The Third Edition. London: Printed for F. Noble
. . . J. Noble . . . T. Lowndes . . . and J. Johnson and B.
Davenport . . . MDCCLXVIII.   tp CtY, tp BM
———— [Another edition] London: Printed by T. Maiden . . .
For Ann Lemoine . . . And Sold by T. Hurst . . . [c.1800].
                                                      tp BM
———— [Another edition] New-York: Printed for Christian
Brown . . . 1802.   CSmH
———— [In *Novels of D.D.*, Vols. VIII-IX] Edinburgh:
Printed by James Ballantyne and Co. For John Ballantyne And
Co. And Brown And Crombie . . . Longman, Hurst, Rees,
And Orme, And John Murray, London. 1810. tp NNC, tp BM
———— [Another edition] New York: Published By Evert
Duyckinck . . . George Long, Printer. 1815.   tp MH
———— [Another edition] Baltimore: Printed by William
Warner . . . [c.1815?].   MWA
———— [Another edition] London: Published By J. Clements
. . . MDCCCXXXIX.   tp Bod
———— [In *The Romancist, and Novelist's Library*, Vol. I, Nos.

11-13] London: Printed By C. Reynell . . . [and published by] J. Clements . . . MDCCCXXXIX.   tp Bod

———— [In *Novels and Miscellaneous Works of D. D.,.* Vol. III] Oxford: Printed By D. A. Talboys, For Thomas Tegg . . . London. 1840.   tp NNC, tp BM

———— [In *Works of D. D.,* ed. William Hazlitt, Vol. II] London: John Clements . . . MDCCCXLI.   tp NN, tp BM

———— [In *D. D.'s Gesammelte Romane,* Bd. 1] Stuttgart, Chr. Belsersche Buchhandlung, 1842.   Ullrich *infra* p. 35

———— Robert und seine Gefährten. Eine Erzählung für die Jugend . . . Nach dem Englischen . . . Stuttgart, Chr. Belsersche Buchhandlung, 1843.   Ullrich *infra* p. 35

———— [In *Novels and Miscellaneous Works* of D. D., Vol. I, Bohn's British Classics] London: Henry G. Bohn . . . MDCCCLIV.   tp NNC, tp BM

———— [In *Novels and Miscellaneous Works,* Vol. I, Bohn's Standard Library] London, G. Bell and Sons, 1880 [more reprintings?].   DLC

———— [Ed. H. Halliday Sparling, in The Camelot Series ed. Ernest Rhys] London Walter Scott . . . 1887. tp NNC, tp BM

———— [In *Romances and Narratives by D. D.,* ed. G. A. Aitken, Vol. VI] London Published by J. M. Dent & Co. . . . MDCCCXCV.   tp NNC, tp BM

———— [In *The Penny Library of Famous Books,* nos. 164-5, ed. C. S. C.] George Newnes Limited . . . London . . . [1899].   tp Bod

———— [In *Romances and Narratives,* ed. Aitken, 2d ed.] 1900.   DL

———— [In *Works* of D. D., ed. G. H. Maynadier, Vol. VI] Limited Edition New York George D. Sproul MCMIII. tp MB

———— [Another edition of the preceding, Vol. VI] New York Fred DeFau & Company [c.1903].   tp MH

———— [Another edition of the preceding, Vol. VI] Boston David Nickerson Company [c.1903].   tp MH, tp Ry

———— [Another edition of the preceding, Vol. III] The C. T. Brainard Publishing Co. Boston New York [1904].   NNC

———— [Another edition of the preceding, Vol. VI] New York

Thomas Y. Crowell & Company [c.1904].   MH (lost)
———— [In *Romances and Narratives,* ed. Aitken, 3d ed.]
London Published by J. M. Dent & Co. MDCCCCIV.   MH
———— [In The Boy's Classics, XI] Henry Frowde Oxford
University Press London, New York And Toronto [1906].
                                              tp BM
———— [In Everyman's Library, No. 74, ed. Edward Garnett]
London: Published by J. M. Dent & Co And In New York By
E. P. Dutton & Co. [1906; many reprintings]. tp NNC, tp BM
———— [In the World's Classics, No. 82, ed. Theodore Watts-
Dunton] Henry Frowde, Oxford University Press London,
New York And Toronto [1906; many reprintings].
                                         tp NNC, tp BM
———— [In *Works,* ed. G. H. Maynadier, Vol. VI] New York
The Jenson Society MCMVII.   tp NNU-H
———— [Abridged, in Blackie's English Texts, ed. W. H. D.
Rouse] Blackie & Son Limited . . . London . . . Glasgow and
Dublin 1909.   tp Bod
———— [In Lebensbücher der Jugend, Bd.26] Kapitän Bobs
erste fahrt oder Quer durch das dunkelste Afrika . . . neu
bearbeitet von Otto Zimmermann . . . Braunschweig, Verlag
von George Westermann [c.1914].   tp DLC
———— Daniel Defoe Kapten Bobs Färder Och Äventyr I
Afrika Bearbetning Av Elias Grip Stockholm Åhlén & Åker-
lunds Förlags A.B. [Andra Upplagan, 1917].   tp BM
———— [In Collection littéraire des romans d'aventures] Les
Pirateries Du Capitaine Singleton Traduction De Maurice
Dekohra . . . Paris L'Édition Française Illustrée . . . [G. Crès
et cie., c.1920].   tp CtY
———— [In *The Shakespeare Head Edition of the Novels . . .
of D.D.*] Oxford: Basil Blackwell Publisher to the Shakespeare
Head Press of Stratford-Upon-Avon 1927.   tp NNC, tp BM
———— [In Daniel Defoe: Freebooters and Buccaneers: Novels
of Adventure and Piracy] New York, The Dial Press, 1935.
                                              tp DLC

This incomplete list needs revision based on a more thorough examination of all editions than I have been able to make. The two German editions for which Ullrich is cited as authority are given in his "Unbekannte Übersetzungen von Schriften Daniel Defoés," *Zeitschrift für Bücherfreunde,* IV (1900-1901), i, [32]-35. For valuable discussions, besides prefaces and treatment of Defoe's fiction in general, see Secord, chap. iii; Dottin, pp. [615]-644; Roorda, chap. iv; J. N. L. Baker, pp. 263-66; and Bonner, pp. 100-110 and *passim.* Cf. my annotation under *Robinson Crusoe.* For briefer comment see Robert P. Utter, "On the Alleged Tediousness of Defoe and Richardson," *University of California Chronicle,* XXV (1923), 179-81.

1720

[Le Sieur Durret]

Voyage De Marseille A Lima, Et Dans Les Autres Lieux Des Indes Occidentales. Avec une exacte Description de ce qu'il y a de plus remarquable tant pour la Geographie, que pour les Mœurs, les Coûtumes, le Commerce, le Gouvernement & la Religion des Peuples; avec des notes . . . Par le Sieur D * * * A Paris, Chez Jean-Baptiste Coignard . . . M.DCCXX. . . .

tp NNC, tp BM

The author explains in the preface that "Le fond de cette Relation est du sieur Bachelier, Chirurgien de la ville de Bourg en Bresse; mais les changemens que j'y ai fait pour adoucir le style, & les notes que j'y ai ajoûtées, doivent la faire regarder comme un ouvrage tout nouveau . . ." (p. ix). This claim to authenticity is vigorously exploded by Jean Baptiste Labat in his *Nouveau Voyage aux isles de l'Amerique* . . . (La Haye, 1724), I,v-xxi. Durret's inventions make him one of "ces Ecrivains qui voyagent sans sortir de leurs maisons. . . . Comme il est trop connu pour hazarder de dire qu'il a fait le Voyage en personne, il se cache sous le nom du nommé Bachelier Chirurgien de Bourg en Bresse, qu'il suppose avoir fait ce Voyage en 1707. . . ." Labat lists his sources, points out that, had he followed them more faithfully, "il ne seroit pas tombé dans une infinité de bevûës & de contradictions qu'on trouve à chaque ligne," and makes a final thrust with "C'est dommage que cet Auteur n'a pas lû Cyrano de Bergerac." Barbier, IV, 1075, does not question Labat's reliability.

1720

[Charles Gildon (1665-1724), *supposed author*]
A Description Of New Athens In Terra Australis incognita. By one who resided many Years upon the Spot [in *Miscellanea Aurea: Or The Golden Medley. Consisting of . . . II. The Fortunate Shipwreck, or a Description of New Athens, being an Account of the Laws, Manners, Religion, and Customs of that Country; by Morris Williams, Gent. who resided there above Twenty Years. . . .*] London: Printed for A. Bettesworth . . . and J. Pemberton. . . . MDCCXX.

tp NNC, tp BM

Morris (or Maurice in the text) Williams is a pseudonym. Parts of the *Miscellanea Aurea* have been ascribed to Thomas Killigrew. No. I, *A Voyage to the Mountains of the Moon . . .* , is a dream.

1720

H. Treby, *pseudonym*
Mr. H. Treby's Narrative of his Unfortunate Shipwreck and Distress, &c. [serially in *The Post-master; Or, The Loyal Mercury*] Exon, Printed by Andrew Brice . . . 1720 [-24].   Wiles

According to Roy McK. Wiles, *Prose Fiction in English Periodical Publications before 1750* (unpublished Harvard dissertation, 1933), II, 431, this narrative was resumed, after an interruption, in No. 193, October 2, 1724, and ended in No. 198, November 6 of the same year. I cannot trace it in the broken set in the Burney Collection at the BM, which does not contain Nos. 193 and 198. The date of No. 1 should be July 29, 1720. Nos. 6 (Sept. 2, 1720), 7, and 9 contain a sea-voyage narrative, which was broken off abruptly in order that the editors might serialize

Captain Singleton beginning with No. 15. It is only a conjecture on my part that the narrative cited by Wiles is a resumption of the one begun in 1720 before *Singleton* attracted the editor's attention. Though this conjecture may be wrong, there is almost certainly one imaginary voyage here, and perhaps there are two.

1720

[Simon Tyssot de Patot]
  La Vie, Les avantures, & le Voyage De Groenland Du Révérend Pere Cordelier Pierre De Mesange. Avec une Relation bien circonstanciée de l'origine, de l'histoire, des mœurs, & du Paradis des Habitans du Pole Arctique. A Amsterdam, Aux Depens d'Etienne Roger . . . M.D.CCXX. 2 vols.

tp NN, tp BM (2 vols. in 1)

———— Des Robinson Crusoe Dritter und Vierter Theil, Oder, Lustige und seltsame Lebens-Beschreibung Peter Von Mesange, Worinnen Er seine Reise nach Grönland und andern Nordischen Ländern, nebst dem Ursprung, Historien, Sitten, und vornemlich das Paradies derer Einwohner des Poli critici, nebst vielen ungemeinen Curiositäten, artig und wohl beschreibet . . . Leyden, Bey Peter Robinson [Moritz Georg Weidmann], 1721. 2 vols.   MiU

For discussions of this see the same books and articles (subsequent pages) referred to on my pp. 218-19, especially Atkinson[b], chap. v, where it is called the first French extraordinary voyage laid in the north. Kippenberg says, pp. 66 f., that the author sets forth his philosophical ideas "in Form einer imaginären Reise" but that "man fühlte bald, dasz es 'gantz keine *Connexion*' mit dem eigentlichen Robinson habe." Van Slee writes, p. 217: "Tyssot a voulu indiquer sans doute que l'empire de la pensée libre et raisonnée s'étend aussi bien aux glaces du pôle Nord qu'aux régions de l'hémisphère austral, au moment où les suppôts de l'intolérance ne voulaient le situer nulle part. Mais, somme toute, la composition relâchée et l'élaboration un peu gauche . . . souligne bien clairement que c'est une œuvre de la vieillesse." Brüggemann, pp. 173-76, discusses it as a utopian romance.

1721

[Johann Gregor Pfeiffer]
Graziani Agricolae Auletis Sonderbahre Reisen In unbekandte Länder, Aus Richtig gehaltenen Diariis, auffgezeichneten Anmerckungen, und angemerckten Entdeckungen, Theils zum eigenen Zeit-Vertreib; Theils aber auch zum Vergnügen anderer Liebhaber abgefasst und an das Licht gestellet . . . Gedruckt zu Hanochia, in der Ophirischen Landschafft Canaan [Bremen?], 1721 [-22]. 3 vols.   tp BM

In three parts, a volume each: *Von der Reise in Ophir; Von der Reise in Crapulien; Von der Reise in den Staat der Sevaramber.* Paludan, p. 48, cites this as an example of German imaginary voyages which imitated *Sévarambes* as a framework model for philosophic and theological reflections. It has also other obvious sources, such as Hall's *Mundus alter et idem.*

1721

Anonymous
Relation D'Un Voyage Du Pole Arctique, Au Pole Antarctique, Par Le Centre Du Monde, Avec la description de ce périlleux Passage, & des choses merveilleuses & étonnantes qu'on a découvertes sous le Pole Antarctique . . . A Amsterdam, Chez N. Etienne Lucas . . . M.DCC.XXI.
                                                      tp DLC, tp BM
———— [Another edition] A Paris, chez Gabriel Amaulry . . . M.DCC.XXIII.   tp NN
———— [Another edition] A Paris, Chez Noel Pissot. . . . M.DCC.XXIII. . . .   RPJCB
———— Seconde Edition. A La Haye, Chez Gerard Block . . . MDCC XXX IV.   tp MH
———— [In *Voyages imaginaires,* ed. Garnier, Vol. XIX] A

Amsterdam, Et se trouve à Paris . . . M.DCC.LXXXVIII.
                                        tp NNC, tp BM

Garnier, pp. xiii f., makes the obvious comparison with Holberg's subterranean voyage, than which, according to Chinard[b],
p. 409 f., this anonymous work has "plus de vérité."

1722

Penelope Aubin
The Noble Slaves: Or, The Lives and Adventures Of Two
Lords and two Ladies, who were shipwreck'd and cast upon
a desolate Island near the East-Indies, in the Year 1710. The
Manner of their living there: The surprizing Discoveries they
made, and strange Deliverance thence. How in their return to
Europe they were taken by two Algerine Pirates near the
Straits of Gibraltar. Of the Slavery they endured in Barbary;
and of their meeting there with several Persons of Quality,
who were likewise Slaves. Of their escaping thence, and safe
Arrival in their respective Countries, Venice, Spain, and France,
in the Year 1718. With many extraordinary Accidents that
befel some of them afterwards. Being a History full of most
remarkable Events. By Mrs. Aubin. London: Printed for E.
Bell, J. Darby, A. Bettesworth, F. Fayram, J. Pemberton, J.
Hooke, C. Rivington, F. Clay, J. Batley, and E. Symon.
M.DCC.XXII.   tp MB, tp BM
———— [Another edition] Dublin: Printed By William Jones
. . . [1730?].   tp BM
———— [In *A Collection of Entertaining Histories and Novels,*
by Mrs. Aubin, Vol. I] London: Printed for D. Midwinter,
A. Bettesworth and C Hitch, J. and J. Pemberton, R. Ware,
C. Rivington, A. Ward, J. and P. Knapton, T. Longman, R.
Hett, S. Austen, and J. Wood. MDCCXXXIX.   MA
———— [In *A Collection of Novels,* Selected and Revised by
Mrs. Elizabeth Griffith, Vol. III] London: Printed for G.
Kearsly . . . MDCCLXXVII.   tp BM
———— [Another edition] Boston, 1797.   Evans XI, 257

————— [Another edition] Danbury: Re-printed by Douglas & Nichols [c.1797].   MWA

————— [Another edition] New-Haven, Printed by Geo. Bunce, 1797.   Evans XI,257

————— [Another edition] New-York: Printed And Sold By John Tiebout . . . 1800.   tp CtY

————— [Another edition] New-York: Printed For Everet Duyckinck. 1806.   tp DLC

————— [Another edition] Belfast: Printed For Simms And M'Intyre. 1812.   tp Bod

————— [Another edition] New-York: Printed for E. Duyckinck . . . By Nicholas Van Riper. 1814.   tp DLC

Briefly considered by Prica, pp. 13 f.

1722

Anonymous

Der Teutsche Robinson Oder Bernhard Creutz das ist Eines übelgearteten Jünglings seltsame Lebens-Beschreibung Darinnen Seine Geburt, Auferziehung, Lehr-Jahre, höchstgefährliche Reisen, Ordens-Standt, Heyrathen, Schiffbruch, Judenthum, Hohe Erhebung, jählinger Fall, verwunderungs-würdige Fata und Begebenheiten erzehlet. Und nebst einer neuen Welt, deroselben Fruchtbarkeit, Justitz-Policey, Sitten, Gewohnheiten und geführte Kriege. Mit glaubwürbiger Feder beschrieben. . . . Hall in Schwaben, Zu finden bey Joh. Ferd. Galli [1722].   Ullrich p. 106

————— Neue Ausgabe, 1727.   Haken IV, [1]

————— Neue Ausgabe, 1737.   Kippenberg p. vii

————— [*In Robinsonaden: eine Sammlung von Abenteurergeschichten* . . . ed. Maximilian Lehnert, Bd.1] Charlottenburg, Raben-Verlag, 1916.   CtY

Discussed in Kippenberg, chap. iv *passim,* and in Brüggemann, pp. 108-10, who says "Das Buch enthält also eigentlich zwei Robinsonaden." Apparently there was also a "first" edition having *glaubwürdiger* on the title page.

1723

Penelope Aubin
The Life Of Charlotta Du Pont, An English Lady; Taken
from her own Memoirs. Giving an Account how she was
trepan'd by her Stepmother to Virginia, how the Ship was
taken by some Madagascar Pirates, and retaken by a Spanish
Man of War. Of her Marriage in the Spanish West-Indies, and
Adventures whilst she resided there, with her return to England. And the History of several Gentlemen and Ladys whom
she met withal in her Travels; some of whom had been Slaves
in Barbary, and others cast on Shore by Shipwreck on the
barbarous Coasts up the great River Oroonoko: with their
Escape thence, and safe Return to France and Spain. A History that contains the greatest Variety of Events that ever was
publish'd. By Mrs. Aubin. London: Printed for A. Bettesworth . . . M.DCC.XXIII.   tp DLC
———— [Another edition] London, 1736.   Sabin, I, 313
———— [Another edition] London: Printed in the Year 1739.
                                                 tp BM
———— [In *A Collection of Entertaining Histories and Novels*
. . . by Mrs. Aubin, Vol. III] London: Printed for D. Mid-
winter, A. Bettesworth and C. Hitch, J. and J. Pemberton, R.
Ware, C. Rivington, A. Ward, J. and P. Knapton, T. Longman,
R. Hett, S. Austen, and J. Wood. MDCCXXXIX.   MA
———— [In *English Nights Entertainments,* Vol. I] London:
Printed by T. Maiden . . . For Ann Lemoine . . . 1800.
                                                 tp DLC

1723

[Philipp Balthasar Sinold von Schütz (1657-1742)]
Die glückseligste Insul auf der gantzen Welt, oder das Land
der Zufriedenheit, dessen Regierungs-Art, Beschaffenheit,
Fruchtbarkeit, Sitten derer Einwohner, Religion, Kirchen-
Verfassung und dergleichen, samt der Gelegenheit, wie solches
Land entdecket worden, ausführlich erzehlet wird, von Con-

stantino von Wahrenberg . . . Gedruckt in Königsberg. 1723.
durch Gottlieb Friedrich Frommann, auch zu finden bey Ernst
Ferdinand Cörner in Leipzig.   IU, tp BM
———— [Another edition] von Ludwig Ernst von Faramund.
Franckfurt und Leipzig, bey Peter Conrad Monath, 1732.
tp BM
———— Neue Ausgabe, Frankfurt und Leipzig, 1737.
Brüggemann p. 177
———— Den Lycksaligaste Ö I hela Wärlden. Eller Nöjsam-
hetenes Land. Desz Regerings-Sätt, Egenskaper och Fruckt-
samhet, Desz Inwånares Seder, Buds-Dyrckan, Kyrckio-
Ordning, Barna-Upfostran, med mera: Samt Tillfället, Huru
detta Landet är blifwit uptäckt. Ifrån Tyska språket öfwersatt.
Westeras, Uplagd af Pet. Devall . . . 1744.   tp CtY
———— [Another German edition] Nürnberg, bey Georg
Peter Monath, 1749. 2 vols. in 1.   tp MH
———— Het gelukkigste Eiland op de gantsche Waereld, of
het Land van Vergenoegzaamheid, 1764.   Staverman p. 91
———— [Another edition] 1776.   Staverman p. 91
———— [Another edition] 1809.   Staverman p. 91

Though Kippenberg considers this a robinsonade, Staverman
questions its inclusion, rightly, says Ullrich⁶, col. 108, "weil es
nur eine Utopie ist." Discussed by Brüggemann, pp. 176-83.

1723

[Christian Stieff (1675-1751), *alleged author*]
Schlesischer Robinson Oder Frantz Anton Wentzels v. C**
eines Schlesischen Edelmanns Denckwürdiges Leben, seltsame
Unglücks-Fälle und ausgestandene Abentheuer, Aus über-
sendeten glaubwürdigen Nachrichten, so wol zur Belustigung
des Lesers, als Unterricht Adelicher Jugend in Druck gegeben.
Breszlau und Leipzig, bey Ernst Christian Brachvogeln . . .
Anno 1723 [-24]. 2 vols. in 1.   MiU, tp BM
———— De Silesische Robinson, Of De Ware en gedenkwaardige Levensbyzonderheden, zeldzame Ongevallen en wonderlyke Ontmoetingen van den Heer Frans Anthoni Wentzel van

C. . . . . een Silesisch Edelman. Zowel tot vermaak als leering
in 't licht gegeven. Uit 't Hoogduitsch vertaalt . . . Te Amsterdam, By de Compagnie Boekverkopers, 1754. 2 vols. MiU
———— [Another edition] Te Amsterdam, By Steven van
Esveldt . . . 1755. 2 vols. in 1.   MiU

Résumé in Haken, III, 308-17, who says: "Kein Robinson in
dem hergebrachten Verstande, (denn so weit und breit auch der
Held des Buchs in mehrern Welttheilen umhervagirt, so führt
er doch . . . nirgends ein insularisches Leben). . .."; discussed
in Kippenberg, chap. iv *passim,* and Staverman, pp. 69-72. See
also Wolfgang Van der Briele, *Paul Winckler (1630-1686): ein
Beitrag zur Literaturgeschichte des 17. Jahrhunderts* (Rostock,
Hinstorff, 1918), pp. 33-35 and n.4.

1724

[Daniel Defoe]
A New Voyage Round The World, By A Course never sailed
before. Being A Voyage undertaken by some Merchants, who
afterwards proposed the Setting up an East-India Company
in Flanders . . . London: Printed for A. Bettesworth . . .
and W. Mears . . . M.DCC.XXV [November, 1724, post-
dated].   tp NN, tp BM
———— [Another edition] London: Printed by G. Read . . .
[1725].   tp MH
———— [Serially as a periodical supplement] Chester; Printed
by W. Cooke . . . [1725].   tp BM
———— [Another edition] London: Printed for F. Noble . . .
MDCCLXXXVII. 3 vols.   tp RPJCB, tp BM
———— [In *Novels of D.D.,* Vols. X-XI] Edinburgh: Printed
by James Ballantyne and Co. For John Ballantyne And Co.
And Brown and Crombie . . . Longman, Hurst, Rees, And
Orme, And John Murray, London. 1810.   tp NNC, tp BM
———— [In *Novels and Miscellaneous Works of D.D.,* Vol.
VII (NNC misnumbered Vol. VIII)] Oxford: Printed By
D. A. Talboys, For Thomas Tegg . . . London. 1840.
                                       tp NNC, tp BM

17

———— [In *Works* of D.D., ed. William Hazlitt, Vol. I] London: John Clements . . . MDCCCXL.   DLC, tp BM

———— [In *Novels and Miscellaneous Works of D.D.*, Vol. VI, Bohn's British Classics] London: Henry G. Bohn. . . . MDCCCLVI.   tp NNC, tp BM

———— [In *Novels and Miscellaneous Works*, Vol. VI, Bohn's Standard Library] London, G. Bell and Sons, 1887 [more reprintings?].   DLC

———— [In *Romances and Narratives of D.D.*, ed. G. A. Aitken, Vol. XIV] London Published by J. M. Dent & Co. . . . MDCCCXCV.   tp NNC, tp BM

———— [Second edition of the preceding] London Published by J. M. Dent & Co. MDCCCC.   MH

———— [In *Works* of D.D., ed. G. H. Maynadier, Vol. XIV] New York Fred DeFau & Company [c.1903].   tp MH

———— [Another edition of the preceding, Vol. XIV] Boston David Nickerson Company [c.1903].   tp MH, tp Ry

———— [Another edition of the preceding, Vol. XIV] Limited Edition New York George D. Sproul MCMIV.   tp DLC

———— [Another edition of the preceding, Vol. V] Boston New York The C. T. Brainard Publishing Co. [c.1904].   tp NNC

———— [Another edition of the preceding, Vol. XIV] New York Thomas Y. Crowell & Company [c.1904].   tp MH

———— [In *Romances and Narratives*, ed. Aitken, 3d ed.] 1904.   DL

———— [In *Works*, ed. G. H. Maynadier, Vol. XIV] New York The Jenson Society MCMVII.   tp NNU-H

———— [In Daniel Defoe: Freebooters and Buccaneers: Novels of Adventure and Piracy] New York, The Dial Press, 1935.   tp DLC

Approach to criticism of this work must be made through references to Defoe's fiction in general, for not much separate attention has been given to it; cf. relevant citations under *Robinson Crusoe*. Specially valuable are, besides prefaces, Roorda, chap. v; J. N. L. Baker, pp. 266-68; and Bonner, chap. vii.

1724

Miles Philips, *pseudonym*
   The Voyages and Adventures Of Miles Philips, A West-
Country Sailor. Containing A Relation of his various Fortune
both by Sea and Land; the inhuman Usage he met with from
the Spaniards at Mexico, and the Salvage Indians of Canada
and other barbarous Nations; and the Sufferings he and his
Companions underwent by their Confinement and Sentence in
the Spanish Inquisition. Together with A Natural Description of the Countries he visited, and particular Observations on
the Religion, Customs and Manners of their respective Inhabitants. Written by Himself in the plain Stile of an English
Sailor. London: Printed for T. Payne . . . and T. Butler . . .
1724.   tp NN, tp BM
   This is not wholly imaginary, but it is a plagiarism, and
"Miles Philips" is both a pseudonym and the name of a 16th-
century seaman who presumably sailed under Sir John Hawkins
and told his uncorroborated story to Hakluyt; cf. J. K. L[augh-
ton] in the *DNB* and Hakluyt, *Principal Navigations* (Glasgow,
1904), IX, 398-445. The 18th-century editor pretends that he is
publishing an old MS, and, after following with alterations the
Hakluyt story, he sends Philips on a second voyage, which, in
fact, Philips did not make and which is a corrupted version of
the first and second voyages of Jaques Cartier, as told in the
translation in Hakluyt, VIII, 183 ff. He also manages to work
in his version of "The travailes of Job Hortop," from Hakluyt,
IX, 445-65; see further *The Rare Travailes of Job Hortop,*
ed. G. R. G. Conway (Mexico, 1928). I wish to thank Professor
R. W. Frantz for kindly turning over to me his detailed notes,
pointing out these relationships and establishing clearly the extent of plagiarism.

1724

Anonymous
   Der Americanische Robinson, In Drey unterschiedenen, curieusen seltsamen und angenehmen Begebenheiten vorgestellet,

und Seiner Vortrefflichkeit wegen aus dem Frantzösischen ins Teutsche übersetzet. Cölln [Dresden, Zimmermann], 1724.

tp NN

————— [Another edition] Cölln, 1734.   Haken III, 318

"Das Buch ist schwerlich eine Uebersetzung . . ." states Ullrich, p. 115. Briefly discussed in Kippenberg, chap. iv *passim*, and Brüggemann, pp. 123 f.

1724

Anonymous
Gvstav Landcron, eines Schwedischen Edelmannes, merckwürdiges Leben und gefährliche Reisen. Auf welchen er als ein warhafter Robinson sich mit einer getauften Türckin bey 12. Jahren, in einer unbewohnten Insel wunderbahr erhalten; auch sonsten die erschrecklichsten Fatalitäten, mit erstaunender Standhaftigkeit erduldet und überwunden hat; Bisz er endlich gantz unvermuhtet zu einer rechten Glückseeligkeit gelangen können. Nach seinem eigenen etwas undeutlichen Concept, mit verbesserter Schreib-Art und darzu gehörigen Kupfern, zum öfentlichen Druck befördert, durch C.F.v.M. Zu finden auf der Franckfurther und Leipziger Mesze. A.1724.

MiU, tp BM

————— [Another edition] Nürnberg, 1726.   Zobelitz p. 388
————— [Another edition] Nürnberg, 1727.   Kippenberg p. x
————— [Another edition] Verlegts Johann Albrecht . . . Nürnberg, Anno 1730.   Ullrich p. [248]
————— [Another edition] Nürnberg, 1731.   Kippenberg p. x
————— De Sweedsche Robinson, Of 't Wonderlyk Leven van Gustav Landcron, Waar in, behalven zyne verscheide togten, door voornaame gedeeltens van Europa, vervat zyn veele verwonderenswaardige gevallen, als onder anderen zyne zwaare gevangenis te Algiers, en by de 12 Jarig verblyf met een bekeerde Turkin op een onbewoond Eiland, zyne zeldzame huishouding en levenswyze op het zelven, en zyne gelukkige verlossing en wederkomst in Duitsland, raakende tegens alle

verwagting en na het uitstaan van veele, byna onbedenkelyke ontmoetingen, in een seer gelukkigen staat in de Wereld. Volgens zyn eige Handschrift in 't Hoogduits uitgegeeven door G.F.V.M. En nu om desselfs aangenaamheid in 't Nederduits Vertaald . . . T' Amsterdam, By Jacob Ter Beek . . . 1733.
             MiU, tp BM
———— [Another German edition] Nürnberg, 1736.
             Kippenberg p. x
———— [Another edition] Verlegts Johann Albrecht . . . Nürnberg, 1738.   Ullrich p. 112
———— [Another edition] Nürnberg, 1739. Ullrich⁴ p. [489]
———— [Another edition] Verlegts Johann Albrecht . . . Nürnberg, 1740.   MiU
———— Gustav Landcronas, en svensk adelsmans märkvärdiga lefverne och fahrliga resa [tr. Eric Humbla] 1740. Böök p. 238
———— [Another German edition] Nürnberg, 1743.
             Kippenberg p. x
———— Den saa kaldede Svenske Robinson eller Gustav Land-krons, en Svensk Herremands, forunderlige Livs- og selsomme Levnets-Beskrivelse, i Dansken overdragen af C[asper] P[eter] Rothe. Kjøbenhavn, 1743.   Bruun IV, 477
———— [Another German edition] Verlegts Johann Albrecht . . . Nürnberg, 1744.   tp CtY
———— [Another edition] Breszlau und Leipzig, verlegts Daniel Pietsch . . . 1753.   Ullrich⁴ p. [489]
———— [Another edition] Breslau, 1754. Kippenberg p. x
———— *Th*ess Svenska Gustav Land-Krons Og *Th*ess Engelska Bertholds Faabreitileger Robinsons, E*d*ur Lijfs Og Æfe Søgur, Ur Dønsku wtlagdar Af Sr. *Th*orsteine Ketels-Syne . . . *Th*rycktar aa Hoolum i Hialltadal, Af Halldore Eriks-Syne, Anno M.DCC.LVI.   tp MH, tp BM
———— [Another Dutch edition] T'Amsterdam, By J. Ter Beek en K. De Veer . . . 1757.   MiU
———— [Another Danish edition, Rothe's tr.] Kiöbenhavn, 1757. Trykt paa F. C. Peltes Bekostning. . . . MiU
———— [Another German edition] Frankfurt und Leipzig, 1770.   Ullrich p. 113

———— [Another Dutch edition] Te Amsterdam; Jan Mor-
terre . . . 1771.   MiU

Critical résumé in Haken, IV, 8-34; discussed in Kippenberg,
chap. iv *passim,* Staverman, pp. 72-77, and Brüggemann, pp. 121-
23.

1725

John Barnard (1681-1770)
Ashton's Memorial. An history of the strange adventures, and
signal deliverances, of Mr. Philip Ashton, who, after he had
made his escape from the pirates, liv'd alone on a desolate
island for about sixteen months, &c. With a short account of
Mr. Nicholas Merritt, who was taken at the same time. To
which is added a sermon on Dan. 3.17. By John Barnard . . .
Boston, New England, Printed by T. Fleet for Samuel Ger-
rish, 1725.   DLC
———— [Another edition] London: Printed for Richard Ford
and Samuel Chandler . . . 1726.   tp BM,DLC
———— [Another edition] Boston: Printed by T. Fleet for
Samuel Gerrish, 1727.   Evans I, 366
———— Der neue Robinson oder die Schicksale des Philipp
Ashton während seines erzwungenen Aufenthaltes unter den
Seeräubern und auf der unbewohnten Insel Roatan. Eine
wahre Geschichte für die Jugend bearbeitet von Gotthilf Hein-
rich von Schubert. Herausgegeben von dem Calwer Verlags-
Verein. Calw, in der Vereinsbuchhandlung; Stuttgart in Com-
mission bei J. F. Steinkopf. 1848.   Ullrich p. 117
———— Zweite, verbesserte und vermehrte Auflage . . . Calw,
in der Vereinsbuchhandlung. Stuttgart, in Commission bei
J. F. Steinkopf. 1849.   tp NNC
———— De Niewe Robinson Crusoë, Of: De Lotgevallen Van
Philip Ashton, Tijdens Zijn Gedwangen Verblijf Onder De
Zeeroovers En Op Het Eiland Roatan. Eene Ware Geschie-
denis. Door G. H. von Schubert . . . Uit het Hoogduitsch
Door T. M. Looman. Amsterdam, H. Höveker. 1851.   MiU
———— Dritte Auflage. Stuttgart, 1853.   Ullrich[d]

———— Philippe Ashton, ou le Nouveau Robinson par G. H. de Schubert, traduit de l'allemand. Paris, 1854. 2 vols.

Ullrich p. 117

———— Sechste Auflage. 1878.   Ullrich p. 117

———— Siebente Auflage. 1887.   Ullrich p. 117

———— Neubearbeitung von B. Schlegel. Stuttgart, Union [1891]. 3 vols.   Ullrich p. 117

———— [In Gresslers neue Jugendbucherei, Vol. II] Langensalza Schulbuchhandlung, 1899.   Ullrich[d]

———— [In Calwer Familien-Bibliothek, Vol. IX] Calw und Stuttgart, Vereinsbuchhandlung, 1902.   Ullrich[d]

———— [In Gresslers neue Jugendbucherei] Zweite Auflage. 1904.   Ullrich[d]

The actual experiences of Ashton and Merritt form the basis of this narrative retold in the first person by Barnard with evident "improvements" and literary ornamentation, including use of the omniscient point of view; and some of the translations are adaptations. It is a borderline inclusion, indebted to *Robinson Crusoe* as well as to the true events. It is abstracted in Cyrus Redding, *A History of Shipwrecks, and Disasters at Sea, from the Most Authentic Sources* (London, 1835), IV, [126]-157, and Denis and Chauvin, pp. 373-76; and commented on briefly in Staverman, p. 59 Prica, p. 14, Ullrich[a], p. 101, and Watson, p. 116. For "Autobiography of the Rev. John Barnard," which throws no light on *Ashton's Memorial,* see *Collections of the Massachusetts Historical Society,* 3S. V (1836), 177-243.

1726

[William Rufus Chetwood]

The Voyages And Adventures Of Captain Robert Boyle, In several Parts of the World. Intermix'd with The Story of Mrs. Villars, an English Lady with whom he made his surprizing Escape from Barbary; The History of an Italian Captive; and the Life of Don Pedro Aquilio, &c. Full of various and amazing Turns of Fortune. To which is added, The Voyage, Shipwreck, and Miraculous Preservation, of Richard

Castelman, Gent. With a Description of the City of Philadelphia, and the Country of Pensylvania. London: Printed for John Watts . . . 1726 [March].   tp MH, tp BM
———— The Second Edition. London: J. Watts, 1727.
Sabin IV, 13
———— The Second Edition. London, Printed: And Sold by Andrew Millar. . . . MDCCXXVIII.   tp NNC, tp BM
———— Les Voyages Et Avantures Du Capitaine Robert Boyle; Où l'on trouve L'Histoire De Mademoiselle Villars, avec qui il se sauva de Barbarie; celle d'un Esclave Italien, & celle de Dom Pedro Aquilio, qui fournit des éxemples des coups les plus surprenans de la Fortune; Avec La Relation du Voyage, du Naufrage & de la Conservation miraculeuse du Sr. Castelman, où l'on voit une Description de la Pensylvanie & de Philadelphie sa Capitale. Traduits de l'Anglois. A Amsterdam, Chez les Wetsteins & Smith, 1730. 2 vols.   tp NN, tp BM
———— Viaggi Ed Avventure Del Capitan Roberto Boyle; Con la relazione del Viaggio, Naufragio, e maraviglioso salvamento del Signor Castelman, in cui si vede una descrizione della Pensilvania, e di Filadelfia sua Capitale. Tradotti dall' Inglese in Italiano. In Venezia A Spese della Compagnia MDCCXXXIV. 2 vols.   tp RPJCB
———— The Third Edition. London: Printed for J. Watts; and Sold by J. Osborn . . . MDCCXXXV.   tp BM
———— Robert Boyles Reisen und Begebenheiten . . . Halberstadt, 1735. 2 vols.   Stuck I, 44
———— De Gedenkwaardige Reizen, en zeldtzame gevallen van Kapitein Robbert Boyle, nevens een naauwkeurig verhaal van de Reize, Schipbreuk en Behoudenis van Richard Castelman; met ene omstandige Beschryving van Pensilvanie en Philadelphia. Uit het Engelsch Vertaalt . . . By Jacobus Hoffman te Amsterdam [1739].   Staverman p. 160
———— The Fifth Edition. Dublin: Printed for George Golding . . . MDCCXLI.   tp MH
———— [Another edition] Liverpool. Printed by Adam Sadler. Wolverhampton. Reprinted by Geo. Wilson. M,DCC,XLIV.
tp NN, tp Bod

―――― [Another German edition] Leipzig, 1744. Price p. 245
―――― The Sixth Edition. London: Printed in the Year,
MDCCLX.   tp MB
―――― De nieuwe Engelsche Robinson, of De overzeldzame
gevallen van capitein Robert Boyle . . . Tweede Druk, veel
vermeerdert en merkelyk verbetert. Te Amsterdam, By Pieter
Spriet en Zoon . . . 1761.   DLC
―――― The sixth edition. London, T. Lownds, 1762.   BN
―――― [Another edition] London: Printed in the Year
M.DCC.LXXI.   tp MdBP
―――― [Another edition] London: Printed for J. Ford . . .
and Sold by S. Gamidge . . . 1772.   tp MB
―――― [Another edition] London, 1777.   Sabin IV, 14
―――― [Another edition] Edinburgh, printed for P. Anderson
. . . 1778.   DL
―――― [Another edition] Edinburgh, 1780.   Sabin IV, 14
―――― [Another edition] London, 1787.   Sabin IV, 14
―――― [Another edition] Edinburgh: Printed For W. Coke
. . . Leith. M.DCC.LXXXVII.   tp BM
―――― [In *Voyages imaginaires,* ed. Garnier, Vols. X-XI] A
Amsterdam, Et se trouve à Paris . . . M.DCC.LXXXVII.
                                    tp NNC, tp BM
―――― [Another English edition] Boston: Printed and sold
by John West Folsom . . . and E. Larkin, jun . . . 1790.
                                    Evans VIII, 16
―――― [Another edition] London: Printed For W. Osborne,
And T. Griffin . . . And J. Mozley . . . 1792.   tp RPJCB
―――― [Another German edition] Leipzig: Weygand, 1793.
                                    Sabin, IV, 14
―――― [Another Dutch edition] Te Amsteldam, By Gerbrand
Roos. MDCCXCIV. 2 vols.   Staverman p. 161
―――― [Another English edition] Printed at Greenfield,
Massachusetts, by Thomas Dickman: for Thomas & Andrews,
and David West . . . in Boston . . . M,DCC,XCIV.   MWA
―――― [Another edition] New-York: Printed By William A.
Davis, For E. Duyckinck, & Co. T. & J. Swords, T. Allen, and
C. Davis. 1796.   ViU

———— First American Edition. Cooperstown: Printed By E. Phinney, For Spencers & Webb . . . Albany. M,DCC,XCVI.

tp NN

———— [Another edition] London: Printed for W. Lane . . . 1797.

tp BM

———— [Another edition] Walpole, Newhampshire: Printed by David Carlisle, For Thomas & Thomas . . . 1799.

tp NN

———— The Twelfth Edition. Dublin: Printed By J. Dunn . . . 1801.

tp NN

———— [Another edition, abridged, n.p.] Printed In The Year 1804.

tp BM

———— [Another edition] New-York: Published By Evert Duyckinck . . . William W. Vermilye, Printer. 1805.

tp NN

———— [Another edition] London: Printed For T. Hughes . . . By J. D. Dewick . . . [1810?]

tp BM

———— [Another edition] Montpelier, Vt. Printed by Wright and Sibley, for Isaiah Thomas & Company. Walpole, N.H. 1812.

MWA

———— [Another edition] Exeter [N.H.]: Published By Abel Brown. 1828. 2 vols.

tp CtY

———— [Another edition] New York: Elton & Co. . . . 1852

tp NN

———— [Another edition] Published By Sykes Syphax & Co. Seekonk, And Quirk O. Jee, Sagadahock, n.d.

tp CtY

In addition this work was broken into parts for separate publication. For the first and fifth below I have no evidence beyond the titles that they are extracts from Chetwood's work:

———— La victime mariée ou histoire de lady Villars, traduite de l'anglais par M.-A. A Londres, et se trouve à Paris, chez Mérigot le jeune, 1775.

Mornet I, 366

———— The Remarkable History Of Miss Villars, Daughter Of An Eminent Merchant Of Bristol In Old England . . . Norwich: Printed and sold by John Trumbull, 1793.

Evans IX, 33

———— An Entertaining History Of An Italian Slave. Norwich: Printed and sold by John Trumbull, 1793. Evans IX, 33

———— The Remarkable History Of Miss Villars . . . Keene
—Newhampshire: Printed & Sold by C. Sturtevant, Jun. & Co.
M,DCC,XCV.   RPJCB
———— The Life Of Don Pedro Aguilio . . . Together With
Many Surprising And Perilous Adventures, Both By Sea And
Land. Cooperstown: Printed by Elihu Phinney, 1797.
                                                      Evans XI, 225
———— The Remarkable History Of Miss Villars . . . Am-
herst, Newhampshire: From the Press of Samuel Preston,
1798.   Evans XII, 38

This is sometimes attributed to Benjamin Victor (d.1778) and
was once thought to be partly from Defoe's hand. A reviewer
in the *Bibliothèque raisonnée des ouvrages des savans de l'Europe,*
VI(1731), 155-63, seemed in doubt about the obvious fictitiousness
of Boyle's narrative but covered himself with "se non è vero,
è ben trovato." Others, however, were generally more severe:
". . . le prémier de ces Voiages est un Roman trés mal écrit, &
encore plus mal inventé. Le second paroit plus réel, mais ne
contient rien, excepté le Naufrage, & les petites Avantures
vraies ou prétendues de l'Auteur, que ce qu'on voit dans les
Relations déja publiées de la Pensilvanie" (*Journal literaire,*
XVII,1731, 226); in *L'Esprit de l'abbé Desfontaines* . . . (Londres, 1757), IV,309, it is called "un tissu d'Avantures fabuleuses
. . . plus propres à amuser la canaille que les honnêtes gens,
mêlées de contes puériles, de réflexions libertines, & de peintures
deshonnêtes;" and according to Evans, VIII,16, "George
Steevens embalmed the author's memory, in the liquid amber of
his remarks, by calling him, 'a blockhead, and a measureless and
bungling liar.'" Staverman discusses it as a robinsonade, pp.
77-80, and Prica notices it, pp. 17 f. See also Bonner, pp. 189-91.

1726

[Daniel Defoe, *alleged author*]
    The Four Years Voyages Of Capt. George Roberts; Being A
Series of Uncommon Events, Which befell him In a Voyage
to the Islands of the Canaries, Cape De Verde, and Barbadoes,

from whence he was bound to the Coast of Guiney. The Manner of his being taken by Three Pyrate Ships, commanded by Low, Russell, and Spriggs, who, after having plundered him, and detained him 10 Days, put him aboard his own Sloop, without Provisions, Water, &c. and with only two Boys, one of Eighteen, and the other of Eight Years of Age. The Hardships he endur'd for above 20 Days, 'till he arriv'd at the Island of St. Nicholas, from whence he was blown off to Sea (before he could get any Sustenance) without his Boat and biggest Boy, whom he had sent ashore; and after Four Days of Difficulty and Distress, was Shipwreck'd on the Unfrequented Island of St. John, where, after he had remained near two Years, he built a Vessel to bring himself off. With a particular and curious Description and Draught of the Cape de Verd Islands; their Roads, Anchoring Places, Nature and Production of the Soils; The Kindness and Hospitality of the Natives to Strangers, their Religion, Manners, Customs, and Superstitions, &c. Together with Observations on the Minerals, Mineral Waters, Metals, and Salts, and of the Nitre with which some of these Islands abound. Written By Himself, And interspers'd with many Pleasant and Profitable Remarks, very instructive for all those who use this Trade, or who may have the Misfortune to meet with any of the like Distresses either by Pyracy or Shipwreck . . . London: Printed for A. Bettesworth . . . and J. Osborn . . . 1726.   tp NN, tp BM
———— [Another edition] 1815.   Wilson III, 544
———— [Ed. A. W. Lawrence, in The Traveller's Library] London Jonathan Cape . . . [1930].   tp BM

Ever since Walter Wilson in his *Memoirs of the Life and Times of Daniel De Foe* (London, 1830), III,543, mentioned that a competent but unnamed friend of his attributed this work to Defoe, decided differences of opinion have existed, but, numerically, authorities have accepted this suggestion, which Wilson himself "left to the judgment of those who are disposed to investigate the matter." J. K. L[aughton] in the *DNB* (article "George Roberts") calls the attribution "unauthorised and unnecessary. The style is rather that of some humble and incompetent imitator of Defoe, whose story is very probably based on fact. No reason can be alleged for doubting the existence of Roberts or the substantial truth of the narrative." However, W. P. Trent in *Daniel Defoe: How to Know Him* (Indianapolis, Bobbs-Merrill [c.1916]), p. 262, believes it is "certainly in part from Defoe's pen. . . . Although noted pirates make their appearance in its pages, and although the description of the inhabitants of the Cape de Verde Islands and of the hero's trying experiences among them is not without interest, this is probably the least readable narrative associated with Defoe's name, and one willingly accepts the theory that there was a real Captain Roberts who was helped by Defoe to put his notes and recollections into shape for publication. In other words, one would like to saddle upon a still hypothetical Roberts and the facts of his career the dulness of a book which one is forced in some way to connect with Defoe on account of a mass of internal evidence of substance and style that points unmistakably either to his editorship or to his authorship." Dottin's theory, pp. 773-78, is that Defoe, unable in 1726 to create a wholly new story, took the memoirs of real experiences and "les modifia si bien qu'il fit de ces relations authentiques, déjà embellies par l'imagination de l'auteur, de véritables romans d'aventures." All these opinions are based solely upon internal evidence, except that Dottin shows that *a* George Roberts, captain of the *Providence,* really existed; there is not a shred of other external biographical evidence. The text itself furnishes the best evidence of its fictitiousness.

The adventures of George Roberts were widely retold in collections of true voyages, notably John Green's *New General Collection of Voyages and Travels* . . . (London, T. Astley, 1745), I, 599-627, which forms the basis of the version in Prevost's *Histoire générale des voyages* (La Haye, 1747), III, 106-224; this went through several editions and translations, by which and by J. J. Schwabe, *Allgemeine Historie der Reisen zu Wasser und Lande* . . . (Leipzig, 1748), II, 106-55, "le nom de Roberts devint célèbre sur le Continent" (Dottin, p. 777). Briefer accounts appear in *A New Collection of Voyages* . . . (London,

John Knox, 1767), II,357-76, and in *The World Displayed; or, a Curious Collection of Voyages and Travels* (London), 3d edition, X (1773), [123]-150; this first began appearing in 1759 and ran through at least seven editions before 1800.

1726

[Jonathan Swift, *dean* (1667-1745)]
Travels Into Several Remote Nations Of The World. In Four Parts. By Lemuel Gulliver, First a Surgeon, and then a Captain of several Ships. London: Printed for Benj. Motte . . . MDCCXXVI [October]. 4 pts. in 2 vols.   tp NN, tp BM
———— Reisbeschryving Na Verscheyde Afgelegene Natien In De Wereld . . . Door Lemuel Gulliver. In 's Gravenhage by Alberts & Vander Kloot. MDCCXXVII [January?]. 4 vols. in 2.   tp BM
———— Voyages Du Capitaine Lemuel Gulliver, En Divers Pays Eloignez . . . A La Haye, Chez P. Gosse & J. Neaulme. MDCCXXVII [January]. 4 vols.   Teerink p. 200
———— Des Capitains Lemuel Gulliver Reisen in unterschiedliche entfernte und unbekandte Länder . . . aus dem Englischen in das Teutsche mit Fleisz übersetzet . . . Hamburg, Gedruckt und verlegt von sehl. Thomas von Wierings Erben . . . 1727. Ist auch in Leipzig bey Philip Herteln zu bekommen. 2 vols.   Teerink p. 214

Besides these first four editions *Gulliver* appeared in five 18th-century translations: Swedish (1744), Italian (1749), Danish (1768-75), Russian (1780), and Spanish (1793); for the Swedish and Spanish, which are not in Teerink, see respectively Böök, p. 258, and *The Growth and Development of the Novel from Antiquity to the Present Day* (London, Maggs Bros. [Cat. No. 621], 1936), p. 173. Altogether there were over one hundred 18th-century editions; I know of no reliable figures for estimating how many have appeared since. The most important information on the early English editions is contained in the edition of Harold Williams (London, First Edition Club, 1926), with which should be compared David Nichol Smith, *The Letters of Jonathan*

Swift to Charles Ford (Oxford, Clarendon Press, 1935), pp. xxxviii-xliv, and Teerink, pp. [173] ff. Also should be noted the good text of John Hayward (Nonesuch Press, Bloomsbury, 1934; New York, Random House). Teerink's valuable *Bibliography* must be used with full recognition of its limitations, some of which he himself mentions and some of which are inevitable, particularly in the insuperable task presented to a bibliographer of *Gulliver:* (1) all editions after 1850 of *Gulliver* in English, French, Dutch, and German are omitted; this means the absence of reference to a number of good introductions like those of Henry Morley, Bernbaum, and Pons; (2) the holdings of only two libraries in America (Yale and Michigan) have been drawn upon, and only slight use is made of the valuable English collections of Harold Williams and Victor Rothschild; cf. the latter's review in *The Library,* 4S. XVIII(1937), 224-28; (3) there is a noticeable absence of American imprints, resulting in either omission or incomplete information about volumes cited under European imprints; (4) critical works listed have not always been themselves examined for further references, e.g., one cannot assume that because Eddy and Goulding (among others) are listed all references that *they* include are in Teerink; and (5) histories of literature and of fiction have been generally disregarded, e.g., E. A. Baker, III, 230-50. See an important review of Teerink in *TLS,* March 20, 1937, p. 228. Many references of first importance will be found in my bibliography (cf. also under Defoe's *Consolidator* and Holberg's *Klimius*); many others which are essential may be found in Teerink: none in either place will be repeated here except to point out that Pons, pp. 144-49, and Bonner, chap. ix, are on *Gulliver.* See also Herbert Davis, "Recent Studies of Swift: a Survey," *University of Toronto Quarterly,* VII (1938), 273-88. Following is a selected list of critical references, arranged alphabetically, which are not in Teerink but which have a more or less relevant connection with *Gulliver* as fiction:

Baildon, H. B. "Robert Louis Stevenson," *Englische Studien,* XXVII (1900), 399-411.
Ball, F. Elrington. "Gay's Works," *N&Q,* 12S., XII (1923), 174.

Brown, Arthur C. L. "Gulliver's Travels and an Irish Folk-Tale," *MLN*, XIX (1904), 45-46.

Brown, Huntington. *Rabelais in English Literature*, Cambridge, Harvard University Press, 1933, pp. 161-72.

Cederschiöld, Wilhelm. "Uppslaget till Gullivers Resor," *Edda Nordisk Tidsskrift for Litteraturforskning*, XXVIII (1928), 215-22.

Chinard, Gilbert, ed. *Dialogues curieux entre l'auteur et un sauvage de bon sens* . . . (de Baron De Lahontan), Baltimore [etc.], Johns Hopkins Press, 1931, pp. 60-62.

Digeon, A[urélien]. " 'Gulliver' et La Bruyère," *Revue anglo-américaine*, III (1925-26), 245-7.

Duff, I. F. Grant. "A One-sided Sketch of Jonathan Swift," *Psychoanalytic Quarterly*, VI (1937), 238-59.

Eddy, William A. *"Gulliver's Travels* and *le Théâtre italien,"* *MLN*, XLIV (1929), 356-61.

Fairchild, Hoxie N. *The Noble Savage: a Study in Romantic Naturalism*, New York, Columbia University Press, 1928, pp. 45-48.

Ferenczi, S[ándor]. "Gulliver Phantasies," *International Journal of Psycho-Analysis*, IX (1928), 283-300.

Frantz, R. W. "Swift's Yahoos and the Voyagers," *MP*, XXIX (1931-32), 49-57.

———— "Gulliver's 'Cousin Sympson,' " *Huntington Library Quarterly*, I (1937-38), 329-34.

———— "Note," *English Literary History*, VI (1939), 82.

Hazard, Paul. "Comment les enfants se sont emparés de Swift," *Les Nouvelles littéraires*, X (12 Sept., 1931), 8.

James, M. R. "Swift's Copy of Dampier." *TLS*, Feb. 26, 1925, p. 138.

McCracken, George. "Homerica in *Gulliver's Travels,"* *Classical Journal*, XXIX (1933-34), 535-38.

McCue, G. S. "A Seventeenth-Century Gulliver," *MLN*, L (1935), 32-34.

Moore, John B. "The Rôle of Gulliver," *MP*, XXV (1927-28), 469-80.

Moore, John R. (See reference on page 276.)

Nicolson, Marjorie. *The Microscope and English Imagination,* Northampton, Smith College Studies in Modern Languages, XVI, No. 4 (1935), 50-56.

———— and Nora M. Mohler. "The Scientific Background of Swift's *Voyage to Laputa,*" *Annals of Science,* II(1937), 299-334.

Niehaus, Agnes. "Defoes Einflusz auf Swifts 'Gulliver,' " *Jahrbuch der philosophischen und naturwissenschaftlichen Fakultät Münster i. W. für 1920,* 1922, pp. 71-75.

Pons, É[mile]. "Rabelais et Swift à propos du Lilliputien," in *Mélanges offerts à M. Abel Lefranc . . . par ses élèves et ses amis,* Paris, Droz, 1936, pp. [219]-228.

Rockwell, Frederick S. "A Probable Source for 'Gulliver's Travels,' " *N&Q,* CLXIX (1935), 131-33.

Rovillain, Eugène E. "Jonathan Swift's *A Voyage to Lilliput* and *The Thousand and One Quarters of an Hour, Tartarian Tales* of Thomas Simon Gueulette," *MLN,* XLIV (1929), 362-64.

Secord, A. W. *"Gulliver* and Dampier," *MLN,* LI (1936), 159.

Seele, [F.] Wilhelm. *Voltaire's Roman Zadig ou La Destinée. Eine Quellenforschung,* Leipzig-Reudnitz, 1891.

Wedel, T. O. "On the Philosophical Background of *Gulliver's Travels,*" *Studies in Philology,* XXIII (1926), 434-50.

Whibley, Charles. "Gulliver's Travels," *Blackwood's Magazine,* CCXX(1926), 549-60.

The article by Niehaus, Ullrich, in *Germanisch-romanische Monatsschrift,* XVII (1929), 467, rightly pronounces "Unsinn! Eine völlig wertlose Arbeit," and I mention it partly to save anyone the trouble of reading it and partly because its very existence points significantly to a neglected subject. It will be noticed that most of these references have to do with Swift's sources and may be regarded as supplementary to Eddy's *Critical Study.* Quintana writes, p. 296, "The extent to which Swift was influenced by the traditional characteristics of this *genre* [imaginary voyage], the extent to which he departed from these characteristics and worked in an original manner—these are matters

18

of far more importance than his specific 'sources.' " In addition to opportunity for much further consideration of these matters, there is real need for a more thorough study of the influence of *Gulliver*. Eddy and Goulding, in particular, have made beginnings, good as far as they go, for the 18th century in England and France; Vera Philippović, *Swift in Deutschland* (Agram, 1903) is superficial.

1727

Eliza Fowler Haywood (1693?-1756)
  The Fruitless Enquiry. Being a Collection Of several Entertaining Histories And Occurrences, Which Fell under the Observation of a Lady in her Search after Happiness. By Mrs. E. Haywood . . . London.   Printed   for   J.   Stephens . . . MDCCXXVII [February].   tp MdBP, tp Bod
  ———— The Second Edition. London: Printed for T. Lowndes . . . MDCCLXVII.   tp CtY, tp BM
  ———— [In *A Collection of Novels,* Selected and Revised by Mrs. Elizabeth Griffith, Vol. II] London: Printed for G. Kearsly . . . MDCCLXXVII.   tp MB, tp BM

"The History of Montrano and Iseria," one of the eight stories in this framework romance, contains the imaginary voyage. The whole work is discussed by George F. Whicher, *The Life and Romances of Mrs. Eliza Haywood* (New York, Columbia University Press, 1915), pp. 31-34.

1727

Eliza Fowler Haywood
  Philidore And Placentia: Or, L'Amour trop Delicat. By Mrs. Haywood . . . London: Printed for Tho. Green . . . and Sold by J. Roberts . . . MDCCXXVII [July?].   tp MH
  Whicher, *op.cit.supra,* p. 63, remarks on the "faint echo of 'Captain Singleton' or of Captain John Smith's 'True Travels' "; cf. Dottin, p. 643.

1727

Samuel Brunt, *pseudonym*
A Voyage To Cacklogallinia: With a Description of the Religion, Policy, Customs and Manners, of that Country. By Captain Samuel Brunt. London: Printed by J. Watson . . . and sold by the Booksellers of London and Westminster. 1727 [July?].   tp MH, tp BM
———— Capitain Samuel Brunts Reise nach Cacklogallinien, und weiter in den Mond, Nebst dem Leben Harvays, des weltbekannten Zauberers in Dublin, Und einigen anderen Moralischen und Satyrischen Schriften Herrn D. Swiffts, aus dem Englischen übersetzt [von G. C. Wolf?] Leipzig [bei Jac. Schuster] 1735.   tp BM
———— Die Zweyte Auflage. Leipzig, 1736.   Teerink p. 61
———— Die Dritte Auflage. Leipzig, 1751.   tp MB
———— Cacklo-Gallinieras Caracter och Afmålning, 1770.
                                                           Böök p. 259.
———— [Russian translation] Moskwa, University Printing-house, N. Nowikow, 1788.   Teerink p. 365
———— [Another German edition] frei übersetzt von J[ohann] F[riedrich] Kinderling. Berlin, 1799. bei Karl August Nicolai, Sohn.   Teerink p. 365
———— [Another edition] Leipzig, Sommer, 1805. Price p. 233
———— [Another English edition, ed. Marjorie Nicolson] Published for The Facsimile Text Society By Columbia University Press New York: MCMXL.   tp NNC

In Philippović, p. 11 n. 2, a Berlin 1880 edition is cited; this I take to be a misprint. Possibly there are two other German editions of 1736 and 1751 both published by Siegert at Liegnitz (cf. Price, p. 233, and Lauchert, p. 96). Also authorities give both *Kindermann* and *Kinderling* for the translator's surname; I have followed Goedeke's *Grundrisz*, 2. Auf., VII, 414. The presence of Swift's name on the title page of German translations has kept alive in Germany the attribution to Swift. On this point Friedrich Lauchert, "Die pseudo-swiftische Reise nach

Kaklogallinien und in den Mond in der deutschen Literatur,"
Euphorion Zeitschrift für Literaturgeschichte, XVIII (1911),
94-98, 478, writes, p. 97: "Es ist eine ziemlich matte und geistlose,
stellenweise herzlich langweilige Gulliver-Imitation, und man
musz sich nur wundern, dasz drei unserer geistreichsten Schriftsteller [Herder, Jean Paul, and Hamann] auf die plumpe
Fiktion hereinfallen konnten, dasz dieselbe von Swift herrühre."
There has even been an attempt by Borkowsky, pp. 356-61, admittedly unfamiliar with the English original, to argue on the
basis of style and satirical method that no one but Swift in
1727 could have written in "dieser art von satirischen reiseroman."
Hence, his amazing theory, p. 361 (cf. O. Glöde, *Englische Studien,* XVIII, 1893, 461-63): "Wir halten dafür, dass die 'Voy. to
Cackl.' alsbald nach ihrem erscheinen verboten wurde, da sie eine
äusserst heftige socialpolitische satire auf England ist und sich
mit verletzender rucksichtslosigkeit nicht nur gegen das englische
volk, den hof und die minister richtet, sondern auch nicht
einmal die person des konigs verschont. Wenn Swift schon seine
'Gull. Tr.' aus furcht vor eventuellen unannehmlichkeiten zuerst
anonym herausgab, und sich erst dann als verfasser bekannte,
als der glanzende erfolg, den sein opus fand, ihn vor solchen
sicherte, so hatte er bei der publikation der in rede stehenden
schrift, deren satire weit bitterer ist und geradezu beleidigend
wird, sicherlich noch eine begrundetere ursache, seinen namen
zu verschweigen."

Pons in his review of Eddy misapplies to *Cacklogallinia* Eddy's
statement, p. 202, that *Gulliver Vol. III* is a forgery. I give Pons's
comment, pp. 153 f., because it has value in itself despite the
misinterpretation and the error about only one copy: "Certainement, M. Eddy n'a jamais eu le livre entre les mains, et nous
ne saurions lui en faire un grief, puisqu'il n'existe qu'un seul
exemplaire au monde (à la Königl. Bibliothek de Berlin) de cet
ouvrage médiocre; mais il eût pu s'en procurer une copie ou des
descriptions exactes. Ce *Voyage* n'est nullement une 'traduction'
ni même une imitation de l'*Histoire des Sevarambes* avec laquelle
il n'a rien de commun; il imite de très près au contraire l'*Histoire du Soleil* de Cyrano, dont il adopte la fable 'ornithomor-

phique' (les habitants de Cacklogallinia sont non des hommes commes les Sevarambes, mais, ainsi que l'indique le tître, des coqs et des poules analogues aux oiseaux de Cyrano, bien que moins divers et moins divertissants), et tout ce qui n'est pas de Cyrano dans le livre vient directement et simplement de *Gulliver.*"

A MS note by W. P. Trent in his copy of *Cacklogallinia* (now MB) reads: "I strongly suspect Defoe to be the author. The book shows the influence of Swift, of French romances like the 'Histoire des Sevarambes,' of Defoe's own 'Consolidator' and 'Robinson Crusoe.' It is throughout a severe satire on Walpole, and it ends with a Journey to the Moon," as quoted by Zoltán Haraszti, "A Great Defoe Library," *More Books,* VI, No. 1(1931), 8, except that I have changed what seems to me obvious misreading of the titles cited. See the introduction by Marjorie Nicolson to the facsimile edition, 1940.

1727

[Armand Léon de Madaillan de Lesparre, *marquis de Lassay* (1652-1738)]
Relation du Royaume des Féliciens [Peuples qui habitent dans les Terres Australes; dans laquelle il est traité de leur Origine, de leur Religion, de leur Gouvernement, de leurs Moeurs, & de leurs Coutumes.] 1727.   Wijngaarden p. 247
———— [In *Recueil de differentes choses,* Par de Lassay, ed. G. L. Calabre pérau, Vol. IV] A Lausanne, Chez Marc-Mic. Bousquet. M.DCC.LVI.   tp CtY, tp BM

Wijngaarden discusses it, pp. 136-45; the author "a profité des spéculations de John Law" (p. 136 n. 19). Several biographical studies have been made, but none gives any attention to the *Féliciens;* e.g., C. A. Sainte-Beuve, *Causeries du lundi,* 3e éd. (Paris, [1869]), IX, [162]-203; Pierre M. M. H. de Ségur, *Gens d'autrefois* (Paris, Levy [1903]), [115]-193; A. L'Eleu, "La Vie romanesque du marquis de Lassay," *Revue historique et archéologique du Maine,* LXXIX (2S. III, 1923), [105]-120, [212]-227; and Max de Marande, "Un Don Juan du grand siècle et de la

Régence," *Revue de France,* X, vi (1930), [238]-266, [420]-448; and XVI, iv (1936), [86]-114, [298]-326, [468]-493.

1727

[Peter Longueville]
The Hermit: Or, the Unparalled Sufferings And Surprising Adventures Of Mr. Philip Quarll, An Englishman. Who was lately discovered by Mr. Dorrington a Bristol Merchant, upon an uninhabited Island in the South-Sea; where he has lived above Fifty Years, without any human Assistance, still continues to reside, and will not come away. Containing I. His Conferences with Those who found him out, to whom he recites the most material Circumstances of his Life; as, that he was born in the Parish of St. Giles, educated by the charitable Contribution of a Lady, and put 'Prentice to a Lock-smith. II. How he left his Master, and was taken up with a notorious House-breaker, who was hanged; how, after this Escape, he went to Sea a Cabbin-Boy, married a famous Whore, listed himself a common Soldier, turned Singing-master, and married Three Wives, for which he was tried and condemned at the Old-Bailey. III. How he was pardoned by King Charles II. turned Merchant, and was shipwracked on this desolate Island on the Coast of Mexico. With a curious Map of the Island, and other Cuts. Westminster: Printed by J. Cluer and A. Campbell, for T. Warner . . . and B. Creake . . . 1727.   tp MH, tp BM
——— [Another edition] The English Hermit . . . by P. L. Gent. [Westminster] Anno Domini, 1727.   tp BM
——— Le Solitaire Anglois, Ou, Avantures Merveilleuses De Philippe Quarll. Par Mr. Dorrington. Traduit de l'anglois. A Rotterdam, Chez Jean Daniel Beman. MDCCXXVIII.
tp CtY
——— De Kluizenaar; of de weergalooze Rampen, en verwonderenswaerdige Gevallen van Filip Quarll, Engelschman. Onlangs ontdekt door den Heer Dorrington, Koopman van Bristol, op een onbewoont Eiland in de Zuid-zee, alwaar hy zich toen ontrent vyftig Jaar gansch alleen had onthouden en

jegenswoordig nog is, zonder met den gemelden Koopman na Engeland te willen keren. Met een kurieuse nodige Kaart van't Eiland . . . Te Rotterdam, By Jan Daniel Beman, MDCCX-XVIII.   ICN

——— Der Englische Einsiedler. Oder: Die wundervolle Begebenheiten und seltene Unglücks-Fälle eines Engländers, Philip Quarll; welcher unlängst von einem Bristolschen Kaufmann, Nahmens Dorrington, auf einer unbewohnten Innsull im Süd-Meere, allwo er sich ohngefehr funffzig Jahre aufgehalten, und noch befindet, ohne nach seiner Heimath kehren zu wollen, entdecket worden. Aus dem Englischen übersetzet . . . Hamburg, Gedruckt und verlegt von seel. Thomas von Wierings Erben . . . 1728.   MiU

——— [Another French edition] A Paris, Chez Etienne Ganeau . . . Guillame Cavelier . . . M.D.CC.XXIX. . . .
                                                                        MiU

——— [Another German edition] Nürnberg zu finden bey Adam Jonathan Felszecker, Anno 1729.   Ullrich p. 121

——— Die zweite Aufflage. Hamburg, Gedruckt und verlegt von seel. Thomas von Wierings Erben . . . 1732. Ist auch in Leipzig bey Philip Hertel zu finden.   MiU

——— Die dritte Aufflage. Hamburg, Gedruckt und verlegt von seel. Thomas von Wierings Erben . . . 1745. Ist auch in Leipzig in der Hertelschen Handlung zu finden.   MiU

——— [Another English edition] London: Printed for J. Osborn . . . MDCCXLVI   DL

——— [Another edition] London: Sold by the Booksellers of London and Westminster [1750?].   tp BM

——— [Another edition] London: Printed for J. Wren . . . J. Jefferies . . . and J. Fuller . . . 1751.   tp Bod

——— [Another Dutch edition] Te Rotterdam, Voor Rekening van de Compagnie, MDCCLII.   tp BM

——— [Another English edition] London, 1752.
                                                        Ullrich p. 119

——— The Third Edition. London: Printed for J. Wren . . . S. Crowder . . . H. Woodgate . . . J. Fuller . . . and J. Warcus . . . 1759.   tp NN, tp BM

———— The Fourth edition. London: Printed for J. Wren . . . S. Crowder . . . H. Woodgate . . . J. Fuller . . . and J. Warcus . . . 1763.   ICN

———— [Another edition London?] 1768.   DL

———— The Twelfth Edition. London: Printed for J. Wren . . . S. Crowder, H. Woodgate, J. Fuller, and J. Warcus.   tp BM

———— [Another German edition] Berlin, 1780. Price p. 147

———— A New Edition. London: Printed for William Lane . . . M.DCC.LXXXVI.   tp NNC

———— [In *The Novelists' Magazine*, Vol. XXI] London: Printed for Harrison and Co . . . M DCC LXXXVI.   tp DLC, tp BM

———— [In *Voyages imaginaires,* ed. Garnier, Vol. IV] A Amsterdam, Et se trouve à Paris . . . M.DCC.LXXXVII.   tp NNC, tp BM

———— [Another English edition] London: Printed by T. Sabine . . . [1788?].   tp BM

———— De Hollandsche Kluizenaar, Of De Verbazende Lotgevallen Van Andries Blank; Zo bevorens als gedurende zyn Veertig-Jarig verblyf op een onbewoond Eiland uitgewischt. Vervattende Eene hoofdzakelyke Beschryving van zyne Geboorte, Opvoeding en t'geen hem verder aanmerkelyks is wedervaren, tot op den tyd dat hy Schipbreuk heeft geleden: Zyne mirakuleuse redding op een onbewoond Eiland, kleding, wooning, huisraad, voedsel en wonderbare Levenswyze op 't zelve, met alles wat hem zeldzaams is bejegend, tot op 't oogenblik dat hy door eenige Reizigers aldaar is ontdekt en medegevoerd geworden. Meerendeels uit des Kluizenaars eigen Aantekeningen zamengesteld. Te Rotterdam, By Cornelis Van Den Dries . . . MDCCLXXXVIII.   MiU

———— [Another English edition] London: Printed and Sold by John Marshall and Co . . . [c. 1789].   tp Bod

———— [Another German edition] Berlin 1790 bei Christian Friedrich Himburg.   Ullrich p. 122

———— [Another edition] Wien, 1790 bey Franz Haas.   MiU

———— The Fifth Edition. London: Printed For The Booksellers. 1790.   tp CtY

———— [Another edition] 1792.   DL

———— [Another German edition; cf. my n. 193] Leipzig, 1792. bey J. D. Kleyb.   MiU

———— [Another edition] Wien, 1793.   Price p. 147

———— First American, From The Sixth London Edition. Printed At The Apollo Press, In Boston, By Joseph Belknap. MDCCXCV.   tp NN, tp BM

———— A New Edition. Printed At Exeter [N.H.], By H. Ranlet, For I. Thomas, And E. T. Andrews . . . Boston. M,DCC,XCV.   tp DLC

———— The Seventh Edition. London: Printed for the Booksellers. [1795?].   tp BM

———— The Seventh Edition. London: Printed by Thomas Martin . . . n.d.   tp Bod

———— [In The Children's Miscellany] First American Edition . . . Boston: Printed And Sold By William Spotswood. 1796.   tp MB

———— [Another edition] Brattleborough (Vt.): Printed by Benjamin Smead, 1797.   Evans XI, 146

———— [Another edition] Hartford Printed by John Babcock. 1799.   CtHi

———— [Another French edition] Leipzig, Sommer [17-?]. 2 vols.   Price p. 148

———— [Another English edition] Gainsborough; Printed For H. Mozley . . . 1801.   tp NN

———— [Another edition] York, Wilson and Spence, 1802.   Block p. 72

———— [Another edition] London: Printed at the Minerva-Press, for Lane, Newman, & Co . . . 1806.   Blakey p. 220

———— [Another edition] London: Printed For J. Brambles, A. Meggitt, And J. Waters, By H. Mozley, Gainsborough. 1807.   tp CtY, tp BM

———— [Another edition] Gainsborough: Printed By And For Henry Mozley. 1814.   MiU

———— [Another edition] London, J. Bysh [c.1815].   Gumuchian I,327

———— [Abridged edition] London: Printed And Sold By Dean and Munday . . . [1815?].   tp DLC

———— [Another edition] London: Printed by T. C. Hansard . . . for Baldwin, Cradock, And Joy . . . John Sharpe . . . and John Marshall . . . 1816.   tp MB, tp BM
———— [Another edition] London, 1821.   DL
———— [Another edition] Revised and corrected, with several Additions, By Mary Elliott . . . London: William Darton . . . 1822.   MiU
———— [Chapbook] London: Printed By And For Hodgson And Co . . . [1823].   CSmH, tp BM
———— [Chapbook] Edinburgh printed by A. Turnbull & Co. [c.1830].   Gumuchian I,113
———— [In The Child's Library, ed. J(oseph) T(homas)] London: Joseph Thomas . . . Sold By Thomas Tegg; And Simpkin, Marshall, & Co. [Palmer & Clayton, Printers] 1839.
                    tp Bod
———— [Another edition] London: Charles Daly . . . 1839.
                    tp NN
———— [Chapbook] Manchester: Printed by J. Wrigley . . . [1840?].   tp BM
———— [Another edition] London: Published By The Booksellers. William Walker, Otley. 1847.   tp CtY
———— [Another edition] Philadelphia: John B. Perry . . . 1855.   tp MB
———— Entirely Re-edited and Modernized. London: William Tegg. 1869.   ICU, tp BM
———— [Abridged in *A Storehouse of Stories,* ed. Charlotte M. Yonge] London Macmillan And Co. 1870.   tp DLC, tp BM
———— [Chapbook] Otley: W. Walker, Printer. [18-?].
                    tp DLC
———— [Another edition] London: Printed And Published By J. Fairburn . . . [18-?].   tp MB
————[Chapbook] Glasgow: Printed For M'Kenzie & Hutchison . . . n.d.   tp Bod

Generally considered among the best of the English imitations of *Robinson, Quarll* remained anonymous until Arundell Esdaile, "Author and Publisher in 1727: 'The English Hermit,'" *The*

Library, 4S.II(1921), [185]-192, discovered a rare edition of 1727 in which the dedication is signed "Peter Longueville," who, according to Esdaile's plausible hypothesis, resented his publishers' alteration of his MS and their invention of Edward Dorrington and who therefore himself published privately his own edition differing from and denouncing the original. Prefaces to both editions are signed "P.L." W. Alfred Jones in an appreciative essay (in which he wrongly lays claim to being the first to write on *Quarll*) in *Literary Studies: a Collection of Miscellaneous Essays* (New York, 1847), I, [91]-104 (reprinted in *Characters and Criticisms,* (New York, 1857, I,82-95), states that it was "first published, in chapters, in a weekly newspaper, called the Public Intelligencer, shortly after the appearance of Robinson Crusoe." Esdaile has been unable to trace this reference. *Quarll* was once attributed to Alexander Bicknell (d. 1796), e.g., by Evans (but not by C. W. Sutton in the *DNB*). Later editors often changed the story considerably, but whether Longueville's own version had any influence on these later editions and translations is a subject not yet investigated. Apparently the most radical alteration occurs in *De Hollandsche Kluizenaar* of 1788 with the Dutch hero Andries Blank, Dutch allusions throughout, a reordering of events to obtain more unity, and a different conclusion; see Staverman, pp. 80-85. For other discussion see Haken, IV, 38-127 (mostly résumé); Kippenberg, pp. 47-49; Prica, pp. 18-22; Brüggemann, pp. 131-33; Mann, pp. 114-19; Dottin, pp. 389-91; John L. Lowes, *The Road to Xanadu* . . . (Boston and New York, Houghton Mifflin, 1927), pp. 458 n. 59,484 n. 40, and 497 n. 41; and Bonner, pp. 192-96, 207-14, where it is shown that the author "transferred many passages unblushingly from Dampier." Dottin calls it a "genre hybride—à mi-chemin entre le récit d'aventures philosophiques et le conte de fées." Besides having wide scholarly consideration the work is the subject of several literary allusions attesting its popularity. Thomas Day wrote an introduction for it (see George W. Gignilliat, Jr., *The Author of Sandford and Merton* . . . , New York, Columbia University Press, 1932, p. 300 n. 138); George Crabbe in "The Parish Register," pt.i,ll. 107-10, ranks it with the Bible and *Pil-*

grim's Progress in rural homes; and Dickens in *Martin Chuzzlewit* (chap. xxxvi; Everyman ed., p. 544) has John Westlock
protest that his chambers are "nothing but . . . the sort of im-
promptu arrangements that might have suggested themselves to
Philip Quarll or Robinson Crusoe. . . ." Lamb twice comments
upon it; once in "Recollections of Christ's Hospital," when some
of the schoolboys "set off from school, without map, card, or
compass, on a serious expedition to find out *Philip Quarll's Island,*" and again in a letter of February 24, 1823, to Walter Wilson: "I do not know who wrote Quarll. I never thought of
Quarll as having an author. It is a poor imitation; the monkey is
the best in it, and his pretty dishes made of shells" (*Works of
Charles and Mary Lamb,* ed. E. V. Lucas, London [1905], VII,
600).

1727.

Anonymous
  Travels Into Several Remote Nations Of The World. By Capt.
  Lemuel Gulliver. Vol. III . . . London: Printed in the Year
  M.DCC.XXVII.   tp DLC
  ———— Voyages Du Capitaine Lem. Gulliver En Divers Pays
  Eloignes. Tome Troisieme. Contenant les Voiages de Brob-
  dingnag & des Sevarambes, & la Clef des deux Tomes précédens.
  A La Haye Chez P. Gosse & J. Neaulme. M.DCC.XXVIII.
                                                    Teerink p. 201
  ———— Reys Na Verscheide Ver Afgelegene Volkeren Der
  Wereld, Door Kap: Lemuel Gulliver. Met De Sleutel, Op
  deszelfs vier Eerste Reyzen. Derde en laatste Deel. In's
  Gravenhage, By Alberts & Vander Kloot. MDCCXXVIII.
                                                    tp CtY, tp BM
  ———— Des Capitains Lemuel Gulliver Reisen in unterschied-
  liche entfernte und unbekandte Länder. Dritter und Letzter
  Theil. In sich haltend Dessen zweite Reise nach Brobding-
  nagg, und von dar nach Sporunda, Severambia, Monatamia &c.
  &c. Nebst des Hrn. Carolini, eines Venetianis. Edelmanns,
  Schlüssel oder Erklärung derer in beyden vorgehenden Theilen

beschriebenen vier Reisen. Wegen ihrer Seltsamkeit, Anmuth und Zusammenhangung mit denen vorigen aus dem Englis. ins Teutsche mit Fleisz übersetzet . . . Hamburg, Gedruckt und verlegt von seel. Thomas von Wierings Erben . . . 1728. Ist auch in Leipzig bey Philip Hertel zu bekommen.

Teerink p. 214

———— [Another French edition] A La Haye, Chez Gerard Van Der Poel. MDCCXXX.   Teerink p. 202

———— [Another German edition] Hamburg, Gedruckt und verlegt von seel. Thomas von Wierings Erben . . . 1731. Ist auch in Leipzig bey Philip Hertel zu bekommen.

Teerink p. 215

———— [Another French edition] A La Haye, Chez Jean Swart . . . MDCCXLI.   Teerink p. 202

———— [Another German edition] Hamburg, Gedruckt und verlegt von seel. Thomas von Wierings Erben . . . 1746.

Teerink p. 215

———— [Another French edition] A La Haye, Chez Jean Swart . . . M.DCC.LXII.   Teerink p. 202

———— [Another edition] A La Haye, Chez Jean Swart . . . M.DCC.LXV.   Teerink p. 203

———— [Another edition] A La Haye, Chez Jean Swart . . . M.DCC.LXVII.   Teerink p. 203

———— [Another edition] A La Haye, Chez Jean Swart . . . M.DCC.LXXIII.   Teerink p. 203

———— [Another edition] A La Haye, Chez Jean Swart . . . M.DCC.LXXVII.   Teerink p. 203

———— [Another edition] A La Haye, Chez Jean Swart . . . M.DCC.LXXVIII.   tp BM

———— Viages Del Capitan Lemuel Gulliver Á Diversos Paises Remotos Traducidos De La Edicion Francesa Por Don Ramon Máximo Spartal, caballero maestrante de la real de Granada, y vecino de la ciudad de Plasencia. Tomo III. Segunda Edicion . . . En Madrid, Año De 1824. Imprenta de I. Sancha.   Teerink p. 222

———— [Another edition] Madrid: Imprenta de la Galería Literaria . . . 1873.   tp BM

No careful study of this spurious continuation has, to my knowledge, been published. Generally dismissed as mainly a forgery of *Sévarambes* (e.g., Swift, *Prose Works,* ed. G. R. Dennis, London, Bell, 1922, VIII,xxxi; Eddy, p. 202; and Goulding, p. 93 n.2), it is also in part an imitation of *Gulliver,* with which it was published in all the continental editions cited above, though not always in the same year. Its relationship to *Sévarambes* raises some problems for solution. Part I of the latter appeared first in English in 1675 (London), the first complete edition in French in 1677-79 (Paris), and a second English part probably not by Veiras in 1679 (London). From which of these publications did the anonymous author of *Gulliver Vol. III* plagiarize? Did the French editions translate literally from this or substitute part of the French *Sévarambes?* And the Dutch and the German (title page notwithstanding), both of which had translations of *Sévarambes* long before 1728 (Amsterdam, 1682, and Sultzbach, 1689, respectively)? The Spanish title page is probably truthful. The author himself alleges in the preface (p. 6): "The following Voyage I wrote Originally in the French Tongue, with a design to have it published at Paris; but losing Part of my Fortune in the Mississippi, gave me such a Disgust for that Nation, that I have at my leisure Hours, Translated it into our Mother Tongue." This is either a downright lie or a clue which indicates that he did not use the English *Sévarambes* at all. The plagiarized part of the French *Tome troisième* of 1728, then, is (if there were no substitution directly from the French *Sévarambes*) either a French translation of an English plagiarism of an English translation of a French original or a French translation of an English plagiarism of a French original—that is, assuming further without evidence that Veiras wrote his romance first in French. For the best treatments of *Sévarambes* see Atkinson[a], Wijngaarden, Lachèvre, and Von der Mühll; but in them none of the problems above is touched. The preface continues with an interesting reference to Swift's original: ". . . which Copy, I should have reposited in my Friend Mr. Simpson's Hands, the Editor of my former Volumes, if I could have had the Opportunity of seeing him; but he avoids me, I suppose, as imagining I am out of Humour

with him upon that Affair, for his Omission of several material
Passages: Yet I freely forgive him; tho' the Bulk of those
Volumes would be considerably increas'd, if he had printed my
Course of Sailing, and many Sea-Terms, fit only to be understood
by the Marine Race. . . ."

1728

Murtagh McDermot, *pseudonym?*
A Trip To The Moon. By Mr. Murtagh Mc.Dermot. Contain-
ing Some Observations and Reflections, made by him during
his Stay in that Planet, upon the Manners of the Inhabitants
. . . Printed at Dublin: And Reprinted at London, for J.
Roberts . . . MDCCXXVIII [February?].   tp BM

This work is introduced by a "Dedication to Captain Lemuel
Gulliver."

1728

Anonymous
[A narrative in letters from L. Gulliver to the editor of *Apple-
bee's Original Weekly Journal*. April 13-October 5] London:
Printed by John Applebee . . . 1728   tp Bod

If this spurious continuation of *Gulliver* had appeared regularly,
there would be 26 installments, but on August 24 the letter is
omitted, and six other numbers between the dates above are
missing from Bodley's files. Each letter occupies approximately
three columns of a single sheet folio, and the series represents the
"remaining Part of my Travels," hitherto kept for the "Entertainment of my worthy Friends." The installments were sus-
pended on October 12, although the narrative was unfinished.

1728

Anonymous
Authentick Relation Of the many Hardships and Sufferings
Of A Dutch Sailor, Who was put on Shore on the uninhabited
Isle of Ascension, by Order of the Commadore of a Squadron

of Dutch Ships. With A Remarkable Account of his Converse with Apparitions and Evil Spirits, during his Residence on the Island. And A particular Diary of his Transactions from the Fifth of May to the Fourteenth of October, on which Day he perished in a miserable Condition. Taken from the Original Journal found in his Tent by some Sailors, who landed from on Board the Compton, Captain Morson Commander, in January 172⅚. London: Printed for J. Roberts . . . M.DCC.-XXVIII. tp BM

——— [Another edition] The Just Vengeance of Heaven Exemplefy'd. In A Journal Lately Found by Captain Mawson, (Commander of the Ship Compton) On The Island of Ascension. As he was Homeward-bound from India. In which is a full and exact Relation of the Author's being set on Shore there (by Order of the Commodore and Captains of the Dutch Fleet) for a most Enormous Crime he had been guilty of, and the extreme and unparallel'd Hardships, Sufferings and Misery he endur'd from the Time of his being left there, to that of his Death. All Wrote with his own Hand, and found lying near the Skeleton. London, Printed: and sold by the Booksellers . . . [1730?]. tp CtY

——— [Another edition] London: Printed for J. Jenkins . . . and sold by the Booksellers and at the Pamphlet-Shops of [last line cut off]. [1730?]. tp BM

——— [In *The Harleian Miscellany*, Vol. VIII] London: Printed for T. Osborne . . . MDCCXLVI. tp BM

——— [Another edition] New-York: Printed and sold by James Parker, 1747. Evans II, 335

——— [Another edition] London, Printed: Philadelphia: Reprinted, and Sold by William Bradford . . . MDCCXLVIII. tp NN

——— [Another edition of *The Harleian Miscellany*, ed. John Malham, Vol. XI] London: Printed For Robert Dutton . . . 1810. tp BM

——— [Another edition of the preceding, ed. Thomas Park, Vol. VIII] London: Printed For White And Cochrane, And John Murray . . . And John Harding . . . 1811. tp BM

1729

[Daniel Defoe]
Madagascar: Or, Robert Drury's Journal, During Fifteen Years
Captivity on that Island. Containing I. His Voyage to the East
Indies, and short Stay there. II. An Account of the Shipwreck
of the Degrave on the Island of Madagascar; the Murder of
Captain Younge and his Ship's Company, except Admiral
Bembo's Son, and some few Others, who escap'd the Hands of
the barbarous Natives. III. His being taken into Captivity,
hard Usage, Marriage, and Variety of Fortune. IV. His
Travels through the Island, and Description of it; as to its
Situation, Product, Manufactures, Commodities, &c. V. The
Nature of the People, their Customs, Wars, Religion, and
Policy: As also, The Conferences between the Author and some
of their Chiefs, concerning the Christian and Their Religion.
VI. His Redemption from thence by Capt. Mackett, Com-
mander of the Prince of Wales, in the East India Company's
Service; His Arrival to England, and Second Voyage thither.
VII. A Vocabulary of the Madagascar Language. The Whole
is a Faithful Narrative of Matters of Fact, interspers'd with
Variety of surprising Incidents, and illustrated with a Sheet Map
of Madagascar, and Cuts. Written by Himself, digested into
Order, and now publish'd at the Request of his Friends. Lon-
don: Printed, and Sold by W. Meadows . . . J. Marshall . . .
T. Worrall . . . and by the Author . . . MDCCXXIX [May].
tp MB, tp BM
———— The Second Edition. London: Printed, and Sold by J.
Brotherton . . . T. Worrall . . . and J. Jackson . . . MDCC-
XXXI.   Oliver, *N&Q* p. 121
———— [Serially in *The Universal Spy: or, London Weekly
Magazine* . . . By Timothy Truepenny, Nos. 1-26] [London]
Printed by J. Nicholson . . . 1739.   tp BM
———— [Another edition] London, Printed, and Sold by W.
Meadows . . . T. Astley . . . and B. Milles . . . 1743.
MiU, tp BM
19

—— [Another edition] London: Printed for and sold by M. Sheepey . . . J. Wren . . . and T. Lownds . . . 1750.
tp NN

—— Now Carefully Revised And Corrected From The Original Copy. London: Printed And Sold By W. Meadows . . . T. Astley . . . And B. Milles . . . 1743. Reprinted For Stodart And Craggs, Hull. 1807   tp DLC, tp BM

—— [In *Autobiography. A Collection Of The Most Instructive And Amusing Lives Ever Published* . . . Vol. V] London:—1826. Printed For Hunt And Clarke . . . [by W. Clowes] 1826.   tp NN, tp BM

—— [Another edition of the preceding] London: Whittaker, Treacher And Arnot . . . [Printed by W. Clowes] MDCCCXXXI.   tp NN

—— [In The Adventure Series, Vol. II, ed. Capt. Pasfield Oliver] London: T. Fisher Unwin . . . MDCCCXC.
tp NNC, tp BM

—— [Another edition of the preceding] London: T. Fisher Unwin . . . MDCCCXCVII.   tp BM

—— [In Collection des ouvrages anciens concernant Madagascar, Vol. IV] Les Aventures de Robert Drury pendant ses quinze années de captivité à Madagascar et son second voyage dans cette île (1701-1717 et 1719-1720) Par MM. Alfred Grandidier . . . et Guillaume Grandidier Paris, Comité de Madagascar . . . 1906.   tp NN, tp BM

On the basis of the text itself and of accumulated opinion Robert Drury's journal is not an authentic voyage, although during the 19th century it was often abstracted as such, e.g., in Cyrus Redding, *A History of Shipwrecks and Disasters at Sea, from the Most Authentic Sources* (London, 1835), IV, [92]-125; *Chambers's Miscellany of Instructive & Entertaining Tracts,* ed. W. and R. Chambers (London and Edinburgh [c.1870]), Vol. III, No. 36; and many others cited in the following references, especially Grandidier and Dottin. Its genuineness was also accepted without question in the *Monthly Review,* n.s. LXIII (1807), 110 f., which expresses "obligations to the editor for rescuing a good book from the danger of falling into oblivion." William Ellis mentions it among his sources for his *History of Madagascar* (London [1838]), I,iv, as does Eugène de Froberville, "Recherches sur la race qui habitait l'île Madagascar avant l'arrivée des Malais," *Bulletin de la Société de géographie,* 2e sér. XI(1839), [257]-274. William Lee, *Daniel Defoe: His Life, and Recently Discovered Writings* . . . (London, 1869), I, 448 f., hesitantly thinks Defoe may have added a few sentences to a work edited by one of his imitators, and Émile Blanchard in a series of articles on "L'Ile de Madagascar," *Revue des deux mondes,* 1 juillet 1872, pp. 69-71, dismisses Drury as unauthentic.

The first detailed investigation came from S. Pasfield Oliver in *N&Q,* 7S.IX (1890), 121-24, 315 f., and in the introduction to his edition of the same year; in the latter, p. 20, he states that "an examination of the evidence tends to disprove the authenticity of Drury's travels in their entirety, although a basis of fact may probably underlie the various strata of fiction piled thereon." C. E. Doble, "The Memoirs of Captain Carleton: Swift or Defoe?" *Academy,* XLIII (1893), 483 n.*, asserts that Defoe's authorship is not only "indicated by a hundred details" but also "unintentionally avowed at p. 299 [ed. Oliver], where the supposed Drury writes of the judicial murder of Captain Green, which might well have kindled the flames of civil war between England and Scotland: 'All I know of the case I have in a proper place related.' It is impossible to doubt that this 'proper place' is Defoe's *History of the Union* (ed. [London] 1786), 78sqq." In Grandidier's excellent edition the opinion is "certain qu'un homme ayant longtemps vécu de la vie des indigènes a pu seul donner les très véridiques et très nouveaux renseignements qu'on trouve à chaque page du livre. . . . Il est certain qu'il n'a pas rédigé lui-même sa relation, en certains points fantaisiste et apocryphe . . ." (p. 6). On the basis of the journal Robert Garnett put Drury into the *DNB* as author of truth "entirely corroborated," although Garnett has to admit the assistance of an editor and the presence of some inconsistencies. W. P. Trent in *Defoe* (Indianapolis, Bobbs-Merrill [c.1916]), pp. 262-65, accepts the work as entitled to a place in the writings of Defoe as editor if not author. The case for Defoe is somewhat strengthened with evidence unknown to Oliver by William Minet, "Daniel Defoe and Kent: a Chapter in Capel-le-Ferne History," *Archæologia Cantiana,* XXXI (1915), 61-75. Dottin, pp. 788-94, comes out strongly for Defoe but not without employing hypothetical evidence. For further remarks see J. T. Hardyman, "Origin and Death of Robert Drury," *N&Q,* CLXXVII (1939), 47, and *idem,* "Shipwrecks and Desert Islands," *ibid.,* pp. 268-69. Though a few definite sources have been established, the line between the supposed real Robert Drury, voyager and writer, and the imaginary Robert Drury, romance hero, still requires to be drawn in detail.—I have allowed this note to stand as originally written, although it has been largely superseded by John R. Moore, *Defoe in the Pillory and Other Studies* (Bloomington [1939], Indiana University Publications: Humanities Series, No. 1), pp. 105-25, who with clarity and cogency has established Defoe's authorship. See also his two forthcoming articles on *Gulliver* in *JEGP* and *Studies in Philology.*

1729

Anonymous

Les Voyages De Glantzby Dans Les Mers Orientales de la Tartarie: Avec Les Avantures surprenantes des Rois Loriman & Osmundar, Princes Orientaux; traduits de l'Original Danois; Et La Carte De Ce Payis. A Paris, Chez la Veuve Delaulne . . . M.DCCXXIX.   tp NNC

———— [Another edition] A Amsterdam. Aux dépens de la Compagnie, M.DCC.XXX.   tp NN, tp BM

"Première des imitations très directes, *Les Voyages de Glantzby* sont vite condamnés, en partie parce qu'elles suivent de près la publication de *Gulliver,* comme la faible copie d'un grand original, copie cependant loin d'être indigne de toute attention, puisqu'elle renferme des maximes solides et louables" (Goulding, p. 89). It was so associated in the *Neue Zeitungen von gelehrten Sachen,* 9 Januarii, 1730, p. 27: "Es scheint, der autor habe den Gulliver nachahmen wollen, dem er aber nicht beykommt."

1730

[Pierre François Guyot Desfontaines, *abbé* (1685-1745)]
Le Nouveau Gulliver, ov Voyage De Jean Gulliver, Fils Du
Capitaine Gulliver. Traduit d'un Manuscrit Anglois. Par
Monsieur L.D.F. A Paris, Chez La veuve Clouzier . . . Et
François Le Breton . . . [De l'Imprimerie de Paulus-Du-
Mesnil] M.DCC.XXX [postdated?]. 2 vols. in 1.   tp NN
———— [Another edition] A Paris, Chez La veuve Clouzier
Et François le Breton. M.DCC.XXX. 2 vols. in 1.   MH
———— [Another edition] A Amsterdam, Aux dépens de la
Compagnie. M.DCC.XXX. 2 vols. in 1.   tp BM
———— The Travels Of Mr. John Gulliver, Son to Capt. Lem-
uel Gulliver. Translated from the French, by J. Lockman.
London: Printed for Sam Harding . . . MDCCXXXI [Febru-
ary]. 2 vols.   tp NN, tp BM
———— De Nieuwe Gulliver, Of Reize Van Joan Gulliver,
Zoon Van Den Kapitein Gulliver. Uit het Fransch vertaalt
. . . In s'Gravenhage, By Isaac Van Der Kloot, MDCCXXXI.
2 vols.   Teerink p. 367
———— [First German translation] Berlin, 1731.
     Teubner p. 30 and Teerink p. 368
———— Der Neue Gulliver, oder Die Reise J. Gullivers, Sohnes
des Capitain Lemuel Gullivers, Aus einem Engländischen
MSSt. ehedem in die Französische Sprache übersetzet durch
den Herrn Abt de Fontenelle, und nunmehr bestmöglichst
verteutschet von Selimantes [Chr. Gottl. Wendt]. Hamburg,
Gedruckt und verlegt von seel. Thomas von Wierings Erben
. . . 1731. Ist auch in Leipzig in Hertels Handlung zu bekom-
men.   tp BM
———— [Another edition] Hamburg, Gedruckt und verlegt
von seel. Thomas von Wierings Erben . . . 1731. Ist auch in
Leipzig bey Philip Hertel zu bekommen.   Teerink p. 367
———— [Another French edition] 1762. 2 vols. Pigoreau p. 198
———— [In *Voyages imaginaires,* ed. Garnier, Vol. XV] A
Amsterdam, Et se trouve à Paris . . . M.DCC.LXXXVII.
     tp NNC, tp BM

———— [Another edition] A Paris, Chez S. B. G. Musier . . . M.DCC.XCV. 4 vols. in 2. tp DLC

————— O novo Gulliver, ou Viagem de João Gulliver, filho do capitão Gulliver. Traduzida de hum manuscrito inglez pelo abbade des Fontaines, trasladada do francez . . . Lisboa, Nova of. de J. Rodrig. Neves, 1804[-5]. 4 vols. DLC

———— [Another French edition] A Paris, Chez Billois . . . 1813. [Vols. III-IV of *Voyages de Gulliver.*] BN

———— [Another edition] A Paris, Chez Genets jeune . . . 1813. [Vols. III-IV of *Voyages de Gulliver.*] Teerink p. 208

———— [Another Portuguese edition] Lisboa, Ma Typografia Rollandiana. 1819 . . . Vende-se em Casa de F. B. O. de M. Mechas . . . 4 vols. in 1. DLC

————[Another French edition] Paris, Lebigre Frères . . . 1836. 2 vols. in 1. tp DLC

By being generally considered in its relations to *Gulliver,* as in Goulding, pp. 90-93, Paludan, pp. 155-57, and Wijngaarden, pp. 157-65, this work becomes the "suite insipide" that Chinard[b], p. 408, called it. It should also be studied as independent, for it seems to have sources other than *Gulliver* and even some "small degree of ingenuity" (cf. Eddy, p. 198). Goulding cites six contemporary periodicals that reviewed it. Schomann discusses it, pp. 83-94. The "manuscrit anglois" is a fiction.

1730

[De Varennes de Mondasse]
La Découverte De L'Empire De Cantahar. A Paris, Chez Pierre Prault . . . M.DCC.XXX. tp DLC

Discussed in Wijngaarden, pp. 145-57; cf. my note 183.

1731

[Louis Adrien Duperron de Castera (1705-1752)]
Le Theatre Des Passions Et De La Fortune Ou Les Avantures Surprenantes de Rosamidor & de Theoglaphire. Histoire Australe. A Paris, Chez Saugrain . . . M.DCC.XXXI. tp MH

———— [Another edition] Paris, Chez Henry . . . M.DCC. XXXI. . . .   tp BM
———— [Another edition] Paris, Brunet, 1731.   BN

Apparently the Brunet edition should be put first, but I have not seen it; in the Henry edition, p. [356], occurs the statement: "J'ai cedé à Messieurs Saugrain & Henri, un tiers pour chacun, suivant l'accord fait entre nous. A Paris, ce 4 Decembre 1730. Brunet, fils."

1731

[Antoine François Prevost, *abbé* (1697-1763)]
Le Philosophe anglois, ou Histoire de Monsieur Cleveland, fils naturel de Cromwell, par l'auteur des Mémoires d'un Homme de qualité. A Utrecht chez Etienne Neaulme, 1731[-39]. 8 vols.   Harrisse p. 152
———— [De Engelsche Filosoof, Of Historie Van Den Heer Cleveland, Natuurlyke Zoon van Cromwel. Behelzende een Verhaal van deszelfs Geboorte, Wonderbaare Opvoeding in een Onderaardsch Hol, Zeldzaame Ontmoetingen in zyn Reizen en Omzwervingen, en verblyf onder Wilden, doormengt met verscheide fraje Geschiedenissen onder en na de Regering van Cromwel voorgevallen. Als mede eene Beschryvinge van een onbekent Eyland, door Christenen bewoont en derzelven Wonderbaare Levenswyze. Door hem zelfs in 't Engelsch beschreven] La Haye, Vom Thol [i.e., Pieter van Thol?] 1731. 4 vols.?   Harrisse p. 157
———— The Life of Mr. Cleveland, natural Son of Oliver Cromwell. Written by himself. [Giving a particular Account of his Unhappiness in Love, Marriage, Friendship, &c. and his great Sufferings in Europe and America. Intermix'd with Reflections, describing the Heart of Man in all its Variety of Passions and Disguises.] London: Printed for N. Prevost . . . and E. Symon . . . 1731. 2 vols.   *Historia Litteraria* II, 285
———— Der englische Weltweise, oder Historie des Herrn Clevelands, Natürlichen Sohnes des Cromwells, von ihm selbst beschrieben, Aus dem Englischen übersetzet [von P.G.v.K] . . . Neue Auflage[?] Berlin, zu finden bey Johann Andreas

Rüdiger 1736[-40]. 7 vols.   Friedrich p. 158
────── Den Engelske Philosoph, eller Clevelands Cromwels
naturlige Søns Historie . . . of det Franske oversatt ved
A[nna] C[atharina] von Passow . . . [og Joh. Herman Mejer]
Kiobenhavn-Trykt og forlagt af Nicolaus Moller . . . 1759
[-68]. 8 vols.   Harrisse p. 400

────── [Another English edition] London: Printed for N.
Prevost . . . MDCCXXXII. 4 vols.   tp NN
────── [Another edition] London: Printed for T. Astley . . .
1734[-35]. 5 vols.   tp BM, tp CtY (Vol. IV wanting)
────── [Another edition] Dublin: Printed by S. Powell, For
William Heatly . . . MDCCXXXVI. 2 vols.
                         tp BM, tp MdBP (Vol. II wanting)
────── The Second Edition . . . London: Printed for T. Ast-
ley . . . 1741. 3 vols.   tp DLC
────── [Another French edition] A Amsterdam, Chez J. Ryck-
hoff, 1744. 8 vols.   tp Bod
────── [Another English edition] Dublin: Printed for Au-
gustus Long . . . and Henry Hawker . . . MDCCL. 2 vols.
                              tp MdBP (Vol. I wanting)
────── The Third Edition, Corrected. London: Printed for
James Rivington and J. Fletcher, and R. Baldwin . . . S. Crow-
der . . . and P. Davey and B. Law . . . 1760. 4 vols. tp NNC
────── [Another French edition] A Amsterdam, Chez J.
Ryckhoff 1770. 8 vols. in 4 [Vol. VII has on tp 1707 for 1770].
                                                 tp RPJCB
────── Nouvelle Edition . . . A Londres, Chez Paul Vaillant.
M.DCC.LXXVII. 6 vols.   tp CtY, tp BM
────── [In *Œuvres choisies* de P., Vols. IV-VII] A Amster-
dam, & se trouve à Paris . . . M.DCC.LXXXIII.
                                          tp NNC, tp BM
────── [Another edition] A Londres. 1788. 6 vols. tp CtY
────── Il Filosofo Inglese O Sia La Storia Del Signor Di
Cleveland Figliuolo Naturale Di Cronvello Scritta de lui
medesimo. Traduzione Dal Francese. Edizione quarta cor-
retta ed emendata. In Venezia, MDCCLXXXX. Appresso

Guiseppe Piotto qu: Pietro. 7 vols. in 3 [Vol. VII: MDCCLXXX. Appresso Domenico Deregni]. tp NN
—————— [Another French edition] Paris, De L'Imprimerie Des Frères Mame . . . 1808. 6 vols. tp NNC
—————— [In *Œuvres Choisies* de P., Vols. IV-VII] Paris, De L'Imprimerie De Leblanc. 1810. tp MH
—————— [In *Œuvres* de P., Vols. IV-VII] A Paris, Chez Boulland-Tardieu . . . 1823. tp CtY
—————— La Colonie Rocheloise Nouvelle Extraite De L'Histoire De Cléveland De L'Abbé Prévost Paris Libraire De L. Hachette Et Cie . . . 1853 (Bibliothèque Des Chemins De Fer Troisieme Série Littérature Française). tp NN

For no other work in my check list is the available bibliography in a more chaotic condition. There is real need for a separate bibliographical study of Prevost that will solve the problems arising from the fact that *Cleveland* came out volume by volume over eight years accompanied by so-called new editions of preceding volumes during which many *contrefaçons* and a spurious continuation appeared. One detailed example of the difficulties will suffice to illustrate. Étienne Neaulme, the Utrecht publisher, brought out in 1734 the spurious *tome cinquième,* followed by a new edition including it, and in 1736 a new edition in five volumes not including the spurious volume, followed in 1738 by an edition containing Prevost's own continuation, which extended the whole to eight volumes by 1739. In the meantime Jean Neaulme at The Hague brought out "Tome cinquième ou tome sixième pour ceux qui ont le tome V d'un autre Auteur" (1738). In addition other publishers, notably at Paris and at Amsterdam, produced varying combinations of volumes in new editions, while translators and pirates were trying to keep up. One obvious result is that many sets today are mixed. The information above (not always in agreement with other evidence) comes chiefly from Henry Harrisse, *L'Abbé Prevost: histoire de sa vie et de ses œuvres d'après des documents nouveaux* (Paris, 1896). His biographical approach often allows ambiguity and incompleteness so that my attempt to reconstruct his information in a systematic bibliography has revealed many possibilities of setting down what is not true. Therefore I have given only those editions which I have seen, except for the first five editions. Harrisse, p. 155, puts publication of the first edition known to him in the summer of 1731, which is certainly too late. The *GM* for April (I, 180) lists the English title under books published in that month, and the *London Evening Post,* as quoted by C. E. Morgan, p. 230n., gives April 10 as the actual day. Several revealing references occur in *Historia Litteraria: or, an Exact and Early Account of the Most Valuable Books Published in the Several Parts of Europe,* a London monthly periodical published by N. Prevost and E. Symon, who published also the English *Cleveland.* On p. 202 of Vol. II, No. 8, the second number of the year 1731 (i.e., February or March), following an announcement that Étienne Neaulme was printing in Utrecht the French *Cleveland,* is added: "The said *Memoirs* are actually printing in *London* from the Original Manuscript," i.e., from the pretendedly existent English MS from which the French is alleged on the title page to be translated. Then in No. 9, pp. 285-92, in March or April, appeared a review of the English *Cleveland.* This is mentioned again on p. 408 in a list of books for April and May, and finally on p. 510 the actual publication of the Utrecht French edition is mentioned for the first time; the sentence which usually states the month in which the listed books were received is unfortunately omitted from this page for lack of space, but the month was presumably June or July. On the basis of the above facts and of Harrisse's incomplete information it seems possible that the first edition may have been English, not French, but I do not feel that I have investigated sufficiently to justify so entering it at the head of my check list. There is a record in Harrisse, p. 156, of an *approbation* and *privilège* granted in April, but this is apparently for the Paris, 1731, edition published by François Didot *after* the Utrecht edition. (After the preceding comment was written, there appeared a helpful note in Jones, pp. 46 f., with which my tentative suggestions on this problem should be carefully compared.) The Dutch title in my list is bracketed because it comes from a 'sGravenhage, 1732, edition in 2 volumes, by the same publisher (MiU). I do not have the date for the first Italian translation. Five German translations and two *Bearbeitungen* are considered in Hugo Friedrich, *Abbé Prevost in Deutschland: ein Beitrag zur Geschichte der Empfindsamkeit* (Heidelberg, Winter, 1929; Beiträge zur neueren Literaturgeschichte . . . N.F.XII), pp. 21-27, 74 f., 158 f.

Since the events connected with "la colonie Rochelloise" form a comparatively minor part in the larger significance of *Cleveland* as a novel of manners or sentimental romance, many otherwise useful references are unimportant; e.g., three particularly detailed studies—Franz Pauli, *Die philosophischen Grundanschauungen in den Romanen des Abbé Prévost* . . . (Marburg a. L., Ebel, 1912), pp. 98-125; Ernest Seillière, "Le Premier Observateur français de l'ame anglaise: l'abbé Prévost et son 'Cleveland,'" *Séances et travaux de l'Académie des sciences morales et politiques*, CLXXXIX (1918) i, [266]-277; and Pierre Trahard, *Les Maitres de la sensibilité française au XVIIIe siècle* (Paris, Boivin [1931]), I, [151]-166—all are more or less irrelevant to its consideration as an imaginary voyage, which I am not the first to call it (see A. J. Tieje, *Theory of Characterization,* p. 105 n. 115). Chinard[b], p. 282, calls it a *roman géographique et utopiste* and Étienne, "La Méthode en histoire littéraire . . . ," *Revue belge de philologie et d'histoire,* V (1926), 372, calls it a *roman d'aventures* and a *voyage extraordinaire.* Moreover, it belongs in part in the tradition of *Robinson Crusoe,* manifested critically by consideration of the relationship between the two in the more relevant studies of V. Schroeder, *Un Romancier français au XVIIIe siècle: l'abbé Prevost* . . . (Paris, 1898), pp. 225-33, 306 n. 2, 333-35; Fernande B. de Bury, "The Abbé Prévost in England," *Scottish Review,* XXXIII (1899), 38-41; Chinard[b], pp. 281-301; Mann, pp. 119-21; Paul Hazard, *Études critiques sur Manon Lescaut* (Chicago, Modern Philology Monographs [1929]), chap. ii *passim* and pp. 91-97; and Engel, pp. 143-47.

Prevost himself writes in the preface: "La *colonie Rochelloise* m'a causé de l'embarras. Il ne me paroissoit pas vraisemblable qu'un établissement si extraordinaire eût été si entièrement ignoré, qu'il ne s'en trouvât nulle trace dans les relations de nos voyageurs, & je ne pus m'empêcher d'en témoigner quelque chose au fils de Cleveland. Il me satisfit aussi-tôt, en me faisant voir quelques endroits d'une relation de la mer d'Ethiopie, composée par *William Rallow, anglois.* Si je n'y trouvai point l'histoire de *Bridge* & de ses compagnons, je fus assuré du moins de l'existence de la colonie, & de la manière déplorable dont elle fut détruite. J'y remarquai même quelques singularités de sa situation, que Cleveland avoit omises, & que j'ai jointes à son récit dans le troisième tome." *Œuvres choisies,* Amsterdam et Paris, 1783, IV, xvii f. This reference to his sources is still, as Hazard remarks, *op. cit.,* p. 91, "à vérifier et à rechercher." Some of the sources have been revealed recently in Engel's excellent study; see especially pp. 112-18, showing that Prevost used Leguat; pp. 198 f.; and p. 203 on the reason for the name *Cleveland.* Several references to contemporary reviews may be found in Harrisse.

Garnier, I, 7 f., makes a curious error in crediting Defoe with the authorship of a romance entitled *Cleveland,* which Prevost presumably knew and used in *his* work. Since Garnier also refers to Defoe's *Colonel Sack* instead of *Jack* and states that Defoe died at Plington, he must have relied on the biographical sketch in the second edition of Feutry's adaptation of *Robinson Crusoe* (Paris, 1775), where, according to Mann, p. 81 n. 5, the same misprint and the same misinformation may be found. Feutry in turn drew on Theophilus Cibber, *Lives of the Poets of Great Britain and Ireland* (London, 1753), IV, 323, where the last entry in a brief list of Defoe's work reads "Cleveland's Memoirs, &c. are also said to be his." This uncertainty is confirmed by Clara Reeve, who as late as 1785 did not know who wrote *Cleveland* but had heard it ascribed to Defoe; see *The Progress of Romance,* ed. Esther M. McGill (New York, Facsimile Text Society [Series I, Vol. IV], 1930), I, 123 f.

1731

[Johann Gottfried Schnabel (1692-c. 1750)]
Wunderliche Fata einiger See-Fahrer, absonderlich Alberti Julii, eines gebohrnen Sachsens, Welcher in seinem 18den

Jahre zu Schiffe gegangen, durch Schiff-Bruch selb4te an eine grausame Klippe geworffen worden, nach deren Ubersteigung das schönste Land entdeckt, sich daselbst mit seiner Gefährtin verheyrathet, aus solcher Ehe eine Familie von mehr als 300. Seelen erzeuget, das Land vortrefflich angebauet, durch besondere Zufälle erstaunens-würdige Schätze gesammlet, seine in Teutschland ausgekundschafften Freunde glücklich gemacht, am Ende des 1728sten Jahres, als in seinem Hunderten Jahre, annoch frisch und gesund gelebt, und vermuthlich noch zu dato lebt, entworffen Von dessen Bruders-Sohnes-Sohnes-Sohne, Mons. Eberhard Julio, Curieusen Lesern aber zum vermuthlichen Gemüths-Vergnügen ausgefertiget, auch par Commission dem Drucke übergeben Von Gisandern. Nordhausen, Bey Johann Heinrich Grosz . . . Anno 1731[-43]. 4 vols.

Ullrich p. 125

I can add nothing to the bibliographic data furnished by Ullrich, pp. 125-36, and Ullrich[d], p. [489], except the information in Böök, p. 239, on 18th-century Swedish translations. The manner of issuing the successive volumes, with different title pages, as independent continuations without edition notes makes impossible the use of the system which I have been following in my check list; i.e., it is possible to enter "another edition" of Volume I, etc., but not of all four volumes together, for there is no way of telling how the volumes go together, or whether they were ever sold in sets. This will be apparent from the following table:

I. Nordhausen 1731, 1732, 1736, 1740, 1744, 1749, 1751
   Halberstadt 1768
II. Nordhausen 1732, 1733, 1737, 1746, 1752, 1763
   Halberstadt 1772
III. Nordhausen 1736, 1739, 1744, 1748, 1751, 1767
IV. Nordhausen 1743, 1746, 1751, 1761, 1769

All these editions were published by J. H. Grosz. The work was translated into Swedish (1754), Danish (1761), and Icelandic (1854), but, apparently for no good reason, not into English, French, or Dutch. There are eight *Bearbeitungen* in sixteen editions (German, Swedish, and Danish) between 1788 and 1876.

By far the best critical work is Brüggemann, but because of different points of view he does not wholly supersede the two less important studies of Becker and Schröder. See also "Bibliographische Bemerkung" in Ullrich, pp. 131 f., Ullrich's review of the three books just cited, and the introductions to Ullrich's and Brüggemann's editions of Volume I. Haken gives a lengthy critical résumé, IV, 150-341, and V, [1]-327, and ten Brink ª, pp. 442-48, a discussion. It is usually stated that Ludwig Tieck's *Bearbeitung* entitled *Die Insel Felsenburg* (Breslau, 1828) is responsible for the name by which Schnabel's work is known, but Reichard in 1783 says, II, 161, that it is known "unter dem kürzern Namen Insel Felsenburg"; Haken in 1807, IV, ii, and V, [i], uses the short title, and Kippenberg, p. 109, quotes a similar usage in 1812; also, Friedrich Bouterwek, *Geschichte der Poesie und Beredsamkeit* . . . (Göttingen), X (1817), 388.

1731

[Jean Terrasson, *abbé* (1670-1750)]
    Sethos, Histoire Ou Vie Tire'e Des Monumens Anecdotes De L'Ancienne Egypte. Traduite d'un Manuscrit Grec. A Paris, Chez Jacques Guerin . . . M.D.CC.XXXI. . . . 3 vols.
                                           tp NN, tp BM
    ——— [Another edition] A Amsterdam, Aux De'pens De La Compagnie. MDCCXXXII. 2 vols.   tp BM
    ——— The Life Of Sethos. Taken From Private Memoirs Of The Ancient Egyptians. Translated from a Greek Manuscript into French. And now faithfully done into English from the Paris Edition; By Mr. [Thomas] Lediard. London: Printed for J. Walthoe . . . M.DCC.XXXII. 2 vols.   tp NN, tp BM
    ——— [Another French edition] A Paris, Chez Desaint . . . M.DCC.LXVII. 2 vols.   tp MH, tp Tay
    ——— Geschichte Sethos, Königs von Egypten. Uebersetzt von Mathias Claudius. Neue Ausg. Leipzig, Sommer, 1794. 2 vols.   Stammhammer II, 129
    ——— [Another French edition] A Paris, Chez Jean-François Bastien. L'an III [1795] . . . 2 vols.   tp MB, tp Bod

———— Sethos: storia o vita tratta da monumenti inediti dell
'antico Egitto, tradotta da un ms. greco. Opera dell 'ab. Terrasson volgarizzata dal professore Gaetano Barbieri. Torino,
Presso G. Cassone e C.ª . . . [18-?]. 6 vols. in 2. (Biblioteca
istruttiva e piacevole, Vols. XXXV-XL)   IU

Though primarily in the tradition of Fénelon's *Télémaque* and
Ramsay's *Cyrus*—see reviews in *Memoires pour l'histoire des
sciences & des beaux arts* (Trevoux), août 1731, pp. [1299]-1324;
Bibliothèque universelle des romans, Décembre, 1776, pp. [3]-68;
Retrospective Review, III (1821), i, 84-97; and *Bulletin du bibliophile,* 1851, pp. 47 f.—*Sethos* is something more than an edu-
cational romance, as Wildstake suggests, p. 22: "Nun verläszt
Terrasson das Thema des Erziehungsromanes und gleitet, sehr
zum Nachteil seines Werkes, in den abenteuerlichen Reiseroman
hinüber, wohl um dem Zeitgeschmack an Reiseabenteuern ent-
gegenzukommen." Also, Wijngaarden in his seven-page analysis
writes, p. 166, that it "n'appartiendrait pas au groupe des voyages
imaginaires à base utopique sans la description de la république
des Atlantes, le jardin des Hespérides." Dunlop in his résumé,
II,350-59, comments on the voyage which unites "the skill of Columbus with the benevolence of Cook and the military genius
of Caesar." See also Schomann, pp. 74-79, and a satire, which I
have not seen, by père Bernard Routh, *Relation fidele des troubles
arrivez dans l'empire de Pluton au sujet de l'histoire de Sethos*
(Amsterdam, 1731), as cited in Jones, p. 46. For connections with
freemasonry see *Histoire de l'ancienne Egypte, avec un précis sur
les expiations, d'après l'ouvrage de l'abbé Terrasson, intitulé
Séthos* . . . (Paris, 1825) and Benj. W. Richardson, "The Legend
of Sethos," *Ars quatuor coronatorum* [Lodge 2076, London], IV
(1891), [158-62] (reprinted, Margate, 1891), containing an unconvincing allegorical interpretation (Sethos=Prince Charles Edward, the Young Pretender). For biography of the author see
Jean le Rond d'Alembert, "Réflexions . . . sur la personne & les
ouvrages de M. l'abbé Terrasson," in *La Philosophe applicable à
tous les objets de l'esprit et de la Raison* . . . (Paris, 1754), pp.
[iii]-xxvi, which dismisses *Sethos* in one paragraph.

1731

Anonymous
Het Leven van Diana Therezia de la Fusiliere, Van hare Geboorte af tot hare Dood toe. Uit het Fransch vertaalt. Te Leiden, By Abraham Ambrullaart . . . 1731. 2 vols.

Staverman p. 168

Discussed in Staverman, pp. 119-21; there is no internal evidence for accepting the assertion of a French original.

1731

Anonymous
De Nieuwe Avanturier, Beschryvende zyne Overzeldzame, Wonderbare, en Aanmerkelyke Gevallen, Op zynen Nieuwe en Gevaarlyke Reis-togt naar het Onbekende Zuid-Land. Uit het Deensch vertaald. Te Leyden by Hendrik En Daniel Van Damme. MDCCXXXI. 2 vols. in 1.   tp NN

Discussed in Staverman, pp. 121-22; the complete absence of anything Danish and the presence of much that is Dutch convinces him that the original is Dutch.

1732

[Alain René Le Sage (1668-1747)]
Les Avantures De Monsieur Robert Chevalier, Dit De Beauchêne, Capitaine De Flibustiers dans la nouvelle France. Rédigées par M. Le Sage. A Paris, Chez Etienne Ganeau . . . M.DCC.XXXII. . . . 2 vols.   tp NN, tp Ry
———— [Another edition] A Amsterdam, Aux Depens De La Compagnie, M.DCC.XXXIII. 2 vols. in 1.   tp DLC
———— The Adventures Of Robert Chevalier, Call'd De Beauchene. Captain of a Privateer in New-France. By Monsieur Le Sage, Author of Gil-Blas . . . London: Printed and Sold by T. Gardner . . . R. Dodsley . . . and M. Cooper . . . M,DCC,XLV. 2 vols.   tp DLC, tp BM

———— [Another French edition] A Maestricht, Chez Jean-
Edme Dufour & Phil. Roux . . . M.DCC.LXXX. 2 vols.   BN
———— [Another edition] A Maestricht, Chez Jean-Edme
Dufour & Phil. Roux . . . M.DCC.LXXXIII. 2 vols. in 1.
                                    tp MB, tp BM (2 vols.)
———— [In *Œuvres choisies de Le S.,* Vol. IV] A Amsterdam,
& se trouve à Paris . . . M.DCC.LXXXIII.   tp NNC
———— Nouvelle Edition. A Mézieres, De l'Imprimerie de
Trécourt. Et se trouve à Lille, Chez C. F. J. Lehoucq . . .
Annee IIe. [1794] de la République. 3 vols.   tp MH
———— [In *Œuvres choisies de Le S.,* Vol. IV] Paris, De L'Im-
primerie De Leblanc. 1810.   tp MH, tp BM
———— [In *Œuvres de Le S.,* Vol. IV] A Paris, Chez Antoine
Augustin Renouard. M.DCCC XXI.   tp DLC, tp BM
———— [In *Œuvres de Le S.,* Vol. IV] A Paris, chez Bouland-
Tardieu . . . 1823.   MH
———— [Another edition] A Paris, Chez Mme Veuve Dabo
. . . 1824. 2 vols.   BN
———— [In *Œuvres de Le S.,* Vol. IV] A Paris, Chez Étienne
Ledoux . . . , 1828.   tp DLC
———— [In *Œuvres de Le S.,* Vol. IV] A Paris, Chez Étienne
Ledoux . . . 1830.   tp NNS
———— [Another edition, ed. Harry Kurz, in The Century
Modern Language Series] New York & London, The Century
Co., 1926.   tp DLC
———— [Abridged edition] Précédées d'une étude par Emile
Henriot avec quatre hors-texte à Paris Editions Excelsior . . .
MCMXXXIII.   tp NN
———— [In Nouvelle bibliothèque illustrée de vulgarisation]
Édition revue à l'usage de la jeunesse [par Léo Claretie] Paris,
Société française d'imprimerie et de libraire, n.d.   BN

LeBreton, p. 369, calls this "une plate imitation du *Robinson.*"
Though Mann, pp. 121-23, shows that it is not, the idea has per-
sisted, e.g., Dottin, p. 413: "Beauchêne est, dans sa simplicité un
peu fruste, un jeune frère de Robinson qui aurait mal tourné."
Mann finds its most striking quality to be "l'exotisme curieux

20

des descriptions et les essais de couleur locale, poussés à un point
jusqu'alors inconnu dans la littérature française. . . . Cet exotisme
tout nouveau a fait pour le roman d'aventures français ce que
Robinson Crusoé avait fait pour ce genre en Angleterre, c'est-à-
dire, lui a donné un air de réalisme et de netteté qu'il ne possédait
guère avant Lesage." Paul Morillot, *Le Roman en France depuis
1610 jusqu'à nos jours* (Paris, [1893]), p. 195, writes: "A la gloire
d'avoir fondé le roman de moeurs réalistes en France Lesage a
joint le mérite de nous avoir donné un de nos premiers romans
de voyages et d'aventures." See for further discussion two works
by Léo Claretie, *Le Roman en France au début du XVIIIe siècle:
Lesage romancier d'après de nouveaux documents* (Paris, 1890),
pp. [60]-73, and *Lesage* (Paris, 1894), pp. [196]-206; and Chinard[b],
pp. 271-79. For a comparison with *Cleveland* see Schroeder (*op.
cit. s.v.* Prevost 1731), p. 306 n. 2. The standard bibliography is
Henri Cordier, *Essai bibliographique sur les œuvres d'Alain-René
Lesage* (Paris, Leclerc, 1910). Both the most recent editions have
good introductions, which consider the real problem behind this
work, as revealed in the following quotation from Kurz, p. xiv:
"Despite the absence of any mention of a Robert Chevalier dit
Beauchêne in Canadian annals or piratical lore, we believe that
Lesage actually had a pirate's notes before him as he transcribed
them in his own graceful style. The writing in the whole work
is recognizably that of Lesage, but the material in Books I, II,
and VI is almost certainly that of the elusive Beauchêne."

Subsequently, Kurz, in "Proving That When a Man Dies, He
Must Have Lived," *Philological Quarterly,* VIII(1929), 309-11,
and Henriot show that a real Robert Beauchêne lived behind
Lesage's relation—so real, in fact, that Charles de la Roncière,
Histoire de la Marine française (Paris, Plon), VI [1932], 508-16,
does not hesitate to take Lesage as basis for detailed information
about Beauchêne! "Bref, où M. de la Roncière dit: Histoire!
M. Gilbert Chinard crie: Roman! Entre ces deux positions, nous
croyons qu'il y a place pour une troisième hypothèse . . . : Les
aventures du chevalier de Beauchesne ne remplissent, dans le
volume de Le Sage, que trois livres sur six. Les trois autres (IIIe,
IVe et Ve) sont consacrés, en hors-d'oeuvre, à l'histoire d'un cer-

tain M. de Monneville, contée par lui-même à bord du navire où
Beauchesne l'a recueilli, et que Le Sage, par un artifice courant
dans la littérature romanesque de l'époque, intercale sous forme
de récit dans les Mémoires qu'il assure tenir de la veuve du
chevalier. Or, autant par le ton, la couleur, la verve et le style,
les aventures de Beauchesne sont vivantes, pittoresques et sentent
le vrai, autant l'épisode Monneville, à quelques détails près, traîne
en longueur et respire à plein nez la littérature. Écrit, dirait-on,
d'une autre encre, c'est de la fabrication de cabinet introduite, pour
gonfler le livre dans le premier travail relatif à Beauchesne, lequel
peut avoir été retouché, mais a eu certainement pour base un
document authentique. S'il y a du roman dans le livre publié par
Le Sage, c'est ce roman du Comte de Monneville, qui n'est pas
du Le Sage des bons jours et ne représente à nos yeux, sous
l'apparence d'une confession personnelle, qu'une de ces utopies
à la mode de 1730. . . ."—Henriot, pp. 18 f. There the matter
rested until Aegidius Fauteux recently came forward in "Les
Aventures de chevalier de Beauchêne," *Cahiers des dix,* II(1937),
[7]-33, to prove convincingly, through errors in dates, places, and
persons, that "l'on peut sans aucune hésitation continuer à ranger
parmi les romans *les Aventures de Robert Chevalier.*"

1733

Madeleine Angélique Poisson, *dame* Gabriel de Gomez (1684-
1770)
    La Jeune Alcidiane. Par Madame de Gomez. Paris, G. D. David
    & Henry, 1733. 3 vols.   BN
    ——— [Another edition] Amsterdam, aux dépens de la Com-
    pagnie, 1734. 2 vols.   BN
    ——— Nouvelle Edition Revuë & Corrigée. A Amsterdam,
    Chez François L'Honore', & Fils. M.DCC.XXXIX. 2 vols.
                        tp NjP

From the preface of the 1739 edition, I, [iii]: "Le Roman de
Polexandre . . . tient une place si honorable entre tous les
Ouvrages de ce genre, qu'il suffiroit de dire, que la jeune Alcidiane
en est une suite pour exciter la curiosité du public, & le prévenir

en sa faveur." Résumé in the *Bibliothèque universelle des romans,* Novembre 1776, pp. 117-214.

1735

[Louis Rustaing de Saint-Jory, *chevalier* (d. 1752)]
    Les Femmes Militaires. Relation Historique D'Une Isle Nouvellement Decouverte . . . Dedié A Monseigneur Le Chevalier D'Orleans. Par le C.D.*** . . . A Paris, Chez Claude Simon . . . Pierre De Bats . . . M.DCC.XXXV.   tp DLC
    ——— [Another edition] A Amsterdam, Chés J. Ryckhoff le Fils . . . M.D.CC.XXXVI.   tp MH
    ——— [Another edition] A Amsterdam, Aux dépens de la Compagnie. MDCCXXXVI.   tp Bod
    ——— [Another edition] A Paris, chez Didot . . . M.DCC. XXXIX.   NjP
    ——— [Another edition] 1750.   Ars
    Discussed in Wijngaarden, pp. 172-81.

1736

[Johann Friedrich Bachstrom (1686-1742)]
    Das Bey zwey hundert Jahr lang unbekannte, nunmehro aber entdeckte vortreffliche Land Der Inqviraner, Aus der Erzehlung Eines nach langwieriger Kranckheit in unsern Gegenden verstorbenen Aeltesten dieses glückseligen Landes, Nach allen seinen Sitten, Gebräuchen, Ordnungen, Gottesdienst, Wissenschafften, Künsten, Vortheilen und Einrichtung umständlich beschrieben, Und dem gemeinen Wesen zum Besten mitgetheilet, Von A B C. Franckfurt und Leipzig. 1736[-37]. 2 vols. MiU
    ——— Neue Auflage. Franckfurt und Leipzig [i.e., Breslau, bei Korn der Aeltere] 1744.   Ullrich p. 137
    ——— Die Inquiraner. Eine Robinsonade. Neu erzählt vom Verfasser der grauen Mappe [J. C. L. Haken]. Chemnitz, 1810, bei Carl Maucke.   MiU
    ——— Neue Ausgabe [of the preceding]. Chemnitz, bei Wilhelm Starke. 1825.   tp BM

———— [Abridgment of the preceding, in Neidls Jugendbiblio-
thek 24] Wien, Verlag von J. Neidl. Druck von M. Pröglhöf.
Wien und Sechshaus [1871].   Ullrich p. 138

For biography see Ullrich, "Johann Friedrich Bachstrom: ein
Gelehrtenleben aus der ersten Hälfte des 18. Jahrhunderts,"
Euphorion Zeitschrift für Literaturgeschichte, XVI(1909), 28-58;
320-49. In this, pp. 320 f., he points out that the *Inquiraner* resembles Tyssot de Patot's *Jacques Massé,* of which the German
translation was probably by Bachstrom.

1736

[Saunier de Beaumont, *abbé*]
Voyage D'Innigo De Biervillas, Portugais, A La Côte De Mala-
bar, Goa, Batavia, & autres lieux des Indes Orientales. Contenant Une description des Mœurs, Coutumes & Religion des In-
diens; les différens établissemens de plusieurs Nations de
l'Europe, & un détail exact du Commerce de Batavia, avec
plusieurs avantures & singularités curieuses. A Paris, Chez
Gregoire-Antoine-Dupuis . . . [De l'Imprimerie de C. Simon]
M.DCC.XXXVI. 2 vols. in 1.   tp DCU-H, tp BM
———— Allerneuste Reisen eines Portugiesen, Innigo von
Biervillas, Nach denen Malabarischen Cüsten, Goa, Batavia,
und andern Ost-Indianischen Orten. Worinnen eine genaue
Beschreibung der Sitten, Gewohnheiten, und Religion der
Indianer; die unterschiedene Wohn-Plätze derer Europäer; eine
umständliche Nachricht von der Handlung zu Batavia, nebst
vielen untermengten sonderbahren und anmuthigen Begebenheiten enthalten sind. Aus dem Frantzösischen übersetzet. Berlin, bey Johann Peter Schmid. 1736. 2 vols. in 1.   tp BM

Noticed briefly as a "voyage romanesque" in *L'Esprit de l'abbé
Desfontaines* . . .(Londres, 1757), III,154.

1736

Anonymous
The History Of Autonous. Containing A Relation how that
Young Nobleman was accidentally left alone, in his Infancy,

upon a desolate Island; where he lived nineteen years, remote
from all Humane Society, 'till taken up by his Father. With
an Account Of his Life, Reflections, and Improvements in
Knowledge, during his Continuance in that Solitary State. The
Whole, as taken from his own Mouth. London: Printed for
J. Roberts . . . M.DCC.XXXVI. 　　　　　　　　　tp BM

———— [Augmented by John Kirkby (1705-54)] The Capacity
and Extent Of The Human Understanding; Exemplified In
the Extraordinary Case Of Automathes; A Young Nobleman, Who Was Accidentally left in his Infancy, upon a desolate
Island, and continued Nineteen Years in that solitary State,
separate from all Human Society. A Narrative Abounding
with many surprizing Occurrences, both Useful and Entertaining to the Reader. London: Printed for R. Manby, and H.
Shute Cox . . . MDCCXLV. 　　　　　　tp MH, tp BM

———— [Another edition of the preceding] Dublin, George
Faulkner, 1746. 　　　　　　　　　　*N&Q,* 6S.XII,177

———— The Second Edition [of the preceding]. London:
Printed for R. Manby and H. Shute Cox . . . MDCCXLVII.
　　　　　　　　　　　　　　　　　　　　tp NNC

———— Die ausserordentlichen Begebenheiten des Automates
eines jungen Edelmanns, der als ein Kind zufälliger weise auf
einem unbewohnten Eilande gelassen worden, und neunzehen
Jahre in diesem einsamen Stande, ohne alle menschliche Gesellschaft geblieben ist. Aus dem Englischen [Kirkby's] übersezt
. . . Franckfurt und Leipzig, bey Georg Peter Monath, 1750.
　　　　　　　　　　　　　　　　　　　　MiU

———— [Another edition of the preceding] Nurnberg, Monath, 1750. 　　　　　　　　　　　　　Price p. 137

———— [Another edition of the preceding] Nach dem Eng-
lischen frey bearbeitet von Karl Ephraim Schmidt. Riga und
Leipzig, bey Wilhelm Christian Andr. Müller, 1798.
　　　　　　　　　　　　　　　　Ullrich[d] p. [489]

———— [Another edition of the preceding] Halle, 1811.
　　　　　　　　　　　　　　　　Strauch XXVII, 248

———— [Kirkby's version, in *Popular Romances,* ed. Henry
W. Weber] Edinburgh, Printed by James Ballantyne and

Company, For John Ballantyne And Company, Silvester Doig
And Andrew Stirling, Edinburgh; Longman, Hurst, Rees,
Orme, And Brown, And John Murray, London, 1812.   tp CtY
———— [Another edition of the preceding, Vol. II] Edin-
burgh: Published, For the Proprietors, By W. & R. Chambers,
Edinburgh; W. Orr, London, And W. Curry, Jun. & Co.
Dublin. M DCCC XXXIII.   tp CtY

The 1736 romance, far from original, being much indebted to
Hai Ebn Yokdhan, was followed, in large sections verbatim, by
Kirkby without acknowledgment. A résumé of Kirkby's version
may be found in the *Retrospective Review,* X(1824), i, 78-88.
Dottin, p. 391, mentions it as an anticipation of Rousseau's *Émile,*
and Prica, pp. 25-32, considers that it "gehört zweifellos zu den
besten, welche die Hochflut solcher Produkte auf den Bücher-
markt gespült hat." Because Kirkby was for 18 months Edward
Gibbon's tutor, he and the book receive a long paragraph in the
Autobiography (Everyman ed., pp. 24-26).

1737

[Simon Berington (1680-1755)]
The Memoirs Of Sig[r] Gaudentio di Lucca: Taken from his
Confession and Examination before the Fathers of the Inqui-
sition at Bologna in Italy. Making a Discovery of an un-
known Country in the midst of the vast Deserts of Africa, as
Ancient, Populous, and Civilized, as the Chinese. With an
Account of their Antiquity, Origine, Religion, Customs,
Polity, &c. and the Manner how they got first over those vast
Deserts. Interspers'd with several most surprizing and curious
Incidents. Copied from the original Manuscript kept in St.
Mark's Library at Venice: With Critical Notes of the Learned
Signor Rhedi, late Library-Keeper of the said Library. To
which is prefix'd, a Letter of the Secretary of the Inquisition,
to the same Signor Rhedi, giving an Account of the Manner
and Causes of his being seized. Faithfully Translated from the
Italian, by E. T. Gent. London: Printed for T. Cooper . . .
MDCCXXXVII.   tp NN, tp BM

———— [Another edition] Dublin: Re-printed by, and for George Faulkner. MDCCXXXVIII.   tp NN, tp Bod

———— Mémoires de Gaudentio di Lucca, où il rend compte aux Pères de l'Inquisition de Bologne, qui l'ont fait arrêter, de tout ce qui lui est arrivé de remarquable dans sa vie, et où il les instruit d'un païs inconnu, situé au milieu des vastes désertes de l'Afrique, dont les habitans sont aussi anciens, aussi nombreux et aussi civilisés que les Chinois, avec l'histoire de leur origine, de leur Religion, de leur coutumes, de leur police, etc. traduits [par Miltz et le chevalier de Saint-Germain] de l'Italien sur une copie d'un manuscrit original de la Bibliothèque de Saint-Marc à Venise, avec des notes critiques et historiques du sçavant M. Rhédi; le tout précédé d'une Lettre du Secrétaire de l'Inquisition à M. Rhédi, dans laquelle il lui rapporte les motifs qui ont engagé ce Tribunal à faire arrêter l'accusé. Amsterdam-Paris 1746.
                                                       Mornet I, 350
———— [Another edition] n.p. 1746. 2 vols.   BN
———— The Second Edition. London, Printed for W. Innys . . . and R. Manby and H. S. Cox . . . And sold by M. Cooper . . . MDCCXLVIII.   tp MH, tp BM
———— Geschichte des Gaudentio di Lucca: oder merkwürdige Nachricht seiner sonderbahren Reise durch die Sandwüsteneyen des innern Africa nach Mezzoranien, nebst der Einwohner Ursprung, Religion, Regierungsart, Sitten, Gewohnheiten u.s.w. mit gelehrten Anmerkungen des Herrn Rhedi. In das Deutsche übersetzt von Johann Bernhard Nack. Frankfurt und Leipzig bey den Gebrüdern van Duren. 1751. 2 vols. in 1.   tp MH
———— The Fifth Edition. Dublin: Re-printed by, and for George Faulkner. MDCCLII.   tp NN
———— Nouvelle édition augmentée par [Jean Baptiste] Dupuy-Demportes, Amsterdam 1753. 4 vols.   BN
———— [In *Bibliothèque de Campagne*, Vols. XIX-XX] 1753.
                                                       BN
———— [Another edition] A Amsterdam Et A Leipzig, Chez Arkste'e & Merkus. MDCCLIV. 4 vols. in 2.   MiU, tp BM

———— [Another German edition] Frankfurt und Leipzig, 1758. 2 vols.   Stuck I, 406

———— [Another English edition] Edinburgh: Printed by A. Donaldson and J. Reid. For Alex. Donaldson. MDCCLXI.
tp MB

———— [Another edition] London: Printed for J. Richardson . . . MDCCLXIII.   MiU

———— [Another edition] Glasgow: Printed by James Knox . . . M.DCC.LXV.   MiU

———— [Another edition] London: Printed for G. Robinson . . . M DCC LXXIV.   tp MH, tp BM

———— Historische Reisbeschryving, Of Gedenkschriften Van Gaudance De Lucques. Gevangene Der Inquisitie Te Boulogne. Vermeerdert met verscheidene Vertoogen, die op den Tol te Marseille waren verlooren geraakt. En verrykt met de Geleerde Aanmerkingen van den Heer Rhedi, Bibliothecaris van St. Marcus te Venetien. Uit het Fransch vertaald. . . . In's Gravenhage, By H. Backhuysen, MDCCLXXV. 2 vols. in 1.
MiU

———— [Another English edition] London: Printed for T. Pridden . . . M.DCC.LXXVI.   tp NN

———— [Another French edition] A Amsterdam & se trouve à Liege, Chez F. J. Desoer . . . M.DCC.LXXVII. 4 vols.
tp DLC

———— [In *The Novelists' Magazine,* Vol. XXI] London: Printed for Harrison and Co. . . . M DCC LXXXVI.
tp NN, tp BM

———— [Another English edition] n.p. [1786].   tp DLC

———— [In *Voyages imaginaires,* ed. Garnier, Vol. VI] A Amsterdam, Et se trouve à Paris . . . M.DCC.LXXXVII.
tp NNC, tp BM

———— [Another German edition] Leipzig und Altona, Joh. Heinr. Kaven, 1792.   Stammhammer II, 129

———— First American Edition. Norwich [Conn.]: Printed and sold by John Trumbull . . . M,DCC,XCVI.   tp NN

———— [Another French edition] A Paris, Chez J. B. Rousseau . . . M.DCCXCVII.   tp DLC

———— [Another English edition] Dublin: Printed By J. And J. Carrick . . . 1798.   IU, tp BM

———— [Another edition] Philadelphia: Reprinted by William Conover, 1799.   tp NNC

———— [Another edition] Baltimore, Printed and sold by Bonsal & Niles. 1800.   tp NN

———— [Another edition] London: Printed For The Proprietor; and sold by Button and Son . . . James, Bristol; Hazard, Bath; Deighton, Cambridge; Annis, Norwich; Purday, Folkstone; Watts, Northampton; Albut, Hanley and Ogle, and Aikman, Edinburgh. 1803.   tp BM

———— [Another edition] By Bishop Berkeley. Author Of The Minute Philosopher, &c. Dublin: For John Cumming . . . 1821.   tp NN

———— [In *The Phoenix Library* . . . , ed. John M. Morgan] London: Charles Gilpin . . . MDCCCL.   tp BM

———— [Another English edition] London: Printed for Thomas Tegg and Co . . . T. Hurst . . . T. Brown . . . and B. Dugdale, Dublin . . . Printed by T. Plummer . . . n.d.
                                              tp MH

An introduction to the history and significance of this is given by Lee M. Ellison, "Gaudentio Di Lucca: A Forgotten Utopia," *PMLA,* L(1935), 494-509. The full references made there to early opinion and to the establishing of the authorship I need not repeat. To them may be added Jas. Crossley's communications to *N&Q* [1S.], II(1850), 327 f., and 4S.XII(1873), 293; and Child, pp. 42-44. One paragraph from Ellison, p. 498, will help to suggest its importance: "It is a question whether the dissociation of the great name of Berkeley from *Gaudentio* does not mark the beginning of the decline from its once high estate. With the great Christian idealist as its supposed sponsor, it attained to a rank and dignity comparable to that of the *Republic* of Plato, the *Utopia* of Sir Thomas More, and the *New Atlantis* of Lord Bacon. But a work emanating from a mere obscure priest could not readily justify such lofty pretensions. Discerning readers, however, must have perceived in *Gaudentio* elements and purposes wholly foreign to its eminent prototypes. In the long interval separating More and Bacon from Simon Berington voyagers and explorers had awakened a strong popular interest in the far places of the earth—in races and peoples, manners, customs, flora, fauna, in the changes and chances of foreign travel, in all the concrete facts and experiences of life in remote regions. This interest Berington undertook to satisfy. The earlier utopias lacked concreteness. In fact, they can hardly be said to exist in an objective sense, but only as abstractions. Berington's Mezzorania, on the other hand, is as real as Mexico and Peru; and integrated with his philosophy and social theory is a narrative that runs the whole gamut from idyllic romance to luscious intrigue and bloody adventure. Nevertheless, as a social and moral philosopher, Berington can stand upon his own merits, and the early appraisal of his work which saw in it the reflection of a wise, humane, and generous spirit does not have to be seriously discounted."

The dissociation of Berkeley's name, beginning with a communication by "W.H." in the *GM*, LV(1785), ii, 757, presenting the right author, was by no means complete; the attribution lived on for a hundred years so that an anonymous writer in the *Dublin University Magazine*, LIX (1862), 341, reprinted in the *Living Age*, LXXIII (1862), 233, could still discern in the plan an opportunity for the "good and learned" Berkeley to give "utterance to many a word of deep wisdom and judicious remark on the mythology and government of the old Pagans" and so that Presley in his bibliography, 4S.XII (1873), 3, knew no other name than Berkeley. Note also the title page of the Dublin edition of 1821, which may have drawn its authority from the *Retrospective Review*, IV(1821), ii, 316-33.

Contemporary criticism was not all praise. From Burkhard G. Struve, *Bibliotheca historica instructa*, ed. Johann G. Meusel, Lipsiae, II(1785), ii, 330 f., comes vigorous condemnation: "Mera figmenta insunt, minime historia vera. Editor seu potius auctor in praefatione impudenter mentitur, dum veram historiam se tradere iactat. Si modo in ipsa narratione verosimilia protulisset, non adeo indignaremur: sed incredibilia ac mirabilia effutit, ut indignatio vehemens inde exoriatur necesse sit. Non viris, sed mulierculis credulis atque pueris narrasse videtur."

Ellison is not concerned with a question that needs a more thorough investigation than has yet been made—the fate of this romance in France. The 1746 translation was considerably augmented, and in 1753 Dupuy-Demportes altered his edition so much that Wijngaarden, pp. 181-89, thinks of and discusses it as a naturalized French work; cf my notes 71 and 179. According to evidence in Lichtenberger and Mornet, Wijngaarden seems to be in error in associating Dupuy-Demportes with the 1746 edition. The *Mercure de France,* mars 1753, pp. 116 f., concluded that "malgré le soin & les Remarques de M. Rhedi, il est bien difficile de ne pas la prendre pour un Roman; les mœurs, les richesses, l'égalité, les Arts, le goût, & la grandeur du peuple Mezzoranien pour une chimere, & son Gouvernement pour une copie de la République de Platon."

1737

De Catalde

Le Paysan Gentilhomme, Ou Avantures De M. Ransav: Avec Son Voyage Aux Isle Jumelles. Par Monsieur De Catalde. Paris, P. Prault, 1737. 2 vols.　　　　　　　　　BN
———— [Another edition] A La Haye, Chez Pierre De Hondt, M.DCC.XXXVIII.　　　　　　　　　　　　　tp BM

1738

Anonymous

Le Solitaire espagnol, ou Memoires de D. Varasque de Figueroas [par le sieur P.B.]. Leyde, B. vander Aa, 1738[-40]. 2 vols.
　　　　　　　　　　　　　　　　　　　　　　　　Ars
———— [Another edition] 1753.　　　　　　　　　　　Ars
———— [In *Voyages imaginaires,* ed. Garnier, Vol. XII] Aventures D'un Espagnol. A Amsterdam, Et se trouve à Paris . . . M.DCC.LXXXVII.　　　　　　　　tp NNC, tp BM

Beyond mere mention in Mann, p. 112, and in Dottin, p. 413, where it is called a robinsonade "à tendances didactiques"; a listing in Mornet, I, 342, as a *roman d'intrigue;* and the extract in Garnier, my information on this is wanting.

1739

[Jean Baptiste de Boyer, *marquis* d'Argens (1703-1771)]
Le Législateur Moderne, Ou Les Mémoires Du Chevalier De Meillcourt. A Amsterdam, Chez François Changuion. M.DCC.XXXIX.   tp BM

For the possibility of another edition of the same year at La Haye see Jones, p. 68. On the author see Elise Johnston, *Le Marquis d'Argens: sa vie et ses œuvres; essai biographique et critique* [Paris, Imprimerie d'art Voltaire, c.1928], especially p. 34.

1739

Joseph Mauritius von Brachfeld, *pseudonym*
Joseph Mauritii von Brachfeld, Curieuse und Wunder-volle Begebenheiten, In den Unbekannten Sud-Ländern, Nemlich In der glückseligen Insul Jaketan, und dem unweit darvon entlegenen sehr grossen Reich Adama, auch andern geraumen Ländern, Wobey merckwürdig vorgestellet, auf was seltsame Art Er dahin gekommen, und durch was für Gelegenheit und Mittel Er die allerhöchste Gewalt über diese vortreffliche und sehr geraume Länder erhalten habe. Alles mit vielen Moral— und Politischen Regeln, Insonderheit aber für die Liebhaber der geheimen Philosophie, Mit einer sehr deutlichen Beschreibung des grossen Wercks dargeboten, auch mit vielen Kupfern versehen von Ihm Selbst. Franckfurt und Leipzig 1739. Verlegts Michael Gottlieb Grieszbach. . . . 2 vols. in 1.
                                              tp NN, tp BM
———— [Another edition] Eisenach, Verlegts Michael Gottlieb Grieszbach . . . 1759.   tp MH

Though Kippenberg, p. xv, lists this under 1739, he knew no copy, and Ullrich in his review of Kippenberg, p. 265, flatly denies the existence of an edition before 1759. It is mentioned briefly by Paludan, p. 48.

1740

Anonymous

Engelænder Berthold, den vidt berømte Robinson Crusoes nær Beslægtede, hans Liv og Levnet, som han i 10 Aar til Lands og Vands har ført, ved at opfinde En ubeboet Insul, men efter udstanden Møye, Lykkelig er kommen til sit Fæderneland. Forfattet med Moralske Anmærkninger. Oversat af det Engelske Sprog. Londen, Paa det Søe-farende Compagnies Bekostning. 1740.   tp BM

―――― *Th*ess Svenska Gustav Land Krons Og *Th*ess Engelska Bertholds Faabreitileger Robinsons, E*d*ur Lijfs Og Æfe Søgur, Ur Dønsku wtlagdar Af Sr. *Th*orsteine Ketels-Syne . . . *Th*rycktar aa Hoolum i Hialltadal, Af Halldore Eriks-Syne, Anno M.DCC.LVI.   tp MH, tp BM

Stangerup, p. 137, calls this practically a plagiarism of *Robinson Crusoe.*

1740

Anonymous

Jean Peter van Anterson's Fataler Schiffscapitain oder merckwürdige Erzehlung dessen unvermutheter Reise nach denen bis dato noch unbekannten südlichen Weltheilen. Aus dem holländischen ins Deutsche übersezt durch Monsieur du Blanchard. Erfurth, druckts und verlegts Joh. David Jungnicol, 1740.   Strauch XXIII, 83

―――― Zwyte vermehrte Auflage. Erfurth. druckts und verlegts Joh. David Jungnicol, 1742.   CLU

―――― [Another edition] Erfurt, druckts und verlegts Joh. David Jungnicol, 1749. 2 vols. in 1.   MiU

The *GPB* (*s.v.* Anterson) lists . . . *Anderwärtige Reise aus Holland nach dem Orient* . . . Theil 2, Erfurt, Jungnicol, 1745.

How to fit this into the listings above I cannot tell. The work shows the influence of Foigny's *Sadeur,* according to Stricher, pp. 32 ff.

1741

[Johann Michael Fleischer]
Der Nordische Robinson, Oder Die wunderbaren Reisen auch ausserordentlichen Glücks- und Unglücks-Fälle Eines gebohrnen Normanns, Woldemar Ferdinand, Wie derselbige Auf eine sonderbare Art nach einer vorhin von einem eintzigen Manne bewohnt gewesenen Insul gelanget, auch sich eine ziemliche Zeit allda aufgehalten, endlich aber nach vielen gehabten Fatalitäten sein Vaterland wieder glücklich erreicht, Nebst untermengten merckwürdigen Begebenheiten anderer Personen, Zum erlaubten Zeitvertreib ans Licht gestellet durch Selimenem . . . Coppenhagen, bey Frantz Christian Mumme, 1741. 2 vols.   MiU, tp BM
———— [Another edition] Copenhagen bey Frantz Christian Mumme. 1749. 3 vols. in 1 [Vol. III, a continuation].   MiU

On the identity of "Selimenes" see Ullrich, p. 125, Ullrich[a], p. 108 n. 50, and Strangerup, pp. 177-85. Mentioned briefly in Kippenberg, chap. iv., and Schröder, p. 81.

1741

[Ludvig Holberg, *baron* (1684-1754)]
Nicolai Klimii Iter Svbterranevm Novam Tellvris Theoriam Ac Historiam Qvintæ Monarchiæ Adhvc Nobis Incognitæ Exhibens E Bibliotheca B. Abelini. Hafniæ & Lipsiæ, Svmptibvs Iacobi Prevssii. MDCCXLI   tp DLC, tp BM
———— Nicolai Klims Unterirdische Reise worinnen eine ganz Neue Erdbeschreibung wie auch eine umständliche Nachricht von der fünften Monarchie die uns bishero ganz und gar unbekannt gewesen, enthalten ist. Aus dem Bücher-Vorrathe Herrn B. Abelins anfänglich Lateinisch heraus gegeben, jetzo

aber ins Deutsche übersetzt. Copenhagen und Leipzig, verlegts Jacob Preusz. 1741.   tp DLC

——— Onderaardsche Reis Van Claas Klim Behelzende Eene Nieuwe Beschryving Van Den Aardkloot Met De Historie Der Vyfde Tot Nog Toe Onbekende Monarchie Uit Het Latyn Vertaalt In's Gravenhage By Isaak Van Der Kloot MDCCXLI.
MiU

——— Voyage De Nicolas Klimius Dans Le Monde Souterrain, Contenant Une Nouvelle Te'orie De La Terre, Et L'Histoire D'Une Cinquième Monarchie Inconnue Jusqu'À-Present. Ouvrage tiré de la Bibliothéque de M^r. B. Abelin; et traduit du Latin par M^r. De Mauvillon. A Copenhague Chez Jaques Preuss MDCCXLI.   tp NNC, tp BM

———Niels Klims Reise Under Jorden, Forestillende En nye Kundskab om Jorden, Og Historie Om det femte Monarchie, Som hidindtil har været os ubekiendt; Funden Blant Abelins efterladte skrevne Bøger paa Latin, Og oversatt af Latin paa Dansk [by Hans Hagerup], samt til Trykken befordret efter special Kongelig allernaadigst Bevilning for Jacob Preusses Fallit-Boed. Kiøbenhavn, 1742. Trykt af Herman Henrich Rottmer.   Ehrencron-Müller III, 237

——— A Journey To The World Under-Ground. By Nicholas Klimius. Translated from the Original. London: Printed for T. Astley . . . and B. Collins . . . Salisbury. MDCCXLII.
tp NNC, tp BM

I give only the Latin original and the first five important translations because an excellent bibliography, to which I can make no additions, exists in one place: Holger Ehrencron-Müller, *Bibliografi over Holbergs Skrifter* (København, Aschehoug, 1933-35; Forfatterlexikon omfattende Danmark, Norge og Island indtil 1814, Vols. X-XII), III (1935), [213]-326. Here are listed 59 editions in 11 languages, 34 of them in the 18th century, which saw translations (besides those given above) in Swedish (1746), Russian (1762), and Hungarian (1783). On the evidence of translations the book was more popular in Germany with 17 editions (10 before 1800) than in Danish, the language of the author, with 13 editions (only four before 1800); in fact, not only two German translations but the Dutch and the French preceded the first Danish edition. Ehrencron-Müller's French edition of 1778 is an error for 1788. The most important book about *Klimius* is Paludan's in 1878, which I have cited on pp. 79 f.; also valuable is C[aspar] W. Smith, *Om Holbergs Levnet og populaere Skrifter* (Kjøbenhavn, 1858), pp. 237-87. Though Holberg composed it some years before he was persuaded to publish, Danish critics agree that it is an imitation of *Gulliver,* not a predecessor. Eddy, pp. 25 f., 28, 30, 67 f., 160 f., and 168 f., urges the probability that it is a source for *Gulliver.* In *Memoirs of Lewis Holberg, Written by Himself* . . . (London, 1827), pp. 179, the author does not say (as Eddy reads him) that *Klimius* was reviewed in the *Hamburg Gazette* for 1732; I have not seen the Latin original of this autobiography, but the German translation, *Eigene Lebens Beschreibung* . . . , 2 Auf. (Copenhagen and Leipzig, 1754), p. 316, agrees with the English: Holberg refers to reviews of other works. In regard to Eddy's statement, p. 67 n. 79, that Scott's is "the only mention of *Klimius* in connection with *Gulliver* that has ever been made" see, besides Paludan, for comparisons between the two, Ehrencron-Müller, III, 217 ff. (references to statements in 1754 and 1786 in French, and 1764 and 1844 in German); *ADB,* XCV (1790), i, 175-77; Weber, pp. xxx f.; J. J. Ampere, "Littérature danoise, sur la vie et les œuvres comiques d'Holberg," *Revue des deux mondes,* VII(1832), 65-68; Smith, *op.cit.,* pp. 239 f. ("Holberg naevner selv som sine Forbilleder i denne Digteart Lucian . . . , Bidermanni Utopia og Swift"); Georg Brandes, *Ludvig Holberg: et Festskrift* (Kjøbenhavn, 1884), pp. 179; Brasch, pp. 33 f.; Kleinwächter, pp. 14-16; Kirchenheim, pp. [206]-227; Böök, p. 258; and Alexander Bugge, "Literaere Forbilleder, Cervantes—Holberg," *Edda Nordisk Tidsskrift for Litteraturforskning,* XIV (1920), 122. See also Kruuse, pp. [48]-67. For additional remarks on *Klimius* see Flammarion, pp. 460-70; Dunlop, II, 619-22; S. C. Hammer, *Ludvig Holberg, the Founder of Norwegian Literature* . . . (Oxford, Blackwell, 1920), pp. 26-30; De la Mare, pp. 172-76; and Stangerup, pp. 76-80.

21

1741

[Johan Krook]

Tanckar om jordens skapnad, eller Fonton Freemassons äfventyr, till högvälborne herr grefven * * * och nu med anmärkningar till trycket befordrat af Antichon. Stockholm, L. L. Grefving, 1741.   Böök p. 260

According to Paludan, pp. 331 f., this is the earliest Swedish moon-voyage; it is based on wide reading in the classics and in Fontenelle and Huyghens, and is specifically influenced by Cyrano, Kircher, Godwin, Swift, and *Cacklogallinia*. Discussed in Böök, pp. 260-62.

1742

Robert Pierot, *pseudonym*

Der Americanische Freybeuter. Oder die mit theils wunderbaren, theils angenehmen Begebenheiten angefüllte Lebens-Geschichte Robert Pierots, Eines gebohrnen Holländers; darinnen desselben Jugend, Auferziehung, Reisen, Gefangenschaft zu Algier, und wunderliche Errettung aus derselben, wie auch mit denen in der Flucht gegen die Türcken davon gebrachten Schiffen verrichtete Caperey und Freybeuterey in America, und deren erfolgte Aussetzung an eine unbewohnte Insul, enthalten: Ingleichen Seine in die zwölff Jahr wunderbarliche Erhaltung und Einrichtung seiner Hauszhaltung, welche er mit Erbauung derselben darauf zugebracht, und endlich von seinen Freunden wiederum angetroffen worden, sammt dem unter denenselben gestiffteten Ritter-Orden der Einigkeit sehr angenehm beschrieben, Und aus dem Frantzösischen ins Teutsche übersetzt [von M.N.O.P.Q., on Vols. II-III only]. Von Ihm selbst. Franckfurt und Leipzig [Bey Frantz Christian Mumme, on Vol. IV only], 1742[-45]. 4 vols. Ullrich p. 140

———— Zweyte Auflage. Franckfurth und Leipzig, Bey Frantz Christian Mumme. 1745.   tp DLC (Vols. I-II wanting)

———— Dritte und verbesserte Auflage. Frankfurt und Leipzig, In der Mummischen Buchhandlung, 1752 [-?]. 4 vols.?
                                        tp DLC (Vols. I-II only)

———— Vierte Auflage. Copenhagen und Leipzig, verlegts Heineck und Faber. 1772 [-?]. 4 vols.   Ullrich p. 142

The listings in Ullrich do not agree with the mixed set of four volumes that I have seen. Reichard gives a résumé, II, 180-91, on the first page of which he says: "Dieser Roman ist eine vermischte Kopie von der Geschichte der englischen Freybeuter und den Robinsons . . . Namen und Styl beweisen, dasz die Uebersetzung aus dem französischen eine blosze Erdichtung ist." Ullrich, p. 142, agrees that it is "höchst wahrscheinlich Original."

1743

[Otto Bernhard Verdion (1719-1800)]
Leben und besondere Begebenheiten Peter Roberts eines gebohr-nen Engelländers, welcher auf wunderbare Art sein Leben auf einer unbewohnten Insul viele Jahre zugebracht, merckwürdig sich verheyrathet, Kinder gezeuget, und nach vielem ausgestan-denen Elende seine grösseste Zufriedenheit erlanget hat. Dres-den, bey Joh. Nicolaus Gerlach. [1743?-45]. 2 vols. [Vol. II, Dreszden und Leipzig].   Ullrich p. 142

———— [Another edition] Dreszden, Bey Johann Nicolaus Gerlachen, 1746[-?]. 2 vols.   Ullrich p. 143

———— [Another edition] Dresden, bey Johann Nicolaus Gerlach und Sohn. 1762[-63]. 2 vols.   Ullrich p. 143

———— [Another edition] Dresden, bey Joh. Nicolaus Gerlachs Wittwe und Sohn. 1771. 2 vols.   MiU

———— [Bearbeitung by Karl Friedr. Benkowitz] Robert, der einsame Bewohner einer Insel im Südmeere . . . Halle 1793 [-98]. In J. C. Hendels Verlage. 4 vols.   Ullrich p. 144

Strauch, pp. 247 f., in his review of Ullrich establishes the authorship.

1743

Anonymous
De Hollandsche Robinson, of wonderlyke Gevallen van den Heer*** Vervattende deszelfs omzwervingen, en wonderlyke

ontmoetingen in Vrankryk, Italie, Turkyen, en West Indiën, Zyn verblyf onder de Engelsche Zeeroovers, Onthouding op een onbewoond Eiland, en zeldzame Regering onder de Wilden. Door Hem zelfs beschreven. Te Gouda, By Franco Bellaart . . . 1743.   Staverman p. 169
——— [Another edition] 1836.   Staverman p. [93]
——— Le Robinson Hollandais ou Journal d'un marin naufragé. Ouvrage amusant et moral en prose et en vers rédigé par l'éditeur du Mnémonique [G. C. Verenet] . . . Amsterdam, Jacobus Radink [c. 1824].   Gumuchian I, 358
——— [Another edition] Amsterdam, Schmidts, 1824.
                                                  Gumuchian I, 358

The comment in Gumuchian makes the addition of these French titles uncertain: "C'est sans doute une imitation du 'Robinson hollandais' paru en 1743." The work, according to Staverman's discussion, pp. [93]-97, follows *Robinson* principally but has other sources which include the *Insel Felsenburg*.

1744

Henrietta de Bellgrave, *pseudonym*
   The True History of Henrietta de Bellgrave. A Woman born only for Calamities: A distress'd Virgin, unhappy Wife, and most afflicted Mother. Wrote by herself for the Use of her Daughter [in *The Lady's Drawing Room. Being a Faithfull Picture Of The Great World. In which the various Humours of both Sexes are display'd. Drawn from the Life: And Interspers'd with entertaining and affecting Novels*]. London: Printed and Sold by M. Cooper . . . and A. Dodd . . . M,DCC,XLIV.   tp NNC, tp Bod
   ——— [In *The Lady's Drawing Room*] The Second Edition. Revised and corrected by the author. London: Printed for A. Millar . . . and Sold by M. Cooper. . . . M,DCCXLVIII.
                                                              ICN
   ——— The True History Of Henrietta de Bellgrave, A woman born to great calamities, a distressed virgin, happy wife, and most afflicted mother, her intended voyage with her parents to

the East Indies; her being taken by pirates, her mothers death
on the seas; being shipwreck'd on the coast of Bombay, where
her father and all the ships crew perished, save herself and two
sailors, one of them attempted her ruin, the other striving to
oppose him lost his life; her being rescued by eight Indians,
where one of them tho' a pagan, fired with resentment, plunged
his javelin through the villains heart, and carried her to their
masters house, where she was used with great tenderness and
afterwards married to the Banyan, who almost adored her, but
not being able to bring her to his way of worship, and one day
he catched her christening her daughter Zoa, for which he never
forgave her, her unhappy life till her daughter was 13 years of
age. [London] Printed and Sold at Bailey's Printing Office . . .
[1750?].   tp BM
———— [Another edition] London: Printed And Sold By
S. Fisher . . . Also Sold By T. Hurst . . . and R. C. Staines,
Chelmsford. 1799.   tp DLC
———— [Another edition] London: Printed And Sold By
T. Sabine And Son . . . [1800?].   tp BM
———— [Another edition] London: Printed And Sold By
S. Fisher . . . [1804].   tp MH
———— [Another edition] London: Printed And Sold By
Dean And Munday . . . [1820?].   tp BM
———— [Another edition] New-York: Published By W. Bor-
radaile . . . 1823.   tp NN
———— [Another edition] Derby: Thomas Richardson; Simp-
kin, Marshall, And Co., London. [1830?].   tp BM

A sequel, not in itself an imaginary voyage, was written, prob-
ably earlier than the date of the only edition I know: *The True
History of Zoa, The Beautiful Indian, Daughter of Henrietta De
Bellgrave; And Of Rodomond, An East-India Merchant, whom
Zoa releases from Confinement And Intended Death; and with
him makes her Escape From Her Father, an India Banyan Of
Bombay; who was the Occasion of Rodomond's Imprisonment
And Dreadful Sufferings. To which is added The True And
Affecting History Of The Shepherdess of Chamouny.* London:

Printed And Sold By S. Fisher . . . Also Sold By T. Hurst . . .
1799 (tp DLC).

1744

[Antoine François Prevost, *abbé*]
Voyages Du Capitaine Robert Lade En Differentes Parties De
L'Afrique, De L'Asie Et De L'Amerique: Contenant L'Histoire
de sa fortune, & ses Observations sur les Colonies & le Commerce des Espagnols, des Anglois, des Hollandois, &c. Ouvrage
traduit de l'Anglois. A Paris, Chez Didot . . . M.DCC.XLIV.
. . . 2 vols.   tp NNC, tp Bod
———— [In *Œuvres Choisies de P.,* Vol. XV] A Amsterdam, &
se trouve à Paris . . . M.DCC.LXXXIV.   tp NNC, tp BM
———— [In *Œuvres Choisies de P.,* Vol. XV] Paris, De L'Imprimerie De Leblanc. 1810.   tp MH
———— [In *Œuvres de P.,* Vol. XV] A Paris, Chez Boulland-
Tardieu . . . 1823.   tp CtY

Harrisse, *op. cit.* p. 281 *supra,* pp. 47 f., approaches this work
from the obvious point of view of Prevost's interest in voyages:
"On doit croire que le roman était un cadre trop étroit pour lui
permettre de satisfaire les besoins de son imagination, car, en 1744,
nous le voyons publier sous le titre de *Voyages du capitaine
Robert Lade* . . . deux volumes remplis de descriptions géographiques, corroborées même par des cartes de Bellin. Les Pères
Jésuites seuls ne semblent pas avoir été complètement dupes, car
leur *Journal de Trévoux,* en rendant compte de l'ouvrage, avertit
que l'on y remarque 'des histoires qui ne dépareraient pas *Cleveland.*' [Cf. *Memoires pour l'histoire des sciences & des beaux
arts,* 1745 (février-mars), pp. 334-48; 528-48, especially p. 347.]
Mais ce fut tout; et le capitaine Lade prit décidément place parmi
les navigateurs dignes de foi. Ses voyages continuent d'être
étudiés; et, hier encore, à la Bibliothèque nationale, un indianiste
venu d'Angleterre y cherchait avec ardeur des renseignements sur
Java, Bantam et Batavia. Nous craignons fort, néanmoins, que ce
capitaine Lade et ses pérégrinations ne soient absolument
apocryphes." It remained, however, for J. Ducarre, "Une 'Su-

percherie Littéraire' de l'abbé Prévost les voyages de Robert Lade,"
Revue de littérature comparée, XVI(1936), [465]-476, to show
specifically that "Robert Lade n'a jamais existé et la traduction
de ses voyages est pure supercherie" and that the geographic
descriptions often parallel the voyages which Prevost was at the
time preparing for his *Histoire générale des voyages,* which in one
place actually cites the invented hero as an authority: "On en
trouve un détail curieux dans le Voïage de Robert Lade. Dampier
en parle aussi . . ." (XII, 1754, 512 n. 6). Ducarre does not consider the possible influence of imaginary voyages also. Neither
Harrisse nor Ducarre mentions that Prevost earlier translated for
Pour et contre Henry Neville's *Isle of Pines* (1668) under the
title "Découverte d'une Isle Inconnue ou Avanture de Georges
Pinès," which was reprinted in Prevost's *Contes, avantures, et
faits singuliers* (Londres et Paris, 1764); also in his *Œuvres
choisies* (Amsterdam et Paris, 1784), XXXV, 267-80. See further
Engel, pp. 128-37 and 199-201: "n'est pas un récit, pas même un
roman: c'est une mosaïque."

1744

Anonymous
Die geschwinde Reise auf dem Lufft-Schiff nach der obern
Welt, welche jüngsthin fünff Personen angestellet, um zu
erfahren, ob es eine Wahrheit sey, dasz der Planet Mars den
10. Jul. dieses Jahrs das erste mahl, so lange die Welt stehet,
mit einem Trabanten oder Mond erschienen? Der untern
Welt zu curieuser Gemüths-Ergötzung und Versicherung
dieser Begebenheit mitgetheilet durch die Allgemeine Fama.
[Lemgo?] 1744.   Klinckowstroem p. 260

1745

Anonymous
Reise eines Europäers In den Mond, Nebst einer Reise-Be-
schreibung eines Monden-Bürgers Von seiner Reise auf unsere
Erd-Kugel, Worinne Absonderlich die Sitten, Gebräuche und

Gewohnheiten derer Innwohner des Mondes und derer
Europäischen Völcker nachdencklich beschrieben werden.
Fingendo scribere verum, quis prohibet? Coppenhagen, 1745.

ICJ

Discussed in Paludan, pp. 324-26, as an "egentligt Plagiat" of
Niels Klim.

1746

Anonymous
Des weitberühmten Seeländers Nil Stairs remarquable und
höchst merkwürdige Reisen nach denen unbekannten Insuln
des orientalischen Oceani, darinnen dessen beträchtliche Schif-
fahrt, jämmerlich erlittener Schiffbruch, eilfjährige Wohnung
unter einer sehr vernünftigen indianischen Nation, angelegte
Plantagen und angestellte Heimreise, bis zu seinem, an der Cap
erfolgten Tode. Nebst andern curiösen Merkwürdigkeiten aus
dessen eigenhändigem Journal, um seiner wunderbaren Vortrefflichkeit willen, ins Hochdeutsche übersetzt und herausgegeben. Frankfurt und Leipzig. 1746.   Haken V, 329
———— [Another edition?] Erfurt, 1746.   Stuck I, 285
———— Zweite Auflage. 1749.   Haken V, 330
———— Dritter Auflage. Frankfurt und Leipzig, 1778.

Haken V, 330

Haken calls it a German original and the *Vorgänger* of *Nil
Hammelmanns Reisen* (1747), *q.v.*

1747

[Jean Baptiste de Boyer, *marquis* d'Argens]
Memoires De Monsieur Le Marquis De St. * * * , Ou Les
Amours Fugitifs Du Cloitre. 1747.   BN
———— [Another edition] A Amsterdam, Aux De'pens De La
Compagnie. M.DCC.XLVIII. 2 vols. in 1.   tp BM
———— [Another edition] 1749.   Ars
———— [Another edition] A Amsterdam, Aux Dépens De La
Compagnie. M.DCC.LIII. 2 vols. in 1.   tp BM

1747

[Charles de Fieux Mouhy, *chevalier* (1701-1784)]
Le Masque de Fer, ou les Aventures Admirables du Pere et du
Fils. La Haye, P. de Hondt, 1747. 6 vols. in 2.   Ars
———— [Another edition] A La Haye, Chez Pierre de Hondt.
MDCCL. 6 parts in 1 vol.   MH
———— [Another edition] 1752.   Mornet I, 339
———— [Another edition] A La Haye, Chez Pierre De Hondt.
M.DCC.LXIV. 3 vols. in 1.   tp BM
———— [Another edition] La Haye, P. de Hondt, 1776. 3 vols.
                                          BN (Vol. I wanting)
———— [Another edition] A La Haye, Chez Pierre De Hondt.
M.DCC.LXXVII.   tp NNC
———— [Another edition] Avignon, Offray aîné, 1829. 3 vols.
                                                          BN
———— [Another edition] 1844. 3 vols.   BN
This popular work undoubtedly went through more editions
than are listed above. For a good biographical sketch see F. C.
Green, "The Chevalier de Mouhy, an Eighteenth-Century French
Novelist," *MP*, XXII (1924-25), 225-37. Mornet gives a brief
résumé, I, 27 f.

1747

Anonymous
Nil Hammelmanns, als tapfern Nachfolgers des weitberühmten
See-Länders Nil Stairs, fortgesetzte merckwürdige Reisen, Nach
denen, nicht allein im Orientalischen Oceano, sondern auch
dem Süd-Pol zu, gelegenen, bishero meistentheils noch unbekannt gewesenen Insuln und Ländern. Wobey dessen
verschiedene Gefährlichkeiten; Treffen mit den See-Räubern,
blutiges Gefecht auf einer Menschen-Fresser-Insul, nahmens
Zelto; ausgestandene Stürme; glückliche Wiederfindung Jobst
Branders Insul, Ulterna genannt; Entdeckung einer bishero
gantz unbekannt gewesenen vortrefflichen Insul, worauf aber
keine Menschen befindlich gewesen; dieser Insul herrliche An-

bauung; Lust-Reise durch die wilde See; allwo er nach aus-
gestandenem schweren Sturm und Strandung, endlich die
beyden Insuln: Grosz- und Klein-Felsenburg angetroffen, Und
nachdem er wieder Flott worden, mit den Einwohnern dieser
beyden letztern, in sehr genaue Freundschafft gerathen, auch
einige Zeit bey ihnen auszuruhen, beschlossen hat, vorgetragen
worden. Aus der holländischen in die teutsche Sprache übersetzt. Zweyte Auflage Erfurt, druckts und verlegts Joh. David
Jungnicol, 1747.   MiU
———— Dritte Auflage. Erfurt, 1749.   Ullrich[d] XI, 489
———— [Another edition] Frankfurt und Leipzig, 1778[-80].
2 vols. in 1.   MiU

Haken gives a critical résumé, V, 328-44. Its relationship to *Nil
Stairs Reisen* (1746), *q.v.*, is not made clear. The date of the first
edition may be 1744; cf. Kippenberg, p. 121; Stuck, I, 136; Ullrich,
pp. 135 f.; and Ullrich[j], p. xxxix. The *Vorbericht* of the 1747
edition is signed "Andreas Speelmann."

                              1749

[Zaccaria Seriman (1708-1784)]
Viaggi Di Enrico Wanton Alle Terre Incognite Australi, Ed
Al Paese Delle Scimmie. [Ne' quali si spiegano il carattere, li
costumi, le Scienze, e la Polizia di quegli straordinarj Abitanti.]
Tradotti Da un manoscritto Inglese. Venice, Giovanni Targier,
1749. 2 vols.   *TLS* p. 112
———— [Another edition] In Napoli 1756. Presso Alessio Pel-
lecchia Ed a spese di Giacomo-Antonio . . . 2 vols.   tp NNC
———— Nuovamente Tradotti Da Un Manuscritto Inglese.
Berna [Venice?] MDCCLXIV. 4 vols.   tp DLC
———— Viages De Enrique Wanton A Las Tierras Incognitas
Australes, y al pais de las Monas; en donde se expresan las
costumbres, caracter, ciencias, y policìa de estos extraordi-
narios habitantes: Traducidos Del Idioma Ingles Al Italiano, y
de este al Español Por D. Joaquin De Guzman, y Manrique,
&c . . . En Alcalà: En la Imprenta de Doña Mario Garcia
Briones . . . Año de 1769[-78]. Se hallará en Madrid en Casa

de Josef Batanero. . . . 4 vols. (Vol. II, En Madrid: En la Imprenta de Pantaleon Aznar . . . 1771; Vols. III-IV, En Madrid: Por Don Antonio De Sancha . . . 1778. Se hallará, y los antecedentes en casa de Don Bernardo Alberá . . .).

tp MB, tp BM

———— Nuova Edizione. In Londra. Presso: Tommaso Brewman . . . M DCC LXXII. 4 vols.   tp BM

———— [Another Spanish edition] En Madrid: Por Don Antonio De Sancha. Año de 1778. 4 vols.   tp MH

———— [Another edition] Madrid. Año De 1781[-85] Se hallará toda la obra en casa de Don Bernardo Alberá . . . 4 vols. (Vol. III, Por Don Miguel Escribano. Año de 1785. Se hallará, y los antecedentes en casa de D. Bernardo Alberá . . .).

tp DLC, tp BM (Vol. II wanting)

———— [Another edition] Madrid En La Imprenta Real. Año de 1800. Se hallará en la librería de D. Gabriel Gomez. . . . 4 vols.   tp NNH

———— Segunda Edicion. Madrid: Se hallará en la librería de Razola . . . 1831 [Febrero-Mayo]. 4 vols.   tp NNC

"For it," says the *TLS,* February 15, 1923, p. 112, "may be claimed a place both in an Australian library and in a collection of aeronautica, and, in addition, it forms an important item in any collection of imaginary voyages, such as 'Gulliver's Travels,' by which probably it was inspired." In a subsequent article, April 19, 1923, p. 276, the same journal comments on the two endings, "one real by its author and the other a 'fake' by its Spanish translator . . . [who in his introduction to Vol. III] explains that the success with which his translation of the two volumes of the travels had met prompted him to search for further manuscripts. . . . A comparison of the last two volumes of the Italian version with those of two Spanish versions shows that they are totally distinct, and the inference is that Don Joaquin de Guzman y Manrique is himself the 'faker' of the third and fourth volumes of the Spanish version. . . ." The English original is a fiction; though the hero is an Englishman and though the Italian edition brought out in London in 1772 is dedicated to

"alla Sacra Reale Maesta' di Giorgio III", the work has come no
nearer an English translation than a few passages in a résumé in
the *Monthly Review,* XLVII(1772), 501-6. Since then it has received virtually no attention. Paludan, pp. 257-61, compares it to
Gulliver and *Niels Klim* and finds it thoroughly in the tradition
of the satiric imaginary voyage but intolerably prolix and com-
monplace ("utaalelig langtrukken og triviel"), especially the
moral reflections of the first volume; however, he adds, the
romantic element predominates strongly over the satiric. In
Michaud, Seriman is called "l'auteur du meilleur et peut-être du
seul roman philosophique que possèdent les Italiens. . . . Il n'a
pas mis de prétention dans son style; mais son ironie est aussi fine
que ses allusions sont piquantes."

1750

[Pierre Charles Fabiot Aunillon, *abbé* Du Guay de Launay
(1694-1760)]
Azor, ou Le prince enchanté; histoire nouvelle, pour servir de
chronique à celle de la terre des perroquets; traduit de l'anglois
du sçavant Popiniay. Londres, Vaillant, 1750. 2 vols. in 1. Ars
——— [In *Voyages imaginaires,* ed. Garnier, Vol. XXI] A
Amsterdam, Et se trouve à Paris . . . M.DCC.LXXXVII.
tp NNC, tp BM
——— [Translation?] Azor des Sohnes Babuk Reise nach
Persepolis oder die verkehrte Welt. Riga, 1793.   Teubner p. 25

1750

Gabriel François Coyer, *abbé* (1707-1782)
A Discovery Of The Island Frivola: Or, The Frivolous Island,
Translated from the French, Now privately handed about at
Paris, and said to be agreeable to the English Manuscripts
concerning that Island, and its Inhabitants. Wrote by Order
of A——l A———n. The Second Edition. London: Printed
for T. Payne . . . and sold by M. Cooper . . . MDCCL.
tp RPJCB

———— Decouverte de l'isle frivole, par M. L'abbe Coyer . . .
La Haye, J. Swart, 1751.   BN
———— A Supplement To Lord Anson's Voyage Round The
World. Containing A Discovery and Description of the Island
of Frivola. By The Abbé Coyer. To which is prefix'd An
Introductory Preface by the Translator. London: Printed for
A. Millar . . . and J. Whiston and B. White . . . M.DCC.LII.
                                            tp NN, tp BM
———— The Second Edition. London: Printed for A. Millar
. . . and J. Whiston and B. White . . . M.DCC.LII.   tp BM
———— Second Edition. Dublin, 1752.   Sabin V,53
———— [Another edition] Dublin: Printed For P. Wilson, and
M. Williamson . . . M.DCC.LII.   tp NNH
———— Seconde édition. n.p.,n.d.   BN
———— [Another edition] n.p.,n.d.   BN
———— [In *Bagatelles Morales*] Londres, P. Walliant, 1754.
                                                       BN
———— [Another edition of the preceding] A Londres, Et se
trouvent à Paris, Chez Duchesne . . . MDCCLIV.   tp BM
———— Seconde Edition [of the preceding] A Londres, Et
se trouvent à Paris, Chez Duschesne . . . M.DCC.LV. tp BM
———— Troisie'me E'dition [of the preceding] Augmentée.
A Londres, Chez Millar . . . 1755.   tp DLC
———— Troisiéme Édition [of the preceding] Revue & corrigée.
A Londres; Et se trouvent, à Paris, Chez Duchesne . . .
M.DCC.LVIII.   tp BM
———— Nouvelle Édition [of the preceding] A Londres, & se
vend à Francfort, Chez Knoch & Eslinger . . . M.DCC.LIX.
                                            tp MH, tp BM
———— [In *Œuvres de M. l'Abbé Coyer*, Vol. I] A Londres, Et
se trouvent à Paris, Chez Duchesne . . . M.DCC.LXV. tp Ry
———— [In *Œuvres complettes* de M. l'abbé C., Vol. I] A Paris,
Chez la veuve Duchesne . . . M.DCC.LXXXII.   tp Tay
———— [In *Bagatelles morales,* publiées par le Bibliophile
Jacob] Paris Libraire Des Bibliophiles . . . MDCCCLXXXIV
(Les Chefs—D'Œuvres Inconnus).   tp MB, tp BM
———— [A Dutch edition]   Sabin V, 52

This "voyage imaginaire de cinquante pages . . . où il s'agit de ridiculiser la vie mondaine de Paris, en attribuant à l'influence d'un nombre de Français naufragés l'existence parfaitement vaine et stupide que mènent les Frivolites, habitants d'une île qu'aurait rencontrée l'amiral Anson dans son voyage autour du monde" (Goulding, p. 98) went through so many editions in its first years that it is impossible without the opportunity of collation to determine their exact number to say nothing of their order. I believe from examination of secondary evidence that all the editions listed are separate and even that there were more. Though 1752 is often given as the date, it will be noticed that even the 1750 edition first in the list carries on the title page "second edition." I have found no trace of an earlier French original. One paragraph on it occurs in the *Monthly Review*, VI (1752), 233, and two pages in Lichtenberger,[a] pp. 47-49. Paul Deslandres, "Un Humoriste Oublié . . . ," *Académie des sciences, belles-lettres & arts de Besançon. Bulletin trimestriel*, 4e Trim., 1931, p. 207, writes: "Si l'on pouvait comparer Coyer à Erasme, l'*Ile frivole* serait son *Eloge de la Folie*. Il n'était pas le premier à raconter un voyage imaginaire, cadre commode pour une satire sociale."

1750

[Johann Michael Fleischer]
Der Dänische Robinson oder die Reisen Niels Bygaard eines gebohrnen Jutländers, Welche Nebst dessen eigenen Begebenheiten auch allerhand lustige Geschichte anderer Personen in sich halten, Ingleichen Wie er Schiffbruch gelitten und auf ein klein Eyland gelanget, von demselben aber zuletzt dennoch wiederum glücklich errettet worden. Copenhagen und Leipzig Bey Friedrich Christian Pelt [1750-53]. 4 vols. in 3 [Vols. I-II, n.d.; Vol. III, 1752; Vol. IV, 1753]   MiU
————— Zweyte Auflage. Copenhagen und Leipzig, bey Friedrich Christian Pelt, 1752. 2 vols.   Ullrich p. 148

Ullrich[d], p. [489], says that a copy exists with 1750 on the title page. On the authorship see Ullrich, p. 125, Ullrich[a], p. 108 n.50, and Stangerup, pp. 177-85. For brief mention see Schröder, pp. 82 f.

1750

[Edward Kimber (1719-1769)]
The Life And Adventures Of Joe Thompson. A Narrative founded on Fact. Written by Himself . . . London: Printed for John Hinton . . . And W. Frederick . . . Bath. MDCCL [August]. 2 vols.   tp CtY, tp BM (2 vols. in 1)
———— [Another edition] Dublin: Printed by S. Powell, For Robert Main . . . MDCCL. 2 vols.
tp MH, tp BM (Vol. I wanting)
———— The Second Edition. London: Printed for John Hinton . . . And W. Frederick . . . Bath. MDCCLI. 2 vols.
tp BM
———— La Vie Et Les Aventures De Joseph Thompson. Traduit De L'Anglois [by P. F. Puisieux] Amsterdam, J. H. Schneider, 1762. 4 vols.   BN
———— [Another edition] A Londres, Et se vend A Paris, Chez Charpentier . . . MDCCLXII. 3 vols.   tp BM
———— The Third Edition. London: Printed for John Hinton . . . And W. Frederick . . . MDCCLXIII. 2 vols.   tp DLC
———— Leben und Begebenheiten des Engländers Joseph Thompsons, aus dem Englischen von J. F. Schröter Magdeburg; Frankfurt und Leipzig, 1764-65.   Black p. 28
———— [Another French edition] A Londres, Et se vend A Paris, Chez Humaire . . . M.DCC.LXV. 3 vols.   tp MH
———— Zweite Auflage. Goslar und Leipzig, 1767. Black p. 28
———— [Another edition] Leipzig und Wolfenbüttel, 1771.
Black p. 28
———— A New edition. London: Printed for John Hinton . . . and W. Frederick . . . Bath. M DCC LXXV. 2 vols.
tp BM
———— [In *The Novelists' Magazine*, Vol. XII] London: Printed for Harrison and Co. . . . M DCC LXXXIII. 2 vols. in 1.   tp NN, tp BM

———— Joseph Thomsens Levnet og Hændelser. Oversat af Engelsk og Fransk. Kjøbenhavn, 1787[-88]. 2 vols.

Bruun IV, 484

———— [Another English edition, abridged] London, E. Newbery [1789 advtd.].   Black p. 28

———— [Another Danish edition] Oversat af Engelsk. Kjøbenhavn, 1799. 4 vols.   Bruun IV, 484

Austin Dobson gives a good introduction to *Joe Thompson,* influenced by Defoe and Longueville as well as by Fielding and Smollett, in "Polly Honeycombe," *Eighteenth Century Vignettes,* Third Series (World's Classics CCXLVII [1923]), pp. 92-96. For a scholarly introduction to the author and his works see Frank G. Black, "Edward Kimber: Anonymous Novelist of the Mid-eighteenth Century," *Harvard Studies and Notes in Philology and Literature,* XVII(1935), [27]-42. In the Dublin edition a portrait frontispiece of Joe Thompson is apparently a bad reproduction of the Patoun portrait of the poet James Thomson; this was first pointed out by W. Roberts, "A Shelf of Eighteenth-Century Novels," *Book-Collector's Quarterly,* XV(1934), 21 f.

1750

[Robert Paltock (1697-1767)]
The Life and Adventures Of Peter Wilkins, A Cornish Man: Relating particularly, His Shipwreck near the South Pole; his wonderful Passage thro' a subterraneous Cavern into a kind of new World; his there meeting with a Gawry or flying Woman, whose Life he preserv'd, and afterwards married her; his extraordinary Conveyance to the Country of Glums and Gawrys, or Men and Women that fly. Likewise a Description of this strange Country, with the Laws, Customs, and Manners of its Inhabitants, and the Author's remarkable Transactions among them. Taken from his own Mouth, in his Passage to England, from off Cape Horn in America, in the Ship Hector. With an Introduction, giving an Account of the surprizing Manner of his coming on board that Vessel, and his Death on his landing at Plymouth in the Year 1739. Illustrated with

several Cuts, clearly and distinctly representing the Structure and Mechanism of the Wings of the Glums and Gawrys, and the Manner in which they use them either to swim or fly. By R. S. a Passenger in the Hector . . . London: Printed for J. Robinson . . . and R. Dodsley . . . M.DCC.LI [December 3, 1750, postdated]. 2 vols.   tp MH, tp BM

———— [Another edition] Dublin: Printed by George Faulkner . . . MDCCLI. 2 vols. in 1.   tp BM

———— Les Hommes Volans, Ou Les Aventures De Pierre Wilkins, Traduites [by Philippe Florent de Puisieux] de l'Anglois . . . A Londres, Et se vend A Paris, Chez la Veuve Brunet . . . M.DCC.LXIII. 3 vols. tp NNC (3 vols. in 1), tp BM

———— Die Fliegenden Menschen oder Wunderbare Begebenheiten Peter Wilkins [tr. by Fr. Wilh. Zachariae]. Braunschweig [Waisenhaus] 1767. 2 vols. in 1.   MiU, tp BM

———— [In *The Novelists' Magazine,* Vol. XII] London: Printed for Harrison and Co. . . . MDCCLXXXIII. 2 vols. in 1.   tp NN, tp BM

———— [Another edition] Berwick: Printed For W. Phorson, And B. Law . . . London. M.DCC.LXXXIV. 2 vols.
     tp NN, tp BM

———— [In *Voyages imaginaires,* ed. Garnier, Vols. XXII-XXIII] A Amsterdam, Et se trouve à Paris . . . M.DCC. LXXXVIII.   tp NNC, tp BM

———— [Another English edition] Dublin: Printed by N. Kelly . . . 1797.   tp BM

———— [Another edition] London: Printed for E. Newbery . . . By J. Crowder . . . 1800.   tp Bod

———— [Abridgment, with change of proper names] The Unrivalled Adventures Of That Great Æronaut And Glum, Peter Wilkins, Taken from the Original MS. of the Author; Containing His Shipwreck On A Loadstone Rock, Near The Southern Pole; His Precipitation into a New Country, Through A Subterraneous Cavern; His Marriage There With Kiekeepewenee, A Whiskeean, or Flying Woman of Korkrdrxt: His Wonderful Conveyance Thro' The Air To King Georgetti; The Rebellion He overturned at Madgaker; with the Customs

22

and Manners of the Inhabitants there. Also, The Extraordinary
Manner Of His being taken on Board the Hector, A South-
Whaler, In Which Ship He Returned to Portsmouth, Where
He Died. By T. Trueman, F.R.S. Peter's Amanuensis on
Board the Hector. London: Printed for Thomas Tegg and
Co . . . T. Hurst . . . T. Brown, Edinburgh; and B. Dugdale,
Dublin. And sold by Champante & Whitrow . . . Wilmot
and Hill . . . T. Hughes . . . London; J. Dingle, Bury; T.
Gibbons, Bath; T. Lamb, T. Matthews, and Messrs. Cowley
and Richardson; Bristol; Messrs. Clarke & Co. M. Swindale,
and J. Reddish, Manchester; N. Rollaston, Coventry; T. Rich-
ards and W. Gray, Plymouth; Harrod and Turner, Notting-
ham; T. Binns, Leeds; T. Newling and M. Wood, Shewsbury;
W. Troughton and W. Jones, Liverpool; J. Legg, Gosport;
T. Crooks, Rotherham; J. Belsher, Birmingham . . . Printed
by T. Plummer . . . [1802].   tp MH, tp BM
———— [Another edition] London: Printed for J. Harris,
(Successor to E. Newberry) . . . by J. Crowder . . . 1804.
                                               tp DLC
———— [In *Popular Romances,* ed. Henry W. Weber] Edin-
burgh: Printed by James Ballantyne and Company, For John
Ballantyne And Company, Silvester Doig And Andrew Stirling,
Edinburgh; Longman, Hurst, Rees, Orme, And Brown, And
John Murray, London. 1812.   tp CtY
———— A New Edition . . . London: Printed For Thomas
And Joseph Allman . . . And John Fairbairn, Edinburgh.
1816. 2 vols.   MiU, tp BM (2 vols. in 1)
———— A New Edition, Revised And Corrected [London]
Printed For A. K. Newman & Co. . . . 1822. 2 vols. in 1
[Added tp: London. Published by Dean & Munday . . . and
A. K. Newman . . .]   MdBG
———— Improved Edition. Boston, Published By J. Shaw And
J. Q. Adams. 1828. [2d tp: Boston: Published By Shaw & Cush-
ing. 1829.]   tp NNC
———— [Another edition] Boston, Published by Baker & Alex-
ander. Rufus Colton, Printer, Woodstock, Vt. 1828. 2 vols. MiU

———— Improved Edition. Boston: Published By Charles Gaylord. 1832.   MiU

———— [Another edition] London: Printed And Published By J. Limbird . . . 1833.   MiU

———— [Another edition] Boston: Published By J. Shaw & J. Q. Adams. 1833.   tp MB

———— Improved Edition. Boston: Published For The Trade. 1835 [Preliminary tp: Published By George Clark. 1838]. tp NN

———— [In Smith's Standard Library London, 1839.]   tp NN

———— [In The Child's Library] London, Joseph Thomas . . . 1839.   MiU

———— Improved Edition. Boston: C. D. Strong. 1840. MiU

———— A New Edition, Thoroughly Revised [by J. C.] London: [Harrison and Co., Printers, for] John W. Parker . . . M.DCCC.XLIV.   tp NN, tp BM

———— Improved Edition. Hartford: S. Andrus And Son, 1846.   tp MB

———— Improved Edition. Boston: T. Bedlington & Son. 1847.   tp MH

———— [Another edition] London: Thomas Dewhurst . . . 1848.   MiU

———— Improved Edition. Hartford: S. Andrus And Son, 1848.   MiU

———— Improved Edition. Hartford: S. Andrus And Son, [184-?].   MiU

———— [In The Universal Library (No.29. Miscellaneous, Vol. I, Pt.3)] London: N. Cooke . . . 1854 [separate tp: London: Nathaniel Cooke . . . n.d.].   tp DLC, tp BM

———— [Another edition. London, 185-?]   MB

———— [Another edition] Philadelphia: Wm. A. Leary [185-?].   CSmH

———— [Another edition] London: George Vickers . . . [1860].   tp BM

———— [Another edition] London George Routledge And Sons . . . New York [Printed by Ballantyne, Hanson And Co. London And Edinburgh] 1883.   tp CtY

——— [Another edition, ed. A. H. Bullen] London: Reeves & Turner . . . 1884. 2 vols.   tp NNC, tp BM

——— [Another edition] London, George Routledge And Sons, Limited . . . [18-?].   MiU

——— [In Everyman's Library, No.676, ed. A. H. Bullen] London: Published by J. M. Dent & Sons Ltd And In New York By E. P. Dutton & Co [1906]   tp NNC, tp BM

——— [Another edition] Dulau & Co. Ltd . . . London . . . 1925.   tp CtY, tp BM

——— [Another edition, ed. A. H. B(ullen)] 1928 J. M. Dent & Sons Ltd. London & Toronto E. P. Dutton & Co. Ltd. New York.   tp NN, tp BM

——— [Abridged by V. H. Collins, in Books within Books series, ed. Richard Wilson] London Edinburgh Thomas Nelson And Sons Ltd [1928].   tp Bod

——— [Another edition] London, John Dicks, n.d.
        Hippe p. 408

——— [Another edition, London?] Hodgson and Co. n.d.
        DL

——— [Another edition] Philadelphia: Jas. B. Smith & Co . . . n.d.   tp MB

Though this work was listed in the *GM* for November, XX (1750), [528], I have taken for the publication date December 3 as given by Ralph Strauss, *Robert Dodsley Poet, Publisher & Playwright* (London and New York, John Lane, 1910), p. 340. I find no convincing evidence for an edition with 1750 on the title page, as sometimes given (e.g., Sabin, XIV,149). The author is supposed to have been unidentified until a pseudonymous contributor in the *Monthly Magazine; or British Register,* XIV (1802), 379, named him; proof was provided in 1835 by the discovery of a signed agreement between the author and his publishers, as stated in the advertisement to the Smith's Standard Library edition of 1839 and restated with fuller details by Jas. Crossley, *N&Q*[1S.],X(1854), 212 f. The authorship, however, was known among Paltock's contemporaries: in *The Adventures of a Rake in the Character of a Public Orator* (London, 1759-60) the author, R. Lewis, refers (I,4) to "the Authors of Giants Histories, *Flying-men, Dog-birds*, &c.," and appends a footnote, "Written by one *P-lt-ck.*" This evidence was first brought to light by E. Phillips Poole, *TLS,* October 4, 1928, p. 711. The "R.S." on the title page is most easily explained as either a misprint or meaningless pseudonym; it has been suggested that it is a telonism of Peter Wilkins (see G. C. Boase and W. P. Courtney, *Bibliotheca Cornubiensis,* London, 1878, II,421) and that it may be intended for Gulliver's Richard Sympson (see W. Roberts, *The Bookworm* . . . , 3S., 1890, p. 199). To the biographical references in the *DNB* should be added W. E. A. Axon, *N&Q,* 10S.,XII(1909),286, and A. J. P. Skinner, *TLS,* May 14, 1925, p. 335.

Comments range from near-condemnation to extravagant praise. "Here," says the *Monthly Review,* IV(1750),157, "is a very strange performance indeed. It seems to be the illegitimate offspring of no very natural conjunction betwixt *Gulliver's* travels and *Robinson Crusoe;* but much inferior to the meaner of these two performances, either as to entertainment or utility. It has all that is impossible in the one, or improbable in the other, without the wit and spirit of the first, or the just strokes of nature and useful lessons of morality of the second. There are likewise many things in this work which appear to be derived from hints drawn from the *Arabian* nights entertainment. However, if the invention of wings for mankind to fly with, is a sufficient amends for all the dulness and unmeaning extravagancies of this author, we are willing to allow that his book has some merit; and that he deserves encouragement at least as an able mechanic, if not as a good writer." Far in the other direction, the *Retrospective Review* in a long résumé, VII(1823),i,120-83, avows, p. 142, that "Certainly this destruction of the immortal fame of the unknown author of *Peter Wilkins,* is the greatest literary delinquency of the last age"; Southey, *Poetical Works* (London, 1838), VIII,231, calls the winged people "the most beautiful creatures of imagination that ever were devised"; and, in the present age, Edmund Gosse, *English Literature: an Illustrated Record* (New York, Macmillan, 1905), III,327, calls it a "beautiful dream of a winged race . . . in its isolated way . . . a minor classic." Whatever its merit, it has again and again been spoken of for its pleasing qualities, from an inquiry in the *Monthly Magazine; or British Register,* XII(1801), 285, down to George Saintsbury and E. A. Baker. The former writes in *The English Novel* (London, Dent, and New York, Dutton, 1913), p. 145: "It was once fashionable to dismiss *Peter* as a boy's book, because it discovers a world of flying men and women; . . . it has more recently been fashionable to hint a sneer at it as 'sentimental' because of its presentment of a sort of fantastic and unconventional Amelia . . . in the heroine Youwarkee. Persons who do not care for fashion will perhaps sometimes agree that, though not exactly a masterpiece, it is rather a charming book"; and Baker, V,44, believes that "Paltock's homely yet sensitive and graphic style might charm any lover of good English." Yet despite such avowals and despite the numerous editions, its record is one of neglect, from Dunlop's evidence in 1814, who states, II,591, that it "has now fallen into unmerited neglect," down to the *TLS,* May 7, 1925, p. 312, which states that it has "never taken its deserved place in the lists of popular literature." Edith J. Morley, *YWES 1925,* VI(1927), 224, strikes the same note: "It is difficult to understand why the book has not been more widely known in recent years, particularly to those interested in the movement of thought in the eighteenth century." This implication that the work is not the last survivor of a dying type of fiction, as regarded by some critics (e.g., Carl Holliday, *English Fiction from the Fifth to the Twentieth Century,* New York, Century, 1912, p. 201), but a forward-looking book, even another contribution to preromanticism, forms the basis of a brief but penetrating comment by Rowland E. Prothero (baron Ernle), *The Light Reading of Our Ancestors* (London, Hutchinson [1927]), pp. 282-84. Partially corroborative are the repeatedly referred-to literary allusions of the 19th century: by Southey ("The Curse of Kehama," vi,2); by Lamb ("Christ's Hospital Five and Thirty Years Ago"); by Coleridge (*Specimens of the Table Talk,* London, 1835,II,337-39, under date of July 5, 1834); and by Leigh Hunt ("Of Peter Wilkins and the Flying Women," *London Journal,* No.32; same essay in *The*

Seer, No.31; and *A Book for a Corner*, London, 1851, I,[68]-92).
Also, Peter and his flying women receive mention in Scott's
Antiquary, chap. xi; in *Martin Chuzzlewit*, chap. xxi; and, anachronistically, in *Henry Esmond*, bk.iii,chap.iv. Two recent
studies show that both Coleridge and Shelley drew poetic inspiration from Paltock: Harold L. Hoffman, *An Odyssey of the Soul:
Shelley's Alastor* (New York, Columbia University Press, 1933),
pp. 78-83, and John R. Moore, "Coleridge's Indebtedness to
Paltock's *Peter Wilkins*," *MP*, XXXI(1933-34), 79-83. The theme
of flying women was recurrently used for stage spectacles and
pantomimes up to 1874 (see the BM Catalogue; Boase and
Courtney, *op. cit.;* and Roberts, *loc. cit.,* p. 202); one, *Peter
Wilkins: or, the Flying Islanders* (New York, Samuel French,
n.d.) was particularly popular, being played in London (1827),
Boston (1828 and 1854), and New York (1852), according to
the performance record given on the inside cover; see further
George C. D. Odell, *Annals of the New York Stage* (New York,
Columbia University Press, 1928-31), Vols. III-VI incl.

To the critical references already cited should be added the
introductions of A. H. Bullen; De la Mare, pp. 64-68; Dottin,
pp. 392 ff.; Prica, pp. [33]-47; Sir Walter Raleigh, *The English
Novel* . . . (London, Murray [1894]), pp. 219 f.; Ullrich[e], col.
112 f.; and Weber, pp. xxxi f.

1751

Oluf Friedrich Jacob Jakobsen, *pseudonym?*
  Der dänische Avanturier. Oder des Herrn von R. eines gebohrnen Dänen und Verwandten des berühmten Engelländers, Robinson Crusoe, wunderbare Begebenheiten und Reisen nach
Frankreich, Ost- und Westindien und in die Südsee, größten-
theils von ihm selbst in dänischer Sprache beschrieben, nach
seinem Tode aber ins Deutsche übersetzet und herausgegeben
von Oluf Friedrich Jacob Jakobsen. Frankfurt und Leipzig.
1751[-52]. 2 vols. in 1.   tp CtY

Haken gives a résumé, I,404 ff., and Mildebrath a criticism,
pp. 104-7, in which he regards the work as a German original

and Jakobsen a pseudonym. Lessing, in a brief review for the *Berlinische privilegirte Zeitung* of 18 September, 1751, says on this point: "Ohne die Wahrheit dieser Umstände zu untersuchen, müssen wir gestehen, dasz er für einen Ausländer ziemlich deutsch und für einen Deutschen ziemlich ausländisch schreibt," as reprinted in *Gotthold Ephraim Lessings sämtliche Schriften,* ed. Karl Lachmann, 3 Auf. (Stuttgart, 1889), IV,357.

1751

[Martigny, *comte de*]
    Voyage d'Alcimédon, ou Naufrage qui conduit au port . . . [Histoire plus vrai que vraisemblable, mais qui peut encourager à la recherche des terres inconnues] Amsterdam, 1751. BN
    ——— [Another edition] Amsterdam, 1759.   BN
    ——— [Another edition] Paris, 1759.   Mornet I, 350
    ——— [Another edition] Amsterdam, 1760.   BN
    ——— [Another edition] Nancy, Leclerc. Paris, Merlin, 1768.
                                      Mornet I, 382
    ——— [In *Voyages imaginaires,* ed. Garnier, Vol. X] A Amsterdam, Et se trouve à Paris . . . M.DCC.LXXXVII.
                                      tp NNC, tp BM

    See my reference to this, n. 277. The *Nouvelle Bibliothèque universelle des romans* (Paris [1800]), 2 Année, III, [88]-203 [i.e.,103], gives a résumé. Servais Étienne, *Le Genre romanesque en France depuis l'apparition de la "Nouvelle Héloïse" jusqu'aux approches de la révolution* (Paris, Colin, 1922), p. 86 n.4., calls it "un fatras où se mélangent les clichés à la Prévost."

1751

Ralph Morris, *supposed author*
    A Narrative Of The Life and astonishing Adventures Of John Daniel, A Smith at Royston in Hertfortshire, For a Course of seventy Years. Containing, The melancholy Occasion of his Travels. His Shipwreck with one Companion on a desolate Island. Their way of Life. His accidental discovery of a

Woman for his Companion. Their peopling the Island. Also, A Description of a most surprising Engine, invented by his Son Jacob, on which he flew to the Moon, with some Account of its Inhabitants. His return, and accidental Fall into the Habitation of a Sea-Monster, with whom he lived two Years. His further Excursions in Search of England. His Residence in Lapland, and Travels to Norway, from whence he arrived at Aldborough, and further Transactions till his death, in 1711. Aged 97 . . . Taken from his own Mouth, By Mr. Ralph Morris. London: Printed for M. Cooper . . . MDCCLI [November?].   tp BM

———— The Second Edition. London: Printed for T. Parker . . . M.DCC.LXX.   tp MH

———— [Another edition] London: Printed and Sold by S. Fisher . . . also sold by T. Hurst . . . and Wilmott and Hill . . . 1801.   tp BM

———— [Excerpt] Flying And No Failure! Or, Aerial Transit Accomplished More Than A Century Ago. Being A Minute Descriptive Account Of "A Most Surprising Engine," Invented, constructed, and used with the greatest success, by Jacob, the son of Mr. John Daniel, of Royston, the latter of whom, who survived his son, died in 1711, aged 97. Reprinted Verbatim From That Excessively-Rare Little Work, "Narrative of the Life and astonishing Adventures of John Daniel . . . by the Rev. Ralph Morris,"—London, 1751 . . . With An Appendix. Totham: Printed by Charles Clark (an Amateur) at his Private Press. 1848.   tp NN, tp Bod

———— [In The Library of Imposters, Vol. I, ed. N. M. Penzer] London Robert Holden & Co. Ltd . . . 1926. tp NN, tp BM

The lack of originality is apparent by reference to those who have commented upon this work, but no careful study of its many sources has been made. Prica discusses it, pp. [48]-51, as an imitation of *Peter Wilkins* (cf. *Monthly Review,* V,1751, 518), but Penzer in his introduction, pp. v-ix, thinks their independence is proved by the mistaken assumption that they appeared too closely together. Baker points out, V, 44 n.3, that *John Daniel* came "exactly twelve months later"; he calls it "a servile copy, only departing from its original by introducing a flight to the moon, after Bishop Godwin and Bishop Wilkins, not to mention others"; but cf. Lawton, "Bishop Godwin's *Man in the Moone*," p. 45 n.1. De la Mare in a brief résumé, pp. 250-52, adds *Isle of Pines* to the probable sources, and Watson, pp. 129 f., mentions *Cacklogallinia*. A reviewer in the *TLS*, March 3, 1927, p. 137, wondering why the work should be reprinted in the Library of Imposters, writes: "Anybody endowed with a rather pedestrian fancy and some industry could have put together Daniel's early career, his shipwreck, the female interest in his adventures, his aeroplane the Eagle, and his monsters, with the help of Robinson Crusoe, a glance or two at 'Moll Flanders,' and a careful look at the island of Laputa." Penzer states that the suppression of the name of Ralph Morris "after the first edition seems to suggest the possibility that he actually was the author, but extensive enquiries have not yielded a single scrap of evidence on the subject." In the *Monthly Review*, VII(1752),470, is brief mention of *Virtue triumphant, and pride abased; in the humorous history of Dicky Gotham, and Doll Clod*, by R. P., who is presumably Robert Paltock. For the "R. P." there is a footnote in the Bodleian copy of the *Monthly Review* in Griffiths's hand reading "author of Charles Osborne, John Daniel &c. all damn'd." This attribution to Paltock is not wholly convincing, for Griffiths went out of his way to review and condemn these novels and several others by grouping them together, and he may have grouped their anonymous authors under one identification without actual knowledge.

1751

Anonymous
Der die Schätze des Reichthums in der Neuen Welt suchende, und nicht findende Tyroler in einer anmuthigen Historischen Beschreibung und Moralischen Vorstellung des Lasters der Unzufriedenheit Dreszden zu finden bey Joh. Nicolao Gerlachen, 1751.   tp MiU

1751

Anonymous

Des zu Wasser und Lande weit und breit herumreisenden und weltberühmten Leonhardi Mirifici, eines Americanischen Passagiers, seltsame und sehr merckwürdige Begebenheiten, Worinnen nicht allein dessen wunderliche mit vornehmen Frauenzimmer gespielte Liebes-Händel angemercket, sondern auch dessen ausgeübte Heldenthaten ausführlich zu lesen sind, Welche der curieusen Welt zum Vergnügen entworffen D.N.H. Franckfurt und Leipzig, 1751.   tp NN

1752

Franz Urban Bawier, *supposed author*

Des See-Capitains Franz Urban Bawiers merckwürdige Reise und Begebenheiten, seine Kriegsdienste zu Land, See-fahrten nach Ost- und Westindien und endliche Wohlfarth, von ihm selbst beschrieben. Franckfurth und Leipzig, G. P. Monath, 1752.   BN

———— [Another edition] Merkwürdige Seereise nach den beeden Indien, in einer Reihe von ausserordentlichen Begebenheiten . . . Frankfurt und Leipzig, bei George Peter Monath, 1777. 2 vols in 1.   tp BM

"Ist eine abentheuerliche Erdichtung," states Stuck, I,20; the *Vorbericht* of the 1777 edition protests against its being considered a robinsonade.

1752

[William Goodall, *supposed author*]

The Adventures Of Capt. Greenland. Written In Imitation of all those Wise, Learned, Witty and Humorous Authors, who either already have, or hereafter may Write in the same Stile and Manner . . . London: Printed for R. Baldwin . . . M.DCC.LII. 3 vols.   tp NNC, tp Bod

"To avoid repetition of the same characteristics, we refer the reader back to our accounts of *John Daniel, Howel ap David Price* . . . [etc.]."—*Monthly Review,* VI (1752), 311.

1752

Franz Lilienstein, *pseudonym*
Der weitbereiste Straszburger, oder des Herrn Franz Lilien-steins, eines gebohrnen Straszburgers, wunderbare Begeben-heiten, durch ihn selbst beschrieben. Copenhagen und Leipzig, bey Friedrich Christian Pelt. 1752.   Ullrich p. 153

The subject of a study by Rod. Reuss, "Le Robinson strasbour-geois," *Revue alsacienne,* II(1878-79), [289]-96; [337]-45.

1752

Howell ap David Price, *pseudonym*
A Genuine Account Of The Life and Transactions Of Howell ap David Price, Gentleman of Wales. Exhibiting A Series of most remarkable Occurrences during his Seven Years Travels Abroad; Five of which were spent with a Lady he had released from Slavery. With farther Particulars since his Return with her to England. Written by Himself. London: Printed for T. Osborne . . . MDCCLII [postdated?].   tp MH

Mentioned briefly by Watson, pp. 131 f. Merits one condemna-tory sentence in the *Monthly Review,* V (November, 1751), 459.

1752

[Stanislaus I, Lesczinski, *king of Poland* (1677-1766)]
Entretien D'Un Européan Avec Un Insulaire Du Royaume De Dumocala. [Paris?] M.DCC.LII.   tp BM
———— Nouvelle Edition. Par le R[oi] D[e] P[ologne] D[uc] D[e] L[orraine] E[t] D[e] B[ar]. M DCC LIV.   tp BM
———— Nouvelle Edition. Par Sa Majesté le R.D.P.D.D.L.E. D.B**. . . A Paris, Chez Duchesne . . . M DCC LV.   tp BM
———— [In *Œuvres du philosophe Bienfaisant,* III, 223-88] A Paris. M.DCC.LXIII.   tp BM

———— [Another edition of the preceding, III,112-45] A Amsterdam, M.DCC.LXIV.   tp BM

———— [Another edition] [Paris? 1790?].   BM (tp wanting)

————[In *Œuvres choisies de Stanislas* . . . , pp. 302-27] Paris, A La Librairie De J. Carez . . . Et Chez Eymery . . . 1825.   tp BM

Briefly noticed in Kirchenheim, pp. 253-55, Lichtenberger[a], p. 371, and Goulding, p. 96; the proportion of narrative to exposition is very small.

1752

Voltaire (François Marie Arouet) (1694-1778)
Le Micromégas De M.De Voltaire. Londres [1752; March?].
      Bengesco I, 440

A bibliography of *Micromégas,* which was composed probably as early as 1747 and perhaps had its origin in his *Voyage de Gangan,* now known by title only, is too formidable an undertaking to be attempted here, and no satisfactorily complete bibliography of Voltaire exists. See, however, Georges Bengesco, *Voltaire: bibliographie de ses œuvres* (Paris, 1882-90), I,440-42; 474-79; IV,xiv f., 50 ff. He does not include translations, some of which may be found in Paul Wallich and Hans von Müller, *Die deutsche Voltaire-Literatur des achtzehnten Jahrhunderts* . . . (Berlin [Liebheit & Thiesen], 1921), pp. 25, 37, 39, 70; about English translations Ronald S. Crane, "The Diffusion of Voltaire's Writings in England, 1750-1800," *MP,* XX(1922-23), 261 n.2, writes, "There is as yet no adequate bibliography of these translations. The list in the British Museum Catalogue is far from complete." See also Gustave L. Van Roosbroeck, "Additions and Corrections to Voltaire's Bibliography," *MLN,* XLIV(1929), 328-30, and Francis J. Crowley, "Corrections and Additions to Bengesco's *Bibliographie,*" *ibid.,* L(1935), 440-41. A list of editions by 1800 would run at least into the thirties. Indispensable for works about Voltaire is the work of Mary-Margaret H. Barr, *A Century of Voltaire Study . . . 1825-1925*

(New York, Institute of French Studies, 1929), and *idem,* "Bibliographical Data on Voltaire from 1926 to 1930," *MLN,* XLVIII(1933), 292-307. See especially Flammarion, pp. 479-87; Goulding, pp. 102 f.; Dorothy M. McGhee, *Voltairian Narrative Devices as Considered in the Author's Contes Philosophiques* (Menasha, George Banta, 1933), *passim* (she calls it on p. 13 an "extraordinary voyage"); Paludan, pp. 161-64; and Pietro Toldo, "Voltaire conteur et romancier," *Zeitschrift für französische Sprache und Litteratur,* XL(1912-13), [131]-185. Goulding writes: "Les douze pages de *Micromégas,* ne sont qu'un *Voyage à Lilliput* exagéré, un *Voyage à Brobdingnag* en sens inverse. L'habitant du monde de Sirius . . . n'est autre que Lemuel Gulliver à Lilliput avec des proportions un peu agrandies, et ses raisonnements sur la nature relative de la grandeur et de la petitesse sont exactement pareils à ceux de Gulliver un peu différemment exprimés. . . . Notons que *Micromégas* est en même temps une satire du roman à la mode. Comme tous les voyageurs imaginaires, Micromégas et son compagnon ont le don des langues cultivé à un degré remarquable. Comme tous leurs semblables, ils se font renseigner par les sages sur les conditions dans lesquelles vit la race qu'ils viennent de découvrir."

1752

Anonymous
De Walchersche Robinson: Zynde Een Zeldzame, Doch Tevens Ware Geschiedenis, Behelzende Deszelfs Geboorte, op een onbekend Eiland: Zeldzame Huishouding aldaar, buiten eenige zamenleving, En wonderlyke Verlossing van hetzelve. Door hem zelven beschreven; En naar zyn eigen handschrift, nu voor de eerste reis in het licht gebracht. Te Rotterdam, By Alardus Van Eyk . . . 1752. tp BM
———Tweede Uitgaaf. Te Rotterdam, By N. Cornel . . . [17-?]. MiU

In Staverman's discussion, pp. 97-101, he includes a comparison with *Hai Ebn Yokdhan,* to which it is very similar and which the author undoubtedly knew.

1753

William Bingfield, *pseudonym*
The Travels And Adventures Of William Bingfield, Esq;
Containing, As surprizing a Fluctuation of Circumstances, both
by Sea and Land, as ever befel one Man. With An accurate
Account of the Shape, Nature, and Properties of that most
furious, and amazing Animal, the Dog-Bird. Printed from his
own Manuscript . . . London: Printed for E. Withers . . .
and R. Baldwin . . . M.DCC.LIII. 2 vols.   tp NN, tp BM
———— The Voyages, Shipwreck, Travels, Distresses, Strange
Adventures, And Miraculous Preservation, Of William Bingfield, Esq. Who, With two others, was cast away on a Desolated
Island, where they discovered the surprising ferocity and
tractable disposition of that amazing Animal called The Dog
Bird. Likewise an account of his dispersing an immense multitude of African Cannibals, Who were feasting on the miserable
wretches they had taken Captives, one of whom our Author
releases. He then reinstates an Indian King, who generously
rewards him for his valour; but at the death of this Monarch is
again reduced to great hardships—Fights for Abluffcar, gains
the victory, and is once more richly rewarded—Makes his
escape, engages his passage, and is taken by Pirates—over-
powers them in a storm, and retakes the Ship—want provision
—cast lots who shall die—eat human flesh—Are released; and,
after many perilous dangers and eminent exploits, arrive safe
in England. London: Printed And Sold By S. Fisher . . .
Also Sold By T. Hurst . . . and R. C. Staines, Chelmsford.
1799.   tp DLC, tp BM
———— [Another edition] London [c.1839?]. Lockhart III, 8

In a letter of November 10, 1814, to Daniel Terry, Sir Walter
Scott expresses the desire to reread *Bingfield* and later writes on
the flyleaf of Volume I of the 1753 edition: "I read this scarce
little *Voyage Imaginaire* when I was about ten years old, and
long after sought for a copy without being able to find a person
who would so much as acknowledge having heard of William

Bingfield. . . . I am therefore induced to think the book is of very rare occurrence," as quoted in J. G. Lockhart, *Memoirs of the Life of Sir Walter Scott* (Boston and New York, Houghton Mifflin, 1902), III,8 n.2. Perhaps the title of the 1799 edition explains why none of Scott's acquaintance would admit knowledge of it, for as Baker says, V,44 f., n.3, it is a story "of the marvellous that more than border[s] on the ridiculous." Prica, p. 51, mentions it as an imitation of *Peter Wilkins,* and E. Phillips Poole, *TLS,* October 4, 1928, p. 711, thinks it not impossible that Paltock wrote *Bingfield* also; cf. the implication in the *Monthly Review,* XII(1755), 394 f., quoted on page 342 *infra.*

1753

[Eléazar de Mauvillon (1712-1779)]
Le Soldat Parvenu Ou Memoires Et Aventures De Mr. De Verval Dit Bellerose. Par Mr. De M***. . . A Dresde 1753. Chez George Conrad Walther. . . . 2 vols.　　　tp BM
———— Nouvelle Edition. A Dresde 1758. Chez George Conrad Walther . . . 2 vols.　　　tp Bod
———— [Another edition] 1759.　　　Mornet I, 352

1753

Paul Wilhem von Meerheim, *pseudonym*
Paul Wilhem von Meerheim eines Obersächsischen Chymici glücklich vollführte Reise-Beschreibung nach denen unbekannten Ost- und Südwerts gelegenen Indianischen Insuln, von wannen derselbe nebst seinen Cameraden glücklich und zur grösten Freude seiner Freunde retourniret ist, vielen zum Vergnügen bekannt gemachet. Erlangen und Leipzig [Nürnberg printed], 1753. Zu finden in dem Müllerischen Buchladen.
　　　tp BM

Stuck remarks, I,195: "Ist eine Erdichtung mit alchymischen Grillen." The "Vorbericht des Verlegers" is signed Johann Caspar Müller. A MS note in the BM copy gives the author's name as Heid of Erlangen, who voyaged to the East Indies.

1753

[Otto Bernhard Verdion, *alleged author*]
Seltsame Lebensgeschichte Zweyer Schwaben Worinnen Derer-
selben Merkwurdigsten Schicksale sowohl zu Wasser, als zu
Lande aufrichtig erzahlet werden Den Liebhabern der Historie
zum ergotzenden Zeitvertreibe ans Licht gestellet von Einem
der mit dabey gewesen Dreszden bey Johann Nicolaus Gerlach
[1753].   tp MiU
The date is from the *Vorrede:* "Geschrieben den 1. Junii 1753."
For the possibility that Verdion wrote this see Ullrich, p. 145,
Strauch's review of Ullrich, pp. 247 f., and Ullrich[a], p. 108 n.49.

1753

Anonymous
Gevallen Van Den Oude En Jongen Robinson. Behelzende de
opvoeding van den jongen Robinson tot Utrecht; zyne deugden,
gebreken en huwelyk. Vertrekt na Madera om zyn Vader
uittevinden bevegt een zee-rover. Gaat hem, die uit de
gevankenisse van de Inquisitie gevlugt was, opzoeken. Strand
op Tabago. Word door zyn Vader van de dood gered, zonder
hem te kennen. Oprechting van een nieuw gemeenebest
aldaar; en keeren te zamen met veele schatten na Europa.
Doormengt met veele Hertaandoenende gevallen en Vaderlandsche Geschiedenissen. Alles door den jongen Robinson
zelfs beschreeven. T' Amsterdam, By Steeven Van Esveldt . . .
1753.   tp BM
———— [Serially in *Maandelyksche Berichten uit den andere
Waereld,* Juli-December] 1764.   Staverman p. 171
———— Tweede Druk . . . Te Amsterdam, By Steven Van
Esveldt . . . 1766. 2 vols.   MiU, tp BM
Discussed in Staverman, pp. 101-10, where reference is made
to an unusually lengthy review in the *Boekzaal* (which I have
not seen) for October, 1753, pp. 437-61, and again in January,
1767, after the second edition, called "dit beroemde werk . . . een

23

der uitmuntenste in zyn soort" and placed in the same class with
Télémaque.

1753

Anonymous
  Die Insul Charlotten-Burg Und der darauf besindliche Her-
  culsberg, oder Liebes-Geschichte der geliebten Charlotte ver-
  lobte Hercules. Franckfurt und Leipzig, 1753. Ullrich p. 157.
  Brief mention in Schröder, p. 83.

1753

Anonymous
  Des maldivischen Philosophen Robine und dessen Sohns und
  Nachfolgers Robinson Leben, Reisen, Thaten und Beherr-
  schung der Philosophen-Insul. Erfurt, druckts und verlegts
  Johann David Jungnicol 1753 [-54]. 2 vols.   Ullrich p. 157

  Schröder in his brief mention, pp. 83 f., calls it "eine Parodie
  der Felsenburg."

1754

Heinrich Löwenthal, *pseudonym*
  Heinrich Löwenthals wahrhaffte und wunderbare Begeben-
  heiten, Welche sich mit ihm auf seinen Reisen in Deutschland,
  Pohlen, Franckreich, Holl- und Engelland; ingleichen in
  Afrika ereignet haben. Von ihm selbst beschrieben. [Alten-
  burg?] Anno 1754. 2 vols. in 1.   tp BM

1754

Drake Morris, *pseudonym*
  The Travels Of Mr. Drake Morris, Merchant in London. Con-
  taining His Sufferings and Distresses in Several Voyages at
  Sea. Written by Himself. London: Printed for the Author:
  And Sold by R. Baldwin . . . M.DCC.LV [postdated].

                                              tp MH, tp Bod

————— The Second Edition. London: Printed for the Author: And Sold by R. Baldwin . . . M.DCC.LV.   tp BM

————— A New Edition. London: Printed By John Abraham . . . For R. Dutton . . . 1797.   tp DLC, tp Bod

The *GM,* XXIV (1754), 534, lists this among the books published in November, and it is mentioned in the same month in the *Monthly Review,* XI, 395. The DLC copy bears on the title page a rubber stamp which covers the date so that it looks like 1707, and therefore a filing card was printed with that date on it. After comparing Sabin, XII, 394, and the BM Catalogue, I asked Mr. Valta Parma, curator of the Rare Book Collection, to make a special examination for me. He reports that "the appearance of the paper and the press work of the volume is that of 1797" and that "all of the advertisements prove this copy to be from the edition of 1797." Advertised are the second edition of *Consequences; or, Adventures at Raxall Castle* and *Which Is the Oracle? Burke or O'Brien;* the first title is a novel of 1796 by Thomas S. Surr. There is no basis for the existence of a 1707 edition of *Drake Morris.*

1755

[Adrian Belek]

Reisebeschreibung um die ganze Welt. Magdeburg, 1755. 3 vols.   Stuck I, 23

After the title Stuck adds in brackets "in alle 4 Welttheile."

1755

[Johann Michael Fleischer]

Der Isländische Robinson, oder die wunderbaren Reisen und Zufälle Gissur Isleif, Eines gebohrnen Isländers. Darinnen insonderheit dessen zehenjähriger einsamer Aufenthalt, auf einer kleinen unbewohnten Insul, und endliche Errettung von derselben beschrieben wird, mit unterlaufenden artigen Liebesbegebenheiten anderer Personen. Nebst beygefügtem

Anhang einer kurzen doch zuverläszigen Nachricht von der groszen Insul Island, auch accuraten Landcharte derselben. Copenhagen und Leipzig, bey Friedrich Christian Pelt, 1755.
                                                tp MH

On the authorship see Ullrich, p. 125, Ullrich^a, p. 108 n.50, and Stangerup, pp. 177-85.

1755

Friga Reveep, *pseudonym*
   The Life And surprizing Adventures Of Friga Reveep, Of Morlaix, in France; Who was Sixteen Years in an un-inhabited Part of Africa, and how he met with a young Virgin who was banish'd; in what Manner they liv'd together, and had two Children, a Son and a Daughter, the latter dying when she was six Years of Age; together with their surprizing Deliverance to their own Country again. With A faithful Relation of all that past during the Time that he was there. Written in French by himself, and translated into English by Mr. Transmarine. 1755. Licensed and entered according to Order. tp BM

The date is by no means certain; having no imprint, it is catalogued by the BM as London? 1770?

1755

[Otto Bernhard Verdion, *alleged author*]
   Der Dreszdner Avanturieur, oder Begebenheiten eines gebohrnen Dreszdners aufgesetzt und beschrieben von ihm selbst. Franckfurt und Leipzig, 1755. 2 vols. in 1.   Ullrich p. 160
———— [Another edition] Frankfurt und Leipzig, 1757. 3 vols. in 1.   tp BM

For the possibility that Verdion wrote this imitation of *Felsenburg,* cf. Ullrich, p. 145, Strauch's review of Ullrich, pp. 247 f., and Ullrich^a, p. 108 n.49. Mildebrath, pp. 110-13, gives an analysis. Apparently the "Dritter Theil" of 1757, which is a continuation, was not published with the 1755 edition.

1755

Anonymous

Der bey Gefangenschaft seiner entfuhrten Mutter in Irrland gebohrne Piccartus Nachmahliger entdeckter Mylord von England nebst dessen seltsamen und gefährlichem Lebenswandel Dreszden bey Johann Nicolaus Gerlach 1755. tp MiU

1755

Anonymous

Der Hartz-Robinson. Oder: Geschichte des Herrn Theophili von B** worinnen dessen wunderbare Geburth, Reisen, Solda-ten-Leben, Gefangenschaft, und andere lesenswurdige Bege-benheiten zu finden sind, von ihm selbst entworffen, nunmehro aber nach dessen Tode zum Druck befordert von Lecrano. [Franckfurth und Leipzig (Vol. II only)] Anno 1755 [-57]. 2 vols. Ullrich p. 161
———— Neue und verbesserte Auflage [of Vol. I]. Franckfurt und Leipzig 1768. tp MiU

Bound with the MiU *neue Auflage* is Volume II ("Fortsetzung und Beschlusz") of the first edition.

1755

Anonymous

Voyage Curieux d'un Philadelphe dans des Pays nouvelle-ment découverts. La Haye, Aux dépens de la Compagnie, M.D.CCLV. Wijngaarden p. 247

Discussed in Wijngaarden, pp. 189-97; cf. my note 183. He refers to it as "une des premières œuvres émanées de l'officine d'une loge de franc-maçonnerie."

1755

Anonymous

A Voyage To The World In The Centre of the Earth. Giving An Account of the Manners, Customs, Laws, Government and Religion of the Inhabitants, Their Persons and Habits described: With several other Particulars. In which is Introduced, The History Of An Inhabitant of the Air, Written by Himself. With some Account of the Planetary Worlds. London: Printed for S. Crowder and H. Woodgate . . . M.DCC.LV.   tp DLC, tp BM

The reviewer in the *Monthly Review,* XII (1755), 394 f., dismisses this as "a moral and philosophical romance, somewhat after the manner of *Bergerac's* voyage to the moon, and the well-known journey of Don *Gonsales;* but inferior to both in the plan, conduct, and writing: it seems to come from the author of the *Dog-Birds, Glums,* and *Gawrys,* and some other later marvelous performances, which we have had the ill luck to peruse." It also derives from Holberg, as Baker has pointed out, V, 44 f.,n.3.

1755

Anonymous
Der zu Wasser und zu Lande reisende Robinson vom Berge Libonon. Franckfurth, 1755.   Ullrich p. 161
——— De Te Water en te Lande Reizende Robinson Van Den Berg Libanon. Uit 't Hoogduits vertaald. Te Leeuwarden, By Abraham Ferwerda En Rud. Joh. Noordbeek, 1757.   MiU
——— [Another edition] De Libanonsche Robinson. . . . Twede Druk. In Friesland, te Herenveen, By T. Roorda . . . [1766]   MiU, tp BM

Discussed in Staverman, pp. 87-90. One copy (Tay) of the second Dutch edition has, written in ink on the title page, the date 1766, which is probably correct.

1756

[Adolphus Bannac, *alleged author*]
The Life And Surprizing Adventures Of Crusoe Richard Davis. London: Printed for F. Noble . . . And J. Noble . . . [1756]. 2 vols.   tp CtY

———— [Another edition] London: Printed and Sold by S.
Fisher . . . also sold by T. Hurst . . . [1801].   tp MH, tp BM
———— [Another edition] London, printed by S. Fisher,
1803.   *N&Q* X(1854), 17

"From some disagreeable peculiarities in the language, and a
parity of nonsense, and ridiculous extravagance, we are led to
conclude, that this is the manufacture of that notable genius,
Mr. Adolphus Bannac. . . . To say no more, is saying enough."
—*Monthly Review,* XV(1756), 656; cf. pp. 535 f. Perhaps Adolphus Bannac is a pseudonym. Prica devotes a few sentences to
it, p. 52, in her section on imitations of *Peter Wilkins,* which it
so obviously resembles that, says Dottin, p. 393, "tout le monde
cria au plagiat." Dottin does not document his "tout le
monde."

1756

[Petrus Lievens Kersteman]
   De Vrouwelyke Cartouche of de doorsleepene Land en Zeeroof-
ster, Behelzende Haare roekelooze en ongebondene Leevens-
loop. Haar ongehoorde Fielteryen en Feitelykheeden: Gaau-
whandige en dappere Uitvoeringen; Geestige en looze Vonden;
Snaakelyke Deugnieteryen, Gevangenschappen en listige Los-
braaken. Mitsgaders Haare klugtige Ontmoetingen in haar
Leeven. Desselfs zesjaarige Huishouding op een onbewoond
Eyland. Haare Ontdekkingen aldaar; Verlossinge van 't zelve,
en daarop gevolgde Bekeering en Overgang in 't Cloosterleeven.
Te s' Hertogenbosch, By Jacobus Palier . . . MDCCLVI.
2 vols.   Staverman p. 171

Discussed in Staverman, pp. 122-25; the author draws not
only upon *Robinson* but also apparently upon *Moll Flanders,*
and the title word comes directly or indirectly from Defoe's
Life and Actions of Lewis Dominique Cartouche (1722).
P[ieter] Haverkorn van Rijsewijk, *De oude Rotterdamsche
Schouwburg* (Rotterdam, 1882), pp. 265 ff., gives a brief biographical sketch.

1756

[Nils Rabenius (1648-1717), *supposed author*]
Peter Sparres robinsonad [in *Små-Saker till Nöje och Tids-fördrif,* V, 65-84] 1756.   Hirn p. 370
Perhaps written about 1700, without, of course, the word *robinsonad* in the title. See, besides Hirn, pp. 370-73, Ullrich[a], pp. 51-52; E. R. Gudde, *JEGP,* XXV(1926), 133; and Nils [G.] Ahnlund, *Nils Rabenius* . . . *Studier i Svensk Historiografi* (Stockholm, Geber [1927]), pp. 153-55.

1756

Anonymous
De Berugte Land- en Zee-Heldin, Of De Wonderbare Levens-gevallen Van Anna Blound, Anders Robert Stafford; Behelzende Haar geboorte, opvoeding, eerste min-avantuur, en duël met haar minnaar, dienstneming onder de Fransche Flybuiters na America, haar eerste zeetogt, landingen, zeegevegt, zee-listen, verhoging, plonderingen van verscheide Spaansche plaatzen, zegen, rampspoeden, schipbreuk, wonderbaare en manmoedige redding, komt met luister weder te voorschyn; zeeslagen, betoonde edelmoedigheid, werd door de Spanjaarden gevangen, listige ontvlugting van daar, by gelegenheid van de liefde van zekere jonge Spaansche Dame voor haar; gaat in dienst van Engeland over, verovering van Jamaica, nieuwe zeegevegten, ysselyke aardbeving, wonderlyk voorval, werd door de Franschen gevangen, haar uitwisseling, helpt St. Domingo veroveren, zeeslag, ongelooflyke stoutmoedigheid, en andere merkwaardige geschiedenissen, werd gekwetst, haar kunne ontdekt, en eindelyk haar huwelyk, en verheffing tot een grote staat . . . Te Amsterdam, By Steven Van Esveldt . . . [1756].
                                                              tp MiU

The date is taken from a reference cited in Staverman, p. 175; he, however, knew no copy of the work. The "zee-amazon's" name in the text is Anna Blount.

1756

Anonymous
Histoire d'un Peuple Nouveau, Ou Découverte d'une Isle à 43. Dégrés 14. Minutes de Latitude Méridionale par David Tompson, Capitaine du Vaisseau le Boston, à son retour de la Chine en 1756. Ouvrage traduit de l'Anglois. A Londres, Aux dépens d'une Société de Libraires, 1756. 2 vols. in 1.
Wijngaarden p. 247
——— [Another edition] A Londres, Aux dépens d'une Société de Libraires MDCCLVII. 2 parts in 1.	tp MH

The "traduit de l'Anglois" of the title page is suspect; for in the words of Wijngaarden in his discussion, pp. 198-203, "l'auteur, non pas le traducteur, dit qu'un voyageur anglais lui propose de raconter en français un de ses voyages extraordinaires. Où est alors l'original anglais dont le livre français serait la traduction?" I wish to thank Mr. Arnold H. Rowbotham for sending me the MS of his unpublished article entitled "The *Histoire d'un peuple nouveau* and Its Relation to the *Supplément au voyage de Bougainville* of Diderot," which he read before a meeting of the Philological Association of the Pacific Coast in November, 1938.

1756

Anonymous
Des Islanders Franz Severin van Dittheffts merkwurdige und neuerliche Reisen zur See und desselben vierzigjahriger Aufenthalt auf der schwimmenden Davids-Insel. aus sehr vielen in englischer und anderen Sprachen enthaltenen Nachrichten übersetzt und in Ordnung gebracht von H . . . L . . . L . . . v.C . . . Frankfurt und Leipzig, 1756.	Ullrich p. 162
——— Zweyte Auflage. Leipzig und Frankfurt, Verlegts Johann Christoph Gollner, 1758.	tp DLC, tp BM

Apparently not a translation.

1757

John Holmesby, *pseudonym*
The Voyages, Travels, And Wonderful Discoveries Of Capt.
John Holmesby. Containing A Series of the most Surprising
and Uncommon Events, which befel the Author in his Voyage
to the Southern Ocean, in the Year 1739. London: Printed
for F. Noble . . . And J. Noble . . . [1757].   tp NN, tp BM
   Listed in the *GM,* XXVII (1757), 605; in the *Monthly Review,*
XVII(1757), 563; and reviewed in the *Critical Review,* IV(1757),
395-402: "This novel is written in a plain style, suited to the capacity of a well-meaning sailor; the allegory is well carried on, and
some of the pictures striking and pathetic." I think Sabin VIII,
393, is clearly wrong in dating this 1739; his pagination agrees
with four copies which I know, three of which (RPJCB,CtY,
and PBL) contain four unnumbered pages at the end advertising
other books for sale, especially the *History of Miss Sally Sable*
("In the Press, and speedily will be published"), a novel by
Mrs. A. Woodfin, which is mentioned in the *Monthly Review,*
loc. cit., and in the *Critical Review* for January, V (1758), 28-32.

1757

[Carl August Thielo (1702-1763)]
   Charlotte eller forunderlige Tildragelser med Frøken von
Weisensøe. Sorøe 1757-58. 3 vols.   Bruun IV, 450
———— Charlotta eller Fröken von Weissensees lefnadshän-
delser. Öfwersättning [af Joh.Pet.Björck]. Götheborg, 1783-84.
2 vols.   Bruun IV, 450
   Discussed in Stangerup, pp. 189-92.

1757

Anonymous
   The Mother-In-Law: Or, The Innocent Sufferer. Interspersed
with the Uncommon and Entertaining Adventures Of Mr.

Hervey Faulconer . . . London: Printed for F. Noble . . .
And J. Noble . . . MDCCLVII. 2 vols.   tp MH

"This performance," writes the *Monthly Review,* XVII (1757),
81, "seems to come from the same hand which obliged us with
the *Guiltless Parricide."* The reference is to the *Impetuous Lover,
or the Guiltless Parricide* (1757) by A. G., Esq., whom I have
not found identified.

1758

[J. J. Hertel?]
Jonas Lostwaters eines Holländischen Schiffsbarbiers Reise
nach Mikroskopeuropien einem neuerer Zeit entdeckten Welt-
körper. Glückstadt [Hamburg], gedruckt bey Johann Jacob
Babst . . . 1758.   tp BM

Dedication is signed by J. J. Hertel.

1758

[Edward Kimber]
The Life, Extraordinary Adventures, Voyages, And Surpriz-
ing Escapes Of Capt. Neville Frowde, Of Cork. In Four Parts.
Written by himself, and now first published from his own
Manuscript . . . London: Printed for J. Wren . . . MDCCVIII
[i.e., 1758].   tp BM
———— [Another edition] London: Printed in the Year
MDCCLXXIII.   tp DLC, tp BM
———— [Another edition] Berwick: Printed For W. Phorson;
B. Law And Son . . . London. M DCC XCII.   tp BM

See Frank G. Black, *loc. cit.* p. 320 *supra.*

1758

[Niels Prahl (1724-1792)]
Lars Larsen, eller Aagerups selsomme Hændelser og forunderlige Tildragelser. En original dansk Roman i sex Bøger. Sorø
og Kjøbenhavn, 1758-62.   Bruun IV, 447

—————[Another edition] Kjøbenhavn, 1777.   Bruun IV, 447
Discussed in Stangerup, pp. 185-89.

1758

Anonymous

De Haagsche Robinson of de Gevallen van Alexander * * * * *
Behelzende zyn Geboorte en Opvoeding, zyne eerste Werelds
ontmoetingen, Dienstneming onder de Moscoviten, en daarna
onder den berugten Thomas Kouli-Kan, plundering der Stad
Delhi en Minavontuur aldaar, zyn gevangneming, en Slaverny
in Turkyen, wonderbaarlycke verlossing van een wreede
dood, werd door den Groten Heer, op enige ontdekkinge
uytgezonden, Schipbreuk, en belanding op 't onbekende Eiland
Tirevas, en zyne over wonderbaarlycke ontmoetingen aldaar;
op wat wyze hy' er de eerst maal, met den Vorst van dat Land
van daan kwam, ysselycken hongersnood en zyn wonderbaarlycke kloekmoedigheid, aankomst op een ander onbekend
Eiland, hun ontmoetingen aldaar, terugkomst op het eerste,
terug komst in Europa, en gelukkig besluyt zyner gevallen &c.
Te Alkmaar, Gedrukt by Jacob Maagh . . . 1758. 2 vols.

tp reproduction ten Brink p. 12.

Jan ten Brink in *Verspreide Letterkundige Opstellen van het
jaar 1888* (Den Haag, 1889), pp. [9]-20, devotes a few general
remarks to this, and Staverman discusses it, pp. 114-16.

1759

[Carl August Thielo]

Matrosen, som blev Keiser i Muratapa og derefter igen Matros.
Sorøe, 1759.   Stangerup p. 194
Discussed in Stangerup, pp. 194-99.

1759

[Voltaire]

Candide Ou L'Optimisme. Traduit de l'allemand de M. le
docteur Ralph. [Paris, chez Lambert] 1759 [February].

Bengesco I, 447

To *Candide* applies also my statement, p. 333, about a bibliography of *Micromégas*, especially for the following: Bengesco, I, 444-53, 474-79, 491;II,xvi f.; IV,xiv f., 68 ff.; Wallich and von Müller, pp. 30-70; Van Roosbroeck; and Barr. Of the eight editions published in the first year, all without name of place or publisher, that by Cramer at Geneva was, after Bengesco's bibliography, designated the first until recently Lambert's Paris edition was reinstated; see Jean Tannery, "L'Édition originale de *Candide*," *Bulletin du bibliophile et du bibliothécaire*, n.s.XII (1933), [7]-15, and n.s.XIII(1934), [62]-70; Norman L. Torrey, "The First Edition of *Candide*," *MLN*, XLVIII (1933), 307-10; and Fernand Vandérem, "Les Deux 'Candide,'" *Bulletin du bibliophile et du bibliothécaire*, n.s. XVI (1937), 151-52. George R. Havens, "The Composition of Voltaire's *Candide*," *MLN*, XLVII (1932), 225-34, kills again the untenable belief that Voltaire wrote it in three days. A list of editions by 1800 would run at least into the sixties. André Morize has published an *édition critique* (Société des textes français modernes, Paris, Hachette, 1913 with an excellent introduction (the first part of which appeared in *Revue du dix-huitième siècle*, I[1913], [1]-27), especially pp. xlvii-lxiii, "Les Sources de *Candide*," to which should be added Dorothy M. McGhee, "Voltaire's *Candide* and Gracián's *El Criticón*," *PMLA*, LII (1937), 778-84. From a large number of commentaries I cite here only those which consider in some degree the form and its relation to the imaginary voyage: Ferdinand Castets, "*Candide, Simplicius* et *Candido*," *Revue des langues romanes*, XLVIII (1905), [481]-91; Émile Faguet, "Les Contes et romans de Voltaire," *Revue politique et litteraire* (*Revue bleue*), 4S., II(1894), 620-25; Gustave Lanson, *L'Art de la prose* (Paris, Librairie des annales politiques et littéraires, 1909), pp. 181-85; McGhee, *op. cit.* p. 334 *supra;* J[ean] Pommier, "Notes sur des sources de *Candide*," *Bulletin de la Faculté des lettres de Strasbourg*, IV (1925-26), 14 f.; Toldo, *loc. cit.* p. 334 *supra;* and "Voltaire's Romances and Their Moral," *Westminster Review*, LXXV(1861), 192-202 (reprinted in *Living Age*, LXIX, 1861, 387-97). *Candide, Seconde Partie* (ICN), 1761, attributed to Thorel de Campigneulles—see Bengesco, I, 449-51, and Emile Henriot, (Paris)

Temps, 17 fév. 1925, p. 3—is not an imaginary voyage; for a long résumé see Pierre Larousse, *Grand Dictionnaire universel* (Paris, 1867), III, 258 f. Nor is *Candide en Dannemarc* (MH), 1769; for other imitations see Mornet's article.

1759

Anonymous
> De wonderlyke Reisgevallen van Maria Kinkons. Behelzende in zig Haare Geboorte. De geheime Vlugt van haar Ouders. Haar Ontmoetingen onder een Mannelyk Gewaad zo te Land als ter Zee; inzonderheid haare Schipbreuk, Stranding en Woonplaats op een onbewoond Eiland; zonderlinge ontmoeting aldaar met een Baviaan; Ontdekkingen van nog andere onbekende Eilanden met derzelver byzonderheden; en eindelyk de te rug komst in haar Geboortestad Hailbron. Doormengd met een meenigte nooit gehoorde en leezenswaardige Gebeurtenissen. Alles naaukeurig beschreeven door A. G. l.m. Te Harlingen, By Bouwe Schiere . . . 1759.
>
> Staverman p. 173
>
> This unoriginal work of many sources, which include *Quarll* and *Robinson* and perhaps *Der teutsche Robinson* and *De Hollandsche Robinson,* is mentioned briefly by Staverman, pp. 125 f.

1760

Rudolph von Senzion, *pseudonym*
> Der Schulmeisters Sohn, oder die wunderbare Geschichte Rudolph von Senzion. Franckfurt und Leipzig. 1760. tp MiU
>
> The foreword is signed "Samuel Grollauf, Secretair."

1763

[Gaspard Guillard de Beaurieu (1728-1795)]
> L'Eleve de la Nature, La Haye et Paris, 1763. 2 vols.
>
> Ullrich[d] p. 490

———— [Another edition] A Amsterdam, & se trouve à Paris, Chez Panckoucke . . . M.DCC.LXIV. 2 vols.

tp MH, tp BM (2 vols. in 1)

———— [Translation?] Der Schüler der Natur. Aus dem Französischen. Leipzig, bei Friedr. Gotth. Jacobäern, 1765.

Ullrich p. 165

———— [Another French edition] A Amsterdam, & se trouve à Paris, Chez Panckoucke . . . M.DCC.LXVI. 2 parts in 1.

tp MB

———— Nouvelle Edition Augmentée d'un Volume . . . A Amsterdam, Et se trouve à Lille, Chez J. B. Henry . . . M.DCC.LXXI. 3 vols.

tp DLC

———— [Another edition] Paris, 1773. 3 vols.

Ullrich p. 165

———— The Man Of Nature. Translated from the French By James Burne . . . London: Printed for T. Cadell . . . M.DCC. LXXIII. 2 vols.

tp BM

———— Nouvelle édition augmentée d'un volume . . . A Amsterdam, et se trouve à Lille, Chez J. B. Henry . . . 1774. 3 vols.

Cohen 467

———— [Another edition] Paris, 1777. 3 vols. Ullrich p. 165

———— [Another edition] Lille, C. F. J. Lehoucq, 1778. 3 vols.

BN

———— [Another edition] Paris, 1783. 3 vols. Ullrich p. 165

———— [Another edition] Lille, G. F. J. Lehoucq, 1783. 3 vols.

BN

———— [Revised edition] Genève, 1790. 2 vols. Ullrich p. 165

———— [Another edition] Paris, 1793. 3 vols. Ullrich p. 165

———— [Another edition] Avignon, chez Jean-Albert Joly, 1793.

Ullrich[d] p. 490

———— [Translation?] Der Zögling der Natur, oder die Wirkung der Natur und der Bildung. Für Erzieher und Zöglinge . . . Prag, J. Buchler, 1794.

Ullrich p. 165

———— [Another French edition] 1796. 3 vols. Pigoreau p. 43

———— Nouvelle Édition. A Paris, Chez les Libraires associés. 1806. 3 vols. in 1.

MiU

So closely does this imitate *Émile* that it was once foisted upon

Rousseau, as Mann points out, pp. 125 f. Furthermore, the heroine's name is *Julie*. Michaud (article "Beaurieu") gives an edition not included above and adds: "L'édition de Genève diffère des autres, en ce qu'on a retranché tout le 3e volume pour y substituer d'autres détails plus liés au corps de l'ouvrage, que Beaurieu publia d'abord sous le nom de J.-J. Rousseau." Lichtenberger[b], pp. 64-76, analyses it; Schomann discusses it, pp. 121-27; and Émile Legouis gives an excellent presentation in the Taylorian Lecture for 1925: *G. G. de Beaurieu et son éleve de la nature* (Oxford, Clarendon Press, 1925).

1763

[Marie Anne de Roumier Robert (1705-1771)]
La Voix De La Nature, Ou Les Avantures De Madame La Marquise De * * * Par Mad. De R. R. Auteur De la Paysanne Philosophe. Amsterdam, 1763.   Mornet I, 359
———— [Another edition] A Amsterdam, Aux Dépens De La Compagnie. M.DCC.LXIV. 5 vols. [Vols. III-V only]   tp BM
———— [Another edition] A Amsterdam, Aux Dépens De La Compagnie. M.DCC.LXX. 5[?] vols. [Vols. I-II only]   tp BM
———— [Another edition] A Amsterdam, Aux Dépens De La Compagnie. M.DCC.LXXIV. 5 vols. in 1.   tp BM
———— A Voz Da Natureza, Ou Aventuras Da Marqueza De . . . [tr. Francisco Manoel do Nascimento, in *Obras Completas de Filinto Elysio,* ed. F. Solano Constancio, Vol. XI] Paris. Na officina de A. Bobée, 1819.   tp BM

1763

[Otto Bernhard Verdion, *alleged author*]
Die Glücks- und Unglücksfälle Martin Speelhovens, eines Kaufmanns aus dem Clevischen gebürtig, welche ihm sowohl in seiner Jugend, als auch auf Reisen nach Amerika begegnet, nebst dessen Gefangennehmung und Flucht, wie auch achtzehnjährigen Aufenthalt auf einer damals noch nie besuchten Insel

und endlichen Befreyung, von ihm selbst beschrieben. Dresden und Leipzig, bey Joh. Nicol. Gerlach und Sohn. 1763.   RPJCB

——— [Another edition] Dreszden und Leipzig bey Joh. Nicolaus Gerlachs Wittwe und Sohn 1769.   tp NN

——— [Another edition] Dreszden und Leipzig [Leipzig, Nauck], 1782.   Ullrich[d] p. 490

——— [Bearbeitung by Karl Friedrich Benkowitz] Der neue Westphälische Robinson . . . Halle, in Joh. Chr. Hendels Verlage. 1799. 2 vols. in 1.   MiU, tp BM

——— [Bearbeitung by Johann Joseph Polt] Abentheuer und Reisen Martin Engelbrechts. Als Seitenstük zum englischen Robinson . . . Leipzig 1801. Im Verlag der Jos. Poltischen Buchhandlung.   MiU

——— [Bearbeitung] Wunderbare Schicksale des Martin Speelhoven . . . bearbeitet von Franz Georg Ferdinand Schläger . . . Hannover. Hahn'sche Hofbuchhandlung. 1858.   tp BM

For the possibility that Verdion wrote this cf. Ullrich, p. 145, Strauch's review of Ullrich, pp. 247 f., and Ullrich[a], p. 108 n.49.

1764

Anonymous

[Wunderbare Reise eines Philosophen in die sehr unbekannten Länder des Mondes, der Lampen-insel, der schwimmenden Inseln, der glückseligen Inseln, der Hölle, der Insel der Träume, der Antipoden, in die Republik der Thiere, in die Insel der Pyrandrier, in das Land der Arpactier, in das Königreich Numismacia, in die Insel der Poeten, Und in die Insel der Pygmeen. Und die Bezauberung, eine scherzhafte Erzählung] Stettin, Drevenstedt, 1764.   Klinckowstroem p. 261

——— [Another edition] Frankfurt und Leipzig, 1765.   Klinckowstroem p. 261

The title is in brackets because it is that of the 1765 edition; I have not found a full title for the first edition.

24

1765

[Charles François Tiphaigne de la Roche (1729-1774)]
Histoire Des Galligènes, Ou Mémoires De Duncan. A Amsterdam, Chez Arkstée, & Merkus . . . Et se trouve à Paris, Chez la Veuve Durand . . . M.DCC.LXV. 2 vols. in 1.

tp BM

———— [Another edition] A Genève, Chez les Freres Cramer. Et se trouve à Paris, Chez Humaire . . . M.DCC.LXX. 2 vols. in 1. tp BM

". . . peut-être un example d'une compréhension de Swift rare au XVIIIe siècle en France. . . . Tiphaigne de la Roche dépeint une société qui a eu toutes les chances d'atteindre à la perfection, mais qui, parce que ses membres sont des mortels avec les caractéristiques innées de la race humaine, se révèle à l'époque où le voyageur européen fait naufrage sur leurs côtes, encore loin d'un état de bonheur complet"—Goulding, p. 100. Lichtenberger[b] gives a résumé, pp. 48-58, as part of a chapter devoted to several works of the author; he says that *Galligènes* was once attributed to Diderot. Schomann discusses it, pp. 131-35. I have not seen J. B. Georges Mancel, *Tiphaigne de la Roche, étude bibliographique* (Caen, 1845).

1766

André Guillaume Contant D'Orville (1730-1800)
La Destinée Ou Mémoires Du Lord Kilmarnoff, Traduits De L'Anglois De Miss Voodwill, Par M. Contant Dorville . . . A Amsterdam, & se trouve A Paris, Chez Claude Herissant . . . M.DCC.LXVI. 2 vols. tp BM

———— [Another edition] 1776. Mornet I, 365

A pretended translation.

1766

[Jean Gaspard Dubois-Fontanelle (1737-1812)]
Aventures philosophiques A. Tonquin [Paris], 1766. BN

———— [Ed. Daniel Mornet, in *Revue du dix-huitième siècle*,

II, (187)-204; (291)-306] A Paris Chez Hachette et Cie . . .
1914.   tp NNC

Lichtenberger[a], p. 380, calls this shipwreck among savages "une
sorte de conte satirique dans le genre de *Candide*"; cf. Mornet,
"Les Imitations du 'Candide' . . ."; his reëdition contains a brief
introduction.

1766

[Christian Gotthold Hauffe]
Merkwürdige und auszerordentliche Begebenheiten einer Kosa-
kischen Standesperson, von ihr selbst zu ihrem und anderer
Vergnügen beschrieben. Regensburg, verlegts Johann Leopold
Montag. 1766.   Ullrich p. 167
——— Zweite Auflage. Regensburg, verlegts Johann Leopold
Montag. 1780. 2 vols. in 1.   tp BM

The dedication is signed "Die Verfasserin Jacobine W * * * ."

1766

Charles Searle, *pseudonym*
The Wanderer: Or, Memoirs Of Charles Searle, Esq; Contain-
ing His Adventures by Sea and Land. With Many remarkable
Characters, and interesting Situations in Real Life; and a
Variety of surprizing Incidents . . . London: Printed for T.
Lowndes . . . M.DCC.LXVI. 2 vols.   tp BM

According to the *Monthly Review,* XXXIII (1765), 490, "to the
highest degree unnatural and improbable, if not utterly impossible"
but "not very ill-written."

1766

Anonymous
Voyage De Robertson, Aux Terres Australes, traduit sur le
Manuscrit Anglois. Aamsterdam MDCCLXVI.   MnU
——— [Another edition] A Amsterdam MDCCLXVII.
                                                       tp BM

———— Robertsons Reise in die mittäglichen Länder oder nach Australien. Amsterdam, 1768.   Teubner p. 29

Discussed in Wijngaarden, pp. 215-25. The fictitious English hero is supposed to have sailed to South America with Sir Francis Drake and later by his narrative to have inspired William Penn to found an ideal city in North America.

1767

Unca Eliza Winkfield, *pseudonym*
The Female American; Or, The Adventures Of Unca Eliza Winkfield. Compiled By Herself . . . London: Printed for Francis Noble . . . And John Noble . . . MDCCLXVII. 2 vols.   tp NN, tp BM (2 vols. in 1)
———— [Another edition] Newburyport [Mass.]: Printed For & Sold By Angier March . . . [c. 1790?].   tp NN
———— [Another edition] Vergennes, Vt. Published By Jepthah Shedd And Co. Wright & Sibley, printers. 1814.
                   tp NN

See Tremaine McDowell, "An American Robinson Crusoe," *American Literature,* I(1929-30), 307-9; Benjamin Bissell, *The American Indian in English Literature of the Eighteenth Century* (New Haven [etc.], Yale University Press, 1925), pp. 99-103; and Heilman, especially pp. 70, 385 n.16, and 386 n.17, where he points out that the anonymous imaginary voyage entitled *The Life and Adventures Of Henry Lanson . . . Put On Shore at an Uninhabited Island, Where . . . He Discovers . . . The Oracle of the Sun . . .* is "unblushingly plagiarized" from the *Female American.* The undated *Lanson* is sometimes given as 1800?, but the MH copy (London: Printed and Sold by S. Fisher . . . also sold by T. Hurst . . .) seems not to have been printed until 1801. In dating the Newburyport edition I have followed Oscar Wegelin, *Early American Fiction 1774-1830 . . .,* 3d ed. (New York, Peter Smith, 1929).

1767

Anonymous
The Adventures Of A Kidnapped Orphan. London; Printed for M. Thrush. . . . MDCCXLVII [i.e., 1767]. tp PU, tp BM

Assuming a transposition of the X and L in the imprint, I have accepted the date 1767 given by Robert Watt, *Bibliotheca Britannica* . . . (Edinburgh, 1824), IV, *s.v.* "Orphan." It is reviewed as a new book in the *Critical Review,* XXIV (1767), 345-49; furthermore, the PU copy carries an advertisement for the *Midnight Spy,* which bears an imprint of London, 1766. It would be difficult to believe that this work could have appeared before *Roderick Random.*

1768

Pietro Chiari (1711?-1785?)
L'Uomo D'Un Altro Mondo O Sia Memorie D'Un Solitario Senza Nome Scritte da lui medesimo In Due Linguaggi Chinese, E Russiano E publicate nella nostra lingua Dall' Abbate Pietro Chiari. In Venezia MDCCLXVIII. Appresso Domenico Battiforo. . . . tp MH

There is a résumé of this in Argenson's *Bibliothèque universelle* for November, 1778, pp. 186-207.

1768

Bernard Le Bovier de Fontenelle (1657-1757), *alleged author*
La Republique Des Philosophes, Ou Histoire Des Ajaoiens. Ouvrage Posthume De Mr. De Fontenelle. On y a joint une Lettre sur la Nudité des Sauvages. A Geneve, MDCCLXVIII. tp MH, tp BM
────── [Another edition?] Amsterdam [1768?].
Wijngaarden p. 203

The supposition that there may have been an Amsterdam edition is based on Jean B. R. Robinet's *Dictionnaire universel des sciences morale, économique, politique et diplomatique* (Londres), I(1777), 603-24, *s.v.* "Ajao." Robinet states, p. 603, that "L'Editeur l'attribue, peut-être sans assez de fondement, à l'illustre Fontenelle. Ce titre pompeux, *la République des Philosophes,* est encore une addition de l'Editeur. J'ai vu cet ouvrage en manuscrit dans une bibliotheque à la Haye, d'où l'on m'a dit qu'il avoit été tiré, pour être livré à la presse, & certainement ce titre n'y étoit point. Du reste, il est fort rare, & presque inconnu en France & dans plusieurs autres pays." Fontenelle's authorship has been consistently denied or questioned, e.g., Lichtenberger[a], pp. 373 f.; Chinard[b], p. 444; and Girsberger, pp. 202-7; but Wijngaarden, pp. 204 ff., tries to prove that it is "une production typique de XVIIe siècle" because of its contents and form—it "renferme tant d'allusions historiques, applicables toutes au XVIIe siècle qu'il est presque impossible de se tromper en attribuant l'odyssée en question à un contemporain de Foigny et de Veirasse" (but see Daniel Mornet, *Revue d'histoire littéraire de la France,* XL, 1933, 129)—and that it is just the kind of work Fontenelle might have written in his early years along with *L'Ile de Bornèo* (1686). This is pure speculation and leaves, as Wijngaarden himself recognizes, several at present unanswerable questions: how did the MS get to a library at La Haye? why did Robinet give Amsterdam instead of Geneva? why would it then have been printed at Geneva? and why did it remain unpublished for nearly a century? Fritz K. Mann, "Fontenelles Republik: eine Dichtung vom besten Staat," *Zeitschrift für Politik,* IV(1911), [495]-521, assumes with some plausible evidence that Fontenelle is the author and makes a thorough study of the political and historical background of the work. On the other hand, the recent detailed study by J. R. Carré, *La Philosophie de Fontenelle ou le sourire de la raison* (Paris, Félix Alcan, 1932), ignores it entirely. Schomann discusses it, pp. 127-31; Hugo, pp. 842-49; Schmitt, pp. 83-85; and Kleinwächter, pp. 86-89, where it is called "ein Flickwerk von Bruchstücken der 'Utopia' und der 'Histoire des Sevarambes,' die in ziemlich

geistloser Weise zu einem Ganzen zusammengestoppelt sind."
Cf. Kirchenheim, pp. 246-48. Toustain de Richebourg's versifica-
tion (*Les Aventures d'Alaine*, 1778) I have not seen.

1768

[Louis Laurent Joseph Gain de Montagnac (1731-1780)]
Les Mémoires du Chevalier de Kilpar. Traduits ou imités de
l'anglais de M. Fielding, par M.D . . . M . . . C . . . D . . .
Paris, chez Veuve Duchesne, 1768. 2 vols.   BN
———— Les aventures ou la vie et les voyages du nouveau
Robinson, chevalier de Kilpar . . . Paris, 1768. 2 vols.
                                                  Ullrich p. 167
———— [Another edition] Liège, 1768. 2 vols.   Ullrich p. 167
———— [Another edition] A Paris, Chez la veuve Duchesne
. . . M.DCC.LXIX. 2 vols.   tp BM
———— [Another edition] A Francfort et à Leipzig, 1769.
Aux Depens De La Compagnie. 2 vols. in 1.   tp CtY
———— Geschichte des Ritters von Kilpar. Aus dem Eng-
lischen [by G. R. Wiedmer]. Leipzig [Gleditsch], 1769.
                                                  Ullrich p. 168
———— Der Wiener Robinson oder seltsame Abentheuer des
Ritters von Kilpar . . . Neu übersetzt und frei bearbeitet.
Hohenzollern bey J. B. Wallishauszer, 1799.   Ullrich p. 168
———— Neue Auflage [of the preceding] Hohenzollern, 1805.
                                                  Ullrich p. 168

In the CtY copy, bound with *Robinson,* an *avis* reads: "Pour
procurer au Lecteur . . . un nouveau plaisir, & non seulement
pour les dédommager de la présente briévité de Lecture, mais
pour leur en continuer l'Agrément d'une maniére, plus variée,
qu'ils ne l'ont eu par les Editions précédentes, nous ajoutons
actuellement (à la Suite de l'Ancien Robinson) La Vie, Les
Avantures, Et Les Voyages Du Nouveau Robinson . . . comme
une trois- & quatrième Partie des Robinsons Anglois." In fact,
Mann in his discussion, pp. 128-32, states, apparently from the
preface of the first edition, that the author intended to entitle the

book *Nouveau Robinson* but changed it when he learned of another under that title, probably Feutry's version of *Robinson*. However, Mann adds later that "l'influence prédominante qui s'y trouve, est celle du genre philosophique et moral inauguré par Rousseau plutôt que le réalisme de *Robinson Crusoé,* et cela, malgré certaines situations et certains incidents communs aux deux livres. Il nous semble, en effet, que l'auteur a voulu créer pour son Robinson une existence idéale. . . . On peut dire aussi que cette petite colonie est le prototype des nombreuses familles naufragées, menant une existence à la Robinson qui ont figuré dans le roman depuis cette époque et parmi lesquelles celle du *Robinson suisse* est assurément le plus célèbre." Fielding had nothing to do with this work, and it is improbable that the author even thought he was imitating him, although he was proud enough of his romance to put on the title pages of two subsequent critical studies "par l'auteur des 'Memoirs du Chevalier de Kilpar.' "

1768

Anonymous

    Voyages Et Aventures Du Chevalier De * * *. Contenant les Voyages de l'Auteur dans les Isle Antilles Françoises du vent de l'Amérique Septentrionale, y compris les Isles Caraïbes de Saint-Vincent, Sainte-Lucie & la Dominique; & dans celle de Saint-Thomas, appartenante aux Danois . . . A Paris, Chez Dessain Junior . . . M.DCC.LXVIII. 2 vols.   tp RPB

    ———— [Another edition] A Londres Et se trouvent A Paris, Chez Dessain Junior . . . M.DCC.LXIX. 2 vols.   tp MB

    ———— [Another edition] A Amsterdam, et se trouve à Paris, Chez Merigot le jeune . . . M.DCC.LXXVI. 4 vols.   MH

Though the 1776 edition has the title *Voyages et Aventures du Chevalier de * * * en différentes parties de l'Europe jusqu'à son retour en France,* it is, according to Sabin, XXVII, 205, a reissue of the 1769 edition. Chinard [b], p. 425, and Mann, p. 133, both imply that there may be some truth in this voyage.

1769

[Johann Daniel Bartholomäi (d. 1790)]
Neue Fata einiger See-Fahrer, absonderlich Gustav Moritz
Frankens eines Deutschen, seine Reisen zu Wasser und Lande,
Glücks- und Unglücksfälle in Europa und andern Weltgegen-
den, dessen sclavischer Aufenthalt in der Türkey, wunderbare
Befreyung, und fernere auszerordentliche Begebenheiten in
einem heidnischen Königreiche u.s.w. Mit untermischten
Lebensbeschreibungen anderer Personen von Ihm selbst his-
torisch-moralisch aufgesetzt und ergötzend beschrieben, an-
jetzo aber zum Druck befördert von * * * . . . Ulm, bey
Albrecht Friederich Bartholomäi, 1769. 2 vols.

tp CtY, tp BM (2 vols. in 1)

Kippenberg, pp. 121 f., writing about imitations of *Felsenburg,*
says: "Vielfach geht man auch ins rein abenteuerliche über, und
es werden, ganz im Stil von Horns Erlebnissen beim Gouverneur
im vierten Teil der Felsenburg, Aufzüge und Festlichkeiten mit
Böllerschüssen und Vergnügungen auf fernen Inseln aus reiner
Lust zur Abenteurerei geschildert, zo z.B. in den 'Neuen Fata
einiger Seefahrer,' 1769."

1769

[Christian Gotthold Hauffe]
Die verkehrte Welt welche anders spricht, wie sie denkt und
anders denkt, wie sie spricht, in dem Leben eines Jünglings,
aus eigener Erfahrung herausgegeben. Frankfurt und Leipzig,
1769.   tp MiU
———— [In *Paszetems bey langen Winterabenden in angenehmen und zeitverkürzenden Geschichten und Erzählungen,*
Vol. IV] Geschichte eines Jünglings. Neue veränderte Auflage.
Frankfurt und Leipzig, 1793.   Ullrich p. 169

1770

[Edward Bancroft (1744-1820)]
The History Of Charles Wentworth, Esq. In A Series Of

Letters. Interspersed With a Variety of Important Reflections, Calculated To improve Morality, and promote the Œconomy of Human Life . . . London, Printed for T. Becket . . . MDCCLXX. 3 vols.   tp MWA, tp BM

Favorably noticed in the *Monthly Review,* XLIII (1770), 67.

1770

[Hans Bergeström (1735-1784)]
Indianiske Bref Eller utförlig beskrifning öfver tvänne obe-kanta rikens moraliska, politiska och oeconomiska beskaffen-het. Carlscrona, 1770. 2 vols.   Böök p. 262

Apparently this appeared also serially in 24 parts in the *Carls-cronas Veckoblad* beginning in No. 18, May 5, 1770. It is dis-cussed in Böök, pp. 262-67, and in Paludan, pp. 332-34; though influenced partly by the *Lettres persanes,* this fantastic voyage is more like *Niels Klim* and *Gulliver,* but is apparently dull and prolix, with a minimum of narrative.

1770

[Isaac Bickerstaffe (1735?-1812?), *supposed author*]
The Life, Strange Voyages, and Uncommon Adventures of Ambrose Gwinett . . . London: J. Barker [c. 1750].

Sabin VII, 517
———— The Life, And Strange, Unparallel'd and Unheard-of Voyages and Adventures Of Ambrose Gwinett, Formerly well known to the Public, As The Lame Beggar Man, Who in the Year 1734, and for a long Time after, swept the Way between the Mews Gate and Spring Gardens, Charing-Cross. Contain-ing, An Account of his being Tried and Convicted, and Hanged in Chains at Deal in Kent, for the supposed Murder of Mr. Collins. His Surprizing Recovery after Hanging in Chains; his Voyages to the West Indies, and being taken by the Spaniards, amongst whom he met with the supposed Murdered Mr. Collins; their Admiration in meeting each other, and pro-

posed to return to England together. The Accident that threw
Mr. Gwinett in the Hands of Pirates; his extraordinary Adven-
tures with them; his being taken again by the Spaniards, and
sent to Old Spain, and there Condemned to the Gallies. His
being taken by the Algerines, and carried into Slavery, and
after many hardships returned to England, &c. Written by
Himself. The Second Edition. London: Printed by John Lever
. . . 1770.						tp BM
———— The Fourth Edition. London: Printed for J. Lever
. . . [1771?]					MH
———— Candide Anglois, Ou Avantures Tragi-Comiques
D'Amb. Gwinett Avant Et Dans Ses Voyages Aux Deux Indes.
A Francfort Et Leipzig, Aux Depens De La Compagnie.
M.DCC.LXXXI.					tp NNC
———— [Another English edition] Newcastle: Printed this
year [1775?].					tp BM
———— [Another French edition] 1778.		Pigoreau p. 89
———— [Another English edition] London: Printed By T.
Sabine . . . [1780?].				tp BM
———— [Another edition, London?] Printed in Stonecutter-
street [1780?].					tp BM
———— The Third Edition. London, Printed: Boston: Re-
Printed and Sold by E. Russell . . . M,DCC,LXXXII. . . .
						tp DLC
———— [Another edition] Norwich: Printed and sold by
John Trumbull, M,DCC,LXXXIV.			MWA
———— [Another edition] Philadelphia: Printed and Sold by
Robert Bell . . . M,DCC,LXXXIV.			PPL
———— Die Wunderbare Geschichte Von Ambrose Gwinnett.
Aus Dem Englischen. Philadelphia: Gedruckt bey Carl Cist,
1784.						Evans VI, 291
———— [Another English edition] Hudson: Printed and Sold
by Ashbel Stoddard, M,DCC,LXXXVI.		tp RPJCB
———— [Another edition] New-London: Printed and sold by
James Springer . . . 1795.			Evans X, 21
———— [Another edition, n.p.] Printed for the traveling book-
sellers. 1798.					Evans XII, 24

———— [Another edition] Printed by M. Angus, and Son . . . Newcastle [1800?]. tp BM

———— [Another edition] Boston. Printed and sold by J. White . . . 1800. tp MB

———— [Another edition] London, Printed by T. Maiden . . . for Ann Lemoine . . . and J. Roe . . . [c. 1805?]. OCl

———— [Another edition] Providence, (R. I.) Printed and published by Miller & Hutchens. 1815. MWA

———— [Another edition] Newcastle: printed by G. Angus . . . [1817?]. tp Bod

———— [Another edition] Glasgow: Printed For The Booksellers. 1850. tp NN

———— Sixth Edition: London, Printed For The Booksellers, And For T. Deighton . . . York [18-?]. tp MH

———— [Another edition] Sold at Henry Fenwick's, Wholesale Book Warehouse, Snow Hill. n.d. tp Bod

———— [Another edition. Printed by G. Wood . . . Liverpool] n.d. tp Bod

———— [Another edition] Preston: Printed by E. Sergent. n.d. tp Bod

The attribution of authorship seems to come solely from a MS note in the 1770 edition in the BM: "Dr. Percy told me he had heard that this pamphlet was a mere fiction written by Mr. Bickerstaff the Dramatic Poet." The preface of the French edition is signed "L. Castilton." If Bickerstaffe is the author and if the date of his birth is 1735, then Sabin's 1750 for the first edition becomes suspect, the more so, perhaps, because he suggests that possibly Defoe is the author. I have therefore entered this work tentatively under the earliest reliable date, 1770, though it seems unwise to remove Sabin's entry from first place. Although H. R. Plomer, *Dictionary of the Printers and Booksellers Who Were at Work in England . . . from 1726 to 1775* (London Bibliographical Society, 1932), cites nothing for John Lever after 1770, the facts that Lever published the second edition in that year, that he probably published a missing third edition, and that he did pub-

lish the undated fourth edition suggest that he may have been
active after 1770.

1770

[François René Turpin (1709-1799)]
   Voyage A Ceilan, Ou Les Philosophes Voyageurs. Ouvrage
publié par Henriqués Pangrapho, Maître ès-Arts de l'Université
de Salamanque. A Amsterdam, Chez Arkstée & Merkus; A
Paris, Chez H. C. De Hansy . . . M.DCC.LXX. 2 vols. in 1.
                                                  tp BM
———— [Another edition] Les philosophes aventuriers par
M.T. . . . , Amsterdam-Paris, Belin, 1780. Mornet *infra* p. 299
   Brief notice in the *Göttingische Anzeigen von gelehrten Sa-
chen,* 39 Stück, 1 April, 1771, p. 332, calls it a *halbphilosophische
Roman,* "mit unwahrscheinlichen Begebenheiten, und vielen phi-
losophischen Unterredungen zwischen einem in einen Weltwei-
sen sich verstellenden Bösewichte. . . ." It is considered by
Mornet in "Les Imitations du 'Candide'. . . ."

1770

[Otto Bernhard Verdion, *alleged author*]
   Merkwürdige Lebensumstände Elias Bendels eines Fischers
Sohns aus Stockholm welche darinn bestehen aus was Ur-
sachen er sein Vaterland verlassen, und sich mit einer holländischen Flotte nach Amerika gewendet wie er auf seiner Reise an
den molokkischen Küsten überfallen, und gefangen worden
auch dessen Flucht und Anlandung an einer unbewohnten
Insel geschehen sein zwanzigjähriger Aufenthalt daselbst
gewesen und endlich sein Tod, mit Hinterlassung eines ein-
zigen Sohnes auf derselben erfolget von ihm selbst aufgezeichnet, und dem Drucke überlassen. Dreszden und Leipzig bey
Johann Nicolaus Gerlachs Wittwe und Sohn 1770.
                                      Ullrich p. 169

———— Dritte Auflage. Dresden und Leipzig, bey Johann
Samuel Gerlach, 1786. tp DLC

For the possibility that Verdion is the author cf. Ullrich, p. 145,
Strauch's review of Ullrich, pp. 247 f, and Ullrich[a], p. 108 n. 49.
The *Anhang* to the third edition is signed "John Stephans Ditten-
holm, kapitain."

1771

[Hans Bergeström]
Om Nahkhanahamahhem eller dumhetens och dårskapens
land. Tryckt uti Carlscrona åhr 1771. Böök p. 267

Issued serially with the *Carlscronas Veckoblad*, Nos. 29-35.
Böök, pp. 267-70, mentions *Gulliver* and Hall's *Mundus* as sources
and calls it the best liked of the "fabulösa reseskildringar" written
in Sweden in the 18th century. Discussed in Paludan, pp. 334-35,
who mentions Cyrano, Brunt, and Holberg as sources.

1771

Anonymous
Le Nagzag, Ou Les Mémoires De Christophe Rustaut, Dit
L'Africain. A Amsterdam, Et se trouve à Paris, Chez J. P.
Costard . . . M.DCC.LXXI. tp MH, tp BM

1772

[Jacob Christian Bie (1738-1798)]
Den fra Maanen hjemkomme Politicus [serially in *Trykke-
frihedsskrifter*, XVIII, Nos. 1-5, beginning January 17] 1772.
Paludan p. 319

1773

Anonymous
Seltsame Fata einiger neuer Seefahrer, Welche auf ihren Reisen
zu Wasser und Land viele Glücks- und Unglücksfälle erfahren,

Und endlich mit groszen Reichthümern wieder in ihr Vaterland zurücke gekommen. Zur Ergötzung curioser Gemüther
von Ihnen selbst zum Druck befördert. Regensburg, verlegts
Johann Leopold Montag und Johann Heinrich Gruner. 1773.

tp MiU

1774

Anonymous
Reise eines Arabischen Weltweisen nach den fünf Planeten
und dem Sternbild des Widders nebst einer Unterredung mit
ihren Einwohnern, von den Absichten der, den 7. und 8ten
Mai bei uns sichtbar gewesenen Zusammenkunft. Aus dem
Arab. übersetzt und mit Anmerkungen vermehrt. Meszhala,
5723. Nürnberg, de Launoy, 1774.	Klinckowstroem p. 263

1774

Anonymous
Wasobyoe [Japan 1774]. 4 vols.	Chamberlain
———— Wasaubiyauwe, The Japanese Gulliver [translated in
part by B(asil) H. Chamberlain, *Transactions of the Asiatic
Society of Japan*, VII, 285-308;311-12; or, in the reprinted *Transactions*, 287-313;316-17] Yokohama: Lane, Crawford & Co.;
Kelly & Co. Shanghai: Kelly & Walsh. London: Trübner &
Co. New York: Appleton & Co. 1879.	tp NNC, tp BM
Brought to the attention of occidental scholarship by Chamberlain, the fiction of this "obscure Oriental Swift" has been discussed in "Swift in Japan," *Saturday Review*, LXII(1886), 392-93,
and in Eddy, pp. 68-71, 131-33, and 169-70. Chamberlain decides
that it contains "too few such points of likeness to favour the idea
of any borrowing on the part of the Japanese author. Swift's
work was so infinitely richer in amusing incidents that had it
been known to the writer of *Wasaubiyauwe* through a Dutch
translation,—in itself a not very probable supposition,—he could
hardly have failed to borrow much more extensively." Eddy con-
jectures plausibly that "the probability is rather of an influence
the other way" on the belief that 1774 is a meaningless date, that

the story is even older than European civilization, and that it may have somehow come to Swift's knowledge through Dutch traders. Eddy does not assert, however, that it is a source for *Gulliver*. A first requirement in any additional theorizing is a complete translation. The original Asiatic Society *Transactions* have *Wasaubiyauwe*, but the reprint adopted the "easier phonetic spelling sanctioned by the Romanization Society and by Dr. Hepburn's Dictionary." The title means the "Japanese Chwang Tsze," that is, a fable in the manner of the Chinese philosopher of that name.

1775

François Thomas Marie de Baculard d'Arnaud (1718-1805)
Makin, anecdote angloise [in *Suite des epreuves du sentiment*]
Paris, Delalain, 1775.   BN
———— [In *Œuvres* de D'Arnaud, Vol. IV] A Paris, Chez
Delalain . . . M.DCC.LXXVII.   tp DLC
———— [In *Epreuves*, Vol. IV] Paris, Le Jay, 1777.   GPB
———— [In *Epreuves*, Vol. V] A Maestricht, Chez Jean-Edme
Dufour & Phil. Roux . . . M.DCC.LXXIX.   tp MB, tp BM
———— [In *Epreuves*, Vol. V] A Paris, Chez Moutard . . .
M.DCC.LXXXI.   tp CtY
———— [In *Epreuves*] Maestricht, J. E. Dufour, 1784.   BN
———·— [In *Œuvres* de d'A., Vol. IV] Paris, Laporte, 1795.
                                                        GPB
———— [In *Œuvres* de d'A., Vol. IV] A Paris, Chez Laporte
. . . [17-?].   tp MH
———— [In *Œuvres* de d'A., Vol. VII A Paris, Chez Le Jay
17-?]   MB (tp wanting)
———— [In *Epreuves*, Vol. IV] Paris, Laporte, 1803.   GPB
———— [In *Œuvres* de d'A., Vol. IV] A Paris, Chez Laporte
. . . [1803?].   tp NNC
———— Robert Makin, eller Uppbäckten af ön Madera [tr. A.
H. Hemmendorf] 1818.   Inklaar p. 365

This bibliography undoubtedly needs revision; *Makin* may have been published separately before 1775 or perhaps may not

have appeared even in the collected *Épreuves* until 1777. Cf.
Cohen, *s.v.* "Arnaud"; Bertran de la Villehervé, *François-Thomas
de Baculard d'Arnaud: son théâtre et ses théories dramatiques*
(Paris, Champion, 1920), p. 159; and Derk Inklaar, *François-
Thomas de Baculard d'Arnaud, ses imitateurs en Hollande et
dans d'autres pays* ('s Gravenhage [etc.], Smits, 1925), p. [28].
The author wrote also *Robinson Cruzoé dans son isle, comédie en
1 acte,* Amsterdam, 1787 (BN).

1776

[Christian Gotthold Hauffe]
Leben und merkwürdige Begebenheiten einer adelichen Pach-
terstochter, welche nach verschiedenen überstandenen Glücks-
und Unglücksfällen zu Wasser und zu Lande, mit vielen
Schätzen bereichert, wiederum in London angelanget, von Ihr
selbst beschrieben. Regensburg, in der Montagischen Buchhandlung, 1776.   tp MiU

1776

[Johann Karl Wezel (1747-1819)]
Belphegor oder die wahrscheinlichste Geschichte unter der
Sonne. Leipzig, bei Crusius, 1776. 2 vols.   Krampe p. 68

"Die äuszere Form des 'Belphegor' ist die des Abenteurer-
oder Reiseromans . . ." states Siegfried Krampe, *Johann Carl
Wezels Leben und Schriften: ein Beitrag zur Geschichte des
Romans* (Berlin, Trenkel, 1911), p. 89, which contains a critical
résumé, pp. 68-103, of this work by the "German Voltaire," including a detailed comparison with *Candide.* Gustav Kreymborg,
Johann Karl Wezel: sein Leben und seine Schriften ([Vechta],
1913) devotes only two pages to *Belphegor.*

1778

Hildebrand Bowman, *pseudonym*
The Travels Of Hildebrand Bowman, Esquire, Into Carnovir-
ria, Taupiniera, Olfactaria, and Auditante, in New-Zealand; in

25

the Island of Bonhommica, and in the powerful Kingdom of
Luxo-Volupto, on the Great Southern Continent. Written by
Himself; Who went on shore in the Adventure's large Cutter,
at Queen Charlotte's Sound New-Zealand, the fatal 17th of
December 1773; and escaped being cut off, and devoured, with
the rest of the Boat's crew, by happening to be a-shooting in the
woods; where he was afterwards unfortunately left behind by
the Adventure . . . London: Printed for W. Strahan; and T.
Cadell . . . 1778.   tp NNC, tp BM

The *Adventure* was Captain Cook's companion ship on his
second voyage; Bowman is an imaginary survivor, for the entire
crew of the cutter was killed by cannibals. See several references
to this work in the index of Heilman, and Jules Duhem, "La
Fiction aéronautique du Pseudo-Bowman," *Bulletin du bibliophile et du bibliothécaire,* n.s.XV (1936), [399]-402, who calls it
"à sa façon un chef-d'œuvre, en plus d'un point semblable à
l'*Icaroménippe* de Lucien, l'archétype du genre." It is reviewed
in the *Monthly Review,* LIX(1778), 409-10.

1778

[Julien Jacques Moutonnet de Clairfons (1740-1813)]
   Les Iles Fortunées, ou les Aventures de Bathylle et de Cléobule,
   par M.M.D.C.A.S. Canarie et Paris, Le Boucher, 1778.   BN
   ———— [In *Voyages imaginaires,* ed. Garnier, Vol. X, "revues,
   retouchées & augmentées par l'Auteur"] A Amsterdam, Et se
   trouve à Paris . . . M.DCC.LXXXVII.   tp NNC, tp BM

The original date is sometimes given as 1771, e.g., in Mornet,
I, 382, perhaps because the author states in his *avertissement*
that "cet ouvrage fut composé pendant l'été de 1771" (Garnier,
X, 98 f.), but I find no record of a publication date before 1778.

1778

Hektor Schkolanus, *pseudonym*
   Seltsame und merkwürdige Schicksale eines Jünglings, genannt
   Hektor Schkolanus, von Reutlingen gebürtig, welche er von

erster Jugend an, und hernach auf Reisen in Pohlen, Deutschland, Frankreich und Spanien, besonders aber auf seiner Fahrt
mit einem Seerauber um Amerika herum gehabt, da er endlich
in der Südsee dieses Welttheils nebst dreyen Kameraden auf
einer unbewohnten Insel von ihm verlassen worden, und
nachdem noch sieben Jahr allein allda zubringen mussen.
Von ihm selbst beschrieben und von dessen Freunden zum
Druck befördert. Frankfurt und Leipzig, 1778.	MiU

Ullrich, pp. 172 f., states that the *Vorrede* is signed "B.G.J."

1781

[Nicolas Edme Restif de la Bretonne (1734-1806)]
La Découverte australe Par un Homme-volant, ou Le Dédale
français; Nouvelle très-philosophique: Suivie de la Lettre d'un
Singe, &c^a . . . Imprimé à Leïpsick: Et se trouve à Paris
[1781]. 4 vols.	tp DLC, tp BM
———— Der fliegende Mensch. ein Halbroman, von dem Ver-
fasser der Zeitgenossinnen [tr. Wilhelm C. S. Mylius] Dresden
und Leipzig, in der Breitkopfischen Buchhandlung. 1784.
	tp DLC
———— Avventure E Viaggi Di Un Uomo Volante. Tradu-
zione dal francese. Milano, Presso Pietro Agnelli . . . 1818.
2 vols.	Tschich
———— [In *Œuvres* de R. de la B.] Paris, Auguste Fontaine
[1875?].	Lacroix (advt.)

A standard reference is Paul Lacroix, *Bibliographie et icono-
graphie de tous les ouvrages de Restif de la Bretonne . . . par
P. L. Jacob* [pseud.] (Paris, 1875), pp. 198-207; see also Eugen
Dühren (pseud. of Iwan Bloch), *Rétif-Bibliothek: Verzeichnis
der französischen und deutschen Ausgaben und Schriften von
und über Rétif* . . . (Berlin, 1906); for the Italian translation
see Günther Tschich, *Rétif de la Bretonne: Katalog einer
Sammlung seiner Werke,* with an introduction by Arthur
Schurig (Berlin, Antiquariat am Lützowplatz [Katalog 4], 1922),
p. 56. Studies of the author are numerous, but of *La Découverte*

australe, few. Brief comment is given by Flammarion, pp. 524-
32; by B[enoît] Malon, "Rétif de la Bretonne: un romancier
polygraphe du dix-huitième siècle, socialiste et transformiste,"
Revue socialiste, IX(1889), 661-71; by Lichtenberger[a], pp. 213 ff.;
by Hugo, pp. 849-57; by Schmitt, pp. 85-86; by Eugen Dühren,
*Rétif de la Bretonne: der Mensch, der Schriftsteller, der Reforma-
tor* (Berlin, Harrwitz, 1906), pp. 498-500; by Schomann, pp. 142-
51; by Chinard[b], pp. 412 f.; by Kleinwächter, pp. 24-26 and 89-
92; by Kirchenheim, pp. 248-51; and by Pierre Trahard, *Les
Maitres de la sensibilité française au XVIIIe siècle* (Paris, Boivin
[1933]), IV, 197-200. Lacroix writes, p. 203: "Restif avait lu
certainement le roman anglais des *Hommes volants* . . . ; les
aventures de Pierre Wilkins lui donnèrent l'idée de faire voyager
son Victorin dans les pays inconnus du globe. Il est à remarquer
que la machine que ce voyageur invente pour s'élever dans les
airs, est antérieure d'un an ou deux à l'invention du *vaisseau
volant* de Blanchard. . . . Le roman . . . accuse une prodigieuse
imagination fantastique. . . . Nous serions tenté de le considérer comme le produit d'une hallucination de malade: *aegri
somnia.* . . . La machine . . . n'est, à vrai dire, qu'une imitation
de celle que Cyrano avait imaginée . . . ; c'est, au reste, dans cet
ouvrage philosophique si remarquable de Cyrano, que Restif a
puisé beaucoup d'idées. . . ."

1782

[Robert Martin Lesuire (1737-1815)]
L'Aventurier français, ou Mémoires de Grégoire Merveil.
Londres; et Paris, Quillau, 1782. 2 vols. in 1.   BN
———— [Another edition] Londres; et Paris, Quillau, 1783.
2 vols.   BN
———— [Bearbeitung] Der Robinson des achtzehnten Jahr-
hunderts; oder Abenteuer und Wanderungen des Herrn Franz
Pelerin . . . Leipzig, in der Weygandschen Buchhandlung
[1783?]. 2 vols.   Ullrich p. 175
———— Troisième Édition . . . A Londres, Et se trouve à
Paris, Chez Quillau l'aîné . . . La Veuve Duchesne . . . Belin

... Mérigot le jeune ... De Senne ... M.DCC.LXXXIV [-IX]. 10 vols. in 5 [a mixed set, especially Vol. VII: A Bruxelles, Chez Dujardin ... Et A Paris, Chez Defer De Maisonneuve ... 1789].   tp NN

———— [Another edition] 1785.   Mann p. 138
———— [Another edition] Paris, Quillau, 1787. 10 vols. in 5.   Ullrich p. 175
———— Der französische Abenteurer oder Denkwürdigkeiten Gregor Merveils. Gera, 1790 [-91]. 4 vols.   Ullrich p. 176
———— The French Adventurer; Or, Memoirs Of Gregoire Merveil, Marquis D'Erbueil. Translated From The French Of M. Le Suire ... London: Printed For John Bew ... 1791. 3 vols.   tp BM

In 1783 the author enlarged this work by sequels of two or more volumes each, which reached the "quatrième suite" in 1803; this explains, for example, the increased number of volumes in the edition of 1787. A complete and accurate bibliography would approach in complexity that of the *Insel Felsenburg* or *Cleveland*. Without being able to examine all the volumes I have no reliable way of deciding just what these successive editions contain; cf. Ullrich, pp. 175 f., and the BN catalogue. For the possibility of an edition at Bruxelles see Vol. IV of the NN set cited above.

Mann in his discussion, pp. 138-44, points out indebtedness to Defoe and Desfontaines. Merveil on his desert island overcomes his hardships with such facility that "on peut aller jusqu'à dire que cette partie du livre est une caricature de *Robinson*" (p. 140); in fact, the whole work is undoubtedly "une parodie des romans d'aventures en général ... s'il n'a pas la plume mordante de Swift ni la pénétration de cet écrivain, il essaie, du moins, de lui emboîter le pas. ... Enfin, pour ce qu'il y a de fantastique et d'utopique dans les descriptions des régions mystérieuses visitées par le héros, nous croyons que l'*Aventurier français* ne le cède en rien aux autres voyages imaginaires que le dix-huitième siècle a produits en si grand nombre" (p. 144). Goulding, pp. 99 f., shows its resemblance to *Peter Wilkins*. The various possibilities of classifying it are indicated by a characterization in Dottin, p. 416: "successivement un roman picaresque, puis une robinsonnade qui, assez réaliste au début, devient vite invraisemblable, et enfin un conte de fées qui se passe dans le royaume des gnomes 'où tout est en or' "; and by a reference to it in Servais Étienne, *Le Genre romanesque en France depuis l'apparition de la "Nouvelle Héloïse" jusqu'aux approches de la révolution* (Paris, Colin, 1922), p. 362 n.1: "Il faudrait signaler aussi, à côté du roman noir, le genre que popularisera Pigault-Lebrun; il est déjà parfaitement constitué avec Le Suire, *L'aventurier français,* 1782, et le chevalier Duplessis, *Mémoires de Sir Georges Wollap,* 1787. Ces auteurs amalgament les souvenirs de Marmontel, de Prévost, de Voltaire, et ils forment une transition entre la littérature des voyages imaginaires et les romans populaires d'Alexandre Dumas et de Sir Rider Haggard." The English translation was noticed in the *Critical Review,* [2S.] II(1791), 234: "these volumes would be uniques, if we had not the extraordinary adventures of Munchausen; the marquis has, however, more ingenuity than the baron, and his adventures are not always contradictory to reason and common sense."

1783

Guillaume Grivel (1735-1810)
L'Ile Inconnue ou Mémoires du Chevalier des Gastines, publiées par M. Grivel, des Académies de Dijon, de la Rochelle, de Rouen, de la Société Philosophique de Philadelphie etc. A Paris, chez Moutard . . . MDCCLXXXIII [-VII]. 6 vols. BN
———— Nouvelle Edition corrigée & augmentée. A Paris, chez Moutard . . . M.DCC.LXXXIV [-VII]. 6 vols. tp MH, tp BM
———— [Another edition] Paris; et Bruxelles, B. Le Francq. 1784. 2 vols. in 1. BN
———— Die unbekannte Insel, oder Reisen und Merkwurdigkeiten des Ritters von Gastines. Gesammelt und herausgegeben von Herrn Grivel. Mitglied der Akademien von Dijon und la Rochelle . . . Aus dem Französischen. Frankfurt am Mayn, bey Johann Joachim Keszler 1784. 4 vols. in 2. MiU

—— [Another French edition] 1786. Mann p. 144
—— [Another edition Paris?] Cuchet, 1787. Mann p. 144
—— [In *Voyages imaginaires,* ed. Garnier, Vols. VII-IX]
A Amsterdam, Et se trouve à Paris . . . M.DCC.LXXXVII.
tp NNC, tp BM
—— [Another German edition "übersetzt von J. F. Simon"]
Frankfurt am Mayn, bei Eszlinger, 1788 [Vol. I only].
ADB XCV, 185
—— [Another French edition Paris?] Bossange, 1793.
Mann p. 144
—— [Another German edition] Frankfurt am Mayne, 1798.
[Vols. I-II only]. Ullrich p. 174
—— [Another French edition] A la Haye, chez les libraires
associés, 1802. 6 vols. Stammhammer I,112
—— [Another edition] Paris, 1804. Ullrich p. 174
—— [Another edition] Paris, 1806. Ullrich p. 174
—— Quatrième Edition. Paris. Briand . . . 1812. 2 vols.
tp MB
—— [Another edition] Paris, Ledoux et Tenré, 1812. 2 vols.
Ullrich p. 174
—— [Another edition] Paris, chez Ledoux et Tenré . . .
1816. 6 vols. Ullrich[d] p. 490

Without opportunity to examine all the editions I am uncertain about the accuracy and completeness of those above, mainly because of the two volumes subsequently added to and presumably accompanied by reëditions of the original four.

"Aucune des imitations de *Robinson Crusoé* n'a été, à son apparition, si vivement critiqué que l'*Ile inconnue,* et très peu en ont eu tant de contrefaçons" states Mann at the beginning of his discussion, pp. 144-53. He gives references to six contemporary journals that compared the work with *Robinson,* including Garnier; cf. pp. 38 f. *supra* and n. 79 referring to Grivel's defense against plagiarism in his introduction to the second edition. Mann calls him "le premier des imitateurs qui, du naufrage, fait la situation principale de son récit. . . . On voit ici, en écartant l'existence sentimentale menée par le chevalier de Kilpar et son épouse, la première esquisse d'une famille naufragée, projet qui se développe plus tard avec tant de succès dans le *Robinson suisse"* (pp. 145 f.). For further detailed discussion see Wijngaarden, pp. 225-35. It is one of the most prolix of the imaginary voyages.

1783

[Joseph Romain Joly, *père* (1715-1805)]
  Les Aventures de Mathurin Bonice, premier habitant de l'Isle de l'Esclavage, ancien ministre du roi Zanfara, tirées de ses mémoires par un académician des Arcades. Paris, Guillot 1783 [-87]. 6 vols. in 3.   BN
  —— Begebenheiten des Mathurin Bonice, ersten Bewohners der Sklaveninsel, ehemaligen Ministers des Königs von Zanfara, aus seinen Berichten gezogen. Aus dem Französischen übersetzt. Frankfurt am Mayn, bei den Gebrüdern van Düren. 1783. 2 vols.   Ullrich p. 175

The 1787 addition to the original four parts of 1783 is entitled *Le Portefeuille de Mathurin Bonice, servant de suite à ses aventures. 5e [-6e] partie* (BN). The *Correspondance secrete, politique & littéraire* (Londres, 1788), XV, 25, disposes of this work: ". . . prenez un livre de Géographie, quelqu'une des mille & une compilations qui existent sur l'histoire naturelle, un volume de sermons; chargez un copiste d'extraire au hasard des morceaux de l'un & de l'autre, amenez ces citations par une fable quelconque, & vous aurez un roman comme les *Aventures de Bonice,* dont l'auteur, pour ne pas se fatiguer l'imagination, a tout bonnement emprunté l'idée dans le roman beaucoup trop vanté de *Robinson Crusoë."* Though this has an air of finality, it cannot be taken seriously. The *Mercure de France,* janvier 1783, i,191-92, says: "quoiqu'il y ait peu d'intérêt pour le cœur, il attache au moins l'esprit. Il est rempli de détails de mœurs & d'Histoire Naturelle qui prouvent ou que le Héros a beaucoup voyagé, ou que l'Auteur est un homme instruit." Mann discusses the work, pp. 153-56.

1783

[Cornélie Pétronille Bénédicte Wouters, *baronne* de Wasse (1737-1802)]

Le Char Volant, ou Voyage dans la Lune. A Londres, & se trouve à Paris, chez la Veuve Duchesne . . . la Veuve Ballard & fils . . . Mérigot l'aîné . . . Mérigot le jeune . . . & Renault . . . 1783.   Klinckowstroem p. 264

———— Der Luftwagen oder Reise in den Mond. Aus dem Franz. der Freifrau v. V††† übersetzt [von Th. Fr. Ehrmann]. Straszburg (i d. akadem. Buchhandlung), 1784.
Klinckowstroem p. 264

Reviewed in *Mercure de France,* 31 janvier, 1784, pp. 210-13.

1783

Anonymous

The Admirable Travels Of Messieurs Thomas Jenkins And David Lowellin Through the Unknown Tracts of Africa: With the Manner how Lowellin lived five Years on an uninhabited Spot; and, having sustained many dangerous Attacks from the wild Beasts and Savages, returned safe to London, in September, 1781, after having been eleven Years in those extensive Regions. London: Printed from the original Manuscript, in October, 1783, by the Author's Consent, for the Benefit of Robert Barker, an unfortunate blind Man.   tp BM

———— [Another edition] London: Printed . . . in January, 1785, for the Benefit of Robert Barker . . . .   tp BM

———— [Another edition] London: Printed . . . in August, 1785, for the Benefit of Robert Barker . . . .   MH

———— [Another edition] London: Printed For W. Clements, J. Sadler, And J. Eves, In The Year 1792.   tp BM

———— [Another edition] London: Printed from the original Manuscript, in May, 1792, by the Author's Consent, for the Benefit of Robert Barker.   tp DLC, tp BM

The duration of Lowellin's isolation and absence increases with successive editions.

1784

[Antoine François Momoro (1756-1794), *alleged author*]
Histoire Intéressante D'Un Nouveau Voyage A La Lune, Et
De La Descente A Paris D'Une Jolie Dame De Cette Terre
Etrangere. A Whiteland Et se trouve à Paris Chez F.-G.
Deschamps . . . M.DCC.LXXXIV.   tp MH

The attribution of authorship is a suggestion made by Paludan,
p. 114.

1784

[Piroux]
L'Art De Voyager Dans L'Air Et De S'Y Diriger. Mémoire
qui va remporter le prix proposé par l'Académie de Lyon . . .
On y trouvera entr'autres, la vraye théorie de la Lune & des
Esprits, & des moyens sûrs & simples d'entretenir les grandes
Routes Terrestres, que l'on devra continuer de fréquenter dans
les tems que les Chemins Célestes seront interdits, &c. A Elli-
venul [i.e., Lunéville], Au Pays de Rianole [i.e., Lorraine]
pendant la mère Lune de 1784.   tp DLC

1784

[Christian Friedrich Timme (1752-1788)]
Wenzel von Erfurt eine Robinsonade. Erfurt 1784 [-86]. bey
Georg Adam Keyser. 4 vols.   tp MiU

The author, in defending his book against his critics, real or
imagined, indicates the title-appeal of the word *robinsonade:*
"Der dritte Vorwurf, den man mir gemacht hat, ist der: das Buch
heist Robinsonade, und noch hat der Held nichts von den
Geschichten eines Robinsons erfahren." But the reader must
wait until the fourth volume before the hero even leaves Europe.
The work is reviewed in the *ADB,* LXIX (1786), ii, 413-15, and
Anhang, 1936 f.

1785

[Rudolf Erich Raspe (1737-1794)]
Baron Munchausen's Narrative Of His Marvellous Travels And Campaigns In Russia. Humbly Dedicated And Recommended To Country Gentlemen; And, If They Please, To Be Repeated As Their Own, After A Hunt, At Horse Races, In Watering-Places, And Other Such Polite Assemblies; Round The Bottle And Fire-Side. Oxford: Printed for the Editor, and sold by the Booksellers there and at Cambridge, also in London by the Booksellers of Piccadilly, the Royal Exchange and M. Smith . . . MDCCLXXXVI [postdated].
tp BM

—————— Wunderbare Reisen zu Wasser und Lande, Feldzüge und lustige Abentheuer des Freyherrn von Münchhausen, wie er dieselben bey der Flasche im Cirkel seiner Freunde selbst zu erzählen pflegt. Aus dem Englischen nach der neuesten Ausgabe übersetzt [by Gottfried August Burger (1747-94)], hier und da erweitert . . . London [i.e. Göttingen] 1786.   tp BM

—————— Gulliver Ressuscité, Ou Les Voyages, Campagnes Et Aventures Extraordinaires Du Baron De Munikhouson. A Paris, Chez Royez . . . M.DCC.LXXXVII.   tp BM

—————— A Sequel To The Adventures Of Baron Munchausen, Containing his expedition into Africa.—How he out-does Alexander.—Splits a rock at the Cape of Good Hope.—Wrecked on an island of ice.—Becomes acquainted with the Sphinx, Gog and Magog.—Overcomes above a thousand lions.—Buried in a whirlwind of sand.—Feasts on live bulls and Kava.—Is declared Sovereign of Africa, and builds a bridge from thence to Great-Britain, supported by a single arch.—Battle of his retinue with the famous Don Quixote.—Becomes acquainted with the Colossus of Rhodes.—Chase of Wauwau through America.—Meets with a floating island.—Visits the islands in the South Sea.—Becomes acquainted with Omai.—Cuts a canal across the Isthmus of Darien.—Discovers the Alexandrian Library.—Besieges Seringapatam.—Overcomes Tip-

poo Saib.—Raises the hull of the Royal George; together with
a variety of other very Surprising Adventures. Humbly Dedicated To Mr. Bruce, The Abyssinian Traveller, As the Baron
conceives that it may be of some service to him, previous to his
making another expedition into Abyssinia: But if this advice
does not delight Mr. Bruce, the Baron is willing to fight him
on any terms he pleases. London. Printed for H. D. Symonds
. . . and J. Owen . . . MDCCXCII.   tp BM
———— The Seventh Edition, Considerably enlarged . . . Gulliver Revived: Or, The Vice of Lying properly exposed. Containing Singular Travels, Campaigns, Voyages, And Adventures In Russia, The Caspian Sea, Iceland, Turkey, Egypt,
Gibraltar, Up The Mediterranean, On The Atlantic Ocean,
And Through The Centre Of Mount Ætna, Into The South
Sea. Also, An Account of a Voyage into the Moon and Dog-
star; with many extraordinary Particulars relative to the Cook-
ing Animal in those Planets, which are there called the Human
Species. By Baron Munchausen. London: Printed for C. and
G. Kearsley . . . M.DCC.XCIII.   tp BM

I give only the generally accepted original, its first translations,
and the seventh edition, enlarged by others, which became the
standard for reëditions, as well as the spurious sequel, which is
not in the seventh edition but often incorporated in later editions.
Only one copy of an *editio princeps* is said to exist. The full title
of the seventh edition shows how many of the elements of the
imaginary voyage manifest themselves in *Munchausen*. Probably
no fiction of similar widespread popularity is more lacking in
thorough and satisfactory scholarly study. A critical bibliography
of the hundreds of editions and translations—an undertaking too
complicated and extensive for my check list—and a critical edition are much needed. At present the best editions are those by
Seccombe; William Rose in the Broadway Translations (London,
Routledge [1923]); Erich Ebstein ([Leipzig, Spamersche
Buchdr., 1925]), by far the most thorough but from the point of
view only of Bürger's translation; and F. J. Harvey Darton (London, Navarre Society, 1930). Ebstein reprints the eighteen

"Münchhausenschen Geschichten" from the *Vade Mecum für lustige Leute* . . . (1781-83). A good introduction to source-study is Müller-Fraureuth, and Werner Schweizer, *Die Wandlungen Münchhausens in der deutschen Literatur bis zu Immerman: ein Beitrag zur Stoffgeschichte* (Leipzig, 1921). For other valuable information and comment, see Dunlop, ed. Wilson, II, 537 n.1; S. A. Allibone, *Critical Dictionary of English Literature* . . . (Philadelphia, 1882), II, *s.v.* "Raspe"; Adams, pp. 128-44; Seccombe, *DNB, s.v.* "Raspe"; and W. L. George, *A Novelist on Novels* (London, Collins [1918]), pp. 177-90. Available records about Karl Friedrich Hieronymus, baron von Münchhausen (1720-97) form the basis of an imaginary biography ("Aber das Wesentliche stimmt genau," p. [222]) by Carl Haensel, *Das war Münchhausen Roman aus Tatsachen* (Stuttgart, J. Engelhorn, 1933).

1785

Anonymous
The Aerostatic Spy: Or, Excursions With An air Balloon. Exhibiting A View of various Countries, in different Parts of the World; and A Variety of Characters in Real Life. By An Aerial Traveller. London: Printed By Edmund Fawcett . . . And Sold By H. D. Symonds . . . MDCCLXXXV. 2 vols.
tp DLC

———— [Another edition] The Balloon, Or Aerostatic Spy . . . London: Printed For W. Lane . . . M DCC LXXXVI. 2 vols. in 1.
tp BM

———— Der äerostatische Zuschauer, oder Streifereien mit einem Luftschiffe, aus dem Englischen. Leipzig 1787. Schneider. 2 vols.
Minor p. 68

———— [Another edition] Leipzig, Schneider, 1788. 2 vols.
Minor p. 68

———— [Part ii in] Wie gehts auf der Welt, oder Besuche in allen vier Welttheilen unter Führung eines Genius . . . Leipzig, Schneider, 1789. 2 vols.
Minor p. 68

———— [Another edition of the preceding] Leipzig, Schneider (Lincke), 1790. 2 vols.
Price p. 31

"An anonymous and very humble precursor of Jules Verne," writes J[oyce] M. S. Tompkins, *The Popular Novel in England 1770-1800* (London, Constable, 1932), p. 190. The work receives one paragraph each in the *Monthly Review*, LXXIII (1785), 466, and the *Critical Review*, LX (1785), 234.

1786

[Marguerite Daubenton (1720-1788)]
Zélie dans le Désert, par Madame D . . . Londres et Paris, Belin 1786 [-87]. 2 vols.   BN
————— [Another edition] A Geneve. Chez François Dufart . . . M. DCC. LXXXVII. 2 vols.   ICN
————— [Another edition] 1788. 2 vols.   BN
————— Zelia In The Desert. From The French. By The Lady Who Translated "Adelaide And Theodore"; And "Anecdotes Of Henry IV. Of France" . . . London: Printed For G. And T. Wilkie . . . MDCCLXXXIX. 3 vols.   tp BM
————— [Another edition] London: Printed For C. Forster . . . M.DCC.LXXXIX.   ICN
————— [Another edition] Dublin; Printed For Messrs. P. Byrne, L. White, P. Wogan, Gruever And Mc. Allister, H. Colbert, J. Moore, B. Dornin. M,DCC,LXXXIX. 2 vols. ICU
————— [Another French edition] A Geneve, Et se trouve, A Paris, Chez Dufart. . . . 1792.   NjP
————— Nouvelle édition. A Paris, an III [1795] . . . 4 vols.
                                                    Cohen 1091
————— [Another edition] 1804.   Mann p. 156
—————Zelia In The Desert, Or, The Female Crusoe. Written By Herself . . . Sidney's Press. For Increase Cooke & Co . . . New Haven. 1812.   tp MH
————— [The fourth French edition] 1819.   Mann p. 156
————— [The fifth edition] 1823.   Mann p. 156
————— [Another edition] 1828. 2 vols.   BN
————— [Another edition] 1835. 2 vols.   BN
————— [Another edition] 1838. 2 vols.   BN
————— [Another edition] 1838. 2 vols.   BN

———— [Another edition] 1840. 2 vols.　　　　　　　BN
———— [Another edition] 1845. 2 vols.　　　　　　　BN
———— [Another edition] 1845. 2 vols.　　　　　　　BN
———— [Another edition] 1846. 2 vols.　　　　　　　BN
———— [Another edition] 1847. 2 vols.　　　　　　　BN
———— [Another edition] 1849. 2 vols.　　　　　　　BN
———— [Another edition] 1851. 2 vols.　　　　　　　BN
———— [Another edition] 1853. 2 vols.　　　　　　　BN
———— [Another edition] 1854. 2 vols.　　　　　　　BN
———— [Another edition] 1855. 2 vols.　　　　　　　BN
———— [Another edition] 1856. 2 vols.　　　　　　　BN
———— [Another edition] 1857. 2 vols.　　　　　　　BN
———— [Another edition] 1861. 2 vols.　　　　　　　BN
———— [In la Libraire populaire des villes et campagnes] Paris, Renault, n.d. 4 vols.　　　　　　　Nisard II, 499
———— [Another edition] Paris, Gennequin aîné, et Nancy, Vincenot, n.d. 4 vols.　　　　　　　Nisard II, 499

"This performance," writes the *Monthly Review,* LXXXI (1789), 363, "is evidently founded on the *Isola Disabitata* of Metastasio,—a circumstance which we think the writer should, in justice to his distinguished prototype, have acknowledged . . . ." Chinard[b], p. 418, n.1, calls this an "imitation de la première partie de *l'Ile inconnue*." Mann discusses it, pp. 156-58. Its popularity brings it within the scope of Charles Nisard, *Histoire des livres populaires ou de la littérature du Colportage* . . . , 2e éd. (Paris, 1864), II,499 f., where he writes: "Il est écrit avec naturel et se fait lire avec intérêt, mais il porte la marque d'un goût qui régnait en tyran sur tous les cœurs, dans le temps de la jeunesse de cette excellente personne. Ce goût était une sensibilité vive et larmoyante que les philosophes avaient mise à la mode. . . ." Servais Étienne, *Le Genre romanesque en France depuis l'apparition de la "Nouvelle Héloïse" jusqu'aux approches de la révolution* (Paris, Colin, 1922), p. 357, writes: "Il suffit de lire *Zélie* . . . pour se rendre un compte exacte de l'influence de Richardson à l'extrême fin de l'ancien régime. Il est certain que Mme Daubenton a fait un effort pour se rapprocher du roman anglais; elle s'éloigne du modèle français par la minutie des détails indifférents, j'ai failli dire inutiles. Le résultat, le seul, c'est qu'elle allonge jusqu'à plus de sept cents pages in-8° un roman qui ne retient plus la moindre trace de psychologie. Elle imagine une robinsonade ridicule à force d'être commode; Richardson n'a pas pu lui donner le génie qu'il faut pour marquer nettement un caractère; il n'a même pas pu la détourner de la fausse naïveté d'*Aline, reine de Golconde,* ni même du pire côté de l'*Astrée;* peut-être, à la rigueur, lui a-t-il fait comprendre combien il est décent pour une jeune fille de seize ans d'aimer le mari de sa bienfaitrice; à coup sûr, l'empreinte de Prévost sur l'esprit de Mme Daubenton était trop profonde pour qu'aucun rival pût prétendre à l'effacer." See for biographical sketch Edmond Pilon, "Madame Daubenton et sa Famille," *Mercvre de France,* XCIV (1911), 30-60. *Zélie* is listed by Pierre Vierge, "Les Lectures de Bonaparte en Égypte," *ibid.,* LXV (1907), 633-40.

1786

[P. Navarre]

Amusemens Géographiques Et Historiques, Ou Les Mémoires De M. * * * Contenant ses Voyages & ses Aventures dans le quatre Parties du Monde . . . A Meaux, Courtois, 1786.

Barbier I, 159

——— [Another edition] A Paris, Chez Méquignon junior . . . 1788. 2 vols. DLC, tp BM

——— [Another edition] Voyages d'un étudiant dans le cinq parties du monde . . . [entièrement refondu] par M. [Georges Bernard] Depping . . . Paris, Méquignon junior, 1822. 2 vols.

BN

——— [Another edition of the preceding] Paris, Delamarche, 1835. 2 vols. DLC, BN

There may have been another edition under the original title in 1822; see Barbier.

1786

[Carl Nyrén (1726-1783)]

Mappa geographica Scelestinae eller Stora-Skälms-Landets geographiska beskrifning. Stockholm, 1786. Paludan p. 335

1787

[Pierre Duplessis, *chevalier* (fl. 1750-1800), *supposed author*]
Mémoires De Sir George Wollap; Ses Voyages dans différentes parties du Monde; aventures extraordinaires qui lui arrivent; découverte de plusieurs Contrées inconnues; description des mœurs & des coutumes des Habitans. Par M. L. C. D . . . A Londres, Chez Thomas Hookham . . . Et se trouve à Paris, Chez la Veuve Duchesne . . . 1787 [-88]. 6 vols.
                                          tp NN
———— Sir George Wollap's Leben, Reisen in verschiedene Welttheile, und auszerordentliche Abentheuer; nebst einer Beschreibung der von ihm entdeckten Länder, ihrer Einwohner, deren Sitten und Gebräuche . . . Aus dem Französischen. Leipzig, im Schwickertschen Verlage. 1788. 3 vols. in
1.   tp BM

Mentioned in Mann, pp. 158 f. See my quotation, p. 374 *supra,* from Étienne.

1788

Giacomo Girolamo Casanova di Seingalt (1725-1798)
Jcosameron Ou Histoire D'Edouard, Et D'Elisabeth qui passèrent quatre vingts un ans chez les Mégamicres habitans aborigènes du Protocosme dans l'intérieur de notre globe, traduite de l'anglois par Jacques Casanova De Seingalt Vénitien Docteur ès loix Bibliothécaire de Monsieur le comte de Walstein seigneur de Dux Chambellan de S.M.J.R.A. A Prague à l'imprimerie de l'école normale [1788]. 5 vols.   tp DLC, tp BM
———— Eduard und Elisabeth bei den Megamikren Ein phantastischer Roman Erste deutsche Bearbeitung von Heinrich Conrad 1922 Benjamin Harz Verlag Berlin/Wien. 2 vols.
                                    tp NNC

J[oseph] Pollio in his full bibliographic description, *Bibliographie anecdotique et critique des œuvres de Jacques Casanova*
26

(Paris, Giraud-Badin, 1926), pp. 134-44, shows that, though this work is often dated 1787 because of the dedication of 20 septembre 1787, it actually did not come off the press until the summer of the next year. As Pollio states, it seems to have been forgotten until the articles of Lorédan Larchey, "Un Voyage de Casanova," *Le Bibliophile français,* III(1869), [314]-318; [374]-380, who says that "ce voyage imaginaire" has never been analyzed anywhere before. A few years later Louis Dépret, "M. Jules Verne et Casanova," *L'Illustration,* 3 mars 1877, p. 139, weakly compares it with Verne's *Voyage au centre de la terre* (1864): "il n'y a seulement analogie de sujet, il y a rencontre (evidemment fortuite) dans le choix de détails singuliers. . . ." Casanova himself writes in his second dedication, II,[iii], "Platon, Erasme, le chancelier Bacon, Thomas Morus, Campanella, & Nicolas Klimius aussi sont ceux qui me firent venir envie de publier cette histoire, ou ce roman." Conrad's recent translation carries a brief *Vorwort* suggesting that its unpopularity may have been caused by the first volume, which takes up 150 pages with a "Commentaire Litteral sur les Trois Premiers Chapitres de la Genese" and an "Introduction." Conrad writes, I,5: "Wenn Casanovas Werk nichts anderes wäre, als eine von den vielen Utopien, die nach der Utopia des Thomas Morus entstanden oder eine der vielen Liliputiaden nach Swift, so brauchte man sich nicht darum zu mühen, es der Vergessenheit zu entreiszen. Aber es ist mehr: es ist das Werk eines tiefen und vor allem auch freien Denkers und es ist vor allem eine sehr unterhaltsame Abenteuergeschichte, die zwar einen Leser verlangt, der gerne denkt, die aber auch ganz abgesehen von ihrem Gedankengehalt durch die bewuszte Fülle der Ereignisse interessiert." (Larchey remarks, p. 380 n.1: "Au moment de la mise sous presse, j'achève la lecture du nouvel ouvrage de madame Clémence Royer, la traductrice de Darwin. Dans ses savantes recherches sur l'*Origine de l'Homme,* madame Royer croit que l'homme primitif et le singe ont pu avoir un ancêtre comme amphibie, hermaphrodite, et pourvu de mamelles lactifères. Cela ressemble fort au *mégamicre* de Casanova." Thus does literary criticism keep up with science!)

1788

[François Guillaume Ducray-Duminil (1761-1819)]
Lolotte Et Fanfan, Ou Les Aventures De Deux Enfans Aban-
donnés Dans Une Isle Déserte. Rédigées & publiées sur des
Manuscrits Anglais, par M. D * * . du M * * ... A Charle's-
Town, Et se trouve à Paris, Chez Maradan ... [1788] [post-
dated?]. 4 vols. in 2.   tp NNC
——— Seconde Édition, Revue & corrigée avec soin ... A
Charle's-Town, Et se trouve à Paris, Chez Maradan ... 1788.
4 vols. in 2.   tp BM
——— [Another edition] Strasbourg, Treutel, 1788.
                                                    Ullrich^d p. 490
——— [Another edition] Neuwied, 1789. 2 vols. Ullrich p. 176
——— Lalotte und Fanfan, oder die Begebenheiten zweier auf
eine wüste Insel ausgesetzten Kinder. In Ordnung gebracht
und herausgegeben nach englischen Manuskripten von M. D * *
du M * *. Aus dem Französischen übersetzt [by F. Schmit].
Liegnitz und Leipzig, bei David Siegert, 1789 [-90]. 4 vols.
                                                    Ullrich p. 177
——— [Another French edition] Paris, 1792. 4 vols.
                                                    Ullrich p. 176
——— Los Dos Robinsones O Aventuras De Carlos Y Fanny
Dos Niños Ingleses, Abandonados En Una Isla De America.
Relacion imitada del Inglés, por D. Justo de la Barra. Segunda
Edicion. En Madrid: En La Imprenta De La Viuda É Hijo
De Marin, 1792 [-97]. 3 vols. [Vol. I, 1797; Vol. II, 1792; Vol.
III, 1793].   tp DLC
——— [Another French edition] Avignon, J. A. Joly, 1793.
4 vols. in 2.   Gumuchian I, 164
——— 6.édition. Paris, 1795. 4 vols.   Ullrich p. 176
——— [Another edition] An III [1795]. 4 vols.   BN
——— Ambrose and Eleanor; Or, The Adventures Of Two
Children Deserted On An Uninhabited Island. Translated [by
Lucy Peacock] From The French. With Alterations adapting
it to the Perusal of Youth, for whose Amusement and Instruc-

tion it is designed. By The Author Of The Adventures of the Six Princesses of Babylon; Juvenile Magazine; Visit for a Week, &c. London: Printed For R. And L. Peacock . . . and sold by Messrs. Hookham and Carpenter . . . 1796.   tp BM

———— Second Edition. London: Printed For R. And L. Peacock . . . And Sold By Hookham And Carpenter . . . And C. Law . . . 1797.   tp CtY

———— [Another edition] Philadelphia: Printed by William W. Woodward. 1799.   Evans XII, 252

———— [Another edition] Baltimore: Printed for Thomas, Andrews and Butler . . . By Warner and Hanna . . . 1799. MWA

———— [Another German edition] Wien und Prag, 1802. 2 vols.   Ullrich p. 177

———— Neuvième edition. Paris, 1807. 4 vols. in 2.
        Ullrich p. 176

———— The Third Edition. London: Printed For J. Johnson And J. Harris . . . R. And L. Peacock . . . C. Law . . . And B. Tabart . . . 1807.   tp BM

———— Dixième Édition. A Paris, Chez Belin-Le-Prieur . . . 1812. 4 vols. in 1.   tp BM

———— Cuarta Edicion. Barcelona: Imprenta de Sierra Y Marti, Ano 1820. 2 vols.   MiU (Vol. I wanting)

———— 11.édition. Paris, Berlin-Leprieur, 1823. 4 vols.
        Ullrich p. 176

———— [Another Spanish edition] Paris, imprimerie de J. Smith, 1824. 2 vols.   BN

———— [Another French edition] Paris, Pillet, 1830. 2 vols. BN

———— The Sixth [English] Edition. Paris, Published By J. H. Truchy, 1839.   MiU

———— [Another Spanish edition] Publicada Por Agustin Masse . . . México. Impreso Por Ignacio Cumplido . . . 1844. 2 vols.   tp MH

———— Nueva Edicion. Barcelona: Imprenta De D. Manuel Sauri . . . 1845. 2 vols. in 1.   tp DLC

———— [Another French edition] 1861. 4 vols.   BN

———— [Another edition, in Bibliothèque des villes et des

campagnes] Paris Renault Et Cie . . . [1865]. 4 vols. in 2.

tp BM

In the *Avant-Propos* of the first edition the author alleges, I, v, that "Ce n'est point *Robinson-Crusoé,* ce n'est point *l'Elève de la Nature,* que j'offre aux yeux de mes Lecteurs. Ces productions, d'ailleurs très-estimables, ne m'ont nullement aidé dans l'Ouvrage que j'ai entrepris: l'Histoire de Fanfan & Lolotte est d'un genre tout-à-fait différent." But the *Monthly Review,* n.s. XX (1796), 346, believes that "while we have Robinson Crusoe in our language, it is little worth while to translate, from another tongue, so inferior a production." Ullrich[a], p. 101, lists it among the "selbständige Jugendrobinsonaden." Dottin, p. 416, explains that "En réalité, ce titre est trompeur: les deux petits héros, allaités comme Romulus et Rémus par un animal qui, en l'éspèce, est une chèvre, ne restent pas longtemps seuls. Un milord anglais est jeté sur l'île par un naufrage et devient leur père adoptif. D'autre part, une baleine philanthrope, qui dormait au fond de la mer, remonte à la surface, apportant sur son dos la carcasse du navire naufragé, qui permettra aux robinsons de se construire une confortable maison de planches." Mann discusses it, pp. 160-62.

1788

Anonymous

The Voyages, Distresses And Wonderful Adventures Of Captain Winterfield. Containing A Genuine Succinct Account of his Transactions in America, during the late War; his disastrous Voyage to England, in which he had the Misfortune to be taken by an Algerine Man of War, near the Coast of Portugal, and carried to Barbary, where he remained in Slavery upwards of six Years; his miraculous Escape from thence, with five more in a Canvass Boat of their own Construction, and safe Arrival at Mayork. With several remarkable Providencies after his Captivity, and his safe Arrival at last in Scotland. Written from his own Memorandums, by an Officer under Captain Cooke, during his last Voyage to the Southern Hemi-

sphere. London: Printed for H. Lemoine . . . J. Sudbury . . .
J. Morgan . . . 1788.   tp MB
———— [Another edition] London. Printed for Ann Lemoine
. . . and sold by Lee and Hurst . . . 1798.   NHi
———— A New Edition. London: Printed For Ann Lemoine
. . . And Sold By T. Hurst . . . 1799.   tp DLC
———— A New Edition. London: Printed by T. Maiden . . .
For Ann Lemoine . . . And Sold By T. Hurst . . . 1800.
                                                    CSmH
———— [Another edition] Glasgow [1800].   Block p. 240
———— [Another edition] London: Printed and Sold by J.
Bailey . . . Sold Also By Champante and Whitrow, Aldgate;
Willmott and Hill, Borough; and Lumsden and Sons, Glasgow
[1800?].   tp BM
———— [Another edition] The Exile in Ireland . . . London:
Printed and Sold by J. Bailey . . . [1800?].   tp NN
———— A New Edition. Printed by A. Swindells . . . Man-
chester: and sold by J. Sadler, and M. Clements [c.1800]. NHi
———— [Another edition] London: Printed by T. Maiden . . .
For Ann Lemoine . . . And Sold By T. Hurst . . . 1802.
                                             MiU-C, tp BM

1789

[William Thomson (1746-1817)]
Mammuth; Or, Human Nature Displayed On A Grand Scale:
In A Tour With The Tinkers, Into The Inland Parts of Africa.
By the Man in the Moon . . . London: Printed For G. And
T. Wilkie . . . MDCCLXXXIX. 2 vols.   tp Bod
———— [Another edition] London: Printed For J. Murray . . .
MDCCLXXXIX. 2 vols. in 1.   tp MH
———— Mammuth oder Darstellung der menschlichen Natur
nach unverjüngtem Maszstabe in einer Reise mit Kesselflickern
nach Afrika, aus dem Englischen von C. A. Wichmann. Leip-
zig, 1792. 2 vols.   Price p. 239
———— Zweite Auflage. Halle, Ruff, 1795.   Price p. 239
See *N&Q*, 5S. VIII(1877), 14.

1789

John Willock, *pseudonym?*
Voyages to various parts of the world, and remarks on different countries in Europe, Africa and America, with the customs and manners of the Inhabitants. By John Willock, Mariner. Penrith: printed by Ann Bell, for the author; And sold by J. Mitchell, Carlisle; T. Hudson, Wigton; Wilson and Branthwaite, Kendal; T. Schofield, Liverpool; S. Hodgson, Newcastle; A. Dunlop, Glasgow; J. Richardson, Penrith; and the booksellers in town and country . . . [1789].   ICN
——— [Another edition] Philadelphia: Printed For George Gibson, By Hogan & M'Elroy . . . 1798.   tp NNC, tp BM

1790

[Balthazard, *abbé* (d. 1801)]
L'Isle Des Philosophes Et Plusieurs Autres, Nouvellement découvertes, & remarquables par leurs rapports avec la France actuelle. [Chartres, Deshayes] 1790.   tp DLC

In brief mention of this work Goulding writes, p. 98: ". . . on se souvient encore de *Gulliver* quand . . . l'abbé Baltazard, pour se moquer de Raynal et de Lamétrie et de leurs théories d'histoire naturelle, raconte un voyage dans un pays merveilleux habité par des ours qui marchent sur leurs pattes de derrière et font tirer leurs charrettes par des hommes 'marchant à quatre pattes avec de grandes ongles comme des griffes, et souvent maltraités par le conducteur.' "

1790

[Karl Ignaz Geiger (1756-1791)]
Reise eines Erdbewohners in den Mars. Philadelphia [i.e., Leipzig, Sommer], 1790.   tp MiU

1791

[Karl Timlich]
Der österreichische Robinson, oder Leben, und merkwürdige Reisen Andreas Geiszlers, eines gebohrnen Wieners, von ihm

selbst beschrieben . . . Frankfurth und Leipzig [Salzburg, Mayrische Buchhandlung] 1791.   MiU

See résumé in Haken, III, 3-144, and discussion in H. F. Wagner, pp. 13-17.

1791

Anonymous

Memoirs Of A Scots Heiress. Addressed To The Right Honourable Lady Catherine * * * * * *. By The Author Of Constance, &c. London: Printed for T. Hookham . . . and sold by J. Carpenter . . . 1791. 3 vols.   DLC, tp BM

Favorably noticed in the *Monthly Review,* n.s. VIII (1792), 340 f.

1791

Anonymous

Der Steyerische Robinson oder Reisen und Begebenheiten des Joseph Müller an der brasilianischen Küste. Wien, 1791.
        Sabin XVII, 414
———— [Another edition] Frankfurt und Leipzig. 1793. MiU

Brief mention in H. F. Wagner, pp. 17 f.

1793

Anonymous

A Voyage To The Moon. Strongly Recommended To All Lovers Of Real Freedom . . . London: Printed For The Author, And Sold By James Ridgway . . . And H. D. Symonds . . . MDCCXCIII.   tp DLC, tp BM

The dedication is signed "Aratus."

1794

Anonymous

Der Jesuit auf dem Thron, oder Das Neue Felsenburg. Ein komisch-politisch-satyrischer Roman. Berlin und Leipzig 1794.   MiU

Résumé in Haken V,345-91. Cited in Ullrich, p. 136, as a continuation and in Schröder, p. 73, as a parody of the *Insel Felsenburg*.

1795

[Thomas Northmore (1766-1851)]
Memoirs Of Planetes, Or A Sketch Of The Laws And Manners Of Makar. By Phileleutherus Devoniensis . . . London: Printed by Vaughan Griffiths . . . And Sold By J. Johnson . . . And J. Owen . . . 1795.   tp NNC, tp BM

1795

Anonymous
The History Of Constantius & Pulchera. Or Constancy Rewarded . . . Printed by T. C. Cushing, Salem [Mass.]; 1795.
tp DLC
————— [Another edition] Norwich: Printed By Thomas Hubbard. M,DCC,XCVI.   tp MB
————— [Another edition] Printed At Leominster, (Mass.) By Charles Prentiss [for Robert B. Thomas, Sterling], 1797.
tp NN
————— [Another edition] A Beautiful Little Novel . . . Portsmouth, N. H. Printed by Charles Peirce . . . 1798.
RPJCB
————— [Another edition] New York, 1801.   Loshe p. 108
————— [Another edition] Baltimore: Printed By Robert R. Maxwell. 1802.   tp MB
————— [Another edition] Boston: Published By Amos B. Parker . . . E. G. House, printer . . . 1821.   tp DLC

1796

[Charles Dibdin (1745-1814)]
Hannah Hewit; Or, The Female Crusoe. Being The History Of A Woman Of uncommon, mental, and personal accomplishments; Who, After a variety of extraordinary and inter-

esting adventures in almost every station of life, from splendid prosperity to abject adversity, Was Cast Away In The Grosvenor East-Indiaman: And became for three years the sole inhabitant of An Island In The South Seas. Supposed To Be Written By Herself . . . London: Printed For C. Dibdin . . . [1796, May] 3 vols.   tp DLC, tp BM

Both DLC and BM date this 1792. I have followed E. Rimbault Dibdin (great-grandson), "A Bibliographical Account of the Works of Charles Dibdin," *N&Q*, 9S., XI (1903), 245; his proposed life of Charles Dibdin, *ibid.*, VIII(1901), 39, has not yet appeared. His revised bibliography was privately printed under the title of *A Charles Dibdin Bibliography* (Liverpool, 1937). In 1798, *Hannah Hewit; or The Female Crusoe, a new Musical Drama in Two Acts* was performed at the Theatre Royal in Drury Lane (*ibid.*, XI,444).

1796

[H. Whitmore]
Modern Gulliver's Travels. Lilliput: Being A New Journey To That Celebrated Island. Containing A Faithful Account Of The Manners, Character, Customs, Religion, Laws, Politics, Revenue, Taxes, Learning, General Progress In Arts And Sciences, Dress, Amusements, And Gallantry Of Those Famous Little People. From the Year 1702 (when they were first discovered and visited by Captain Lemuel Gulliver, the Father of the Compiler of this Work), to the present Æra 1796. By Lemuel Gulliver, Jun . . . London: Printed For T. Chapman . . . 1796.   tp DLC, tp BM

Halkett and Laing, IV,99, give the name of H. Whitmore. Mrs. Elizabeth Susanna Graham used the pseudonym of Lemuel Gulliver, Junior, for her *Voyage to Locuta* (London, 1818), and so *Modern Gulliver's Travels* has sometimes been attributed to the same author.

1796

Anonymous

Berkeley Hall: Or, The Pupil Of Experience. A Novel . . .
London: Printed For J. Tindal . . . 1796. 3 vols.   tp MH
———— Second Edition. London: Printed At The Minerva
Press, For Lane And Newman . . . 1803. 3 vols.   tp MB

The imaginary voyage is a long inner-story told by Sancho
beginning with chapter xxvi (I,186), entitled "The History of
Prince Pangoleen, Alias George Silverheels, Heir Apparent to
the Crown of Angola." See numerous references to the main
story in the index to Heilman. Lois Whitney, *Primitivism and
the Idea of Progress in English Popular Literature of the Eighteenth Century* (Baltimore, Johns Hopkins Press, 1934), pp. 271-
76, gives a partial résumé of the story but does not refer to
Pangoleen. The work is favorably noticed in the *Monthly Review,* n.s. XXII (1797), 92 f.

1796

Anonymous

Der Böhmische Robinson oder Traunholds des Jüngern wunderbare Begebenheiten, Reisen, widrige Zufälle, dann glück
liche Wiederkunft im Vaterlande. Ein Beytrag zur Menschen-
kenntnisz, auch Belehrung der unerfahrenen Jugend . . .
Prag und Leipzig 1796[-1800], bei Johann Buchler. . . . 2 vols.
                                                       Ullrich p. 178
———— Der Robinson aus Böhmen . . . Zwote verbesserte
Auflage. Prag 1802[-1800]. Bey Johann Kuchler [Buchler?].
. . . 2 vols.   Ullrich[d] p. 490
———— [In *Robinsonaden: eine Sammlung von Abenteuer-
geschichten* . . . ed. Maximilian Lehnert, Bd.5] Charlotten-
burg, Raben-Verlag [1920].   tp MiU

Discussed in H. F. Wagner, pp. 18-20.

1796

Anonymous

Letters From Mr. Fletcher Christian, Containing A Narrative Of The Transactions On Board His Majesty's Ship Bounty, Before and after the Mutiny, With His Subsequent Voyages And Travels In South America. London: Printed For The Proprietor, And Published By H. D. Symonds . . . 1796.

tp NN, tp BM

———— [Another edition] Voyages And Travels Of Fletcher Christian . . . [London] Printed for H. Lemoine. 1798.

tp BM

Obviously, as J. K. L[aughton] says in the *DNB*, this is "an impudent imposture."

1797

[Royall Tyler (1757-1826)]

The Algerine Captive; Or, The Life And Adventures Of Doctor Updike Underhill: Six Years A Prisoner Among The Algerines . . . Printed At Walpole, Newhampshire, By David Carlisle, Jun . . . 1797. 2 vols.   tp NN, tp BM (2 vols. in 1)

———— [Another edition] London: Printed for G. and J. Robinson . . . by S. Hamilton . . . 1802. 2 vols.   MH

———— [Serially in *The Lady's Magazine, or Entertaining Companion for the Fair Sex,* Vol. XXXV] London, Printed by G. & J. Robinson, 1804.   MNF

———— [Another edition] Hartford: Printed by Peter B. Gleason and co. 1816.   DLC

The best discussion of the author and of this work may be found in Frederick Tupper, "Royall Tyler: Man of Law and Man of Letters," *Proceedings of the Vermont Historical Society for the Years 1926-1927-1928,* pp. [65]-101.

1798

[Carl August Engelhardt (1768-1834)]

Karl Bruckmann oder William Sterne Findling des Harzge-

birges und Bewohner einer einsamen Insel der Südsee. Frankfurt und Leipzig, 1798[-1801]. 5 vols.   Ullrich p. 179
——— [Another edition] Zittau und Leipzig, bei J. D. Schöps, 1801. 5 vols. [Vols. II-V: Frankfurt und Leipzig, 1799-1801]   tp CtY
——— [Another edition] Zittau und Leipzig, bei J. D. Schöps, 1811. 5 vols.   MiU

1798

Christian Olaus Ewald, *pseudonym*
Der Ost- und Westindienfahrer. Oder Geschichte Christian Olaus Ewald. Eine Robinsonade. Grätz, gedruckt und verlegt bey Joh. Andr. Kienreich. 1798.   tp MiU

1798

[Joseph Alois Gleich (1772-1841)]
Edwin und Blanka oder Abentheuer eines Schottländers in zweyerlei Welttheilen, eine Robinsonade aus der ersten Hälfte dieses Jahrhunderts . . . Zweyte Auflage Vom Verfaszer des schwarzen Ritters [Leipzig, Schmidt] 1798.   tp MiU

I have found no trace of a first edition, which was probably in the same decade.

1798

Anonymous
Découvertes Dans La Mer Du Sud. Nouvelles De M. De La Peyrouse, Jusqu'en 1794. Traces de son passage trouvées en diverses isles et terres de l'Océan pacifique; grande Isle peuplée d'émigrés français. A Paris, Chez Everat . . . [1798]. tp NNC
——— Ontdekkingen In De Zuidzee, En Berichten Aangaande De La Pérouse En Zijne Tochtgenoten, Opgemaakt Uit Sporen Van Zijne Reis. Op Onderscheidene Eilanden En Landen Der Stille Zee Gevonden; alsmede aangaande een Groot Eiland, Thans Door Fransche Vluchtelingen Bevolkt.

Uit Het Fransch Vertaald. Te Haarlem, Bij François Bohn. MDCCIC.   tp DLC

The opening sentence, p. [3], reads: "Ce qu'on va lire est l'extrait d'une lettre écrite par un Français . . . datée de l'Isle hospitalière, dans la mer du Sud, le 28 janvier 1795," and this letter is signed at the end, p. 397, "C. . . . ." The attributed date comes from information in the second official catalogue of the DLC: the work is listed among the "Livres nouveaux" in the *Journal typographique et bibliographique,* No. XVII (9 Fév. 1798), p. 131; Sabin gives 1795. This apocryphal voyage suggested by the disappearance of Jean François de Galaup, comte de Lapérouse (1741-88), is listed by Gabriel Marcel, "Bibliographie: ouvrages se rapportant à Lapérouse ou à son expédition . . . ," *Bulletin de la Société de géographie,* 7S., IX(1888), 329 f., and by Jean d'Estampes, "Catalogue descriptif et méthodique . . . ," *ibid.,* p. 371. For a full account of Lapérouse see P[eter] Dillon, *Narrative and Successful Result of a Voyage in the South Seas . . . to Ascertain the Actual Fate of La Pérouse's Expedition . . .* (London, 1829), I, [xi]-lxix.

1798

Anonymous
Human Vicissitudes; Or, Travels Into Unexplored Regions . . . London: Printed For G. G. and J. Robinson . . . 1798. 2 vols.   tp MH

1799

Louis François Jauffret (1770-1850?)
Les Voyages de Rolando et de ses compagnons de fortune autour du monde. Par L. Fr. Jauffret. Paris, Adr. Leclerc 1799[-?]. 6 vols.   Ullrich p. 239
——— Reisen und Abenteuer Rolando's und seiner Gefährten. Ein Robinson für Kinder zur Erlernung geographischer und naturhistorischer Vorkenntnisse. Nach dem Französischen des Jauffret. Weimar, gedruckt und verlegt bey den Gebrüdern Gädicke. 1800.   tp CtY (Vol. I only)

———— [Another edition] Mulhouse (en Alsace), Bisler, 1800.
Reboul p. 108

———— [Another French edition] Publ. p. Lang, Stuttgart 1802[-4]. 6 vols.   Ullrich p. 239

———— [Another edition, with notes by Meynier] Cobourg, 1803[-4]. 3 vols.   Ullrich p. 239

———— The Travels Of Rolando; Containing, In A Supposed Tour Round The World, Authentic Descriptions Of The Geography, Natural History, Manners, And Antiquities Of Various Countries. Translated [by Lucy Aikin] From The French Of L. F. Jauffret. London: Printed For Richard Phillips . . . By J. Taylor . . . And Sold By Tabart And Co. . . . 1804. 4 vols.   tp BM

———— [Another German edition] Wien, bey B. Ph. Bauer. 1804. 6 vols. in 3.   tp NN

———— Third Edition. London: Printed For Richard Phillips; Sold By John Souter . . . 1813. 4 vols.   tp MH

———— Reizen van Rolando en zijne medgezellen van fortuin rondom de wereld . . . door L. F. Jauffret. Uit het fransch vertaald. Amsterdam, J. Tiel, 1813.   BN

———— A New Edition. London: Printed For R. Phillips, By A. Applegath . . . Sold By John Souter . . . 1822. 2 vols.
tp Bod

———— A New edition. London: Printed For Sir R. Phillips And Co. . . . 1823. 2 vols.   tp BM

———— [Another edition] London: George Routledge & Co. . . . 1853.   tp MH

———— [Spanish translation.]   Reboul p. 108

"C'est un cours amusant et instructif d'histoire naturelle, de géographie, de littérature et de morale, sous la forme d'un conte" writes Robert M. Reboul, *Louis-François Jauffret, sa vie et ses œuvres* (Paris [etc.], 1869), p. 26.

1799

Zacharias Taurinius, *pseudonym*
Beschreibung einiger See- und Landreisen nach Asien, Afrika

und Amerika, vorzüglich von Holland und England nach
Batavia, Madras, Bengalen, Japan und China, ingleichen vom
Vorgebirge der guten Hoffnung durch die Kafferey und die
Wüste Sahara nach Aegypten von einem gebohrnen Aegyptier
Zacharias Taurinius. Mit einer Vorrede von Johann Jacob
Ebert, Professor zu Wittenberg. Leipzig, bey Friedrich Gott-
hold Jacobäer. 1799[-1801]. 3 vols.
                                    tp NN (Vol. III wanting), tp BM
———— Lebensgeschichte und Beschreibung der Reisen durch
Asien, Afrika und Amerika des Zacharias Taurinius, eines
gebornen Aegyptiers. Nebst einer Vertheidigung gegen die
wider ihn in verschiedenen gelehrten Zeitungen gemachten
Ausfälle, vorzüglich in Rücksicht der unter dem Nahmen
Damberger von ihm herausgegebenen Landreise durch Afrika
. . . Wien, bey Anton Doll. 1804. 2 vols.   tp NNH

Joseph Schrödter, *pseudonym*
See- und Landreise nach Ostindien und Aegypten, auf die
Berge Sinai und Horeb, nach Gaza, Rama, Damascus, Sydon,
Tyrus, Jerusalem, Bethlehem, nach dem todten Meere u.s.w.
in den Jahren 1795-1799. Von Joseph Schrödter. Leipzig, bey
Pet. Phil. Wolf und Compagnie 1800.   tp BM

Christian Friedrich Damberger, *pseudonym*
Christian Friedrich Dambergers Landreise in das Innere von
Afrika, vom Vorgebirge der guten Hoffnung durch die Kaf-
farey, die Königreiche Mataman, Angola, Massi, Monoemugi,
Muschako u.a.w.; ferner durch die wüste Sahara und die
nördliche Barbarey bis nach Marocco. In den Jahren 1781 bis
1797 . . . Leipzig, bey Martini, 1801. 2 vols.
                                    Neue ADB infra p. 450
———— Voyage Dans L'Intérieur De L'Afrique Depuis Le
Cap De Bonne-Espérance, A Travers La Cafrérie, Les Ro-
yaumes De Mataman, D'Angola, De Massi, De Monoémugi,
De Muschako etc. En Continuant Par Le Désert De Sahara
Et La Partie Septentrionale De La Barbarie, Jusqu'a Maroc.

Commencé en 1781 et achevé en 1797 Par Chr. Fr. Damberger Traduit De L'Allemand Par L. H. Delamarre . . . A Paris chez Amand König . . . A Strasbourg même maison de commerce . . . An IX [1801]. 2 vols.   tp NN
——— Travels In The Interior Of Africa, From The Cape Of Good Hope To Morocco, From The Years 1781 To 1797; Through Caffraria, The Kingdoms Of Mataman, Angola, Massi, Monoemugi, Muschako, &c. Likewise Across The Great Desert Of Sahara, And The Northern Parts Of Barbary. Translated [by William Tooke] From The German of Christian Frederick Damberger . . . London: Printed For T. N. Longman And O. Rees . . . J. Cuthell . . . And C. Geisweiler . . . By G. Woodfall . . . 1801. 2 vols. in 1.   tp NNC
——— [Another edition] London: Printed For R. Phillips . . . And Sold By T. Hurst, And J. Wallis . . . By Elphinstone Balfour, Edinburgh; J. Archer Dublin . . . 1801.   tp BM
——— [Another edition] London: Printed for J. Lee . . . By J. Rhynd . . . 1801.   tp BM
——— [Another edition] London: Printed For The Translator, And Sold By C. Chapple . . . Wynne And Scholey, And Wallis . . . Lackington, Allen, And Co. . . . And Mundell And Son, Edinburgh. 1801.   tp MB
——— [Another edition] Dublin: Printed For P. Wogan . . . 1801. 2 vols.   tp Bod
——— [Another edition] New-York, W. Durell, 1801. 2 vols. in 1.   tp DLC
——— [Another edition] Charlestown: Printed By Samuel Etheridge, For E. And S. Larkin . . . Boston. 1801.   tp NN

These three forgeries appearing in successive years must be grouped together because the three pseudonyms are unquestionably those of one man who with the help of one Magister Junge succeeded for a short time in deceiving geographers and publishers in three countries. The fabrication is explained in part in *Of the Shoe-Maker, Schrödter, the Printer, Taurinius, and the Cabinet-Maker, Damberger, Three Travellers Who Never Travelled at All, but Fabricated Their Accounts in One Manufactory*

27

(London, 1801) and in "Erdbeschreibung, Reisebeschreibung und Statistik," *Neue ADB,* LVIII(1801), 442-59. The English editions represent at least three different translations.

1800

Anonymous
The Sailor Boy. A Novel . . . London: Printed At The Minerva-Press, For William Lane . . . 1800. 2 vols. in 1. tp BM

1800

Anonymous
Speelhofen der Jüngere oder Begebenheiten des neuen Robinsons auf dem stillen Meere Original Ausgabe. [Linz, Eurich] 1800.   tp CtY
———— Speelhofen mladšij ili priključenija novago Robinsona na tihom morju, podlinoe izdanie prevedens s Německago na Serbskij j ě zyk. V Budině gradě Pismeny kral. Vsenčil Vengerskago 1809.   Ullrich[d] p. 490

Bibliography

The following bibliography does not contain all the books and articles referred to in this book. Instead it confines itself to a list of works on the imaginary voyage in general or on two or more imaginary voyages; references to works discussing only one imaginary voyage are cited in the check list or at appropriate places in the notes. This explains, for example, why some works on *Gulliver* appear below and others appear only under *Gulliver* in the check list. All authors cited, however, are listed in the index. One book—Hirn—which clearly belongs in the bibliography for the sake of completeness is in parentheses because I have used it only superficially. Two or more works by the same author are arranged chronologically. A surname in parentheses following a title indicates the symbol that I have used for reference in the check list. I have given the names of publishers only for books published since 1900.

Adams, H[enry] C. Travellers' Tales: a Book of Marvels. New York, Boni & Liveright, 1927.

Andrews, Charles M., ed. Ideal Empires and Republics. Washington & London, Dunne, [c.1901] (Universal Classics Library).

Anonymous. "Voltaire's Romances and Their Moral," Westminster Review, LXXV (1861), 192-202; *reprinted in* Living Age, LXIX (1861), 387-97.

———— "Travellers' Tales," All the Year Round, ed. Charles Dickens, VI (1862), 356-60.

———— "Sea-Thoughts of Two Races," (London) Times Literary Supplement, August 7, 1930, pp. [633]-634.

———— "Scientific Romances," (London) Times Literary Supplement, August 3, 1933, pp. [517]-518.

———— [Review of W. H. Bonner, *Captain William Dampier*], (London) Times Literary Supplement, August 9, 1934, p. 551.

Atkinson, Geoffroy. The Extraordinary Voyage in French Literature before 1700. New York, Columbia University Press, 1920 (Columbia University Studies in Romance Philology and Literature). (Atkinson[a])

———— The Extraordinary Voyage in French Literature from 1700 to 1720. Paris, Champion, 1922. (Atkinson[b])

———— Les Relations de voyages du XVIIe siècle et l'évolution des idées contribution à l'étude de la formation de l'esprit du XVIIIe siècle. Paris, Champion, [1924].

———— Les Nouveaux Horizons de la Renaissance française. Paris, Droz, 1935.

Babcock, William H. Legendary Islands of the Atlantic: a Study in Medieval Geography. New York, 1922 (American Geographical Society Research Series, 8).

Baker, Ernest A. The History of the English Novel. London, Witherby, 1924-[1938]. 9 vols.

Baker, J[ohn] N. L. "The Geography of Daniel Defoe," Scottish Geographical Magazine, XLVII (1931), [257]-269.

Baldensperger, F[ernand]. [Review of Goulding, *Swift en France*], Revue de littérature comparée, IV (1924), 702-4.

Barbeau, Marius. "Cartier Inspired Rabelais," Canadian Geographical Journal, IX (1934), 113-25.

Beazley, C. Raymond. The Dawn of Modern Geography: a History of Exploration and Geographical Science. . . . London, Murray, 1897-1906. 3 vols.

Becker, Franz K. Die Romane Johann Gottfried Schnabels. Bonn, Foppen, 1911.

Begley, Walter. "Bibliography of Romance from the Renaissance to the End of the Seventeenth Century," *in* Nova Solyma, the Ideal City; or Jerusalem Regained: an Anonymous Romance [by Samuel Gott]. . . . London, Murray, 1902, II, 355-400.

Béquet, Étienne, ed. Histoire véritable de Lucien. Paris, 1828 (Collection des romans grecs, t. XII).

Bernbaum, Ernest, ed. Gulliver's Travels. New York, Harcourt, Brace, [1920].

Bobertag, F[elix]. "Ueber einige den Robinsonaden verwandte Erscheinungen in der deutschen Literatur des 17. Jahrhunderts," Abhandlungen der schlesischen Gesellschaft für vaterlandische Cultur. Philosophisch-historische Abtheilung, 1872/73, pp. [11]-26.

Bonner, Willard H. Captain William Dampier, Buccaneer-Author. Stanford University, Stanford University Press, [c.1934].

Böök, Fredrik. Romanens och Prosaberättelsens Historia i Sverige intill 1809. Stockholm, Bonnier, 1907.

Borkowsky, Th. "Quellen zu Swift's 'Gulliver,'" Anglia. Zeitschrift für englische Philologie, XV (1893), [345]-389.

[Bougeant, Guillaume H.]. Voyage merveilleux du Prince Fan-Férédin dans la romancie; contenant plusieurs observations historiques: géographiques, physiques, critiques & morales. Paris, 1735.

Brandl, Leopold. "Vordefoesche Robinsonaden in der Weltliteratur," Germanisch-romanische Monatsschrift, V (1913), 233-61.

———— "Krinke Kesmes und Defoes *Robinson*," Neophilologus, XI (1926), 28-40.

Brasch, Moritz. Socialistische Phantasiestaaten: ein historisch-politischer Essay. Leipzig, 1885.

Brecht, Walther. [Review of Mildebrath, *Die deutschen Aventuriers*], Anzeiger für deutsches Altertum und deutsche Litteratur, XXXIV (1910), 175-77.

Brink, Jan ten. "De Romans van Jules Verne," *in his* Verspreide Letterkundige Opstellen van het jaar 1887. Den Haag, 1888, pp. [31]-63.

———— Romans in Proza. Leiden, [1899].   (ten Brinkᵃ)

Brown, Huntington, ed. The Discovery of a New World (Mundus alter et idem) . . . by Joseph Hall, ca. 1605. . . . Cambridge, Harvard University Press, 1937.

Brüggemann, Fritz. Utopie und Robinsonade. Untersuchungen zu Schnabels Insel Felsenburg (1731-1743). Weimar, Duncker, 1914 (Forschungen zur neueren Literaturgeschichte, XLVI
(Brüggemann)

———— ed. Vorboten der bürgerlichen Kultur Johann Gottfried Schnabel und Albrecht von Haller. Leipzig, Reclam, 1931 (Deutsche Literatur, Reihe Aufklärung [14], Bd. IV).

Brun, Pierre. Savinien de Cyrano Bergerac, gentilhomme parisien: l'histoire et la légende de Lebret à M. Rostand. Paris, Daragon, 1909 (Bibliothèque du vieux Paris).

Burger, D. "Over Boekillustratie van fantastische Reisverhalen," *in* Handelingen van het Tweede Wetenschappelijk Vlaamsch Congres voor Boeken Bibliotheekwezen. Gent, Vyncke, 1933, pp. 139-47.

Case, R[obert] H., ed. The Post-Captain or the Wooden Walls Well Manned: Comprehending a View of Naval Society and Manners, by John Davis [1805]. London, Scholartis Press, 1928.

Chassang, A[lexis]. Histoire du roman et de ses rapports avec l'histoire dans l'antiquité grecque et latine. 2 éd., Paris, 1862.

Chauvin, Victor. "Les Vrais Robinsons," Revue des cours littéraires . . . , II (1864-65), 294-96.

——— *See also* Denis, Ferdinand.

Child, Harold. "Some English Utopias," Essays by Divers Hands, Being the Transactions of the Royal Society of Literature of the United Kingdom. n.s.XII (1933), [31]-60.

Chinard, Gilbert. L'Exotisme américain dans la littérature française au XVIe siècle d'après Rabelais, Ronsard, Montaigne, etc. Paris, Hachette, 1911. (Chinard[a])

——— L'Amérique et le rêve exotique dans la littérature française au XVIIe et au XVIIIe siècle. Paris, Hachette, 1913. (Chinard[b])

——— [Review of Atkinson[a] and Atkinson[b]], Modern Language Notes, XXXVII (1922), 491-98.

——— ed. Diderot supplément au voyage de Bougainville. Paris [etc.], Droz, 1935.

Conant, Martha P. The Oriental Tale in England in the Eighteenth Century. New York, Columbia University Press, 1908 (Columbia University Studies in English and Comparative Literature).

Dallas, Dorothy F. Le Roman français de 1660 à 1680. Paris, Gamber, 1932.

Dege, Charlotte. Utopie und Satire in Swifts Gulliver's Travels. Frankfurt, Trowitzsch, 1934.

Deisch, Noel. "The Navigation of Space in Early Speculation and in Modern Research," Popular Astronomy, XXXVIII (1930), 73-88.

De la Mare, Walter. Desert Islands and Robinson Crusoe. New York, Farrar & Rinehart, 1930.

Denis, Ferdinand, and Victor Chauvin. Les Vrais Robinsons: naufrages, solitude, voyages. Paris, 1863.

Dodds, Muriel. Les Récits de voyages sources de l'esprit des lois de Montesquieu. Paris, Champion, 1929.

Dottin, Paul. Daniel De Foe et ses romans. Paris, Les Presses universitaires de France, 1924.

Dunlop, John C. History of Prose Fiction, ed. Henry Wilson. London, 1896.

Eddy, William A. "A Source for *Gulliver's Travels*," Modern Language Notes, XXXVI (1921), 419-22.

———— "A Source for Gulliver's First Voyage," Modern Language Notes, XXXVII (1922), 353-55.

———— "Rabelais,—a Source for *Gulliver's Travels*," Modern Language Notes, XXXVII (1922), 416-18.

———— "Cyrano de Bergerac and *Gulliver's Travels*," Modern Language Notes, XXXVIII (1923), 344-45.

———— Gulliver's Travels: a Critical Study. Princeton, Princeton University Press, 1923. (Eddy)

Engel, Claire E. Figures & aventures du XVIIIe siècle: voyages et découvertes de l'Abbé Prevost. Paris, Editions "Je Sers," [1939] (Études de littérature, d'art et d'histoire, 5).

Esdaile, Arundell. A List of English Tales and Prose Romances Printed before 1740. London, Bibliographical Society, 1912.

Faguet, Émile. "Les Contes et romans de Voltaire," Revue politique et littéraire (Revue bleue), 4S.II (1894), 620-25.

Firestone, Clark B. The Coasts of Illusion: a Study of Travel Tales. New York and London, Harper, 1924.

Flammarion, Camille. Les Mondes imaginaires et les mondes réels: voyage pittoresque dans le ciel et revue critique des théories humaines scientifiques et romanesques, anciennes et modernes sur les habitants des astres. 17e éd., Paris, 1880.

Fournel, Victor. La Littérature indépendante et les écrivains oubliés: essais de critique et d'érudition sur le XVIIe siècle. Paris, 1862.

Frantz, R[ay] W. The English Traveller and the Movement of Ideas, 1660-1732. Lincoln, 1934 (Nebraska University Studies XXXII-XXXIII).

Fürst, Rudolf. Die Vorläufer der modernen Novelle im achtzehnten Jahrhundert: ein Beitrag zur vergleichenden Litteraturgeschichte. Halle, 1897.

[Garnier, Charles G. T., ed.]. Voyages imaginaires, songes, visions, et romans cabalistiques. Amsterdam et Paris, 1787-89. 36 vols.

Gilbert, Eugène. Le Roman en France pendant le XIXe siècle. Paris, 1896.

Giles, Edward L. "Shipwrecks and Desert Islands," Notes & Queries, CLXXVII (1939), 218-20.

Girsberger, Hans. Der utopische Sozialismus des 18. Jahrhunderts in Frankreich und seine philosophischen und materiellen Grundlagen. Zürich, Rascher, 1924 (Zürcher volkswirtschaftliche Forschungen, 1).

Goebel, Julius. "The Dutch Source of Robinson Crusoe," Journal of English and Germanic Philology, XXII (1923), 302-13.

Goodrick, A.T.S. "Robinson Crusoe, Imposter," Blackwood's Magazine, CLXXXIII(1908), 672-85.

Goulding, Sybil. Swift en France: essai sur la fortune et l'influence de Swift en France au XVIIIe siècle, suivi d'un aperçu sur la fortune de Swift en France au cours du XIXe siècle. Paris, Champion, 1924 (Bibliothèque de la revue de littérature comparée, XV).

Gourcuff, Olivier de. "Deux Voyages imaginaires écrits par des Bretons," Revue de Bretagne de Vendée & d'Anjou, VI(1891), [215]-223, [306]-315.

Gudde, Erwin G. "Grimmelshausen's Simplicius Simplicissimus and Defoe's Robinson Crusoe," Philological Quarterly, IV (1925), 110-20.

———— [Review of Ullrichᵃ], Journal of English and Germanic Philology, XXV (1926), 132-34.

Günther, Max. Entstehungsgeschichte von Defoe's Robinson Crusoe. Greifswald, Abel, 1909.

[Haken, Johann C. L.]. Bibliothek der Robinsone: in zweckmäszigen Auszügen vom Verfasser der grauen Mappe. Berlin, 1805-8. 5 vols.

Haviland, Thomas P. The *Roman de Longue Haleine* on English Soil: a Study of the Manner, Form and Content of the French Heroic Romance in Translation, and of Those English Productions Which Fall within the Class, with Some Account of the Popularity of Both and of Their Influence on the Modern English Novel in Its Earliest Years. Philadelphia, 1931.

Hazeltine, Mayo W. "Jules Verne's Didactic Fiction," *in his* Chats about Books Poets and Novelists. New York, 1883, I, 337-46.

Heidler, Joseph B. The History, from 1700 to 1800, of English Criticism of Prose Fiction. Urbana, University of Illinois, 1928 (University of Illinois Studies in Language and Literature, XIII, No. 2).

Held, Felix E. Johann Valentin Andreae's Christianopolis, an Ideal State of the Seventeenth Century. [Urbana], University of Illinois, 1914.

Hettner, Hermann. Literaturgeschichte des achtzehnten Jahrhunderts. 4th and 5th ed. Braunschweig, 1893-94. 3 vols.

Hippe, M[ax]. [Review of Ullrich], Englische Studien, XXVI (1899), 405-11.

(Hirn, Yrjö. Ön I Världshavet. Stockholm, Schildt, [1928].)

Hodgson, J. E. The History of Aeronautics in Great Britain from the Earliest Times to the Latter Half of the Nineteenth Century. London, Oxford University Press, 1924.

Hönncher, E[rwin]. Fahrten nach Mond und Sonne. Studien insbesondere zur französischen Litteraturgeschichte des XVII. Jahrhunderts. Oppeln und Leipzig, 1887.

———— "Quellen zu Dean Jonathan Swifts 'Gulliver's Travels,'" Anglia. Zeitschrift für englische Philologie, X (1888), [397]-427.

Hubbard, Lucius L. Notes on the Adventures and Surprizing Deliverances of James Dubourdieu and His Wife: a Source for *Gulliver's Travels;* Also the Adventures of Alexander Vendchurch. Ann Arbor [for private distribution], 1927.

Hübener, Gustav. "Die Entstehung von *Gulliver's Travels* und die 'Curiosity'-Kultur," Neophilologus, VII (1922), 35-57.

Hugo, C. Die Vorläufer des neueren Sozialismus, *in* Die Geschichte des Sozialismus in Einzeldarstellungen, ed. E. Bernstein and K. Kautsky, Bd.I. Stuttgart, 1895.

Hutchins, Henry C. [Review of Secord, *Narrative Method*], Journal of English and Germanic Philology, XXVIII (1929), 443-52.

Kästner, Abraham G. "Ob Robinson Crusoe auch Robinson I. ist?" *in his* Poetische und prosaische schönwissenschaftliche Werke. Berlin, 1841, II, 135-38.

Keltie, J. Scott. "Fictitious Travel and Phantom Lands," Harper's Monthly Magazine, CXV (1907), [186]-194.

Kippenberg, August. Robinson in Deutschland bis zur Insel Felsenburg (1731-43). Hannover, 1892.

Kirchenheim, A[rthur] von. L'Éternelle Utopie: étude du socialisme à travers les ages, ed. A. Chazaud des Granges. Paris, 1897.

Kleemann, Selmar. "Zur Geschichte der Robinsonaden," Euphorion Zeitschrift für Literaturgeschichte, I (1894), 603-4.

Kleinwächter, Friedrich. Die Staatsromane: ein Beitrag zur Lehre vom Communismus und Socialismus. Wien, 1891.

Klinckowstroem, Carl von. "Luftfahrten in der Literatur," Zeitschrift für Bücherfreunde, N.F. III, ii (1911-12), [250]-264.

Koerting, Heinr[ich]. Geschichte des französischen Romans im XVII. Jahrhundert. 2 Ausg., Oppeln und Leipzig, 1891. 2 vols.

Kruuse, Jens. "Holberg og Swift," *in* Fem Danske Studier tilegnet Vilh. Andersen. . . . Copenhagen, Branner, 1934 (Studier fra Sprog- og Oldtidsforskning, Nr.167).

Lachèvre, Frédéric. . . . Les successeurs de Cyrano de Bergerac. Paris, Champion, 1922 (Le Libertinage au XVIIe siècle, X).

(Lachèvre)
———— ed. . . . Le Royaume d'Antangil (inconnu jusqu'à

présent) réimprimé sur l'unique édition de Saumur, 1616, avec des éclaircissements. Paris, La Connaissance, 1933 (Collection "Les Textes," 12).

Lanson, Gustave. "Origines et premières manifestations de l'esprit philosophique," Revue des cours et conférences, XVI (1907-8) and XVII (1908-9). [A series of 17 articles.]

────── "Formation et développement de l'esprit philosophique," Revue des cours et conférences, XVII (1908-9) and XVIII (1909-10). [A series of 18 articles.]

Lawton, Harold W. "Notes sur Jean Baudoin et sur ses traductions de l'Anglais," Revue de littérature comparée, VI (1926), [673]-681.

────── "Bishop Godwin's *Man in the Moone*," Review of English Studies, VII (1931), 23-55.

LeBreton, André. Le Roman au dix-huitième siècle. Paris, [1898] (Nouvelle Bibliothèque littéraire).

Lefranc, Abel. Les Navigations de Pantagruel: étude sur la géographie rabelaisienne. Paris, Leclerc, 1904.

Letts, Malcolm. "Of Lying Travellers," Contemporary Review, CXVIII (1920), [95]-100.

Lichtenberger, André. Le Socialisme au XVIIIe siècle: étude sur les idées socialistes dans les écrivains français du XVIIIe siècle avant la Révolution. Paris, 1895.   (Lichtenberger[a])

────── Le Socialisme utopique: études sur quelques précurseurs inconnus du socialisme. Paris, 1898.   (Lichtenberger[b])

Liddell, Scotland. "Travellers' Tales," English Review, XLII (1926), 622-31.

McColley, Grant, ed. The Man in the Moone and Nuncius Inanimatus for the First Time Edited, with Introduction and Notes, from Unique Copies of the First Editions of London, 1629, and London, 1638. Northampton (Smith College Studies in Modern Languages, XIX, No. 1, 1937).

Magendie, Maurice. Le Roman français au XVIIe siècle de l'*Astrée* au *Grand Cyrus*. Paris, Droz, 1932.

Mann, William E. Robinson Crusoé en France: étude sur l'influence de cette œuvre dans la littérature française. Paris, Université de Paris, 1916.

Margry, Pierre. Les Navigations françaises et la révolution maritime du XIVe au XVIe siècle. . . . Paris, 1867.

Martino, Pierre. L'Orient dans la littérature française au XVIIe et au XVIIIe siècle. Paris, Hachette, 1906.

Matthes, Heinrich. "Die Verschleierung der Verfasserschaft bei englischen Dichtungen des 18. Jahrhunderts," Beiträge zur Erforschung der Sprache und Kultur Englands und Nordamerikas, IV (1928), [33]-112.

Messac, Régis. "Voyages modernes au centre de la terre," Revue de littérature comparée, IX (1929), [74]-104.

Mildebrath, Berthold [W.]. Die deutschen "Aventuriers" des achtzehnten Jahrhunderts. Gräfenhainichen, Schulze, 1907.

Miller, Francis T. The World in the Air: the Story of Flying in Pictures. New York and London, Putnam, 1930. 2 vols.

Minor, Jacob. "Die Luftfahrten in der deutschen Literatur. Ein bibliographischer Versuch," Zeitschrift für Bücherfreunde, N.F. I (1909), i, [64]-73.

Mohler, Nora M. *See* Nicolson, Marjorie.

Moncrif, François A. Paradis de. "Réflexions sur quelques ouvrages faussement appelés ouvrages d'imagination," *in his* Œuvres, nouv. éd., Paris, 1768, II, 93-105.

Morgan, Charlotte E. The Rise of the Novel of Manners: a Study of English Prose Fiction between 1600 and 1740. New York, Columbia University Press, 1911 (Columbia University Studies in English and Comparative Literature).

Morize, André, ed. Candide ou l'optimisme: édition critique avec une introduction et un commentaire. Paris, Hachette, 1913 (Société des textes français modernes).

Mornet, Daniel. [Review of Chinard, *L'Amérique*], Revue d'histoire littéraire de la France, XXI (1914), 800-802.

———— "Les Imitations du 'Candide' de Voltaire au XVIIIe siècle," *in* Mélanges offerts par ses amis et ses élèves à M. Gustave Lanson. Paris, Hachette, 1922, pp. [298]-303.

———— "Roman français de 1741 à 1760," *in* J.-J. Rousseau: La Nouvelle Héloïse: nouvelle édition publiée d'après les manuscrits et les éditions originales avec des variantes, une intro-

duction, des notices et des notes. Paris, Hachette, 1925 (Collection des grandes écrivains de la France, 2e Série). Vol. I.
(Mornet)

Müller-Fraureuth, Carl. Die deutschen Lügendichtungen bis auf Münchhausen. Halle, 1881.

Neubert, Fritz. Die französischen Versprosa-Reisebrieferzählungen und der kleine Reiseroman des 17. und 18. Jahrhunderts. Ein Beitrag zur Geschichte der französischen Rokoko-Literatur. Jena und Leipzig, Gronau, 1923 (Zeitschrift für französische Sprache und Litteratur. Supplementheft XI).

Newton, Arthur P., ed. Travel and Travellers of the Middle Ages. London, Paul, Trench, Trubner; New York, Knopf, 1926.

Nicolson, Marjorie. A World in the Moon: a Study of the Changing Attitude toward the Moon in the Seventeenth and Eighteenth Centuries. Northampton (Smith College Studies in Modern Languages, XVII, 1936, No. 2).

——— "Cosmic Voyages," ELH: A Journal of English Literary History, VII (1940), 83-107.

——— and Nora M. Mohler. "Swift's 'Flying Island' in the *Voyage to Laputa*," Annals of Science, II (1937), 405-30.

Oliver, [S.] Pasfield. "The Land of Parrots," Scottish Geographical Magazine, XVI (1900), [1]-17, 68-82, 583-96.

Paludan, J[ulius]. Om Holbergs Niels Klim, med saerligt Hensyn til tidligere Satirir i Form af opdigtede og vidunderlige Reiser. Et Bidrag til Kundskab om fremmed Indvirkning paa det attende Aarhundredes danske Literatur. København, 1878.

Parks, George B. "More's Utopia and Geography," Journal of English and Germanic Philology, XXXVII (1938), 224-36.

Parsons, Coleman O. "Lunar Craters in Science and Fiction," Notes & Queries, CLXIV (1933), 346-48.

Pastor, Antonio. The Idea of Robinson Crusoe. Watford, Góngora Press, 1930. Vol. I.

Peyre, Henri. [Review of Von der Mühll], Romanic Review, XXX (1939), 302-4.

Planhol, René de. Les Utopistes de l'amour. Paris, Garnier, 1921.

414   *BIBLIOGRAPHY*

Polak, Léon. "Vordefoesche Robinsonaden in den Neiderlanden," Germanisch-romanische Monatsschrift, VI (1914), 304-7.

Poll, Max. The Sources of Gulliver's Travels. Cincinnati, University of Cincinnati Bulletin No. 24, [1909] (Publications of the University of Cincinnati Series II, Vol. III).

Pons, Émile. [Review of Eddy, *Gulliver's Travels*], Revue de littérature comparée, IV (1924), [149]-154.

—— "Le 'Voyage' genre littéraire au XVIIIe siècle," Bulletin de la faculté des lettres de Strasbourg, IV (1925-26), 97-101, 144-49, 201-7.   (Pons)

—— ed. Gulliver's Travels (Extraits). Paris, Hachette, [1927].

—— "Les Langues imaginaires dans le voyage utopique un précurseur: Thomas Morus," Revue de littérature comparée, X (1930), [589]-607.

—— "Les Langues imaginaires dans le voyage utopique les 'Jargons' de Panurge dans Rabelais," Revue de littérature comparée, XI (1931), [185]-218.

—— "Les Langues imaginaires dans le voyage utopique les grammairiens: Vairasse et Foigny," Revue de littérature comparée, XII (1932), [500]-532.

Presley, James T. "Bibliography of Utopias and Imaginary Travels and Histories," Notes & Queries, 4S. XI (1873), 519-21; XII, 2-3, 22-23, (41), (62), 91, (153); 5S. I (1874), (78-79), (237); II, 252; VI (1876), 38, (118); VII (1877), 458; VIII, (13-14); 6S. IX (1884), (84).

Prica, Zora. Daniel Defoe's Robinson Crusoe und Robert Paltock's Peter Wilkins. Budapest, Serbische Buchdruckerei, 1909.

Prinsen, J[acob]. De Roman in de 18e Eeuw in West-Europa. Groningen, Wolters, 1925.

Prÿs, Joseph. Der Staatsroman des 16. und 17. Jahrhunderts und sein Erziehungsideal. Würzburg, Staudenraus, 1913.

Quintana, Ricardo. The Mind and Art of Jonathan Swift. London and New York, Oxford University Press, 1936.

[Reichard, Heinrich A. O.]. Bibliothek der Romane. Zweyter Band. Berlin, 1778.

Richter, Karl. Die Entwicklung des Seeromans in England im 19. Jahrhundert. Leipzig, 1906.

Robinson, Charles N. The British Tar in Fact and Fiction: the Poetry, Pathos, and Humour of the Sailor's Life. New York and London, Harper, 1909.

Rogers, Stanley R. H. Crusoes and Castaways. London [etc.], Harrap, [1932].

Rohde, Erwin. Der griechische Roman und seine Vorläufer. Neue Auf., Leipzig, Breitkopf und Härtel, 1914.

Roorda, Gerridina. Realism in Daniel De Foe's Narratives of Adventure. Wageningen, Veenman, 1929.

Ross, Ernest C. The Development of the English Sea Novel from Defoe to Conrad. Ann Arbor [192-].

Ross, Harry. Utopias Old and New. London, Nicholson and Watson, 1938 (University Extension Library).

Rötteken, Hubert. "Weltflucht und Idylle in Deutschland von 1720 bis zur Insel Felsenburg. Ein Beitrag zur Geschichte des deutschen Gefühlslebens. I. Die Robinsonaden," Zeitschrift für vergleichende Litteraturgeschichte, N. F. IX (1896), 1-32.

Rovillain, Eugène E. "Sur le *Zadig* de Voltaire; quelques influences probables," Publications of the Modern Language Association, XLIII (1928), 447-55.

———— "Sur le 'Zadig' de Voltaire; quelques autres influences," Publications of the Modern Language Association, XLVI (1931), 533-39.

Rümann, Arthur. "Robinson und Robinsonaden in der Buchillustration des 18. und 19. Jahrhunderts," Philobiblon eine Zeitschrift für Bücherfreunde . . . , IX (1936), 9-21.

Russell, Frances T. Touring Utopia, the Realm of Constructive Humanism. New York, Lincoln MacVeagh, 1932.

Salverte, François de. Le Roman dans la Grèce ancienne. Paris, 1894.

Schmitt, Eugen H. Der Idealstaat. Berlin, Räde, 1904 (Kulturprobleme der Gegenwart, VIII).

Schneider, Arno. Die Entwickelung des Seeromans in England im 17. und 18. Jahrhundert. Leipzig, 1901.

Schneider, Paul, ed. Erlebte Robinsonaden: abenteuerliche Fahrten und Schicksale aus den Zeiten der Entdeckungsreisen, nach Originalberichten. Berlin, Ullstein, [c.1925].

Schomann, Emilie. Französische Utopisten des 18. Jahrhunderts und ihr Frauenideal. Berlin, [Felber], 1911.

Schotel, G[illes] D. J. Vaderlandsche Volksboeken en Volkssprookjes van de Vroegste Tijden tot het Einde der 18e Eeuw. Tweede Deel. Haarlem, 1874.

Schröder, Karl [B. F.]. J. G. Schnabels "Insel Felsenburg." Marburg, Schaaf, 1912.

Seccombe, Thomas, ed. The Surprising Adventures of Baron Munchausen. . . . New York, 1895.

Secord, Arthur W. Studies in the Narrative Method of Defoe. Urbana, 1924 (University of Illinois Studies in Language and Literature, IX).

———— [Review of Eddy, Gulliver's Travels], Journal of English and Germanic Philology, XXIII (1924), 460-62.

Smith, Alpheus W. Collections and Notes of Prose Fiction in England, 1660-1714. [Unpublished Harvard dissertation, 1930.]

Stangerup, Hakon. Romanen i Danmark i det Attende Aarhundrede: en komparativ Undersøgelse. København, Levin & Munksgaard, 1936.

Starr, Nathan C. The Sea in the English Novel from Defoe to Melville. [Unpublished Harvard dissertation, 1928.]

Staverman, Werner H. Robinson Crusoe in Nederland. Een Bijdrage tot de Geschiedenis van den Roman in de XVIIIe Eeuw. Groningen, de Waal, 1907.   (Staverman)

———— "Een Nederlandse Bron van de Robinson Crusoe," Nieuwe Taalgids, XIX (1925), [16]-26.

———— [Review of Dottin, Defoe et ses romans], English Studies, VIII (1926), 189-93.

———— "Robinson Crusoe in Holland; on the Two Hundredth Anniversary of the Death of Daniel Defoe," English Studies, XIII (1931), [49]-58.

Strauch, Philipp. [Review of Kippenberg, Robinson in Deutschland], Anzeiger für deutsches Altertum und deutsche Litteratur, XXIII (1897), 79-84.

——— [Review of Ullrich], Anzeiger für deutsches Altertum und deutsche Litteratur, XXVII (1901), 245-48.

Streeter, Harold W. The Eighteenth Century English Novel in French Translation: a Bibliographical Study. New York, Institute of French Studies, [1936].

Stricker, W. "Ueber Robinsonaden und fingirte Reisen," Jahres-Bericht des frankfurter Vereins für Geographie und Statistik, XXXV (1870-71), [29]-38.

Thibaudet, Albert. ". . . Le Roman de l'aventure," Nouvelle Revue française, XIII (1919), 597-611.

Thierkopf, Paul. Swift's Gulliver und seine französischen Vorgänger. Magdeburg, 1899 (Dreiszigster Jahresbericht über die Guericke-Schule zu Magdeburg).

Thompson, D. W. "Japan and the *New Atlantis*," Studies in Philology, XXX (1933), 59-68.

Tieje, Arthur J. "The Expressed Aim of the Long Prose Fiction from 1579 to 1740," Journal of English and Germanic Philology, XI (1912), 402-32.

——— "A Peculiar Phase of the Theory of Realism in Pre-Richardsonian Fiction," Publications of the Modern Language Association, XXVIII (1913), 213-52.

——— "The Critical Heritage of Fiction in 1579," Englische Studien, XLVII (1913-14), [415]-448.

——— The Theory of Characterization in Prose Fiction Prior to 1740. Minneapolis, 1916 (University of Minnesota Studies in Language and Literature, No. 5).

Tieje, Ralph E. The Prose Voyage Imaginaire before 1800. [Unpublished University of Illinois dissertation, 1917.]

Tilley, Arthur. "Rabelais and Geographical Discovery," *in his* Studies in the French Renaissance, Cambridge, Cambridge University Press, 1922, pp. [26]-65.

——— " 'Extraordinary' Voyages," *in his* Decline of the Age of Louis XIV or, French Literature 1687-1715. Cambridge, Cambridge University Press, 1929.   (Tilley[b])

Toldo, Pietro. "Les Voyages merveilleux de Cyrano de Bergerac et de Swift, et leurs rapports avec l'œuvre de Rabelais," Revue des études rabelaisiennes, IV (1906), [295]-334; V (1907), [24]-44.

28

———— "Voltaire conteur et romancier," Zeitschrift für französische Sprache und Litteratur, XL (1912-13), [131]-185.

Treneer, Anne. The Sea in English Literature from Beowulf to Donne. London, Hodder & Stoughton, 1926.

Ullrich, Hermann. [Review of Kippenberg, *Robinson in Deutschland*], Zeitschrift für vergleichende Litteraturgeschichte N. F. VI (1893), 259-66.   (Ullrich^h)

———— "Eine Replik," Zeitschrift für vergleichende Litteraturgeschichte, N. F. VII (1894), 230-31.   (Ullrich^b)

———— Robinson und Robinsonaden: Bibliographie, Geschichte, Kritik: ein Beitrag zur Vergleichenden Litteraturgeschichte, im Besonderen zur Geschichte des Romans und zur Geschichte der Jugendlitteratur. Teil I. Bibliographie. Weimar, 1898 (Litterarhistorische Forschungen, VII).   (Ullrich)

———— ed. Die Insel Felsenburg . . . erster Theil. Berlin, Behr, 1902 (Deutsche Litteraturdenkmale des 18. und 19. Jahrhunderts, No. 108-20. N. F. No. 58-70).   (Ullrich^j)

———— "Zur Bibliographie der Robinsonaden. Nachträge und Ergänzungen zu meiner Robinson-Bibliographie," Zeitschrift für Bücherfreunde, XI (1907-8), ii, 444-56, [489]-498. (Ullrich^d)

———— "Robinson und Robinsonaden in der Jugendliteratur," *in* Enzyklopädische Handbuch der Pädagogik, ed. W. Rein, 2 Auf. Langensalza, Beyer & Söhne, VII (1908), 567-76.
                                                      (Ullrich^c)

———— [Review of Mildebrath, *Deutschen Aventuriers*], Euphorion Zeitschrift für Literaturgeschichte, 9 Ergänzungsheft, 1911, pp. 21-23.

———— "Zur Robinson–Literatur," Literaturblatt für germanische und romanische Philologie, XXXIII (1912), 105-13.
                                                      (Ullrich^e)

———— [Review of Becker (1911), Schröder (1912), and Brüggemann (1914), on *Insel Felsenburg*], Literaturblatt für germanische und romanische Philologie, XXXVI (1915), 6-11.
                                                      (Ullrich^k)

———— "Der zweihundertste Geburtstag von Defoes Robinson," Zeitschrift für Bücherfreunde, N. F. XI (1919), i, 35-41.
                                                      (Ullrich^f)

———— [Review of *Robinsonaden, Abenteurergeschichten* . . . , Berlin, Harrwitz, Vols. I-IV], Zeitschrift für Bücherfreunde, N.F. XII (1920), Beiblatt, 61-63. (Ullrich[1])

———— Defoes Robinson Crusoe: die Geschichte eines Weltbuches. Leipzig, Reisland, 1924. (Ullrich[a])

———— [Review of Secord, *Narrative Method*], Englische Studien, LIX (1925), 457-67.

———— [Review of Dottin, *Defoe et ses romans*], Englische Studien, LX (1925-26), 364-70.

———— [Review of Hirn, *Ön I Världshavet*], Literaturblatt für germanische und romanische Philologie, L (1929), [321]-332. (Ullrich[g])

Utter, Robert P. Studies in the Origins of the English Novel, with Special Reference to the Influence of the Periodical Essay. [Unpublished Harvard dissertation, 1906.]

Valkhoff, P. "De wonderbaarlike Reizen van Simon Tyssot de Patot," De Gids, XCV (1931), i, [239]-260.

Von der Mühll, Emanuel. Denis Veiras et son histoire des Sévarambes 1677-1679. Paris, Droz, 1938.

Wackwitz, Friedrich. Entstehungsgeschichte von D. Defoes "Robinson Crusoe." [Berlin, Mayer & Müller, 1909].

Wagner, Henry R. "Apocryphal Voyages to the Northwest Coast of America," Proceedings of the American Antiquarian Society, N. S. XLI (1931), 179-234.

Wagner, H[ermann] F. Robinson in Oesterreich: ein Beitrag zur Geschichte der deutschen Robinson-Litteratur. Salzburg, 1886.

———— Robinson und die Robinsonaden in unser Jugendliteratur. Wien, Im Selbstverlage des Verfassers, 1903.

Watson, Harold F. The Sailor in English Fiction and Drama 1550-1800. New York, Columbia University Press, 1931 (Columbia University Studies in English and Comparative Literature).

Weber, Henry [W.] Popular Romances: Consisting of Imaginary Voyages and Travels. Edinburgh, 1812.

Wells, H[erbert] G. *Preface to* The Scientific Romances of H. G. Wells. London, Gollancz, 1933.

Werl, Adolph. Robinson's Stammbaum: eine Skizze der Robinson-Jugendliteratur: nebst einer Abfertigung der Herren Julius Petzholdt und Emil Hallier. 3 Auf. Leipzig, 1862.

[Whiting, Sydney]. Heliondé; or Adventures in the Sun. London, 1855.

Wijngaarden, Nicolaas van. Les Odyssées philosophiques en France entre 1616 et 1789. Haarlem, Vijlbrief, 1932.

Wildstake, Karl. Wielands Agathon und der französische Reise- und Bildungsroman von Fénelons Telemach bis Barthélemys Anacharsis. Murnau Obby, Fürst, 1933.

Wolff, O[scar] L. B. Allgemeine Geschichte des Romans, von dessen Ursprung bis zur neuesten Zeit. 2 Ausg., Jena, 1850.

Wolff, Samuel L. The Greek Romances in Elizabethan Prose Fiction. New York, Columbia University Press, 1912 (Columbia University Studies in English and Comparative Literature).

Wright, John K. The Geographical Lore of the Time of the Crusades . . . New York, 1925 (American Geographical Society Research Series, No. 15).

Wurzbach, Wolfgang von. Geschichte des französischen Romans: von den Anfängen bis zum Ende des XVII. Jahrhunderts. Heidelberg, Winter, 1912.

Yardley, Edward. The Supernatural in Romantic Fiction. London, 1880.

Zobelitz, Fedor von. "Eine Bibliographie der Robinsonaden," Zeitschrift für Bücherfreunde, II (1898-99), ii, 386-88.

Index

Italic page numbers indicate the main entries in the check list. In general, titles do not appear in the index under such initial words as *adventure, history, life,* and *voyage* or under initial nondescript and stereotyped adjectives, but rather under key words, especially proper names whenever possible. Eponymous heroes are entered under their surnames, except when the Christian name has become almost inseparable (e.g., *Tom Jones*). It has seemed impracticable and unnecessary to enter here variations in spelling of proper names when translated. Titles are usually entered in the wording of the original language and not in their translated forms, except when the latter vary significantly. Thus, Prevost's *Philosophe anglois* does not appear under *Englische Weltweise, Engelsche Filosoof,* or *Filosofo Inglese,* and Longueville's *Hermit* does not appear under *Solitaire anglois, Kluizenaar,* or *Englische Einsiedler;* but Ducray-Duminil's *Lolotte et Fanfan* has an entry under its English translation entitled *Ambrose and Eleanor.* Likewise, literary terms are given in English unless their foreign equivalents have been used in the text almost exclusively; thus, *Picaresque romance,* but no entry under *Schelmenroman,* although some of the pages indexed may employ only the latter word. Besides authors and titles of imaginary voyages and of all other works mentioned, the index includes the names of translators, adaptors, editors, commentators, and critics; it does not include the printers and publishers listed in the imprints, the titles of scholarly and literary periodicals (excepting a few which serialized imaginary voyages), the libraries cited, or names cited as authority for the existence of various editions.

INDEX

Castelman, Richard, *see under* Chetwood

Castera, *see* Duperron de Castera

Castets, Ferdinand, cited, 349

Castilton, L., 364

Castle of Otranto, 64

Catalde, De, *300*

Caylus, Comte de, 29

Cederschiöld, Wilhelm, cited, 256

Ceilan, Voyage à, 365

Cervantes Saavedra, Miguel de, 16, 305; *Don Quixote,* 18, 26, 64, 82 *n*131, 151 *n*233, 379

Cessares, Account of the, 158

Céton, Milord, 50, 177

Chadwick, William, quoted, 206

Chamberlain, Basil H. (translator), 104 *n*164, 367

Chambers, W. and R., 229, 274

Chandler, Frank W., quoted, 162-63, 164-65

Chapelle et Bachaumont, 55, 58

Charles Edward Stuart, Prince, 287

Charlotte, 346

Charlotten-Burg, 338

Char Volant, Le, 377

Chassang, Alexis, quoted, 7, 17-18

Chauvin, Victor, 41 *n*81, 152 *n*236, 201, 202, 204, 210, 220, 247

Ch'en Shou-yi, cited, 225

Chetwood, William R., *Captain Robert Boyle* (and *Richard Castelman*), 32 *n*70, 33, 39, 40, 247-51; *Captain Richard Falconer* (and *Thomas Randal*), 42 *n*82, 227-29

Chevalier de ***, Voyages du, 360

Chew, Samuel C., cited, 177 *n*278

Chiari, Pietro, *357*

Child, Harold, cited, 298

Chinard, Gilbert, 33-34, 99, 101, 108 *n*167, 115 *n*174, 118, 166 *n*262, 172, 218, 237, 256, 278, 283, 290, 358, 360, 372, 383

Chivalric romance, 11-12, 80, 88

Christian, Fletcher, 396

Christianopolis, by Andreae, 93 *n*148

Chronique scandaleuse, 7, 89

Church, Alfred J., cited, 103 *n*162

Church-Man's Last Shift, The, 201

Cibber, Theophilus, 122, 284

Civitas Solis, see Campanella

Clairfons, *see* Moutonnet de Clairfons

Claretie, Léo, cited, 289, 290

Clarissa, 26

Clarke, James S., quoted, 41 *n*81, 229

Claudius, Mathias (translator), 286

Cleveland, Monsieur, see under Prevost

Cohen, Henri, cited, 28 *n*65, 369

Coleridge, S. T., cited, 326, 327

Collett, Robinson Crusoe, 153 *n*236

Collins, V. H., 324

Columbus, Christopher, 287

Conrad, Heinrich (translator), 385, 386

Consequences, 339

Consolidator, The, see under Defoe

Constancio, F. Solano (editor), 352

Constancy Rewarded, 393

Constantius & Pulchera, 393

Contant D'Orville, *see* D'Orville

Conte de fées, 7, 9, 21, 23, 24, 28, 29 *n*67, 69-70, 73, 88, 89 *n*141, 111, 174, 374

Conway, G. R. G., cited, 243

Cook, Capt. James, 5, 26, 170 *n*268, 287, 370, 389

Cooper, J. Fenimore, 124 *n*190, 166 *n*260

Cordier, Henri, cited, 290

Couret de Villeneuve, Martin (editor), 44 *n*85, 56-57

Courtney, W. P., cited, 325, 327

Coyer, Gabriel F., *Frivola, 316-18; Letter to Dr. Maty,* 176

Crabbe, George, 267-68

Crane, Ronald S., quoted, 8 *n*15, 333

Crapulia, see Hall

Crater, The, 124 *n*190

Creutz, Bernhard, see Teutsche Robinson

Criticón, El, 349

Cromwell, Oliver, natural son of, 279-84

Crossley, Jas., cited, 298, 324

Crowley, Francis J., cited, 333

Hermsprong, 13
Herodotus, 92-93 *n*148
Heroic romance, 7, 83, 89
Hertel, J. J., *347*
Hettner, Hermann J. T., 8, 132-34,
135, 136 *n*210, 167
Hetzel, J., quoted, 168 *n*264
Hewit, Hannah, 393-94
Hieronymus, Karl F., 381
Hippe, Max, cited, 128 *n*198, **224**
Hirn, Yrjö, cited, 152 *n*235, 344,
403
Historia Litteraria, 282
Hoadley, Benjamin, cited, 122 *n*186
Hoffman, Harold L., cited, 327
Holberg, Ludvig, ix, 25, 32, 50, 61,
64, 68, 79-80, 94 *n*148, 104, 112,
113, 134, 155, 183, 237, 255, 303-5,
312, 316, 342, 362, 366, 386
Hole, Richard, cited, 202, 203-4
Holländische Robinson, Der, 124
Hollandsche Kluizenaar, De, 264, 267
Hollandsche Robinson, De, 307-8, 350
Holliday, Carl, cited, 3 *n*1, 326
Holmesby, John, *pseud., 346*
Holy Land, journeys to, 80
Homer, 7, 16, 19, 20 *n*50, 71, 83-84,
103 *n*163, 117, 166, 168, 202,
256
Hönncher, Erwin, cited, 25 *n*57
Hoogewerff, G. J., 213, 215, 216
Horn, Franz, cited, 132 *n*199
Horne, Charles F., cited, 16 *n*37
Hortop, Job, 243
Howell, John, 68
Hubbard, Lucius L., 148 *n*230, 213,
214, 215, 216, 225, 227
Hubbard Collection of Imaginary
Voyages, 148 *n*230
Huet, Bishop Pierre, 20, 201
Hugo, C., cited, 358, 372
Human Vicissitudes, 398
Humbla, Eric (translator), 245
Hume, David, 77
Hunt, Leigh, cited, 326-27
Hutchins, Henry C., 36 *n*77, 41 *n*80,
140 *n*219, 154, 224, 225

Hutchins Collection of Robinsonades,
154 *n*239
Hutchinson, Thomas, cited, 205
Huyghens, Christian, 306
Hymans, Ella M., x

Iambulus, 10
Icaromennipus, 370
Ideal commonwealth, *see* Political ro-
mance; Utopia
Idée d'un regne doux, see Lesconvel
Ile de Borneo, L', 358
Ile inconnue, see Grivel
Imaginary voyage, *see* Voyage, imag-
inary
Impetuous Lover, The, 347
Indianischen Insuln, 336
Indianiske Bref, 362
Infortunes sur mer, 27 *n*65, 32 *n*70
Inklaar, Derk, cited, 369
Inquiraner, Die, see Bachstrom
Insel Felsenburg, see Schnabel
Insul Charlotten-Burg, Die, 338
Insul Jaketan, 301-2
*Isländers Franz Severin van Dittheffts
Reisen, Des,* 345
Isländische Robinson, Der, 339-40
Isle de la Vertue, 175
Isle des philosophes, L', 391
Isleif, Gissur, 339-40
Isle imaginaire, L', 32 *n*70
Isle of Pines, see Neville
Isles fortunées, Les, 40, *370*
Isola Disabitata, 383
Iter Lunare, 200

J., B. G., 371
Jackson, Henry E., cited, 226
Jacob, P. L., *pseud., see* Lacroix
Jacobs, Joseph, quoted, 7
Jaketan, Insul, 301-2
Jakobsen, Oluf F. J., *pseud., 327-28*
James, M. R., cited, 256
Jansénie, Pays de, 83, 96
Japanese Gulliver, The, 103-4, *367-68*
Jason, 16, 20 *n*50
Jaucourt, Chevalier de, 13 *n*31
Jauffret, Louis F., *398-99*

Wells, H. G., 167, 204
Wendt, Christian G. (translator), 277
Wentworth, Charles, 361-62
Wentzel, Frantz A., 240-41
Wenzel von Erfurt, 378
Wezel, Johann K., *369*
Whatley, Stephen (translator), 217
Whibley, Charles, cited, 257
Whicher, George F., cited, 258
Which Is the Oracle? Burke or O'Brien, 339
Whitcomb, Seldon L., cited, 178 *n*279
Whiting, Sydney, 75, 78 *n*126
Whitmore, Charles E., cited, ix
Whitmore, H., 112, *394*
Whitney, Lois, cited, 395
Wichmann, C. A. (translator), 390
Wiedmer, G. R. (translator), 359
Wie gehts auf der Welt, 381
Wiener Robinson, Der, 359
Wijngaarden, Nicolaas van, 110 *n*171, 117-22, 198, 199, 218, 261, 270, 278, 287, 292, 300, 341, 345, 356, 358, 376
Wildstake, Karl, quoted, 287
Wiles, Roy McK., 234-35
Wilkins, Bishop John, 206, 330
Wilkins, Peter, see Paltock
Wilkinson, Clennell, cited, 152 *n*235
Williams, Harold, cited, 254, 255
Williams, Morris, *pseud.,* 234
Williams, Ralph C., cited, 20 *n*53
Willock, John, *pseud., 391*
Wilson, Henry, cited, 70 *n*111
Wilson, Walter, quoted, 206, 252
Winckler, Paul, 241
Winkfield, Unca Eliza, *pseud., 356*
Winterfield, Capt., 389-90

Wohleingerichtete Staat, see Ophir
Wolf, G. C. (translator), 259
Wolff, O. L. B., cited, 132 *n*199
Wollap, Sir George, 374, 385
Woodbridge, Benjamin W., quoted, 163-64
Woodfin, Mrs. A., 346
Woolf, Virginia, cited, 225
World Displayed, The, cited, 254
World in the Centre of the Earth, 341-42
Wouters, Cornélie P. B., *see* Wasse
Wright, Ernest H., xi
Wright, Thomas, quoted, 205, 206
Wright, Wyllis, cited, 6 *n*6
Wunderliche Fata einiger See-Fahrer, see Schnabel
Wurzbach, Wolfgang von, quoted, 11
Wyer, Malcolm G., cited, 185 *n*3
Wyss, Johann R., 360, 376

Yokdhan, Hai Ebn, *see* Tophail
Yonge, Charlotte M. (editor), 266

Zachariae, Fr. W. (translator), 321
Zacharie de Lisieux, 83, 96
Zadig, 257
Zandvoort, R. W., 148 *n*230
Zayde, 20n 51
Zélie dans le désert, 382-84
Zevort, Charles, quoted, 7
Zimmermann, Otto, 232
Zoa and Rodomond, 309
Zotenberg, Hermann, cited, 201, 203
Zucchelli, Antonio, 125
Zu Wasser und Lande, 331
Zu Wasser und zu Lande, 342
Zweyer Schwaben, 337